Between Berlin and Slobodka: Jewish Transition Figures from Eastern Europe
Augmented Edition

ALSO BY HILLEL GOLDBERG
ISRAEL SALANTER:
TEXT, STRUCTURE, IDEA
THE FIRE WITHIN:
THE LIVING HERITAGE OF THE MUSAR MOVEMENT

Between Berlin and Slobodka: Jewish Transition Figures from Eastern Europe
Augmented Edition

Hillel Goldberg

KTAV PUBLISHING HOUSE, INC.
JERSEY CITY, NEW JERSEY

Passages from these volumes are reprinted 1w permission Harvard University Press:

Against the Apocalypse: Responses to Catastrophe in Modern Jewish Culture, by David
G. Roskies

Grescas' Critique of Aristotle: Problems of Aristotles Physics in Jewish and Arabic Philosophy. by Harry Austryn Wolfson

The Philosophy of the Church Fathers: Faith. Trinity. Incarnation, by Harry Austryn Wolfson

The Philosophy of Spinoza: Unfolding the latent Processes of His Reasoning. by I harry
Austryn, Wolfson

Rabad of Posquieres: A Twelfth-Century Talmudist, by Isadore Twersky

COPYRIGHT © 1989, 2010
HILLEL GOLDBERG

ISBN 978-1-60280-135-6

Published by
KTAV Publishing House, Inc.
930 Newark Avenue
Jersey City, N.J. 07306
www.ktav.com
Email: orders@ktav.com

For those who nurture my muse
My wife Elaine,
and Jerusalem

The wisdom of philosophers is not a commodity that can be produced on demand. Their books are not responsa. We should not regard them as mirrors, reflecting other people's problems, but rather as windows, allowing us to view the author's soul. Philosophers do not expend their power and passion unless they themselves are affected, originally or vicariously. The soul only communes with itself when the heart is stirred.

Abraham Joshua Heschel

Once Rabbi Eliyyahu Lopian arrived in Slobodka and lectured. All went to listen, the Elder of Slobodka among them. The lecture was passionate, admonitory, and the Elder was moved to tears.

The next day, when Rabbi Lopian came to take his leave, the Elder rebuked him, asking rhetorically, "How could you admonish such a distinguished group of talmudic scholars? Rabbi Lopian remained silent, accepting the rebuke.

Afterwards, Isaac Hutner questioned the rebuke, noting that the Elder himself had wept during the lecture.

Said the Elder:

"A thing and its opposite–contradictions–these are among the ways of God himself."

Contents

Preface..........xi
1. Introduction 1
2. Rabbi Israel Salanter..........15
3. Professor Harry Austryn Wolfson..........37
4. Rabbi Isaac Hutner..........63
5. Rabbi Joseph Baer Soloveitchik..........89
6. Professor Abraham Joshua Heschel..........115
7. Rabbi Joseph Zev Lipovitz..........137
8. Conclusion..........147

NOTES..........157
    Chapter One..........157   Chapter Five..........190
    Chapter Two..........161   Chapter Six..........199
    Chapter Three..........169   Chapter Seven..........210
    Chapter Four..........181   Chapter Eight..........210

BIBLIOGRAPHY..........211
    Prefatory Note..........211
    I. Interviews..........212
    II. Primary Sources..........213
    III. Secondary Sources..........221

INDEX..........261

Introduction to the 2010 Augmented Edition

I am an inveterate rewriter. Long after I finished *The Fire Within: The Living Heritage of the Musar Movement* (1987), I discovered that my computer program kept track of the number of drafts for each chapter: between 77 and 144. *Between Berlin and Slobodka: Jewish Transition Figures from Eastern Europe* was just the opposite. I did not even use a computer. I wrote the book by hand — no cut-and-paste — so certain I was of what I wanted to say. My certainty was not that I was right about the preeminent thinkers in this book — that, the reader will have to judge. My certainty was that what I wrote accurately reflected my convictions. Often, writing is a process of self-discovery; the author himself is not certain how his thinking will unfold until pen is put to paper (or, finger to keyboard). *Between Berlin and Slobodka*, while the product of extensive research, nonetheless acquired its essentials over the course of a quarter century of thought; the research added flesh to sinews already in place, awaiting only the discipline — and the moment — to be articulated. There is no other way to explain the boldness and independence with which I approached these charismatic figures: the book sprung as much against my will as a consequence of it, phrase by phrase, very slowly, very surely, as if a higher truth came into being and I was merely the amanuensis, absent all but minimal rewriting, by hand, on paper — just like this new introduction.[1]

Rereading the book a quarter century after I wrote it (though published in 1989, it was written primarily in 1985), two types of comment present themselves. The first is what the intervening years have revealed about the figures themselves, and about the transition experience generally. The advancement of time and of scholarship has added information unknown, or only sketchily known, in 1985. The second type of comment reflects changes in my perspective.

In the single case of Rabbi Joseph B. Soloveitchik, of much greater moment than the intervening scholarship is the pivotal fact that when I wrote Rabbi Soloveitchik was living, albeit disabled, but now, more than 15 years since he died, the new writing about him (and the posthumous volumes by him) shift in poignance. So much more about his impact has been revealed by his passing and the response to it.

Scholarship published since the publication of this book has left two of its subjects, Professor Harry Austryn Wolfson and Rabbi Joseph Zev Lipovitz, essentially untouched, if possibly more rounded; while other subjects have benefitted from the additional knowledge. However, as if in unintended negative compensation, the new scholarship often has dressed itself in simplicities and other images of the transition figures that they themselves would little recognize. This yields

— for example — a Joseph [Soloveitchik] that knew not Joseph. A new generation's master is eisegetically read to affirm the centripetal needs of a segment of Orthodox Jewish society whose contours bear only elementary resemblance to the Orthodox Jewish society that Rabbi Soloveitchik sought to shape. He who needed no self-justification for his bold philosophical explorations and their integration into his halachic commitment and being is posthumously colored by admirers who scour his corpus for instructions on how to justify secular curricula and professions, how to define and delimit a differentiated, "modern" Orthodoxy. Either that, or they puzzle over his unself-conscious use of secular material. The notion that justification of secular involvement is unavoidable and unself-conscious involvement is impossible has become an idee fixe.

Or — for example — the negative compensation leads to an Abraham Joshua Heschel limned as a new generation's icon, reconstructed to affirm theological positions he never held. Subsumed under a new liberalism, anachronistically tied back to his social action, the iconic Heschel yields an equation and a fallacy: his embrace of civil rights in the 1960s is tantamount to the liberal side of the culture wars of now. Or, for another example, Rabbi Israel Salanter — a master halachist and exemplary pietist in relentless search of a unified spiritual field — is, in some circles, now bifurcated and segmented to yield introspection, personal growth, and spirituality, calmly detached from the halachic minutiae and the immersion in halachic study that were Rabbi Israel's hallmarks.

Of course, the new scholarship also expands our knowledge often without a narrowing edge and in that sense is a beauty to behold. This list is long. One may cite, by way of inadequate representation, the translation of most of the elliptical corpus of Israel Salanter, by Zvi Singer (*Ohr Yisrael*, 2004); the translation of Joseph B. Soloveitchik's recalcitrant "And from There shall You Seek" (*U-Vikashtem mi-Sham*), by Naomi Goldblum (2008); the publication of critical communications by Soloveitchik, edited by Nathaniel Helfgot in *Community, Covenant, Commitment* (2005); Manfred Lehman's discoveries about the early Soloveitchik, particularly his education in Warsaw; Samuel Dresner's and Edward K. Kaplan's first of a projected two volumes, *Abraham Joshua Heschel: Prophetic Witness* (1998); the open access to Yitzhak Hutner's *Pahad Yitzhak*; the astonishing treasure trove of information, including an exhaustive review of pertinent incidents in the life of Israel Salanter, in Nathan Kamenetsky's *The Making of a Godol* (2002); and Marc Shapiro's *Between the Yeshiva World and Modern Orthodoxy: The Life and Works of Rabbi Yehiel Jacob Weinberg, 1884-1966*.

On the transition experience generally, *The Great Escape: Nine Jews Who Fled Hitler and Changed the World*, by Kati Marton (2006), extends to the Hungarian context the timbre that I assayed in the Polish and Lithuanian context.

In two instances, publications have been decisive. I have been asked why I selected the figures I did. One critical reason was the availability of primary sources, written and oral. In the 1980s, I attempted, without success, to ascertain and to confirm pertinent information about Menachem Mendel Schneerson, the seventh Lubavitcher Rebbe. I submitted a lengthy, written query to the rebbe himself, which was not answered. Had Shaul Shimon Deutsch's two biographical volumes, *Larger Than Life: The Life and Times of the Lubavitcher Rebbe* (1995, 1997), been available, I likely would have supplemented them with sufficient oral history to yield a chapter on the rebbe. Similarly, in the case of Professor Saul Lieberman, the publication of Saul Lieberman, the Man and His Work, by Elijah J. Schochet and Solomon Spiro (2005), would have led, together with oral history, to a chapter on Lieberman. I have now articulated its essence in a review essay, "Discontinuities: The Case of Saul Lieberman" (Tradition, Fall, 2007), showing Lieberman as a foil for the other transition figures from Eastern Europe.

No doubt, as I re-read Between Berlin and Slobodka, I would now make certain adjustments, due to changes in perspective. For example, I wrote then: "Joseph Baer Soloveitchik, not having created a cadre of profound talmudic-religious personalities who would win the Diaspora for talmudic Judaism . . ." (pp. 11-12.). This remains true. But it is also true that through prodigious first- and now second-generation disciples, the reach of Rabbi Soloveitchik became more extensive than was then predictable. However, just as life itself has no integrity if one tries to revise it in retrospect, in light of subsequent accomplishments or regrets, so, too, a book of this kind. It has only one author, not two, even if those two bear the same name. I, the potential second author, may not now revise or reimagine Between Berlin and Slobodka and also sustain its integrity, the certainty of its correspondence to my convictions, any more than I can revise my own life.

An authorial moment, if truly blessed, is not to be revised. It may, however, be transcended. If a book has merit, its author may revise not it, but himself. An author may grow. To be committed to one's authorial vision is not necessarily to clutch it, but to distill it and plant it in new soil. The last thing I might have envisioned upon publication of *Between Berlin and Slobodka* in 1989 was that a year later in Salt Lake City, Utah, I would perceive holiness in cement, halachically configured, and begin an 18-year trajectory to my Hebrew halachic work, Hallel Hakohen (2008).

To write such a work was to transport myself into the animating spirit of most of these transition figures more organically than I ever dreamed. Hallel Hakohen unfolds the elusive and elliptical formulation of the laws of mikveh as understood by the man who, in a way, was the premise, the datum, the starting point behind all of the East European transition figures: the Vilna Gaon. Circles complete themselves in unexpected ways.

[1]. There is one exception: passages translated from the Hebrew. I labored over these, endlessly rewriting, especially the passages by Rabbi Isaac Hutner, trying to capture the tone and rhythm, and not just the meaning, of his rich, poetic, and allusive Hebrew.

Preface

It was autumn, 1965. I had transferred to Yeshiva College in Manhattan from the University of California in Berkeley; the scene remains etched in my imagination.

I entered Rubin dormitory, strode half-right with the flow of the walking traffic.

But I stopped.

Something caught my eye, as if a magnetic pull made me look to the left. Standing next to the dormitory's mailboxes, facing into the student synagogue just outside its glass door, a man was praying.

Late afternoon, sun declining, clear light: a man prayed; steady body movement, but no unusual gesticulation; steady, barely audible pronunciation of each and every word of the Eighteen Benedictions.

Students and others turned half-right, proceeded in the normal fashion; I lingered. Something about that man, that prayer, fascinated and held me. His prayer was passionate and restrained, at once. He was dressed in an ordinary suit, with no distinguishing mark.

The secretary at Rubin dormitory was extraordinarily solicitous of this man's needs the moment he completed his afternoon prayer (*minhah*).

In their brief exchange, I heard her address him, "Rabbi Soloveitchik."

Another scene remains similarly etched.

I entered what would be called a courtyard if it were in the open air. Off to the side of the main foyer of Yeshiva's Furst hall was an area lined on three sides with doors leading to administrators' offices. The rectangular area between them was filled with lounge chairs and coffee tables.

Again, I lingered.

Sitting together were an internationally renowned talmudic scholar, a broad shouldered man with a distinguished mien and presence, and the smaller Rabbi Soloveitchik. This time he was not reverential and restrained; he was animated, even loud, articulating each and every word, not steadily, not rhythmically. He was talking Talmud. He gesticulated in the manner of talmudic debaters, meeting each question or challenge with a firm response whose intellectual power was accentuated by its accompanying gesture.

Both word and gesture were absolutely definitive. Rabbi Soloveitchik's debater, whose own intellect and demeanor commanded deference, sat as his own students sat before him. He deferred not for deference's sake.

He was in need of illumination; he posed difficulties, summoned sources, marshalled arguments. One by one, Rabbi Soloveitchik met them with vigor, totally absorbed, totally in control. The exchange was fierce and friendly, at once. His mind sparked, his words satisfied. After one half hour his discussant arose, in gratitude.

The two sides of Rabbi Joseph Baer Soloveitchik's piety–passion and intellect–recurred in other scenes I witnessed during those undergraduate years at Yeshiva College, and then when I was in graduate school in Boston, his home. On the side of passion, there was, for example, his unabashed baring of soul during his Saturday evening lectures at the Maimonides School in Brookline. In remarkable, public pining for his late wife, he would say: "What I would not give for just five minutes of conversation with her. In poignant yearning for his late father, he would say: "All the praise and admiration, from whatever source, can never match one brief compliment from your own father.' In a comment on nostalgia (a frequent topic), he would note how music penetrated memory, most pervasively, how it, of all submerged psychic forces, most readily reemerged. A person hearing a time for the first time in several years or even decades–a time associated with a pivotal personal experience-this person will respond with the same visceral pain or pleasure originally associated with the experience. In saying this he winced, and one wondered at the source of his own nostalgia. He continued his passionate musings–forcefully yet somehow delicately delivered through a microphone to a full hall–on the side of intellect. He would say that if it were not for Torah study–not for his intensive and extensive grappling with knotty talmudic texts–he "could not continue," Clearly, here was a man of intellect in need of expressing emotion.

Later, as I began to read Rabbi Soloveitchik systematically, I was profoundly surprised to learn that what I, the observer, regarded with admiration, he himself regarded with suspicion. I learned that to him intellect is unqualifiedly valuable, worthy of unrestrained communication, while passion is an endless source of philosophical difficulty, requiring the most carefully defined and delimited legitimization. I learned that Rabbi Soloveitchik, at least consciously and intellectually, was more complex than he seemed (Chapter Five).

Perhaps I unconsciously realized this during those early years at Yeshiva College, for as moving and fascinating as I found him, it was other figures at Yeshiva who touched me more deeply, turning my absorption of "human data" into personal search. Of Lithuanian background (like Rabbi Soloveitchik), these figures lived and formulated the integration of passion and intellect in a way that I found more appealing, because more serene, and more penetrating in self-analysis. Elsewhere 1 have drawn memoirs of Rabbi Jacob Moses Lesin, emodiment of a different Lithuanian Talmudic tradition: Musar. In a subliminal way. Rabbi Lesin kindled my interest in the Musar movement, founded by Rabbi Israel Salanter. Without hesitation, Rabbi Israel valued both passion and intellect (Chapter Two). The subtle combination was so difficult to achieve that those who did so successfully thereby exhausted themselves. They were unable to put to writing the insightful interpretations of text and psyche that their success engendered. An exception is Rabbi Joseph Zev Lipovitz (Chapter Seven), If Rabbi Soloveitchik, from both personal inclination and family heritage, rejected the Musar approach, others modified it with profoundly illuminating intellectual consequences, and uniquely opaque personal ones, both fruitful (Rabbi Isaac Hutner, Chapter Four) and unfruitful (Professor Harry Austryn Wolfson, Chapter Three). With or without Musar, the Lithuanian talmudic tradition entailed a definitiveness and direction that, in a hasidic scion, are subject to elasticity and indistinctness (Abraham Joshua Heschel, Chapter Six).

For several years I never regarded these figures as other than Jewish resources whose thought and deeds I could accept or adapt in my own quest, which was both consummated and initiated by my arrival at Yeshiva College. As I made my choices, accepting, adapting, or rejecting ever more conclusively, I developed an academic interest in all of these figures. All of them genuinely struggled to bridge two cultures, to integrate their background with thought and society in their new West European, American, or Palestinian homes. However one evaluates them personally, they collectively illuminated the range of problems and possibilities inherent in the transposition of a seemingly sealed, especially fertile, spiritual and intellectual seedbed to seemingly inhospitable surroundings.

The pioneers who undertook this unusual transposition tended to conceal the personal quandaries that generated it. It was my own observation of Rabbi Soloveitchik that became the foundation of my skepticism about the adequacy of formal writings in understanding the cross-cultural urge. I learned that exclusive reliance on formal works could mislead, that intellectual honesty and academic comprehensiveness required many types of knowledge and tools of research. Personal observation when possible, re-imagining when impossible, personal interviews with friends and disciples (or disciples of disciples), as well as textual analysis and search for sources, were all indispensable, notwithstanding the methodological difficulties they introduced-difficulties obviated by narrow concentration on texts alone.

From my concentration on the individual and his relation to ideas, a thesis about pioneering Jewish intellectuals from Eastern Europe emerged. Briefly stated, the thesis is this. Underneath the complexities and subtleties of cross-cultural figures who originated in Eastern Europe, there rests an elemental fissure. This fissure, an experience of life, gave a distinct force and fascination to intellectual work. Thinkers who set forth complex ideas, eloquently expressed in languages not their mother tongue, found their primary nurture in a simple, searing decision: to fulfill expectations of family or culture in absorbing and enriching their received tradition, or to disappoint and confound those expectations-to absorb another tradition, perhaps just emerging, not yet born. The decision of these thinkers to blend received tradition with unheralded ideas made them complex. At the inception of their journeys, however, the dominant note was simplicity: to turn this way or that, to conform to expectations or to defy them, to choose continuity or independence.

My method, then, is twofold biographical analysis: the search for a simple, if agonizing, incubus at the root of a complex, if salient, position. My subjects were not disembodied spirits. Their thought grew from life, responding to its crises, flowing from its decisions, flowering from its commitments. Their thought-psychological, theological, philosophical, political-pressed through a prism that refracted idea from action, persuasive formulation from personal struggle.

The key conceptual term that defines this prism is "transition." Sketched here, fleshed out in Chapter One, transition, as I use it, identifies a type of cross-cultural thinker who, broadly speaking, has surfaced in Jewish history at least since the time of Philo of Alexandria, down through the golden age of Spain, on to modem times (to name the most well known of his stopping points). The transition figure has been a recurrent phenomenon, emerging in different guises and garbs, ever since Judaism first took seriously the claims of another intellectual world. Scholars of Philo argue whether Philo was primarily Jewish or primarily Greek, primarily a believing commentator on Jewish scripture or primarily a Hellenistic philosopher, but the scale is not responsibly tipped wholly in one direction or the other. Caught in the middle, whatever the proportions of the definitive configuration, Philo is a transition figure, a dealer in two cultures, two worlds. The prism that is transition refracts two foci, two disjunct patterns of life and thought that try to become one.

I have concentrated on transition figures from Eastern Europe for a reason besides personal history and inclination. The reason is objective need: the neglect of East European Jewish thinkers relative to the attention lavished on such West Europeans as Moses Mendelssohn, Hermann Cohen, Franz Rosenzweig, and Martin Buber. A corollary neglect is the decisive idea, book, parent, teacher, or institution at the genesis of transition figures from Eastern Europe. One such critical, catalytic element for the figures examined in this book is the institution-idea that is also the teacher-model. Examples: the third-generation Musar school, "Slobodka," an institution-idea whose teacher-models were Rabbis Nathan Zvi Finkel ("the Elder of Slobodka") and Moses Mordechai Epstein (Slobodka's dean of talmudic studies); and the innovative Beth Midrash Elyon of Berlin, an institution-idea whose teacher-model was Rabbi Hayyim Heller. Cities and institutions, Slobodka and Berlin were also sobriquets-metonymies, if you will-for types of Jewish learning that were indispensable to Jewish transition figures from Eastern Europe. In different, sometimes diametrically opposed ways, both ideas stood for broadening of talmudic study. Slobodka broadened with piety, grounded in self-analysis; Berlin broadened with knowledge, grounded in "secular" study. The Jewish transition figures passed through one or both of these two poles as if through magnetic fields. The tugs and pulls left them permanently reshaped. It was not the quantity but the quality of their shifts that was decisive. In some cases, residence in Berlin or Slobodka was short. Nonetheless, East Europeans who studied in one or both of these institution-ideas emerged radically different from their contemporaries.

Of necessity, I freeze-frame the six transition figures at various stages of documentary development. For Isaac Hutner, both personal letters and extensive, published writings are available. At the other end of the spectrum, Israel Salanter's personal correspondence (if he ever even wrote it) will probably never he available, and his writings are sparse. In between there are Harry Austryn Wolfson (many finished volumes readily available, personal letters less accessible), Joseph Baer Soloveitchik (personal correspondence unavailable but, to compensate, published writings that are at least as much personal outpouring as they are critical analysis), Abraham Joshua Heschel and Joseph Zev Lipovitz (published writings in abundance-though most of Lipovitz's posthumous works did not have the benefit of his immaculate editing-personal correspondence either nonexistent or unavailable). In one case, Israel Salanter, my earlier study of his sparse writings helped to offset the brevity of the information itself. And so, if the documentation on the transition figures examined here is not as complete as the historian would wish, neither is it without its solidity, and, in some cases, without its abundance. What is more, with respect to all of the six figures, extensive oral tradition has been recorded in numerous studies or gathered by me personally through observation or in conversations with scholars and disciples for over twenty years.

In an unexpected and telling way, the long arm of transition figures was conveyed through the cooperation of several disciples who were both extremely helpful and unqualifiedly insistent that I neither thank them by name nor cite them in footnotes or bibliography. The authority of some of the figures examined in this book is such that disciples will not agree to be associated even indirectly with critical study of their mentors, for fear of missing the mark, offending the mentors' relatives, or other reasons. To those whom I cannot thank by name, I thank you for your generosity in anonymity.

Others I am happy to thank by name: all the interviewees listed in Bibliography I, who generously shared their knowledge, and are not responsible for the uses to which it has been put; my former students at the Hebrew University, invariably a motivated, intellectually curious, and stimulating group; the administration at the University, particularly Herbert Weinberg and Aaron Singer, for interest in this project stretching beyond technical aid to substantive comments, respectively, on the chapters on Wolfson and Heschel; Henry F. May, the American intellectual historian, for continual encouragement, insight, and example, extended since my days at Berkeley; Walter Wurzburger, for genuine encouragement and kindness; and, to Nathan Bulman, a truly prodigious thinker, of whose razor-sharp distinctions and vast knowledge I hope I have absorbed a little, ever since his first overflowing gift of knowledge to me. This occurred as I sat in a pay phone booth in a Manhattan subway station, calling, simply, to make an appointment to meet him, finding myself suddenly scrambling for any shred of paper to take down his instantaneous jet of information, released at the drop of the name of the subject about which I was inquiring, Novorodock Musar. His intellectual openness and giving, I have come to learn, are typical responses to countless seekers in the vineyards of Jewish thought. To my revered teacher and friend, the late, learned, and tragic Eliyahu Sobel, my debt is incalculable and wide-ranging. In the context of the present work, it was his first-hand, expert knowledge of the talmudic method as taught in Slobodka that helped me understand the intellectual roots of Harry Austryn Wolfson; and it was his person that helped me understand Wolfson on a deeper level.

To Frankie Goldberg, Joel Mandel, and Seiji Kondo, my thanks for help with the bibliography. I owe a special expression of appreciation to James Sheehy–a student mature beyond his years-for all manner of technical assistance and perceptive queries.

No diacritical marks appear in names of people. Unless otherwise noted, all translations from the Hebrew are my own.

Rabbi Hillel Goldberg, Ph.D.
Denver, Colorado

CHAPTER ONE

Introduction

"To talk of . . . culture in transition is also to imply a coherent and self-conscious cultural tradition that survived the transfer. Transition thus has as its countertheme (or better, complementary theme) the tenacious continuities of an old tradition perpetuating itself in a new cultural environment."

Bernard Septimus

I.

Transition must connote the simultaneous persistence of the old and the new—the tenacious continuity and the conscious transformation. Otherwise, transition, as a concept, becomes meaningless, for either slowly or quickly all epochs and individuals are in transition. "It is said," writes Robert Wohl, paraphrasing Jose Ortega y Gasset,

> that all epochs are epochs of transition. This, [Ortega] admitted, was true. But some epochs were marked by sudden jumps and subterranean crises that produced a radical deviation in the center of gravity of the public consciousness. When this happened there arose two nations that coexisted and yet were completely foreign to each other: an official nation that obstinately repeated the gestures of a dying age, and a vital nation, blocked by the other, that was unable to push its way onto the stage of history.[1]

Coexistence of foreign thrusts—crisis that illuminates abstract discourse about transitional "epochs" and "nations"—by the same token illuminates twists and turns in individual Jews originating in Eastern Europe, in epochs of transition. This is certainly the case for the six nineteenth- and twentieth-century transition figures examined in this book. For them, "coexistence," or transition, connotes radical reevaluation of Judaism or Jewish society, in tandem with tenacious clinging to the East European tradition or society they seemingly reject.

To these creative and influential thinkers whom I label "transition figures," there was a critical difference between their double burden and Ortega's. To Ortega, a radical deviation in consciousness produced two trajectories "completely foreign to each other." To transition figures from Eastern Europe, both their old and new worlds were vital. Their struggle was not between one dying and one emerging culture or spiritual constellation, but between two living and legitimate though conflicting claims on their conscience. For all their personal or intellectual transformation, these transition figures retained at bottom a full, double loyalty, a commitment to that which supposedly they had transcended, an uncertainty arising from ultimate indecision, a view of the world and of themselves that was complex. Unicultural self-definition was profoundly alien to them.

Transition figures from Eastern Europe constitute some of the most puzzling, ubiquitous, significant representatives of Ashkenazi Jewry in its encounter with the West since the birth of Moses Mendelssohn over 250 years ago. From Israel Salanter to Harry Wolfson to Isaac Hutner, from J. Z. Lipovitz to A. J. Heschel to J. B. Soloveitchik, the psychological, the scholarly, the theological, the literary, the political, and the philsophical landscape of modern Jewry was irretrievably altered by individuals who embodied a prevailing, usually premodern Jewish conception of man, God, or society, and who then transposed that conception with both vigor and recoil into another culture.

Not always using the term, Jewish historians have applied transition adumbratively to dissimilar individuals in dissimilar settings; for example, to halakhist-philosophers, politicians, and lawyers in, respectively, medieval Christian Spain, nineteenth-century Western Europe, and twentieth-century America.[2] I use transition in order to bring a broader canvas to high focus, to illuminate a central development in modern Jewish intellectual history: the Jewish thinker from Eastern Europe who occupied a new, uneasy middle ground that distinguished him from familiar types in both medieval and modern Jewish society. The Marrano who renounced either his conscience-stricken Judaizing or Christianizing tendencies and then blended into Jewish or Christian society; the early nineteenth century German Jew who converted to Christianity and lost touch—religious, social, psychological—with Judaism; the pre-Nazi twentieth-century German Orthodox Jew who grew up naturally in two cultures; the pious and secularly ignorant East European Jew; the Jewish revolutionary, artist, or scholar whose Jewishness is defined strictly in relation to his sociological status as outsider; the halakhic convert to Judaism who spurns his family and former religion; the self-hating Jew who removes himself from Jewish faith and peoplehood; the contemporary returnee *(ba'al teshuvah)* who leaves career, secular learning, and American culture to become a hasid in Israel; the unapologetic Jew-in-name only—rarely would any of these types describe the transition figure from Eastern Europe, for he located himself in more than a single Jewish intellectual or social ambience, in more, even, than two separate ambiences. He did more than move from one world to another; he bridged worlds, linked them. He created a compound—a new world.

By contrast, nontransition figures from Eastern Europe failed to encounter Western culture or mores, or, if they did, and consequently transformed their Jewishness, they then failed to reevaluate the transformation; or, indeed, reevaluated it repeatedly, only finally to generate an undifferentiated rejection of or return to Judaism. In its purest form, nontransition is structurally antipodal to transition. The purest antipode to the East European transition figure is neither the culturally unidimensional, reclusive pietist nor the cosmopolitan Jewish renegade. Rather, he is that nontransition figure who is doubly bound, separated from both Judaism and the West, reflective of a twofold marginality that nurtures a singularly objective perspective from which to peer back into society, to perceive microcosmically (as with Freud) the relativity of human emotion,[3] or macrocosmically (as with Einstein) the relativity of the cosmos.[4] In twofold opposition stands the East European transition figure who, too, is doubly bound, not in a double exclusion but in a double participation, in a double inclusion—in an urge to step not out of but beyond one society or culture into another, resulting in a nonobjective perspective on both, illuminating with lucid flashes of insight the parts but not the whole of his multiple loyalties.

The transition figure from Eastern Europe was not an abortive radical or reactionary (though he may have been viewed that way by the society he left). He was a person who tried to get *control*, to seize power at the center of the society into which he moved. His beginning at the fringes, say, of American life, his coming in from the outside, was not just a necessity but a tactic given to effective exploitation: what is more attractive to Americans than the assimilated immigrant who remains just foreign enough—and in just the right way—to be enticingly exotic?

Transition figures from Eastern Europe both fascinate and frustrate; they are intuitively understandable, yet inaccessible. They lived on the edges of one culture, leading it, expressing it, and creating it, yet were also deeply part of another world. They both spoke for and reached past their native context. In trying to articulate the underlying assumptions of their particular Jewish milieu, they reshaped those assumptions under the impact of a different, usually non-Jewish milieu. The result was a highly personal vision that transformed either the thought or the social fabric of their native world. They were illustrative of a context, yet atypical; successful and admired, yet restless and questing; the culmination of one milieu and the beginning of another. Their search was a conscious and often trying one, and eventually dominated their concerns. Their search, in short, reflected a subtle dynamic in autonomous Jewish encounter with the West, in which the Jewish component was neither overwhelmed nor protected, but distinctly exposed—controlling and controlled, salient and subdued, victorious and vulnerable.

If abstract truisms about "transitional epochs" do illuminate individual transition figures from Eastern Europe, these truisms, or definitional categories, cannot bring to light all of the desired details. With some exceptions, the full explanation for the emergence of these transition figures must remain obscure because the requisite information is lacking. As we shall see, one characteristic of these transition figures was their attempt to mystify or shield their origins generally and their inability or unwillingness to speak about their late adolescence particularly. Accordingly, the surest way to understand the idea of transition in Eastern Europe, especially as it reached the United States, is to work inductively, to probe individual lives with the aim of identifying commonalities in the transition experience. Not every transition figure who originated in Eastern Europe evinced all of the commonalities that form a profile reflective of most of these figures most of the time. In detailed exploration of individual figures in the chapters to come, we shall observe both a fleshing out and a partial dismantling of this profile, in a different way for each figure. If too complex to yield a wholly uniform pattern, transition figures did evince strong similarities. No single common thread can explain transition. All of the threads woven together, like the transition figures themselves, fascinate and frustrate, reveal and conceal.

II.

Common to all of the transition figures from Eastern Europe was, of course, geographical dislocation, and this in two senses. All of these figures underwent significant stages of development in the aftermath of changes in locale, and their influence was greatest outside their native locale. The twofold shape of their dislocation—extensive travel and displaced influence—was interlinking. Had their travel been without clear necessity, then lessons learned from it could have become important anywhere, whether close to or far from the transition figures' starting point. They traveled, however, not as wanderers between many worlds, perpetually departing without agenda or itinerary, but as dwellers in one world in search of the realization of an as yet not fully defined political, spiritual, or academic commitment. They pined not for flight but for arrival, not for movement but for the knowledge and the impact that only movement could bequeath. It was a search born not of accident, but of essence; not catalyzed preponderantly by a Europe or an America transformed by modern transportation and communication, but by the subtler ways that ideas have of penetrating the seemingly sealed hamlets and cultures of even those transition figures who predated the modern technological developments. Witness the indiscriminate presence of travel in East European transition figures: they were peripatetic before, during, and after the invention of the telegram and the automobile.

Israel Salanter (1810–1883), the East European talmudist and founder of the pietistic Musar movement, first articulated his understanding of the unconscious (the foundation of his psychological interpretation of Judaism) in letters written after he left Vilna for Kovno in 1849. He developed that foundation both in articles (1861–62) written after he left Kovno for Prussia, and in an essay (1881) written after a quarter of a century of peregrinations in Germany, France, and Lithuania.[5]

Harry Austryn Wolfson (1887–1974), the historian of Western philosophy, first read secular literature when he left Kovno for Vilna in 1902, first expressed antitraditional ideas when he left Eastern Europe for New York in 1903, first received a systematic secular education when he left New York for Scranton, Pennsylvania, in 1905, and first published an article that would become indicative of a lifetime of research three years after he left Scranton for Cambridge in 1908.[6]

Isaac Hutner (1906–1980), the secretive and social yeshiva dean in the United States and Israel, first embraced Musar piety when he left Warsaw for Slobodka in 1921, first obscured his Musar piety, and embraced Zionism and anti-Zionism, when he left Eastern Europe for Palestine in 1925, first accepted and rejected secular study when he left Eastern Europe for Western Europe in 1929, and first put his dialectical qualities to public purpose when he left Europe for America in 1934.[7]

Joseph Baer Soloveitchik (born 1903), talmudic master and scion of one of the most distinguished rabbinic families in Eastern Europe, first developed his synthesis of talmudic Judaism and existentialism when he left Halusk, Russia, for Berlin in 1925, and first developed his notion of modern Orthodoxy as both unavoidable and mandated by tradition when he left Berlin for Boston in 1932.[8]

Joseph Zev Lipovitz (1889–1962), the Israeli pietistic philosopher and Bible commentator, first encountered the pietistic Musar movement when he left Bialystock for Slobodka in 1905, first encountered philosophy when he left Rituva, Lithuania, for Berlin in 1922, and first set forth his synthesis of piety, philosophy, and Zionism when he left Europe for Tel Aviv in 1924.[9]

Abraham Joshua Heschel (1907–1972), born in Warsaw to the expectation that he would become a hasidic mentor (rebbe), openly associated with secular Jewish poets only when he left for Vilna in 1924, acquired the tools for his later researches, philosophic syntheses, and impressionistic tracts when he left Vilna for Berlin in 1927, learned the language and the culture of his most influential writings when he left Europe for Cincinnati in 1940, and set the stage for his religious existentialism and political activism when he left Cincinnati for New York in 1945. He became influential only after moving to New York—just as most transition figures were most influential outside their native environment.[10]

Israel Salanter of Lithuania was most influential in Russia, Poland, and Israel; Harry Austryn Wolfson and Joseph Baer Soloveitchik of Lithuania, in the United States; Isaac Hutner of Lithuania, in the United States and Israel; Abraham Joshua Heschel of Poland, in the United States.

This displacement of influence was an inevitable consequence of the East European transition figures' desire not to wander but to peregrinate with purpose, to turn the discoveries precipitated by their travels into solutions to quandaries that prompted the travels to begin with. The psychological, philosophical, or academic discoveries of the transition figures reflected, yet also represented a transformation of, the transition figures' original matrix. Consequently, their discoveries—their commitments—could not resonate in that matrix. They could become important only elsewhere. And this was true without respect to the Holocaust, since such figures as Wolfson, Hutner, and Soloveitchik began to attain a stature in the United States—before the Holocaust—that they could not have attained in Europe.

A critical impetus that fed symbiotically upon the East European transition figures' urge to travel was their strong interest in and talent at languages. They knew many languages and spoke or wrote with unusual power. They both sought and confirmed limitations and possibilities in a cultural-linguistic matrix as they struck roots in another matrix. Their linguistic dexterity nurtured the transcendence of both the constricting and the liberating elements in their native context while it also deepened roots in that context. Talent for articulation and thirst for expression reflected the need to sort out cross-cultural subtleties of concept and language. It made no difference which languages were acquired and which were the mother tongues; the transitional experience wound it's way through a wide range of Semitic and Indo-European languages.

Israel Salanter's knowledge of Hebrew and Aramaic traditional texts was encyclopedic, his oratorical power in Yiddish, renowned.[11] Harry Austryn Wolfson combined a reading knowledge of Spanish, French, Italian, German, Dutch, and Yiddish with an eloquent English style, a knowledge of rabbinic texts in Aramaic, and a mastery of philosophic texts in Latin, Arabic, Hebrew, and Greek.[12] Isaac Hutner, who consciously concealed his knowledge of languages, math, physics (and other fields, too?) read, as far as is known, Yiddish, German, English, Aramaic, and Italian, and wrote Hebrew with crystalline clarity, stylistic originality, and dignified verve.[13] Joseph Baer Soloveitchik, an orator in Yiddish and English, a haunting writer in English, Hebrew, and Yiddish, has mastered Aramaic talmudic texts and read deeply in Latin, Greek, and German philosophic texts.[14] Abraham Joshua Heschel, who read Polish, Latin, Greek, and German, wrote a uniquely beautiful English and an elegant Hebrew and Yiddish.[15] Of the 150 pietistic volumes written by Israel Salanter and his disciples, none is more elegantly styled than Joseph Zev Lipovitz's commentary on the *Scroll of Ruth*.[16]

What conditioned interanimative linguistic talents and geographical displacements? Transition figures' loneliness, dexterity, impressionability, and eloquence germinated in childhoods both rich and lean, disciplined and disrupted. Their early lives were marked by a stern compression of circumstances that imposed both adversity and freedom—the isolating opportunity to develop intellectual energy or artistic sensibilities far in advance of peers. Extreme disconnection from regulated environments of family or school (or both) nurtured great independence, great expectations, and fears of great failure.

At age twelve, Israel Salanter was sent away from home, never to return (except, perhaps, for brief periods, of which there is no record). A prodigy, he was sent to study with a preeminent talmudic scholar in Salant, Lithuania (whence his surname). His reputation as a throwback to incomparable scholars of the medieval period, his transforming spiritual meeting with and subsequent intensive tutelage under a self-scrutinizing pietist, and his early marriage (which endured)—all this by the time he was fourteen—marked Israel Salanter with that unusual degree of audacity and self-criticism, of certainty of mission and uncertainty of tactics, that animated his unsettling innovations (for example, teaching females), his uneven success with his Musar movement, and his ceaseless curiosity about the unconscious roots of personality and behavior.[17]

At age nine, Harry Austryn Wolfson left home to spend the next four years in three talmudic academies in three different cities. The first year he lived with grandparents, the rest of the time as a boarder. He returned home briefly at thirteen, and then, when his father left for America, Wolfson went to his fourth academy (and fourth city). He stayed for two years of independent study, then went to a fifth city, Vilna, to read classical and modern Hebrew literature independently. When he left Lithuania to be reunited with his father after a three-year separation, the rest of the family stayed behind and he did not see his mother or siblings for almost five years. In New York he studied at still another talmudic academy, in which he fought to widen the curriculum and told witty, irreverent stories, and then left for Scranton, where he received a high school diploma, wrote Hebrew poetry, and learned English. By the time he reached Harvard in 1908, he was twenty-one, had pursued independent study in eight schools on two continents for twelve years, had endured long periods of separation from family, and had developed the extreme reserve, the extreme ambivalance about Judaism, and the extreme dedication to study that marked the rest of his life.[18]

At age fifteen, Isaac Hutner left home for twelve years (save one visit after eight years), keeping his parents at arm's length with letters both affectionate and inaccessible; drawing intimately close to and remaining brazenly independent of talmudic, philosophical, and pietistic masters, many of whom stood in opposition to each other; commuting, as it were, between Lithuania and Palestine, traveling also to Western Europe. In all this he built a formidable array of intellectual, spiritual, and pedagogic powers, which he deployed for four decades to the utter delight, or utter consternation, of students and colleagues in the United States, before returning, again, as he would put it, to the "Land of Israel."[19]

At age seven Joseph Baer Soloveitchik was sent to school for one year.

It was his only formal schooling until he entered the University of Berlin. Until Soloveitchik was twenty-two, his father was his teacher in Talmud, his mother was his teacher, surreptitiously, in literature. Even tutors were not employed until he was past high school age. Never did Soloveitchik interact with his own peers, in study or in play, in the sustained rhythm or regularity of school life. Engraved in childhood were his extreme intellectual acuity, social awkwardness, and painful loneliness—the enduring themes in both his life and work.[20]

Abraham Joshua Heschel, whose father died when he was very young, was raised by his uncle (a hasidic rebbe) and by his mother—the one inculcating the traditional talmudic and hasidic teaching, the other unable (as a father might have been) to prevent the prodigious tyro from surreptitiously learning Polish and Latin, from leaving home to associate with secular poets (while still wearing sidecurls and traditional black frock coat), and from going to Germany to enter a university. Heschel undertook all this in explicit defiance of the wishes of his family, to most of which he became a scandal, to most of which he tried to remain attached. The stage was set for the complexity of Heschel—his wide acclaim and narrow following, his deep tradition and distinct modernity, his outpouring of scholarly, poetic, impressionistic, and theological writings—and his utter silence about himself.[21]

One does not have to be impervious to biographical differences to notice how a strange and similar constellation of yearning, disorientation, and direction animated these special childhoods. They were both creative and crippling. Already in their early years these transition figures were given much and accomplished much, but they also were wrenched (or wrenched themselves) out of natural cultural or familial contexts. They either openly defied or quietly resisted the norms associated with those contexts. And yet, they remained emotionally and sometimes morally or intellectually tied to them. These deep ties, together with the transition figures' certainty about the existential or intellectual necessity of making new departures, account for their silence about, or deliberate romanticization of, their origins. Their most intense period of transition—the late teenage years—was too painful, too full of ambivalence, of both a real sense of disloyalty and an equally strong sense of authentic discovery, to be recollected accurately, if at all. Autobiographical muteness or deception was doubly tempting for those East European transition figures who ended up in the United States—Wolfson, Hutner, Soloveitchik, and Heschel—because most Americans had had no direct contact with Eastern Europe and hence, after the destruction of East European Jewry, no way of either verifying what they were told about it or discovering what they were not told.

Heschel's silence about his teenage years, then, was no rarity, even as it was extreme. There is no record of why the hasidic, traditionally dressed Heschel suddenly appeared with secular poets in Vilna at age seventeen; and Heschel's closest disciples, though privy to many reminiscences and stories, recall Heschel only very rarely talking revealingly about this period.[22] To his very closest followers, Joseph Baer Soloveitchik sometimes drops hints about why he went against the wishes of his father, whom he revered, in enrolling at the University of Berlin—hints, but nothing more. Isaac Hutner permitted not even his closest disciples more than the briefest glance (and, usually, not even that) into the secrets of his intellectual development, sartorial comportment, and pedagogic purposes. The impenetrable side to this hermetic privacy was its pervasiveness since the time he was a teenager, notwithstanding his posthumously published personal letters, which even from his teenage years poignantly reveal a wide range of concerns.[23] Harry Austryn Wolfson, the favorite of a number of yeshiva deans, the young man whose father took great care to ensure his talmudic development—hopes that the young prodigy fulfilled—never identified the point at which he became an "unobservant Orthodox Jew" (his own acutely ambivalent self-definition) by the time he reached Harvard at twenty-one.[24] Past the age of forty, Israel Salanter told his disciples about his preteenage transforming experience with the self-scrutinizing pietist, Joseph Zundel Salanter, and about the dynamics of his decision when he was twenty-eight to break with the reclusive path of Joseph Zundel, but there is no record of his having told his disciples anything about what happened in between.[25] The very fact that the Israeli pietist Joseph Zev Lipovitz studied in Berlin was unknown to virtually all of his followers and omitted from biographical information published about him.[26]

The reluctance of transition figures from Eastern Europe to divulge significant, accurate information about the inner dynamics of their most crucial period of change entailed two dissimilar responses, a complex and self-critical one by the transition figures themselves, and a simplistic and hagiographical one by disciples or admirers. Although these transition figures had to be fiercely independent to follow the forces pulling them away from their native context, it was difficult wholly to shake off the opinion and appraisal of the culture that had left its imprint in their earliest formative stages. Either embarrassed by the betrayal of their past or unable to locate anyone who could understand the forces tugging at them from two or more directions, the transition figures remained silent; only they themselves could know their own complexities and conflicts. Precisely this silence added a mysterious aura to their subsequent accomplishments, an aura of transcendence of the normal limits of culture, an aura that led generally literate and intellectually disciplined disciples or admirers to slip into an exaggerated estimation of their mentor's power or achievements—into an extreme piety that surpasses the usual gratitude and nonobjectivity of someone for another to whom he is in great intellectual or spiritual debt.

Israel Salanter, his admirers thought, would stem the onrush of secularization in East European Jewry; Harry Austryn Wolfson would set right the history of all Jewish, Christian, and Islamic philosophy; Isaac Hutner would unlock the hitherto unfathomable unity within all major categories of Jewish thought; Joseph Baer Soloveitchik would resuscitate talmudic learning and observance throughout the Diaspora; Abraham Joshua Heschel would save the Jewish spirit; Joseph Zev Lipovitz would scrape away the layers of wrong or superficial understanding encrusted upon the Hebrew Bible and unveil its true meaning.

The great expectations that East European transition figures and their disciples or comrades harbored were matched only by the ultimate, great distance between the mentors and the followers. As the follower's estimation of the mentor expanded, the mentor's estimation of himself contracted. Most of these transition figures reached old age (or early death) with great regret or in the specter of great failure.

Israel Salanter, not having stayed the spiritual corrosion of traditional East European Jewry, virtually withdrew into a shell, traveled as far as Paris to undertake a relatively menial task, below his rank, mourned the shrunken size of East European Orthodoxy, and wrote fearfully of himself as "an old man."[27]

Harry Austryn Wolfson, not having convinced Western scholarship of the validity of his bold restructuring of Western philosophy as spurred by Philo until it was spurned by Spinoza, bitterly if unrealistically berated himself in the last year of his life for not having married, for not having published in Hebrew, and for having spent too much time on the Kalam.[28]

Isaac Hutner, never having revealed his innermost feelings on anything (the success of his career included), typically illuminated and obscured himself when, on his deathbed, someone rearranged his pillow and asked whether he was comfortable. "You ask about comfort, but I am already holding by 'Get thyself out! [*lekh le-khah*]' (Genesis 12:1)."[29]

Joseph Baer Soloveitchik, not having created a cadre of profound talmudic-religious personalities who would win the Diaspora for talmudic Judaism, has partially turned to a mystical, or kabbalistic, approach.[30]

Abraham Joshua Heschel, not having transformed the Jewish spirit or ended the Vietnam war, turned into himself, as if in suspension of his social activism, shifting his research from a theological examination of human grandeur to a psychological examination of human mendacity and self-deception.[31]

III.

Shriveled vision, biting remorse, or peculiar diversion constitutes an ironic final self-image to an experience originally suffused with broad talents, goals, and sensibilities. The overblown aspirations and exaggerated failures of the transition figures from Eastern Europe reflect the danger of unrealistic visions of Jewishness since the reentry of Ashkenazic Jewry into Western culture at the end of the eighteenth century. Between the radical alternatives of apostasy or assimilation, and of unalloyed Orthodoxy, there lies a web of interlinking spiritual, intellectual, psychological, and nationalistic commitments whose adoption, these transitions figures found, is both existentially urgent and ultimately unsatisfying. They found no ready way to integrate cross-cultural intellectual aspiration with personal tranquility and societal integrity, notwithstanding their many and diverse attempts to forge the ideal synthesis.

And yet, we should look beyond the danger, should avoid putting too strict a construction on the remorse or sense of defeat in these figures. Their deathbed disappointments should not preclude an analysis of their remarkable achievements, nor yet of the price they paid for them. The chapters shortly to follow constitute the twofold analysis of the achievements and the costs. We shall then be in a position to analyze whether a fundamental quality of Judaism enables the synthesis of an indigenous Jewish culture, such as was found in Eastern Europe, with a contemporaneous culture elsewhere.

Because Salanter, while a psychologist, was still a talmudist; Wolfson, while an objective scholar still a Jewish partisan; Hutner, while a dialectician still a simple sermonizer; Soloveitchik, while a radical existentialist still a talmudist; Heschel, while a social activist still a Polish hasid; Lipovitz, while a self-conscious commentator still an unselfconscious believer—because all of these transition figures from Eastern Europe in the nineteenth and twentieth centuries spanned two worlds, always with toil, sometimes with moving failure and sometimes with dazzling success, their legacy is both a challenge and a quandary. To fashion an integrated Jewish life in the culture of the West is the challenge. The quandary is that, short of the radical alternatives, history permits no evasion of that challenge by Jews touched both by Western civility, freedom, ideas, or promises of glory, and by their God, people, land, or history. There are those who do not simply acknowledge the challenge or wish they could evade it. They welcome it with an intensity that dominates their lives. These are the transition figures to whose lives we now turn.

CHAPTER TWO

Rabbi Israel Salanter

"Anxiety is forbidden,
with one exception:
anxiety over anxiety."

In approaching the early psychologist of the unconscious, Rabbi Israel Salanter (1810–1883), it is not answer, or resolution, but question, or quandary, that predominates. The record of his life and thought in Lithuania and Germany—the documents, the oral traditions, the writings—tantalize to the point of frustration, not fruition. Hints, gaps, unspokenness between the lines, upon reading and rereading, thinking and rethinking, persuade that we can hear the voice behind the silence—but we can never be certain. In his own time an admired pietist, acknowledged scholar, and mysterious bridge figure between East and West European Jewry, he left nothing behind save a few scraps—stories, letters—to push his posthumous profile just one level above anonymity. Frustration with the shreds of evidence led to the fascination he exercized over the traditional Lithuanian Jewish mind. Frustration also led to consistency. Since so little information was left behind it engendered but little interpretation: few documentary hooks upon which to peg disagreement.

For all this, the evidence, if fragmentary, is telling—poignant or dense writings and thematically consistent reports of critical decisions, all bearing Rabbi Israel's typically conscious and considered imprint. The evidence, if spotty, is rich. It is possible to press and knead it until it yields an intensive complexity and more than merely suggestive pattern. The pattern to be built up out of the complexity begins with a series of oscillations between competing concerns that emerged, one after the other, in each successive stage of Rabbi Israel's life.

The son of a Talmud scholar, Israel Salanter, in early childhood displayed the talent of a prodigy in the Talmud's complicated logic, and great devotion to mastering it; yet even before he was thirteen he evinced what became a life-long interest in the logically uncomplicated, psychological, and imaginative Musar, or ethical, literature. This began his first oscillation: between logical and psychological ways of thinking. The congenial disciple of a reclusive, pietistic master of both talmudic and Musar literature, Israel Salanter pursued his studies quietly for some sixteen years, then undertook to propagate the Musar teachings publicly, and secured the appropriate position—a prized chair of Talmud in a renowned academy in Vilna, Lithuania—from which to do so. This began the second oscillation: between private personal growth and public responsibility. The punctilious practitioner of talmudic law, ritual and moral, he founded the Musar movement in Vilna, positing the centrality of Talmud study yet innovatively setting forth a protopsychoanalysis as both prerequisite and helpful concomitant to effective study and practice of talmudic law; doubly innovative in including females within the embrace of a fresh religiopsychological norm. This began the third oscillation: between tradition and innovation. The would-be social revolutionary began to revamp traditional society in Vilna, yet abruptly left in 1849 to narrow the focus of his activity from "society"—the learned and unlearned, the scholar and businessman, male and female—to the young, learned, budding, male scholar, in Kovno, Lithuania. This began the fourth oscillation: between working with masses and working with an elite. Rabbi Israel, the successful founder of a countermovement to modernism in Kovno, trained disciples who personally, or through their own disciples, set the tone by which most of traditional Lithuanian Jewry flourished or against which it rebelled for the next ninety years, until 1939. Yet, Rabbi Israel, at the height of his influence, abruptly left Kovno in 1857 or 1858 for the heartland of modernism (Haskalah)—Prussia—to grapple with it almost continuously until his death in Koenigsberg in 1883. This lengthy and mysterious sojourn recapitualted all previous oscillations.

The oscillations in Rabbi Israel's life were matched by a similar dialectical form in his thought. Life and thought in Rabbi Israel, suggested one commentator, were akin to the procedure of a research physician without the means for a controlled experiment.¹ Continually testing and refining a potent, beneficial drug, he has no one on whom to test it but himself. In the end he produces a wonder drug, but the conclusion to all of the experimental injections is his death.

I.

By the time of Israel Salanter's birth, in 1810, Hasidism had transformed almost all of East European Jewry. In Poland, in Vohlynia, in White Russia, in the Ukraine, and in Galicia, the teachings of the Baal Shem Tov and his disciples had evolved into a number of schools, those appreciative and those skeptical of miracle-working rabbis, those with their own philosophic systems and those without them, those that downplayed talmudic study and those that cultivated it instrumentally, to induce God-consciousness. All of these schools fostered an emotional tonality (often expressed in dancing, drinking, and singing) and, above all, the submission to or overwhelming appreciation of the charismatic religious adept, the rebbe. Only in Lithuania was Hasidism found wanting. Lithuania, notwithstanding its pockets of Stolin and Lubavitch Hasidism, and its interest in the prehasidic Lurianic mystical tradition, followed the lead of the towering talmudic authority, Elijah of Vilna, "the Vilna Gaon" (1720–1797). Under him, Lithuania sustained a deeply ingrained rationalism, a steady, unruffled appreciation of the scholar and the academy, of calm and seriousness, of the Talmud and its supremacy—and the intrinsic value of its study. In Zagory, Lithuania, near the Prussian border, Israel Lipkin (not yet surnamed Salanter) was born to a rabbinical family.² His father, Zev Wolf Lipkin (died 1858), authored commentaries on the Talmud and the codes of Alfasi, Maimonides, and Asher.³ Israel Lipkin's first teacher was his father, the entire curriculum was Talmud. When he was about twelve, his father sent him to the town of Salant (whence his surname) to study with a leading talmudic scholar, Rabbi Zvi Hirsh Broide. Israel Salanter never went to school.

He pursued formal studies under his new teacher assiduously, but grew close to another man, Rabbi Joseph Zundel Salanter (1786–1866), a leading student of Rabbi Hayyim of Volozhin, who, in turn, was the leading student of the Vilna Gaon.⁴ It took time for Israel Salanter to learn the intellectual pedigree of Rabbi Joseph Zundel Salanter, for he dressed without the customary rabbinical robe, held no rabbinic or teaching post, earned his living as a laborer, and talked little. He was self-effacing, hid his knowledge, esteemed privacy, and disguised a pietistic bent. Israel Salanter made a habit of stalking Rabbi Joseph Zundel, observing him at a distance. He learned, through the punctiliousness of Rabbi Joseph Zundel's observance of the talmudic laws, that he could only be a scholar—no one else could know so many details about which to be punctilious.[5] Israel Salanter learned Rabbi Joseph Zundel's unusual ways of humility and of masking aid to unfortunates.[6] As Rabbi Israel told his disciples over thirty years later, he would stealthily follow Rabbi Joseph Zundel into the fields. There, Rabbi Joseph Zundel was in the habit of formulating ethical and pietistic duties of particular relevance to him. Once, he spotted his young spiritual suitor, turned on him, and said, "Israel, learn Musar that you may become one who fears Heaven."[7]

This, reported Rabbi Israel decades later, was the formative experience of his youth. Rabbi Joseph Zundel had revealed a protean code word: Musar. It was the code in which the secrets of Rabbi Joseph Zundel's allure were encased. It was the source of the oscillation between Israel Salanter's attraction to Rabbi Joseph Zundel and his devotion to talmudic study. Musar, as a multifaceted corpus of ethical and pietistic Jewish literature,[8] may have been known to young Israel Salanter even before his encounter with Rabbi Joseph Zundel, but as a competing source of authority, as a practical guide to piety ("fear of Heaven"), as something more than a niche in Jewish intellectual history, as a means for emulating Rabbi Joseph Zundel, Musar, we may assume, was unknown to Israel Salanter prior to the unexpected confrontation in the field. "Rabbi Joseph Zundel's words pierced the chambers of my heart like searing flames," Rabbi Israel told disciples.[9] It was a simple, transforming moment whose reverberations threaded their way through not only the personal life of Rabbi Israel but also the lives, the schools, or the rebellions of Nathan Zvi Finkel ("the Elder of Slobodka"), Harry Austryn Wolfson, Isaac Hutner, Joseph Baer Soloveitchik, and Joseph Zev Lipovitz. They would not likely have developed as they did had Israel Salanter not been vulnerable to the person and the teachings of Rabbi Joseph Zundel.

How Israel Salanter developed these teachings initially can only be surmised. We know virtually nothing about his life for some sixteen years after his confrontation other than that he married, studied Talmud intensively, and remained in close contact with his mentor.[10] Their association was twofold. On the one hand, Rabbi Joseph Zundel was the master. He had read the unasked questions on his fledgling disciple's face—how can I become like you? how can lowly I not succumb to despair, seeing how even lofty you must scrutinize, criticize, your actions? He had read the boy's soul. We must presume this, for otherwise Rabbi Joseph Zundel's one short sentence could not have penetrated with such decisive effect. Clearly, it was well aimed. Rabbi Joseph Zundel knew how to guide. He knew that the pupil needed to emulate his method—Musar study—to advance. As a consequence, he wielded power; he was both adept and analyst. He could, if he wished, not only teach and guide Israel Salanter, but fashion, mold, control him. On the other hand, Rabbi Joseph Zundel instilled independence in the impressionable pupil—either that, or nurtured an independence already there. For if Israel Salanter's sense of unworthiness in the face of the mentor necessitated long years of tutelage under him, unworthiness did not entail imitation or stultification. Rabbi Israel, after a period of accounting of the relative merits of private practice and public teaching of Musar, decided that his role was to differ from his mentor's.[11] It is Rabbi Israel, not Rabbi Joseph Zundel, whom we recall as the founder of the Musar movement. Rabbi Israel, while rooted in Rabbi Joseph Zundel's pietistic teachings, broke from his reclusive path—though the break was hardly complete, Rabbi Israel remaining keenly sensitive to the advantages of privacy even as he opened to public responsibility.

The immediate occasion of Rabbi Israel's reorientation was his mentor's departure. In 1838, Rabbi Joseph Zundel "went up" to Jerusalem,[12] leaving his disciple alone for the first time. How the talmudic talent and pietistic quandaries of the twenty-eight-year-old rabbi came to public attention illustrates the special sense of self-imposed exile—the oscillation between private and public practice of Musar—that grew out of Rabbi Israel's departure from the reclusive path of his teacher.

To seek a position of public responsibility in Lithuania, Rabbi Israel understood that he must first establish his credentials as a talmudic scholar. Setting out on what was to become a lifetime of travel, he circulated throughout small towns (*shtetlekh*) in Lithuania. In each *shtetl* he would post a list of talmudic sources and announce a lecture. It amounted to a challenge to local scholars to review the sources, to entangle him in a web of contradictions. Invariably, however, Rabbi Israel bested his challengers. Soon fame, and jealousy or animosity, preceded him. In one *shtetl*, after Rabbi Israel had posted his list of references, jesters removed it, substituting an unrelated listing. Later, when Rabbi Israel ascended the podium to lecture, he was handed what he thought would be his own listing. Taken aback, he stood silent for minutes. Then he proceeded with his usual mastery of sources, as if his lecture had been prepared on the basis of the new listing.

In relating the incident to disciples long afterward, Rabbi Israel commented that he had not needed time to prepare a new lecture; this he could do instantaneously. The interval, when he stood silent, was a time of inner debate, whether to announce that he had forgotten his lecture, disgracing himself but concealing his acumen; or to remain loyal to his original intentions, revealing his acumen to establish his credentials.[13] The ambivalence, the oscillation between self-concealment and self-revelation, between personal and intellectual growth and public responsibility, defined the particular spiritual pain that Rabbi Israel's break with Rabbi Joseph Zundel's solitariness engendered.

Rabbi Israel's inner debate, we may imagine, was perplexing. To reveal himself—to unveil his knowledge and serenity, to propagate the study of Musar and raise questions about Lithuanian Jewry's ethical standards—would be at once helpful and unhelpful, salutary for the community but corrosive of inner peace, beneficial for the community's integrity but not for his own. Rabbi Israel's decision to become a public figure paradoxically radicalized his penchant for privacy since the new, public stance radically constricted the opportunity for the old, quiet pursuit of piety. And so, dialectically, simultaneously, he thrust himself into the center of Lithuanian Orthodox society and turned ever deeper into himself. He became both public leader and intellectual recluse, a counselor of the women, the students, the rich, and the scholars, and also a resident expatriate; one who taught and argued and struggled for the poor, a leader at the hub of the community, yet also an occupant of its outer rim, one who recoiled from society to create his own refuge. The refuge was both literal—a periodic withdrawal (as under Rabbi Joseph Zundel)—and mental—an internal disengagement, a carving of private space in which spiritual quests, achievements, and setbacks were known not to friends, disciples, even to family, but only to himself.

The framework in which all this first occured was his residence in Vilna, to which he moved from Salant in 1840 or 1841 as a consequence of the intended outcome of his lecture tour—an invitation from a leading talmudic academy, or yeshiva, to assume a senior position.[14] His scholarship confirmed by his position at Rameiles Yeshiva in Vilna, he turned to his larger program: establishing conventicles (*Muser shtiblekh*) for study of Musar literature; moving beyond the classroom to lecture publicly for scholars, laymen, women, and the unlettered; and showing an interest in the poor and troubled.[15] All of this, especially the teaching of women and the establishment of study rooms outside the framework of the advanced talmudic college, broke with communal mores.[16] Externally he seems to have weathered the opposition these innovations generated, his scholarship and unthreatening manner muffling criticism. Internally, however, a web of introspective concerns about fame, sin, purity, arrogance, repentance, and the unconscious springs of behavior and their implication for fear of God, filled his private world. Undertaken originally as a means of self-protection, of guarding integrity while meeting responsibility, Rabbi Israel's private, Zundel-like world—consisting as it did of self-analysis; in particular, scrutiny of the psychological impact of both the enthusiasm and the hostility his innovative program generated—came to expression in his first statements on the power, the malevolence, and the malleability of the unconscious, in homilies of 1845–1846 and letters of 1849.[17]

II.

Rabbi Israel's thought in his early Vilna period, particularly in the letters, is the most complex and compressed of all his thinking. As he grew older he narrowed the range of his concerns even as he developed those few topics that continued to command attention.[18] His Vilna letters (the most important of the Vilna writings), however, represent a whole spectrum of issues, so long "simmering in his uncommunicative mind that it was boiled down to a concentrated essence," and it is this concentrated essence that he set forth in language so elliptical and disjointed that it is as if he used words "not as a means of expression but as a system of mnemonic symbols," words standing not "for simple ideas but for complicated trains of thought."[19] These trains of thought, subjected to exegesis and then interlinked by theme, yield a series of polar concepts whose formal integration was less important to Rabbi Israel than two interrelated messages—the one rhetorical, the other psychological—emerging from his method of presentation. These are the polar concepts: instinct and intellect, emotion and ratiocination, subjectivity and objective truth (Torah), introversion and extroversion, exploitation and altruism, this world and the next world.[20]

Rhetorically, Rabbi Israel shielded his resolution of these polarities behind aphorism and digression. He did not want to be understood in the ordinary sense. He devised a style in which staccato, not flow, predominated, a manner of expression in which each phrase, each element of apparent contradiction, would be absorbed individually. A pithy and jarring idiom was his way of nettling his readers, stinging them to turn into themselves, to absorb, to embody, and ultimately to integrate the fundamental pairings of his thought. The understanding of it would come in the living of it. The resolution of polarities would come not intellectually but internally, not in felicitous formulation but in integrated experience. Rabbi Israel wished not to persuade people but to move them, not to bring a theory of action to high polish but to stimulate its actualization.

This style of rhetoric had a still more direct psychological goal in countering the pietistic risk of self-absorption. On the one hand, Rabbi Israel's stress on man's rootedness in controlling and evil psychic forces necessitated self-scrutiny, the identification and transformation of malevolent motivation, mood, sensibility. On the other hand, self-scrutiny could slip into self-love. Introspection could turn the Musar practitioner wholly into himself, transforming piety and ethics into solipsism and hypocrisy. It was to counter these twin dangers that Rabbi Israel used a pithy, unsystematic idiom. Typically, after hammering away at his reader with a dour epigram ("tormented we are, tormented, by our lusts, whose fulfillment is imaginary gain"),[21] Rabbi Israel shifted to a range of lofty human possibilities such as inner peace or comprehensive intellectual achievement.[22] Rabbi Israel wished to militate against fixation on either the malignant reality or the exalted possibility of man, for to be transfixed by evil, or by the inwardness required to transcend it, was to sink into despair or self-centeredness, and to be transfixed by ideal types was to flee from reality to abstraction, to ignore the inward analysis and behavioral transfiguration required to actualize high ideals. Rabbi Israel used dialectics to coerce the self from out of self-enclosure to reckoning simultaneously with its own radical contingency and with the ethical and spiritual norms that talmudic Judaism commanded.

Of Rabbi Israel's six polar concepts, instinct and intellect received his special attention and elaboration. This pairing forms a particularly clear window to his turn to mind, revealing more vividly than his treatment of other pairings the dialectical goal of his rhetoric and paradoxical mode of his thinking. Man, wrote Rabbi Israel, teems with uncontrollable and unpredictable instincts, wills, desires, inclinations, urges, and "raging character traits"[23] (all were synonymous for Rabbi Israel), all of which subjugate man's intellect, reducing it to a subordinate extension of his inner psyche, robbing it of the power to understand and control itself. In Rabbi Israel there is nothing of the subtle philosophic discussion found, for example, in the Cambridge Platonists about an intricate interrelation of faculties and subfaculties of intellect and will. In Rabbi Israel there is a vision of inner warfare—unsubtle, powerful, incendiary—a vision, as

Karen Horney put it, of "war to the death . . . between fiery giants and icy queens." It is the fiery giant, the unconscious, that triumphs, according to Rabbi Israel. Unconscious desire turns reason into bias, righteousness into selfishness, passion into malevolence; it creates a discrepancy between declared and underlying intentions, a stormy inner world of conflict and self-deception. The malignant desire "confounds and dances within us," wrote Rabbi Israel.[24] "We are sick any way you look at it."[25] Irrationality, evil, and disquietude freely roam.

And yet, said Rabbi Israel, intellect remains an ineradicable substratum; it is never erased. It is a hidden power, a latent ember at any time able to be kindled, revivified, galvanized. Hope is never wholly lost; evil need not be eternally triumphant. Through arduous, persistent labor at Musar study in all its branches, but especially in the impassioned recitation of pithy epigrams in Scripture ("create within me a pure heart, o God!"),[26] intellect gradually reawakens. It quickens; its fiber toughens; its energy returns. It sheds the bonds of raw passion through the extended contemplation and the unmediated absorption of arresting normative phrases of Scripture. Intellect, through the ceaseless repetition of holy words in the white heat of emotion, becomes a burning coal, a fiery giant itself, scorching the inner being word by word, norm by norm, etching in the behavioral and the character patterns of the Torah, until ultimately the unconscious psychic pool, the malignant will, is transfigured into a collectivity of unrestrainable impulses to normative perfection. The intellect, natively all but extinguished by instinct, now extinguishes, or, rather, transmutes instinct.[27]

Intellect, however lucid or acute, cannot shape the inner being and impel action, yet instinct cannot be molded in the absence of intellect. Intrinsically impotent, intellect is still the key to personality refashioning, ironically rendered efficacious by a very stratum that it seeks to mold, the emotions. Transfigured under the impact of renascent intellect, man's erstwhile instincts to evil are now instincts to the good, the healthy, the holy—for Rabbi Israel they are all one.

Dialectic in thought paralleled oscillation in life. Both built in intensity under the impact of two incidents that compelled Rabbi Israel to leave Vilna. In the first instance, Rabbi Israel ran afoul of the talmudic authorities. In 1848 he ruled that it was obligatory to eat on Yom Kippur, the holiest day in the Jewish calendar, on account of a cholera epidemic that was taking lives daily. Not to eat would be to lower resistance to the point of danger, he said. His experience with the epidemic was direct;

he had established a makeshift hospital to treat the ill. There, to lower fatalities, he had issued lenient rulings making it easier to prepare hot food on the Sabbath. This, in combination with the Yom Kippur ruling, provoked open opposition, also spreading his name throughout Lithuania.[28] His image as an iconoclastic Orthodox scholar reached all the way to Tsar Nicholas I, whose emissary, Count Sergei Uvarov, was dispatched some months later to persuade Rabbi Israel to head an "enlightened" rabbinical seminary.[29] His mere association with the seminary, a front for conversion to the Russian Orthodox Church, against the rumblings over his rulings during the epidemic, convinced him that his position in Vilna was no longer viable.[30] For him, the collaboration of Jewish modernizers (*maskilim*) with the actively anti-Semitic tsarist authorities was particularly telling, bringing to the fore a destructive inclination.[31] He altered his view that internal dissolution of the community was a distant threat. The threat, he now believed, was immediate.[32] It would no longer be fruitful to work with masses, as he had in Vilna, no longer realistic to expect that history would grant him time to fortify communal solidarity single-handedly. He would have to found a movement—a Musar movement—and to do so, he chose Kovno, Lithuania, for the site of a new, elite academy.[33]

The shift from teaching a broad spectrum of people to educating an elite cadre of Musar personalities accentuated the importance of pedagogic skill, particularly in tying piety and character development to talmudic study, for in Lithuania it was not raw talmudic talent that Rabbi Israel had to locate. The challenge, rather, was to integrate intellectual achievement with piety, to mold a scholarly personality embodying also the ethical practices, the humility, and the helpfulness prescribed and studied in the talmudic and Musar texts. To train the Musar leader-scholar, the interrelation of instinct and intellect, of emotion and ratiocination, would have to be clear to Rabbi Israel himself. Here, the two incidents that urged him out of Vilna were helpful in his influential nurture of the small, elite academy in Kovno—the cradle of coming generations of the Musar movement. His rulings during the cholera epidemic brought him, a man who had deliberately refrained from deciding the narrowest questions of Jewish law in Vilna so as to avoid all competition or appearance of conflict with the rabbinate there,[34] into open defiance of much of it. The ensuing uproar was such that he announced a public discourse to defend himself. Against expectations, he made no reference to the sources and the reasoning for his lenient rulings, but delivered a talmudic lecture on other topics with such erudition that his detractors were silenced—a scholar of this stature could not err.[35]

The calculated response indicates a strength of detachment, a continuing rootedness in his private Musar world of independent evaluation and pietistic endeavor. Responding to events rationally and clinically, he could not fail to have been instructed by the sudden, emotion-laden outbursts on the part of intellective and balanced legal scholars in response to his own legal rulings. These outbursts must have confirmed and strengthened the direction in which his thought was moving. A year after the cholera epidemic, Rabbi Israel first described the unconscious, particularly its power to erupt unexpectedly and to corrupt absolutely: "Suddenly man will sin greatly [such that] he cannot morally recoup" and "in a split second man will sin grievously; there is no restraining his spirit, he will execute the most evil and abominable actions under the sun," and in all this he will be unable either to perceive his minute transgressions or to "reveal the roots of his heart."[36] "We are sick any way you look at it"; "we tread in darkness"; "our character traits are corrupted" and "raging"; "inclination confounds and dances within us, effortlessly executing its every machination."[37]

Pungent observations on the power of the unconscious (formulated in more explicitly psychological terminology in later writings)[38] were matched by prescriptions for harnessing and transfiguring the unconscious psychic energy. The twofold agenda for raising up Musar disciples was clear: not to exempt the motivations of even the most talented young scholar from biting scrutiny, and not to underestimate the influence that a transformed scholarly personality could wield.

If the uncompromising honesty upon which Rabbi Israel's Musar teachings rested was not to degenerate into a formula routinely invoked yet substantively emasculated—not to harden into a code, a shibboleth, repeatedly uttered yet actually avoided, becoming a rationalization for the very self-deception that it was supposed to uproot—then Rabbi Israel's disciples would have to differ from each other. Since honesty, by both mentor and disciple, could only reveal that each psyche differed from every other, honest analysis of weakness and effective refining of talent would have to yield masters not fashioned in a uniform mold. The unlikeness of Rabbi Israel's three major disciples, all trained in his early years in Kovno, testifies to his concentration on inculcating the importance of scalpel-like introspection—both razor sharp and finely calibrated—and his drawing out talent, individually rendered.

The three major disciples were Rabbis Simhah Zisl Ziv (1824–1898), Naphtali Amsterdam (1832–1916), and Isaac Blazer (1838–1906), whom Rabbi Israel designated, respectively, "the wise," "the pious," and "the learned."[39] Passionate and brilliant, Rabbi Blazer ("the learned") was called to the most lucrative and prestigious rabbinical post in all of Russia—at St. Petersburg (Leningrad)—when he was only twenty-five, and published an enduring work of halakhic discourse when he was forty-three. Then he headed the first Musar *kolel*, or institute for advanced talmudic study, and struggled to institute Musar study in all of the yeshivas of Lithuania. His struggles were usually successful but sometimes controversial, emblematic of the Musar movement's failure to win over the Soloveitchik rabbinical dynasty. In a confrontation with Rabbi Hayyim Soloveitchik that still reverberates in the writings of his grandson, Rabbi Joseph Baer Soloveitchik (Chapter Five), Rabbi Hayyim Soloveitchik maintained that only sick souls were in need of Musar study, that for the rest—such as his own healthy students—study of Talmud was sufficient. Rabbi Blazer maintained that now everyone was sick, in need of Musar teaching and analysis, only some realized this and some did not.[40]

Self-effacing and reclusive, Rabbi Naphtali Amsterdam ("the pious") harked back tonally and temperamentally to the private path of Rabbi Joseph Zundel and was most responsive to that strain in Rabbi Israel's personality. Zealous in his desire to avoid all communal activity, he served as rabbi in Helsingfors and other cities only when economic necessity pressed. Like Rabbis Joseph Zundel and Isaac Blazer he spent his last years in Jerusalem, and also like Rabbi Joseph Zundel he took no part in public activity there, nurturing private devotion and diligent but unrevealed talmudic scholarship until the end of his long life.[41]

Calm and complex, Rabbi Simhah Zisl ("the wise") best preserved the Salanterian dialectic. A pedagogue, like his master, he constituted the channel through which the Salanterian teachings reached those transition figures whose traditional roots were formed by the two different yet cooperative colleagues in the Slobodka yeshiva, Rabbi Moses Mordechai Epstein and "the Elder of Slobodka," Rabbi Nathan Zvi Finkel—the former affecting Harry Austryn Wolfson (Chapter Three), the latter affecting Isaac Hutner and Joseph Zev Lipovitz (Chapters Four, Seven). Rabbi Simhah Zisl founded and headed an academy in Kelm, Lithuania, the first yeshiva in Eastern Europe in which secular studies were taught. Although they were not extensive, it was in Kelm that the Salanterian breadth of intellectual interest was latent, available for students who wished to build upon it, and to which most of the most talented second-generation disciples of the Musar movement came, if only to be stimulated to develop their own reading of the Musar tradition in modification of or opposition to that of Rabbi Simhah Zisl.[42] The Elder of Slobodka's decisive Musar influence was in Kelm, yet the independence of mind that Rabbi

Israel nurtured in Rabbi Simhah Zisl was in turn absorbed by the Elder. His opposite number, Rabbi Joseph Jozel Hurvitz, the Elder of Novorodock (1850–1919), was a radically ascetic nontransition figure who practiced a joyous, one-dimensional self-transcendence. He, too, was influenced by Rabbi Simhah Zisl (and also by Rabbi Isaac Blazer in Kovno), and yet, like the Elder of Slobodka, departed from the orientation in Kelm.[43]

The future of the Musar movement was secured in Kovno with the training of the three major (and other) disciples. Rabbi Israel must have sensed this because by the mid-1850s he was no longer devoting all energy to his yeshiva, but again lecturing in the community, founding Musar *shtiblekh,* turning his energies to laymen.[44] One such layman was Shraga Frank (died 1887), a wealthy businessman in Alexot, a suburb of Kovno, who made his attic available to Rabbi Israel and his disciples. There Rabbi Israel taught his most talented pupils privately, and both he and his students used the attic for periods of solitary study and introspection, especially during the forty days preceding Yom Kippur. The attention Rabbi Israel paid to laymen, a diversion from the institutional goals of his concentration on superior students upon his arrival in Kovno, often served in a roundabout way the same goal; for as the second generation built the Musar movement throughout Lithuania it was often these laymen who supported the institutions it founded. In the case of Shraga Frank and his wife, Golda, more direct aid was provided. Golda Frank, after her husband's death, made certain to seek budding Talmud scholars for sons-in-law and free them of financial worry. One of these scholars was Rabbi Moses Mordechai Epstein, who supplied the intellectual backbone to the influential Slobodka center of Musar for thirty-five years.[45]

III.

It is critical to distinguish between Rabbi Israel's opposition to Haskalah ("Enlightenment") as it was constituted in Jewish circles in Vilna and Kovno and his attitude toward it in principle. The modernization of East European Jewry went through a pronounced assimilatory phase in the 1840s and 1850s, according to which Jewish languages and customs were not to be complemented but replaced by Russian language, religion, or culture.[46] Lithuanian Haskalah seemed particularly dangerous to Rabbi Israel since its emphasis on secular study, not in tandem with but in opposition to Talmud study, could be especially compelling in a cultural environment readily inclined to use of the mind. The Musar movement, with its emphasis on knowing and transforming the psyche, was an attempt to ground the Lithuanian inclination to intellection solidly in the will, such that the respective allure of secular and religious study would be unevenly matched. On the one side would be the cultural and economic advantages of secular study. On the other side would be the integrated religious personality. His commitment to talmudic study and custom would encompass but also reach below his intellect into what Rabbi Israel conceived to be the more powerful, determinative unconscious, or will, able to resist an allure that, whatever its intrinsic merits, entailed the abandonment of Jewish study, custom, and community.

Rabbi Israel's estimate of the intrinsic merits of Haskalah was clouded by his fierce opposition to it in Vilna and Kovno, yet a positive estimate contributed to his early successes there. In a traditional society breaking down, the endeavor to preserve it has a better chance of success if some of the corrosive forces acting on it can be accepted as consonant, on a profound level, with the tradition that, on the manifest level, they attack. It was differentiated vision of this kind that Rabbi Israel's seemingly blind opposition to Haskalah masked, for Rabbi Israel sought to raise to the consciousness of traditional Lithuanian Jewry certain tendencies of Haskalah that bathed in light forgotten segments of tradition, while staunchly attacking Haskalah generally on account of its assimilatory impulse. Haskalah's humanistic stress on individual development and its pungent critique of ethical laxity in the community—these were precisely the segments of tradition that Rabbi Israel's own Musar studies had irradiated, and that he worked to propagate. And yet, Haskalah, notwithstanding its merits, could not be countenanced.

It was the explosion of this unstable tension that took Rabbi Israel's fourth oscillation—between working with masses and working with an elite—to extremity: leaving Eastern Europe altogether. The positive evaluation of Haskalah, even if only partial, could not forever be hidden if it was precisely the Musar teachings of Rabbi Israel that dovetailed with the positive aspect of Haskalah. And yet, Haskalah could not be praised—and yet, it was increasingly victorious in the struggle for Lithuanian Jewry, so its positive elements could not wisely be hidden. A vicious circle—especially since any praise of Haskalah would destroy Rabbi Israel's credibility in the Orthodox rabbinical community. Impasse.

A way out was to turn to a culture in which individual elements of Haskalah could be praised against a background in which the essential failure of Haskalah could be presumed. Rabbi Israel explained his unexpected decision to remain in Western Europe (to which he had traveled temporarily in 1857 for medical treatment) with a parable:

> When horses panic on a mountaintop and begin to gallop downhill, they cannot be restrained. Whoever tries to halt them will endanger his life; the horses will surely trample him. Once the horses have reached level ground, however, it is possible to bridle them, to bring them under control. So it is with rejuvenation of Judaism. In Russia, the large Jewish communities gallop on a downward spiritual slope; it is impossible to bring them to order. But the German communities have been on level ground for some time; it is possible to halt them, to restore them.[47]

The revitalization of Orthodoxy in Lithuania, Rabbi Israel seems to have said, could not be achieved so long as Haskalah was alluring, while in German lands Haskalah, precisely because it had already taken its toll and was predominant, was no longer uncommonly attractive. Haskalah in Germany had been a movement of promise. It had offered enticing visions of intellectual, religious, social, and occupational emancipation, but a promise half-fulfilled and half-aborted, thought Rabbi Israel, was not so alluring as a promise envisioned. Haskalah in Germany was therefore amenable to being openly challenged no less than openly, if partially, appreciated.[48] And in this the quandary over working with masses or elites could receive a hitherto impossible resolution. German Jewry, the source of Haskalah, had the power of a vanguard. If Haskalah could be successfully remolded at its ideological root, then the danger to Russian Jewry could be diminished. All of German Jewry fell into the category of an elite with respect to Lithuanian Jewry. To work in Germany was to work, in effect, with masses and an elite simultaneously; in other words, to reduce tension in the fourth oscillation.

Residence in Germany and later in Paris reduced tension also in the third oscillation, between private personal growth and public responsibility. The probability of spiritual trials owing to revelation of knowledge and piety was diminished since the number of people in the German Jewish communities who could understand and appreciate keen talmudic intellect and Musar spirituality was far smaller than in Lithuania. In the West Rabbi Israel would not have to strain to veil his knowledge and spirit, nor would he have much to fear if he incautiously revealed them. There was a reverse and almost a perverse spiritual comfort in working with Jews whose Jewishness was neither so intense nor so informed as in Eastern Europe. Rabbi Israel's wanderings—he infrequently remained in any single locale for more than a year at a time[49]—further reduced the risks of self-revelation. If spiritually less trying, work and travel in Western Europe nevertheless constituted the acceptance of public responsibility, and in simpler terms of self-sacrifice the travels were both a physical and psychological strain, as he was so often on the move and separated from family hearth. In leaving Lithuania he could pursue his Musar studies and self-analytical experiments privately without either renouncing public responsibility or, in carrying it out, bearing the full burden of the peculiar Musar suffering of self-revelation.

Not unintended, we suspect, was an ineluctable corollary of Rabbi Israel's move westward: the ease of covering his tracks, of suppressing or simply precluding the existence of documents that would inform contemporaries and posterity of what he did in the West. His extant personal letters from this quarter century add up to just over one hundred pages, and many of them are riddled with ellipses, rendering them partially or wholly unintelligible.[50] One slim work, written by a grandson, describes his activities in his German period.[51] There is no extant picture or drawing of Rabbi Israel—again, we suspect, not an accident. If self-revelation was a trial to be avoided at all costs, Rabbi Israel succeeded at much cost to historian and biographer.[52]

Residence in Western Europe accelerated and radicalized Rabbi Israel's penchant for pedagogic innovation, but here, too, the tension in the second oscillation—between tradition and innovation—was reduced. The Orthodox who could find Rabbi Israel's innovations objectionable were culturally, if not geographically, distant, in Lithuania, while the Orthodox of Germany were themselves the originators of new departures. More important, little to nothing came of Rabbi Israel's innovations, which amounted mostly to suggestions and projects that he could not bring to fruition. The one success, the first journal of talmudic investigations and Musar thought, lasted less than two years (*Tevunah*, 1861-1862). The stillborn suggestions included: the preparation of an Aramaic-Hebrew dictionary to facilitate the study of the Talmud by beginners; the translation of the Talmud from Aramaic to make Talmud accessible to non-initiates; the elucidation of methodological principles of Talmud study, to make it understandable to a systematic mind; the introduction of Talmud into university curricula to increase respect for it among Gentiles (this, as a way of establishing a locus of respect for Talmud that would speak to the assimilating mentality of West European Jewish students, who did not respect Talmud in its own right); and finally, the publication in Russian of Jewish books for assimilating East European Jewish students.[53]

All of these ideas, except for the last one, derived from Rabbi Israel's contact with German and Parisian Jewry that, as far as can be ascertained, included informal teaching of Jewish university students, counseling Jewish community councils (especially in Memel and Paris), educating individual lay and academic devotees of both West and East European origin, and supervising ritual slaughter *(shehitah)*.[54] During the long sojourn in Western Europe, Rabbi Israel stayed in touch with Lithuanian Jewry by sending emissaries to his disciples and by returning frequently on brief trips, once (perhaps twice) for two years.[55] The opposition to whatever reached Lithuania of his innovative ideas was muffled by his heroic image as the first, ranking Lithuanian talmudic scholar to try to "save" West European Jewry; and upon his return to the West his innovative streak agitated no one.

Finally, we may imagine that also the first oscillation, between Musar and talmudic study, received a certain quieting over the years, for Rabbi Israel's writings develop with progressive clarity the interrelation of the two—the subsuming of Musar under the rubric of talmudic teaching, the understanding of talmudic norm as the substance of the Musar personality.[56] And yet, if tension in Rabbi Israel's oscillations did recede, tension surely persisted. First and foremost, on the scale that mattered to Rabbi Israel, he failed. Many of his projects in Western Europe failed; his Musar movement in Eastern Europe never took hold of the community as did its analogue, Hasidism, in other parts of Eastern Europe. In 1881, two years before he died, Rabbi Israel wrote mournfully about the spiritual decomposition of the community he had set out to fortify in 1838.[57] Then there was his illness, never posthumously diagnosed. Symptomatically he suffered from migraine headaches and fits of melancholia. Some link these symptoms to Musar excesses of self-criticism, but they apparently were a hereditary disorder, as his brother and one of his sons (neither of whom was identified with the Musar movement) suffered from similar symptoms.[58] In any case, he was often ill and sometimes virtually disabled, especially in his last years. And finally, he grieved over another one of his sons, Lippman Lipkin, who apparently inherited his father's intellectual ability but turned it, against the wishes of his father, to mathematics *(the Lippman parallelogram)* instead of to Talmud, dying at the age of thirty.[59] Rabbi Israel's wife also predeceased him, leaving him a widower for thirteen years.[60] And here we reach the ultimate oscillation in Rabbi Israel Salanter, the struggle between struggle and tranquility. Struggle: his oscillations, travels, projects, tragedies. And tranquility: memoirs paint a picture of a man of self-transcendence and serenity, calming and soothing by his presence.[61] Contradictory poles coalesce as dynamic equilibrium.

IV.

The legacy of Rabbi Israel has divided into several faults, with his strata of multifaceted interests posthumously colored by a diversity of perspectives, both ideological and institutional.

Rabbi Israel's lengthy exploration of how subjective, preeminent talmudic scholars could be transformed into objective teachers not only in the narrow sense of masters of received tradition but also in the wider sense of teachers and counselors in all areas of life, individual and communal, found its way to the heart of the ideology of the Orthodox political movement, Agudath Israel. It was founded to unite West and East European Orthodoxy in 1914, subsequently active in interbellum Poland, and now, after the Holocaust, is active in both Israeli politics and American Jewish communal life. Agudath Israel owes the essence of its ideology—the preeminent Talmud scholar as the final authority in Jewish life—to Rabbi Israel, not only substantively but, equally important, terminologically. For, as Harry Austryn Wolfson has written, "beliefs and ideas ride on the back of terms, and wherever there is a transmission of a belief or an idea from one . . . setting to another, there is always a transmission of the fundamental terminology of the belief or the idea transmitted, either by translation or mistranslation."[62] Rabbi Israel's term, *da'at Torah* ("the Torah opinion"),[63] was taken over by Agudath Israel as both translation and mistranslation: a translation of Rabbi Israel's intent in the sense that Agudath Israel uses the term to connote formally the kind of leadership Rabbi Israel intended; a mistranslation in the sense that all that lay behind the term—the conscious, self-analytical process of transfiguring the subjectivity of the talmudic scholar[64]—is not widely appreciated.

A related area of the Salanterian legacy is the *kolel*, in which newly married men are supported financially to free their energy for advanced talmudic study. Rabbi Israel's decision led to the allotment of a large, unearmarked donation for the founding of the first *kolel*, in Kovno, in 1877[65] (there are now hundreds throughout the world). As Rabbi Israel believed that a besieged Orthodoxy required a new kind of leadership, so, too, he believed that the institutional training for this kind of leadership must dominate communal priorities. Communal breakdown required new institutional and ideological approaches. And beyond—or, perhaps, behind—all this, his struggle for tranquility was not just a psychological need or Musar ideal, but a way of coping with the disappearance of the familiar landmarks of traditional society.

Rabbi Israel's intellectual legacy is the incorporation of psychology into Jewish thought. His own treatment of a range of philosophical and theological issues was rooted in a new understanding of man. Psychology as an irreducible prism through which other disciplines of Jewish thought were to be refracted was both assumed and put to use with greater force and comprehensiveness by Rabbi Israel than by any Jewish thinker before him. If the antinomy of free will and divine foreknowledge, or of free will and the unconscious, for example, could be resolved only by Rabbi Israel's resignation to its being irresoluble—to its irrationality—then this logically unsatisfactory solution acquired a new reasonableness by virtue of Rabbi Israel's new recognition of man's own irrationality.[66] If the problem of evil, the antinomy of righteousness and suffering, could be resolved only by reference to the inscrutability of righteousness—the self-deception and exploitation never with certainty wholly uprooted from even those who appear to themselves or to others to be most pious[67]—then, again, man and his psychology were at the heart of the quandary. Rabbi Israel was both medieval and modern. He did not shift Jewish thought from its medieval God-centeredness, but rendered the modern focus on man, in all his complexity and unpredictability, no less central than the focus on God.

Rabbi Israel's penchant for paradox and inclination to innovation bequeathed the receptivity to Judaism-as-a-dynamic, a life pattern to be shed or adopted, rebelled against or existentially embraced. Ever since Rabbi Israel's Judaism took as its base the human receptacle of holiness ever in need of analysis and change, ever deficient in apprehending and embodying the will of the Divine, a dynamic was set in motion, according to which Judaism spoke to the whole gamut of the experiential, became the traversal of a whole continuum. In the aftermath of Salanterian Musar, Jews could climb on or off that continuum at any point. This idea has had its most direct resonance in the returnee movements in Russia, Israel, and the United States that began in the 1960s.[68] Particularly in Israel, the long arm of this idea took form not in a resonance but in a delayed influence, as disciples of third-generation Musar yeshivas became the first to attract in large numbers the type of assimilated Jewish students who, a century earlier, had become the object of Rabbi Israel's solicitude in Germany.

Finally, Rabbi Israel left behind a fresh image of righteousness, in which the upshot of his Musar analysis, the goal of his communal activity, the content of his talmudic and philosophic knowledge, and the behavioral confluence of his oscillation between struggle and tranquility, all met. Ultimately, what gave Rabbi Israel and the Musar movement power can best be expressed by the anecdotal, for the image of the Musar personality that one would predict or imagine on the basis of literary remains is often at odds with the results of direct observation and analysis. If, perhaps, oral tradition exaggerates or alters details, representative anecdotes preserve a tonality still discerned in fourth-generation Musar disciples.

Ascending the bridge on the way to deliver a talmudic lecture in Zaritsche, across the river from Vilna, Rabbi Israel noticed a woman rushing toward the river. He descended, stopped her, asked the cause of her distress. She was evasive, told him to let her go. He grabbed her bodily. She told him that her two children had recently taken ill and died. Her husband then suffered a breakdown. She hired someone to operate his horse-and-buggy taxi, but he had to be paid and there was almost no income. Today, she said, the horse died. She was going to end her life. Rabbi Israel searched for words. He observed that her problems were correctable. She was young, could yet bear children. Her husband could recover. And as for the horse he would send money the next day to buy a new one. She was calmed, returned home. Rabbi Israel proceeded to his lecture, sent money the next day for a horse. A year later he received an invitation to a ritual circumcision (*brit milah*).[69]

Rabbi Simhah Zisl Ziv was traveling together with Rabbi Eliezer Shulevitz from the town of Lomza. As dinnertime approached, they came upon an inn and entered to rest and eat. The presence of these two men caused quite a stir in the inn. The proprietress, in particular, treated them with great respect and solicitude. While serving their meal, she began to chatter about her affairs and rambled on for some time, detailing her family problems and her difficulties in running the inn. Throughout, Rabbi Eliezer sat with his head in a book, paying no attention to the lady, but Rabbi Simhah Zisl listened attentively, responding to her questions and asking questions in turn. When it came time to pay for the meal, the proprietress refused to accept payment from either of them. On the road again, Rabbi Simhah Zisl turned to Rabbi Eliezer, "Don't you think you transgressed the prohibition, *Thou shall not steal?* You ate and drank and did not pay for it." Rabbi Eliezer responded, "What are you saying? We offered to pay for the meal but were refused!" "That is so," replied Rabbi Simhah Zisl, "but you didn't realize that the woman was pouring out her heart to us and found emotional relief and satisfaction in speaking to us. You refused to listen to her, so that you, in fact, enjoyed her meal without paying anything at all for it."[70]

This is the story about Rabbi Isaac Blazer at the *hadran* (lecture marking the completion of a talmudic tractate) that he delivered in Kovno. He asked the other scholars to speak first. They did so with great brilliance, since they were masters of the Talmud. They wove intricate patterns, and engaged in most subtle reasoning and explanation. But when Rabbi Isaac took his turn, he delivered a brief Musar talk on *Torah lishmah* (the importance of studying Torah for its own sake, free of any ulterior motive) and the great happiness which such study bestows. The audience was taken aback, for they knew that he could have outshone the other speakers. But this was his way of calling attention to the teachings of Musar.[71]

Although Rabbi Naphtali Amsterdam set a rigid schedule every day, not varying his plans by a hairsbreadth despite all vicissitudes, he would relax on Purim by drinking and relating stories about his teacher and noted friends. He spoke of the virtues of Rabbi Israel's great disciples and repeated his description of them. "Rabbi Isaac was learned and Rabbi Simhah Zisl was wise." He did not even mention what his teacher said about him. Due to indulgence in strong drink, I was impudent enough to ask him in Purim style: "What did your teacher say about you?" Rabbi Naphtali looked at me sharply with astounded eyes and exclaimed: "Do you think it is permisslble to mock an old man even on Purim?"[72]

On the last night of his life, Rabbi Israel found himself in Koenigsberg. The representatives of the Jewish community there had assigned a watchman to sit with him, since he was a luminary, and family, friends, and disciples were away in Lithuania. The watchman was upset—frightened at the prospect of spending the night with a dead body. As a preacher of self-scrutiny, Rabbi Israel, we may assume, would have liked to take these last moments to review his life and repent. Inwardly, perhaps he did. Outwardly, he talked with the watchman, to try to convince him that there was no danger in remaining alone with a corpse—his own.[73]

As realized in his last moments, Rabbi Israel's experiments in producing and propagating a potent new drug—a fresh understanding of righteousness, rooted in self-analysis and talmudic study, realized in the integration of talmudic ritual, ethical, and character norms into the personality—gave his life the heroic character of the undaunted explorer. This legacy was subjected to ramified interpretation—adopted and adapted, attenuated and amplified, a medicine that incubated research, rebellion, and reverence—but, in all cases, taken as a fundamental datum of human experience.

CHAPTER THREE

Professor Harry Austryn Wolfson

"Every Jew who in his own experience has broken away from the old moorings and is set adrift, driven on and on, not knowing whither, has this longing uppermost in his heart, to land somewhere, to fall in harmony with the rest of the world, to share with the rest of mankind their common ideals and tasks and joys and sorrows. . . . For to lose one's self in the multitude, body and soul, is one of the elemental human passions."

"Some are born blind, some deaf, some lame, and some are born Jews."

Harry Austryn Wolfson unraveled with aplomb and erudition the mystery of the "parentage" (as he called it) of unknown or seemingly unrelated, seminal terms and ideas in Greek, Arabic, Latin, and Hebrew philosophic texts. He put a unique stamp on intellectual history, but in so doing he sealed his own history in mystery. A man who produced a mass of learned monographs and magisterial volumes on the history of Greek, Christian, Islamic, and Jewish philosophy—all grounded in an unusual method of research—he could not help but obscure the parentage of his method, for it was grounded in his own history. And his own history he could not illuminate, for its first half was a progressive slide into impotence; and its second half, impotent as it was, could only be borne in helpless silence—in a loneliness so pervasive that he could not even say, with his fellow Lithuanian emigre to Boston, Joseph B. Soloveitchik: "There is a redemptive quality for an agitated mind in the spoken word and a tormented soul finds peace in confession."

The search for the roots and contours of Wolfson's research method, and for Wolfson himself, are one and the same, for in the mature Wolfson all that remained of his first half was his method alone. He had systematically squeezed out every other trace of earlier allegiance: to doctrinal and behavioral Orthodoxy, to Hebrew poetry, to essay writing, to Zionist revival. The early Wolfson is a study in the relentless denuding of Jewish attachments and the evisceration of human attachment generally—a study in the self losing itself in the multitude—while the mature Wolfson is a study in the stubborn persistence of the burden of Jewishness, reduced and attenuated to a transformed talmudic method and unadmitted partisanship. "Some are born blind, some deaf, some lame, and some are born Jews," mourned Wolfson.[1] Just as the blind, the deaf, and the lame cannot escape their condition, so, too, the Jew. But just as the handicapped can, with immense effort, modify their circumstances, so, too, can the Jew: so ran the logic of Wolfson's life. It was an effort to transform an onerous, unasked-for, "Fate."[2] Wolfson's radical transformation of the original uses to which his research method were put, and his radical transposition of the spiritual seedbed in which it was nourished, account for the twofold tonality of his embrace of both method and seedbed: his rootedness in both, his distance from both.

An unraveling of Wolfson's dialectic in his own lifetime had to contend not only with his reticence but with an almost legendary aura that grew up around him: Lithuanian Talmud student who, by way of Scranton, Pennsylvania, entered Harvard University as a freshman at the age of twenty-one, soon to occupy the first chair in Jewish studies in any American university in the twentieth century, created by Harvard especially for him; extraordinarily assiduous bachelor scholar holed up in his Harvard study ten to fourteen hours daily, seven days per week, living among manuscripts; master of countless languages, accomplished English stylist, philosophic visionary of three world religions; "priestly guardian of scholarship" (as he alluded to himself) "zealous for its purity and fearful of its being contaminated by the gaze and touch of the uninitiated"[3]—all this, in application of "the Talmudic hypothetico-deductive method of text interpretation."

The method originated in Rabbi Israel Salanter's third-generation Musar school, Slobodka, but before it assumed its scholarly form in Wolfson's agile hands he passed through an anguished crucible of pulverization and reconstitution.

I.

Harry Austryn Wolfson, nee Zvi Hirsh Wolfson, was born in Ostrin, Lithuania, in 1887.[4] On a certain level—chronological segmentation—his life bore an uncanny resemblance to that of Rabbi Israel Salanter. For both Lithuanians, there first came intensive introduction to Talmud study and fundamental reorientation toward it, a period in which only dates and places of residence are known, the internal workings of mind and soul, largely unknown (dates, places, for Rabbi Israel: birth to age twenty-eight, in two hamlets in Lithuania; for Harry Austryn Wolfson: birth to age twenty-one, in seven hamlets in Lithuania and three cities in the United States).[5] Then came the two Lithuanians' period of semi-extroversion; study, teaching, and analysis of the Jewish community for Rabbi Israel (age twenty-eight to forty-seven, in Vilna and Kovno); study, analysis of the Jewish community, and a degree of socializing for bachelor Wolfson (age twenty-one to forty-two, in Cambridge, Massachusetts, save a brief stint in the Army).[6] Finally, for both, came withdrawal, concealment, a movement inward—an aura of inaccessibility due to reputation for extreme intellectual attainment and extreme personal reserve, as if only another world could understand. Rabbi Israel almost literally disappeared, preponderantly wandering about Prussia and France, covering his tracks, leaving scant record even of dates and places, let along of what he studied, whom he taught, and what impressions he left. Wolfson remained externally present, teaching and publishing at Harvard, but internally absent, withdrawn, married to research and cloistered in his carrel.

The similarity in life patterns ends with the structural parallel. Withdrawn and private as he was, Rabbi Israel's acute self-consciousness periodically bequeathed telling reports of the state of his consciousness—reports that enable a skeletal reconstruction of the ground of major decisions and quandaries that shaped his life. Wolfson, however, sealed his consciousness almost hermetically. Few leaks, or telltale recollections, enable a reconstruction of the ground of his major decisions and quandaries. His personal remarks illuminated either a single or a temporary fiber of consciousness—an enduring or momentary mood—but no ganglion of conflicts from out of which he came to turning points, let alone a pattern of internal development. Wolfson was solitary, self-absorbed,[7] both incapable and unwilling[8] to commit to anything but intellectual problems[9] (save the movies, mystery novels, and television).[10] In this enveloping privacy, if Harry Wolfson diverged from Rabbi Israel's Musar sensibility, he also derived from it, or, at the least, found nurture in it.

The occupational hazard of Rabbi Israel's teaching of introspection as an essential step to effacement, to the bending of selfish impulse to service of God and man, was self-absorption. In the in-turning to self for the sake of purifying it, one could become stuck in the self. The dialectic between self and society could become lost. Self-absorption, precisely the opposite of the Musar goal of self-effacement, could spring from the process of abnegating the self. This occupational hazard had its different filters. It was generated in one school of Rabbi Israel's disciples in a different way from in another school. In the Slobodka school, characterized by quiet intensity, ratiocinational rather than emotional passion, and the penchant for resolving pietistic quandaries less in conjunction with mentors, comrades, or disciples than by oneself, the particular filter of the Salanterian occupational hazard was extreme self-containment.[11] To root Harry Austryn Wolfson's extreme reserve, clothed in single-minded devotion to study, in his experience in Slobodka, must be done hesitantly in the absence of information about his inborn or prior inclinations. But we may safely say that the trappings and the teachings of Slobodka's pietistic strain did not run against the grain of Wolfson's native tendencies—and we may say more.

Harry Austryn Wolfson was not enrolled in Slobodka by elders or teachers; he voluntarily snuck into it in defiance of them. He was brought by his uncle not to Slobodka but to Kovno. These twin towns, separated by a river, had witnessed a bitter split within the Slobodka yeshiva not long before Wolfson's arrival. The split was generated by a fractious dispute in Lithuanian Jewry, of which Slobodka was only one of the foci—a dispute about the propriety of study and practice of Musar in Lithuanian yeshivas. The better part of the Slobodka student body sided with the opposition to Musar, and, to house that opposition, anti-Musar proponents founded a new yeshiva, Knesset Bet Yitzhak, in neighboring Kovno in 1897.[12]

It was in this anti-Musar yeshiva that young Wolfson was enrolled in about 1900. But he used to sneak across the bridge connecting Kovno to Slobodka in order to listen to what represented a kindred intellectual spirit, the talmudic discourse of the Slobodka yeshiva dean, Rabbi Moses

Mordechai Epstein.[13] Wolfson did not stumble upon Slobodka; he sought it out, and he stayed there longer than at any other stopping point between leaving home at age nine and leaving Lithuania at age sixteen.[14] It is clear, as we shall see, that the impact of Rabbi Epstein's lectures on Wolfson's method of research was deep and lasting. If Slobodka was sufficiently alluring to draw Wolfson to it from a climate of opinion opposed to it, and if its impact on his mind was enduring, then its broader strictures about the surpremacy of personal dignity, deliberateness in demeanor, restraint in decorum, and control of desire at least did not violate his sensibility. And if they reinforced and served as justification for his bent toward an extreme privacy and abstemiousness, leading to lifelong bachelorhood, devotion to intellect, and lucid exposition, then Wolfson was not the only one of his kind to have emerged from Slobodka.[15]

Arriving in the United States, Wolfson studied at the Rabbi Isaac Elchanan yeshiva, as if in default. There was nothing else for a Yiddish-speaking, talmudically trained teenager to do, except to work. His father would not hear of that. When the first chance to move beyond the rebellion of telling irreverent stories at the yeshiva presented itself, he jumped. After an abortive attempt to learn to cut men's suits, he answered an advertisement for a teacher at a new Hebrew school in Scranton, Pennsylvania.[16]

Employed in the late afternoon, his thirst for knowledge of American ways and general knowledge was sufficient to enable him to swallow pride, to enroll in elementary school. Completing his "degree" in three months, he entered Central High School, graduating three years later with an average of nearly 100. Already he was an enigma. "Absorbed in his own thoughts, he would sometimes pass the [Hebrew school's] principal and some of the lay directors in the halls without recognizing them."[17] Not the least object of his concentration was the English language. An aesthetic concern for style occupied him also in experiments in Hebrew verse and short story writing. Through a fortuitous turn of circumstances, Wolfson learned of scholarship aid available from Harvard, applied, and was admitted.[18] His first publications were in the Hebrew press in New York City on life at Harvard and on literary criticism ("The American Trend in Hebrew Literature").[19] One of two surviving undergraduate term papers is an essay in the philosophy of art.[20] The sureness and lightness of touch evident in this paper, and throughout his subsequent writings, could not have come without sustained labor.

A poor East European, an exceptionally bright Jewish youth, a *yeshiva bochur*, falls in love with America, above all with the English language.

(In what other language does lyric poetry rise so effortlessly to pure song? Maybe Heine's German.) He is determined to master the language, so he becomes one of the finest creators of expository philosophical prose on both sides of the Atlantic: never misty, always lucid; never fumbling with immigrant dialect; never retreating behind metaphysical jargon because the substance is technical or ponderous; always thoroughgoing in review of the primary sources. The labors to achieve this felicity, in addition to mastering classical languages and Semitic ones, were labors he must have loved, to be sure, but they forced him into loneliness and hard work in all hours and all seasons—learning, remembering, testing, forming hypothesis, deducing, revising, writing, writing, and rewriting.[21]

"Forced him into loneliness." No. These labors constituted an outlet for a loneliness already deeply ingrained. "When . . . long ago, [I was] a boy far away from home in a strange city, weighed down with lonesomeness and homesickness, walking aimlessly the unfamiliar streets and looking with wistful eyes at the shuttered doors and windows . . . ."[22] Wolfson goes on to describe the solution to his loneliness (cited in this chapter's epigraph)—falling into harmony with the common ideals, tasks, joys, and sorrows of mankind. The solution, set forth in an essay, "Escaping Judaism" (1921), was cast in code words whose meaning and evolution had overtaken Wolfson, as if in tragic inevitability, beginning at some unknown point after he had left home (1896). The belief in the commonality of mankind, into which he could merge, was the end point of a journey whose earliest reconstructible moment was Wolfson's recoil from the ethical, worldly demand, or side, of the Musar dialectic in Slobodka, and whose earliest external evidence was his renunciation of Judaic observance sometime between his residence in the lower east side yeshiva and his entrance to Harvard. The shedding of halakhic observance by East European literary *maskilim* on theological or passionate grounds was not unusual, but in Wolfson's case the abandonment of observance sprang from a deeper wellspring; since that which he substituted for formal religion—Hebrew poetry, essay writing, Jewish philosophy, and Zionism—he abandoned as well. Wolfson's loneliness entailed an unremitting stripping himself of Jewishness, until he reached a synthesis so strange and idiosyncratic that no one else could share in it. Any number of points along the continuum of this denudation may be isolated as affirmative on literary, scholarly, nationalistic, or even religious grounds. But in the context of Wolfson's slide into impotence, these affirmations shrivel to brief, shining moments.

Wolfson's impotence was not neutrality. It was the inability to act upon commitments clearly perceived, once within reach. Wolfson's deformation of sensibility proceeded through three stages: affirmation, grotesque and successful struggle to suppress affirmation, and, finally, a compliant and isolated submission to what he took to be "Fate." Affirmation: Wolfson's student years at Harvard found him not only equipping himself with scholarly tools of languages, philology, and philosophy.[23] He also wrote Hebrew poetry, played a role in student Zionist circles and in the Intercollegiate Menorah Association,[24] and published an award-winning undergraduate essay that broached grounds for the revival of Jewish philosophy.[25] For four years Wolfson was the Hebrew poet at the Harvard Menorah dinners[26] (one of these poems, in English translation, played a key role in Louis D. Brandeis' conversion to Zionism). Even then, however, during Wolfson's brief flirtation with nonscholarly pursuits his attenuation of sensibility was evident. Wolfson's instructor, George Santayana, commented on an undergraduate paper of 1910: "You have a firm, resolute way of arguing; but I am not so sure that your psychological analysis is adequate or final in every case . . . probably, in every instance you mention, various natures would be found to act in various ways . . . you have the *power* of analysis if only you can acquire the necessary scope in experience, or by sympathy. Don't let premature certitude prevent you from doing so with an open mind."[27]

Young Wolfson: Analysis and certitude coupled with dearth of experience and sympathy. Nerve endings, singed, burned, precisely in combination with analytical power, make possible a rendering of psychological reality especially acute, and certain. How much more searingly the contours of experience can be evoked by one essentially denied them yet perpetually, infinitely, close to them. Asymptotically close to life, one impossible step from full participation, Wolfson can imagine its texture and radiance especially powerfully. "[He] keeps himself aloof," wrote Wolfson of a fictional, modern Jewish intellectual, "he is observant, absorbent, discriminative, but not a participant . . . disinterested, frigidly clear-visioned, unblinded by love or by prejudice . . . ."[28] Harold E. Stearns, the literary critic who, like Wolfson, entered Harvard in 1908: "I found [Wolfson] devastatingly well-informed on almost any subject brought up, except the subject of girls . . . ."[29] "Devastatingly well-informed": the power of analysis. "The subject of girls": narrow experience and sympathy.

Graduating with an M.A. in 1912, Wolfson thought seriously of becoming a poet and novelist, or of studying medicine.

But chance, the agent of necessity, . . . decreed otherwise. Shortly before graduation, Professor David Gordon Lyon, the chairman of the Semitics Department, asked Wolfson what he would do if he were awarded a Sheldon Traveling Fellowship. On the spur of the moment, Wolfson replied that he would study Crescas. The reason was, said Wolfson, that Crescas was the one medieval Jewish philosopher who had broken with Aristotle on logical grounds. . . . Wolfson spent the next two years at European universities and libraries. He wasted some time in Italy, he said, with a circle of artists and writers, but mostly he copied passages from manuscripts and books, accumulating two suitcases full in that era before xeroxing, and then returned on the eve of the First World War to the United States.[30]

II.

Upon his return, Wolfson published the first of four essays (1915 to 1921), which mark his passage to a permanent position of narrow experience and sympathy. Only in this seven-year span of his eighty-seven year life does Wolfson provide significant glimpses into his deepest consciousness. "Jewish Students in European Universities" (1915) was published with a picture of the twenty-eight-year-old graduate student. If not for the absence of yarmulke and beard, the visage would be that of a young master in Slobodka: perfect grooming, starched collar, neatly clipped hair, immaculately ironed suit, aristocratic glance. The appearance of Slobodka persisted, the substance did not.

Wolfson writes with a chilling distance, deftly ridiculing "Parlor Judaism" and "Cricket Judaism" in England, playing the role of the proverbial second son in reference to German Jewish students and "their" problems, poking fun at Jewish beggars,[31] comparing Italian Jews with his own native Lithuanians yet describing his visit to an Italian synagogue as if he were an amateur anthropologist who had never seen the scene ("many interesting gesticulations and genuflections . . . a monotonous sing-song not unlike what one often hears in the chapel of St. Peter").[32]

The one affirmative note is his allegiance to Zionism as a personal ideal. "Personal devotion and loyalty to two causes are not psychologically a self-deception . . . ."[33] Even this is overturned by 1918, when he anonymously published "Pomegranates," a venomous, splenetic attack on Judaism in various garbs, unlike anything he ever published before or after, a supremely agitated exercise in self-hatred, a piece parts of which, dripping with acid, could not be better duplicated by an anti-Semite: the last gasp of Harry Austryn Wolfson's personal engagement with the Jewish cause.[34]

From the outset of the essay is removal from life. "Social life is not the only distraction of the college student from his studies; social service is perhaps doing more harm, because it has the public sanction."[35] Undistracted by social life or social service, Wolfson's "pomegranates," or divisions, are exercises in self-reflection. The strangeness and idiosyncrasy of these reflections is that their apoplectic ragings are all cast in the form of a defense of a true and pure Judaism against those who would mongrelize it.

The chief culprits are speakers of Yiddish, "the dumping ground of whatever is filthy, pestilential and unwholesome in the subterranean sewerages of European letters."[36] Then, just after Brandeis had moved from the melting pot to acceptance of Horace Kallen's cultural pluralism, Kallen's erstwhile protege—Wolfson[37]—regarded his once precious, American Zionist pockets as but part of the American problem of "the unfused scrap-heap," the prospect of "a million parochial schools and as many quaint outlandish cook shops."[38] To Wolfson, the true purpose of Zionism now became the facilitation of assimilation. Zionism is no longer a personal ideal, as it was in 1915. It is the establishment of Jewish nationality in its homeland, whose direct consequence is "the complete and harmonious assimilation, in a cultural and political sense, of the Jews living in the Diaspora."[39] Without Jewish nationalism, the individual Jew must bear the burden of perpetuating Judaism, but with the realization of Zionism, the individual Jew is freed of the task. Wolfson foreshadows his watchwords of 1921: assimilation, accomodation, adaptation, adjustment. Unfortunately, there still remains an obstacle, "the Yidds," with their "Yiddish empire," stretching its fangs from Poland to London, Paris, and New York, reaching even to Palestine, there to thwart the "casting off the accumulated filth and dirt of centuries."[40]

By 1921, Wolfson has quieted. His passion is spent, his agenda forgotten, his barbs gone, his new world, his final world: scholarship. The rescue of manuscripts, the publication of research, the sponsorship of fellowships ("The Needs of Jewish Scholarship in America").[41] In "Escaping Judaism," published later in 1921, Wolfson's own conception of Judaism reaches its final form: impotence. At the outset of its description, Wolfson declares, "I shall confine myself to a mere analysis of the situation, for I believe that more than to solve a problem it is important to understand it."[42] The real reason it must simply be understood, however, is that it is insoluble. One can neither escape Judaism, for to throw off a "social inheritance" is impossible, nor endow Judaism with religious, salvational meaning, for the time when that was possible is "gone forever."[43] The logic of this position, one might think, is religious reform. But for that Wolfson has only contempt. However, religious reform is wrong not because it is wrong, but because it says what it thinks. "It will not do," objects Wolfson, "to coin a new term for God every time we change our conception of him . . . I cannot tolerate the many breaches in theological good taste on the part of our liberal Jews."[44] Wolfson's final position is aesthetic, to be measured in terms to taste and comfort, not content.

Judaism, writes Wolfson, is now intellectually obsolete, spiritually narrow and dry, and, practically speaking, "all sacrifice and no reward."[45] The threefold solution is to adjust Judaism intellectually to the truth of the time, to understand that so-called spiritual narrowness is but a cover for a social coveting of the beauties of Christianity, and, practically speaking, to sacrifice allegiance to Jewish law in acknowledgement of an internal, ingrained Jewishness that needs no outer expression.[46] For Wolfson, the intellectual solution to the problem of Judaism is assimilation, accomodation, adaptation, adjustment.[47] Tellingly, once the spiritual problem is diagnosed as a social one, Wolfson need pursue the matter no further. Social problems require no attention; Wolfson, the nonsocial, self-absorbed scholar, has emerged. Practically, he sacrifices his expression of Judaism on an altar of perfect impotence—sacrifice in order

> not to upset our native habits and characters, our timidities, our natural reserves, our bashfulness, our sense of propriety, of right and goodness. How many things do we leave undone, how many words do we leave unsaid, how many objects do we leave unattained, and how often do we let our highest happiness remain unrealized, all because of an inner inhibition, an inner restraint! Happy the Jew to whom his Judaism is so ingrained in his character as to constitute an inner inhibition and restraint.[48]

Wolfson cannot choose either to exercise his Jewishness or to abandon it, only to inhibit it. Carried into his scholarship, Wolfson's principle of indecisiveness expands from Judaism to all scriptural religion. In 1956 he writes in his introduction to his work on the Church Fathers:

> While [*The Philosophy of the Church Fathers: Faith, Trinity, Incarnation*] is primarily a study of the Church Fathers, chapters on the New Testament seemed to be necessary as background. A friend, on reading these chapters, commented: "As a Christian who believes in the teachings

of the Church as transmitted by tradition, I cannot accept the view that the doctrines of the Trinity and the Incarnation as contained in the New Testament had a human origin and a piecemeal development. However, I am prepared to concede the propriety of such inquiries in these New Testament teachings, provided they are taken not as dealing with the true origin of these teachings but with what may appear to the human mind with regard to their origin from the verbal expressions in which these teachings were made known." To which I answered: "Even in the study of nature, philosophers often wonder whether the laws discovered by science, upon which men ultimately rely for the building of bridges and the flying of airplanes, are based upon a knowledge of nature as it really is or only upon appearances. No historian investigating texts of Scripture, whether of the Jewish or of the Christian Scripture, should therefore object to being considered by theologians as dealing only with appearances."[49]

Perfect equivocation. Either Wolfson's entire life work—setting forth the history of Western philosophy from Philo to Spinoza—is but a dealing in appearances, reality behind the appearance being Scripture, between two of whose radically different versions, however, he cannot decide, or, Scripture does not constitute reality, the history of philosophy of Scripture does, between whose verisons, too, he has no preference. Perfect impotence.

In "Escaping Judaism," the spring to Wolfson's plea for inhibition and restraint of Jewish expression is an observation about "a great university in this country where examinations for admission sometimes fall on our Day of Atonement."[50] The university is Harvard, and Wolfson characterizes those applicants who protest the conflict, as driven by "outer convenience," while those who violate the Day of Atonement in order to take the examination are driven by "inner duty."[51] The single, unequivocal, openly expressed duty in Wolfson's life became Harvard. He entered in 1908, died as Professor Emeritus sixty-six years later, and never left in between, save his research period in Europe (on a Harvard scholarship) and a few months in the Army. Above all, Wolfson had to honor Harvard, and never challenge it, even if that meant not standing up for Jewish students,[52] for Jewish sensibility,[53] or even for Jewish refugee scholars.[54] In one of the most prominent institutions of the world, one of its most prominent Jews sat silent before, during, and after the Holocaust. With reference to Jewish students, Lewis Feuer defends Wolfson's alternative inaction and restraint on the grounds that a genteel anti-Semitism was pervasive throughout the Harvard community in the 1920s and 1930s; and that for Wolfson to have been more assertive might have provoked opposition and slowed progress.[55] This sociological perspective—whether protest advances or slows progress—cannot displace or cloud the psychological reality: Wolfson's renunciation of all but his Jewish name and Yiddish accent rendered it impossible for him to act otherwise. Wolfson never got over standing in awe of himself—the little boy from Slobodka who made it to the tenured faculty at Harvard.

The role of economic insecurity in Wolfson's decision to remain at Harvard and abandon a literary career cannot be ignored. When his two-year traveling scholarship ended, he quickly completed his doctorate, at which time the only job offer was from Harvard. Then, with his future as an instructor still unclear, and with no funds available to publish his first book, senior colleague George Foote Moore warned him in 1919 or 1920, with reference to his essays in the *Menorah Journal*, "Be careful or you'll become a successful journalist."[56] From then until his death, over fifty years later, Wolfson suppressed his interest in writing poetry and fiction, and published only his two essays of 1921, on the needs of Jewish scholarship and "Escaping Judaism." Moore, whom Wolfson admired, would have an important say in Wolfson's academic future, but if economic necessity was influential in Wolfson's taking a cautionary word about scholarly image to connote also a warning against public expression on Jewish issues, it was not economics, but psychological deformation, to which Wolfson continued to allude. In *The Philosophy of Spinoza: Unfolding the Latent Processes of His Reasoning* (1934), there is an abundance of personal reflection needing only a conscious look to unfold it from latent to actual.

> ... recluses are not made by philosophies, not even by philosophies which, unlike the philosophy of Spinoza, preach retirement from life as an ideal virtue; they are made, rather, by the inhospitableness of the social environment and by the ineptitude of their own individual selves.[57]

In the following, amplifying passage, Wolfson lets the ineptitude of his self stand, but adds an important qualification regarding social environment. It is not only inhospitable, robbing one of unhesitant self-expression, but paradoxically kind, reinforcing self-attenuation.

> In this strange environment, to which externally [Spinoza] seems to have fully adjusted himself . . . [he] became cautious, hesitant, and reserved. It was a caution which sprang not from fear but from an inner sense of decorum which inevitably enforces itself on one in the presence of strangers, especially strangers who are kind.[58]

In the subtle economy of relation between life and work, Wolfson's work on Spinoza occupied a special place. *Spinoza* was preceded by *Crescas' Critique of Aristotle* (1929), a textual monograph growing out of the circumscribed rigors of doctoral dissertation research, and succeeded by the philosophy of *Philo, The Philosophy of the Church Fathers,* and *The Philosophy of the Kalam*—the mature, inaccessible Wolfson, sealed safely behind text, footnote, and concept.[59] *Spinoza's* postdissertation exhilaration and expansiveness ventilated a continuing textual concentration. The passage in *Spinoza* that is most pregnant in autobiographical implication is the most expansive.

> Perhaps, also, despite differences in theology, [Spinoza] would have joined the Lutheran church of his friend Doctor Cordes in The Hague. And I can picture him, once of a Sunday, at the invitation of the good old Doctor, taking the services in the church. He preaches a sermon which is an invective against what he styles "the prejudices of the theologians of our time." In it he inveighs against prevailing credulous beliefs in the spirituality of God, His personal relation to men, His direct guidance of human affairs, the divine origin of the Scriptures, human freedom of the will, the separability of soul from body, and the survival of the soul after death as an individual entity. The sermon over, he pauses and says, "Now let us pray." And in his prayer he thanks God, "the creator of the universe," for His bountiful goodness; he begs for the forgiveness of "our sins," asks for divine enlightenment in the true understanding of "Thy revealed Word," and petitions for divine grace in "guiding us" in the paths of righteousness, to the end that "we may inherit" life everlasting and enjoy eternal bliss in the presence of "Thy glory." As he is about to close his prayer, he catches a glimpse of the congregation and suddenly realizes that he is in a Christian church. Immediately he adds: "In the name of Christ, the mouth of God, whose spirit is the idea of God, which alone leads us unto liberty, salvation, blessedness, and regeneration. Amen."[60]

Harry Austryn Wolfson's unexpressed Judaism inveighs against credulous beliefs; Zvi Hirsh Wolfson's Orthodox Judaism prays to, begs, asks, and petitions God; *Wolfson of Harvard's* suppleness pays homage to the shibboleths of what he takes to be the churchly demands of his surroundings, to the strangers of Harvard who are kind, to the place in which no need was felt to write an apologetic preface to his critical examination of the sacred literature of Judaism or Islam, but in which the need was felt to write an apologetic preface to his critical examination of the sacred literature of Christianity.[61]

In referring to Wolfson as Harry Austryn and Zvi Hirsh, I have alluded to the deepest level of autobiographical revelation in *Spinoza*. It is mediated through Wolfson's literary device of distinguishing between the explicit Benedictus Spinoza and the implicit Baruch Spinoza, between the skeptical, modern, Latin mouthpiece and the traditional, medieval, Hebrew mind. "Benedictus is the first of the moderns; Baruch is the last of the mediaevals. It is our contention that we cannot get the full meaning of what Benedictus says unless we know what has passed through the mind of Baruch."[62] In unfolding the latent reasoning behind this device we locate Zvi Hirsh Wolfson, whose mouthpiece, Harry Austryn Wolfson, translates into critical scholarship a traditional, talmudic method. Just as the implicit Baruch was not conscious of how and why he formulated the words of the explicit Benedictus, so, likewise, the implicit Zvi Hirsh was not conscious of how and why he formulated the "Talmudic hypothetico-deductive method of text interpretation" of the explicit Harry Austryn. The method, no less than Benedictus Spinoza's philosophy, has its own source, and if Wolfson wrote *Spinoza* out of the conviction that he had to "undertake to do for Spinoza what Spinoza had failed to do for himself," namely, to show what he meant by what he said,[63] it is equally necessary to do for Wolfson what he failed to do for himself, namely, to understand that source of Zvi which became the method of Harry.

We return to Slobodka.

III.

Fact and circumstance converge fortuitously to reconstruct the intellectual atmosphere in Slobodka to which Zvi Hirsh Wolfson, it will be recalled, surreptitiously betook himself. First, Wolfson's biographer reveals that Wolfson arrived in Slobodka when he was thirteen, or in about 1900.[64] Second, the title page of the first volume of *Levush Mordekhai*, the talmudic investigations of the Slobodka yeshiva dean to whose lectures young Wolfson was attracted, reveals that it was published in 1901,[65] or about one year after Wolfson's arrival. Third, the introduction to these published investigations reveals that they constitute the record of lectures that Rabbi Epstein delivered in the Slobodka yeshiva.[66] From all this we may gather that that talmudic method used in the lectures to which Wolfson was attracted is the very method of which we have a concrete record in the first volume of *Levush Mordekhai*. Now, given Wolfson's expressed preference for Rabbi Epstein's talmudic lectures, and given Wolfson's attribution of his research method to a talmudic method of text interpretation, we may hypothesize that the particular characteristics of Rabbi Epstein's method constitute Wolfson's description and practice of his own method. Then we may compare Wolfson's scholarly work to Rabbi Epstein's *Levush Mordekhai* to see whether the hypothesis is correct. In drawing this comparison, we shall find that the professor's treatment of philosophic texts is a virtual translation of the rabbi's treatment of talmudic texts. The mind of Harry Austryn Wolfson, historian of philosophy, took root in the mind of Moses Mordechai Epstein, talmudic lecturer of Slobodka.

Harry Austryn's words on the research method that he applied to philosophic texts constitute but "floating buoys which signal the presence of submerged, unuttered thoughts."[67] The implicit Zvi Hirsh, working from a background in Slobodka while sitting in a study at Harvard, was not always manifest in what the explicit Harry Austryn was saying about his method. In fact, the implicit Zvi Hirsh is but elliptically represented in Harry Austryn's most elaborate and well-known description of his talmudic hypothetico-deductive method of text interpretation. We have emphasized certain key phrases, to which we shall refer in analyzing this description.

> Confronted with a statement on any subject, the Talmudic student will proceed to raise a series of questions before he satisfies himself of having understood its full meaning. If the statement is not clear enough, he will ask, "What does the author intend to say here?" If it is too obvious, he will again ask, "It is too plain, why then expressly say it?" If it is a statement of fact or of a concrete instance, he will then ask, "What underlying principle does it involve?" If it is a broad generalization, he will want to know exactly how much it is to include; and if it is an exception to a general rule, he will want to know how much it is to exclude. He will furthermore want to know all the circumstances under which a certain statement is true, and what qualifications are permissible. Statements apparently contradictory to each other will be reconciled by the discovery of some subtle distinction, and statements apparently irrelevant to each other will be subtly analyzed into their ultimate elements and shown to contain some common underlying principle. The harmonization of apparent contradictions and the inter-linking of apparent irrelevancies are two characteristic features of the Talmudic method of text study. And similarly every other phenomenon about the text becomes a matter of investigation. Why does the author use one word rather than another? What need was there for the mentioning of a specific instance as an illustration? Do *certain authorities differ* or not? If they do, why do they differ? All these are legitimate questions for the Talmudic student of texts. And any attempt to answer these questions calls for in-

genuity and skill, the *power of analysis and association,* and the *ability to set up hypotheses*—and all these must be bolstered up by a wealth of accurate information and the use of good judgement. No limitation is set upon any subject; problems run into one another; they become intricate and interwoven, one throwing light upon the other. And there is a logic underlying this method of reasoning. It is the very same kind of logic which underlies any sort of scientific research, and by which one is enabled *to form hypotheses, to test them and to formulate general laws*. The Talmudic student approaches the study of texts in the same manner as the scientist approaches the study of nature. Just as the scientist proceeds on the assumption that there is a uniformity and continuity in nature so the Talmud student proceeds on the assumption that there is a uniformity and continuity in human reasoning. Now, this method of text interpretation is sometimes derogatorily referred to as Talmudic quibbling or pilpul. In truth it is nothing but the application of the scientific method to the study of texts.[68]

Imbedded in this deceptively lucid passage are both universal aspects of the talmudic method and four other aspects, three of which derive specifically from Slobodka's Rabbi Epstein. His method represented a threefold variation on a larger development in talmudic methodology in Lithuania at the turn of the twentieth century. This larger development is the fourth aspect of talmudic method hinted at by Wolfson. We may most readily understand Rabbi Epstein's threefold method, and that of Wolfson, by setting it in the context of this larger development, to whose description we now briefly turn.

The originator of this development is Rabbi Hayyim Soloveitchik (1853–1918; grandfather of Rabbi Joseph Baer Soloveitchik, Chapter Five). Rabbi Hayyim Soloveitchik's method is terminologically "the Brisker method" (after the Lithuanian city, Brisk, *Brest Litovsk,* in which he served as rabbi) and substantively a critico-conceptual technique traceable to a twelfth-century talmudist, Rabad of Posquières. It is often through a conceptualizing of the distinctions between Maimonides and Rabad's glosses on Maimonides' Code that Rabbi Hayyim Soloveitchik practiced his method. The method is designed to reconcile overtly contradictory talmudic and post-talmudic sources by postulating a purely hypothetical, abstract distinction between them and then seeing whether the contradictory sources are, in fact, reconcilable in accord with the postulated distinction. The Brisker method devised several types of abstract distinctions. The following is an illustration of the *gavra* type—the separating out of two distinct halakhic personalities from an apparently interdependent context. The two distinct personalities posited to resolve the contradiction in the following illustration on disqualified testimony are *the witness as testifying about himself*, and *the witness as testifying about a relative*.

Sometimes the Talmud has a case where the testimony of disqualified witnesses is totally discarded, while sometimes part is retained as valid and part is rejected. Talmudic commentators were hard put to reconcile these various [contradictory] cases. Rabad elaborated an abstract principle which determines and explains this juristic distinction. When a witness testifies, among other things, about some matter pertaining directly to himself, when he is directly involved and the testimony concerns his own person, then the court may split his testimony. The part concerning his person is rejected, while the rest remains valid. On the other hand, a relative or any technically disqualified witness who offers testimony is invalidated. This distinction is imbedded in the divergent character of the disqualifying traits. In the first case, there are no reservations concerning the very truthfulness and reliability of the witness, except that what he states about himself is not valid. Therefore the court dismisses this part of the testimony as irrelevant, or simply deletes it from the record as if it had never been presented; the rest is retained independently. In the second case, the witness is initially disqualified because of an a priori reluctance on the part of the court to accept his testimony. There is some question concerning his reliability and trustworthiness as an individual. Consequently, there is no reason to discriminate between various portions of his testimony: if part is nullified, all of it is nullified, for his very trustworthiness is doubted.[69]

Rabbi Hayyim Soloveitchik's penchant for resolving contradictions or other difficulties in talmudic texts by means of postulating distinctions—in the fashion of Rabad's distinction between the technically and the intrinsically disqualified witness—engendered four self-imposed methodological restrictions: (1) concentration on purely hypothetical approaches to resolving talmudic contradictions; (2) concentration on especially problematic talmudic material, to the relative neglect of other, simpler material; (3) dispensing with the aid of vast stretches of contextually relevant, but noncritico-conceptual, post-talmudic commentary; and (4) dispensing with the aid of contextually irrelevant, conceptually relevant talmudic discussion. The Brisker agenda was highly concentrated: attention paid to problematic material given to purely hypothetical distinctions catalyzed by the material itself.[70] To all four of Rabbi Soloveitchik's restrictions, Rabbi Epstein—and Professor Wolfson—objected.

First of all, Rabbi Epstein often alloyed his purely critico-conceptual analysis to another conceptual approach. Second, to him all talmudic material was of primary interest, and, third, all later talmudic commentary was potentially of interest. Fourth, he fished in apparently irrelevant contexts, drawing implications from the primary context to many others.[71]

Now, in his lengthy description of his hypothetico-deductive method, cited above, Wolfson's reference to "the ability to set up hypotheses" was a floating buoy signaling a large, unuttered reality, the general Brisker development of critico-conceptual talmudic method. When Wolfson referred to "the power of analysis and association," to consultation with differing authorities, and to the formulation of general laws arising out of the testing of hypotheses, he signaled his agreement with specific variations on that general development—the variations of Rabbi Epstein. Wolfson agreed, respectively, with the first, the second and third, and the fourth reservations of Rabbi Epstein about the first, the second and third, and the fourth self-imposed methodological limitations of Rabbi Soloveitchik. Wolfson's "power of analysis and association" (1) is a compressed summation of Rabbi Epstein's expanded, alloyed use of the critico-conceptual method. Wolfson's reference to consultation with differing authorities (2 and 3) is a compressed summation of Rabbi Epstein's use of all talmudic and commentatorial sources, whether conceptual or not. Wolfson's "formulation of general laws" (4) is a compressed summation of Rabbi Epstein's use of texts and contexts, related or ostensibly unrelated, with which to form a large canvas from specific investigations.

All of this may be illustrated, comparing the professor with the rabbi, point by point. We shall take the major points of comparison in an order different from their listing above in order to begin with what is most salient in both writers, the fourth and last point—the thirst for largeness, the drawing of implications from seemingly unrelated contexts in order to formulate general laws. This we shall label *comprehensiveness*. The next commonality between both writers (corresponding to Rabbi Epstein's first, conceptual modification of the Brisker method) we shall label *creative interpretation*. And the final commonality between the writers (corresponding to Rabbi Epstein's second and third, "source" modifications of the Brisker method) we shall label *universal interests*.

I. *Comprehensiveness.* In Rabbi Epstein, comprehensiveness expresses itself in three ways: length, breadth, depth.[72] *Length*, in two senses: first a nonelliptical style, a way of *explication de texte* radically unlike that which is being explicated, an effusive elucidation of complex, fragmentary, or conceptually difficult texts, often with a degree of repetition for the sake of clarity but not in a burdensome way, not giving a sense of repetitiveness; second, the linking of the point at hand to its appearance in other texts, in similiar contexts, until all such related texts have been cited with their point of commonality or difference laid bare. *Breadth:* consideration not just of a given point and its reappearance in related texts, but of the relation between this point and the larger context of which it is an integral part, such that the entire topic subsuming this point is made clear. *Depth:* the penetration to the heart, the animating idea or concept, within the topic in all of its parts.

In Wolfson: length, breadth, depth.

Length: One could quote hundreds of examples of his nonelliptical style, elucidating complex, fragmentary, or conceptually difficult texts, often with a degree of repetition for the sake of clarity,[73] and always linking the point at hand to its appearance in other texts, in similar contexts, to lay bare the point of commonality or difference. We refrain from quotation since lengthy introduction to the technical terminology within the appropriate citations would be necessary. Suffice it to say (to summarize but two instances, one from Wolfson's first scholarly volume, *Crescas,* and one from his last scholarly volume, *Kalam*) that when Wolfson explicates the Aristotelian notion and terminology of "corporeal form" he does so, in a few sentences, in conjunction with the alternative interpretations of Avicenna, Algazali, Averroes, and Crescas, with extensive footnote amplification also in reference to Abraham Ibn Daud, Isaac Abravanel, Simplicius, Plotinus, Narboni, Sharastani, Abu Bekr ibn Turfail, Altabrizi, Alfarabi, Joseph ibn Aknin, Plutarch, Joseph ibn Zaddik, Saul ha-Kohen Ashkenazi, and Judah Abravanel;[74] and that when he explicates the Christian origin of the Muslim belief in divine attributes, he does so, in one paragraph, in conjunction with the views of Abulfaraj, Adad al-Din al-Iji, David al-Mukammis, Saadia, Joseph al-Basir, and Maimonides.[75] Rabbi Epstein's linking the point at hand to its appearance elsewhere, with points of commonality and difference laid bare in a nonelliptical, lucid, flowing style: this is vintage Wolfson.

Breadth: One encounters Wolfson's linkage of a given point, in its appearances throughout the history of Western philosophy, to the larger topic at hand, in three frameworks: in chapters, in monographs, in the structure of his entire scholarly enterprise. In chapters, one witnesses (to take one of scores of examples) Wolfson linking the Aristotelian notion of corporeal form to the larger topic of matter and form, such that elucidation of the entire topic—matter, form, substance, spheres, force, eternity of motion, universals, immaterial Intelligences, and the like—would collapse without this linkage of part to whole.[76] In monographs, one witnesses Wolfson not following flights of fancy but doing technical spadework for large volumes. Only four of Wolfson's intended twelve volumes were completed, but spadework for all of them constitutes almost all of his three volumes (1,543 pages) of collected monographs.[77] "Points" within the larger topic of *The Philosophy of the Kalam* (1976), for example, are thirteen earlier monographs (1943 to 1969).[78] Traversing chapter, monograph, and volume, one reaches, finally, Wolfson's projected, twelve-volume "Structure and Growth of Philosophic Systems from Plato to Spinoza." Breadth!

> Anticipating the publication of the two volumes of *The Philosophy* of *Kalam* in 1964, he planned to proceed with the second volume of *The Philosophy of the Church Fathers*; a volume to be entitled *Greek Philosophy*, dealing with problems in Greek philosophy as they evolved in the development of philosophy to Spinoza and including a prolegomenon to the methodology of the study of the history of philosophy; a volume to be called *The Muslim Philosophers*, examining Muslim philosophy from Alfarabi to Averroes; a volume on *The Philosophy of Halevi and Maimonides*, explicating the major systems of medieval Jewish philosophy with reference to all the other Jewish philosophers within that framework; and finally a volume on *Latin Philosophy from St. Thomas Aquinas to Descartes*, dealing with the systems and principles of the Scholastic Christian philosophers and their descendants. Thus he projected the completion of his twelve-volume series . . . following which he planned a definitive revision of *Spinoza*, with cross-references to all the previous books of the series.[79]

Depth: penetration to the heart of the topic in all of its parts. This, in Wolfson's eyes, is precisely what he did (a) by unifying all of Western religious philosophy—Jewish, Christian, Muslim—under the rubric of "Scriptural philosophy," of that procedure "by which philosophy, the product of erring human reason, had to be tested and purged and purified" in light of "inflexible principles, of a divinely revealed origin";[80] (b) by, on this criterion, identifying a seventeen-century trend in philosophy, begun by Philo and ended by Spinoza;[81] and (c) by, also on this criterion, regarding Greek philosophy as but prologue and modern philosophy as but epilogue to real, Scriptural philosophy.[82]

II. *Creative interpretation*. In Brisk, we recall, the critico-conceptual method was used to draw purely hypothetical distinctions in order to reconcile contradictory texts. The distinctions of Rabbi Epstein and Professor Wolfson, however, are often not hypothetical. Their distinctions reconcile contradictions by reinterpreting the problematic texts. Their use of the critico-conceptual method leaves one with material that, reconceived, constitutes the basis of a hitherto unseen distinction between its contradictory parts; not with a purely hypothetical distinction according to which hitherto problematic material reclassifies neatly, ingeniously, along the lines of the distinction. To use a Kantian metaphor, in Brisk, distinction produces itself out of pure thought, after the manner of neo-Kantian Hermann Cohen; while in Slobodka, distinction produces itself under the impact of material drawn from sensation—the text—after the manner of Kant himself.

To present a comprehensible illustration would take us afield in pages of laying bare technical terminology and complex talmudic analysis.[83] The point is that the Epstein-Wolfson distinction is not pulled out of the air and then neatly seen to fit the text. It is not the purely hypothetical, purely mentally devised distinction between *the witness testifying about himself* and *the witness testifying about a relative*. The Epstein-Wolfson distinction is pulled out of the text itself—the reinterpreted text. It is not the reinterpretation *per se* that resolves the contradiction between this and other texts, but the distinction arising out of the reinterpretation. Now, we may view Wolfson's "power of analysis and association" as hinting at his own latent process of reasoning, as connoting the power to *associate* a problematic text with a seemingly unrelated text or distinction, the upshot of this association being a new *analysis* of the original text, giving rise to a distinction according to which the text's problematic aspect falls away. And this procedure is precisely what Rabbi Epstein follows with his modified, alloyed critico-conceptual approach: conceptual distinction alloyed to creative interpretation. In almost this very language, Wolfson sets forth his method in *Spinoza*, the telling passages of which I have emphasized.

> But problems of still greater difficulty [than linking together apparently disconnected propositions into a coherent argument] presented themselves to us on frequent occasions, such, for intance, as apparent misuse of terms on the part of Spinoza, or apparent contradictions in his own statements, or apparent misrepresentations of the views of others. Invariably in the solution of such problems we set up some distinction *in the use of the term* which Spinoza seemed to misuse, or we discerned some new aspect *in the statement of the idea* in which Spinoza seemed to contradict himself, or we assumed the possibility of some new interpretation *of the view* in which Spinoza seemed to misrepresent others.[84]

III. *Universal interests:* Wolfson's consultation with other authorities, who may or may not differ; Rabbi Epstein's interest in all talmudic and commentatorial material, whether or not given to critico-conceptual interpretation.

A fundamental distinction in approach to Talmud study took on new importance in nineteenth-century Lithuania as Rabbi Hayyim Soloveitchik honed his critico-conceptual method, passing it on to disciples such as Rabbi Baruch Ber Lebowitz, stimulating its modification in authorities such as Rabbi Epstein, and generally popularizing it such that it spread in one form or another, to one extent or another, throughout Lithuanian yeshivas. This distinction, for which various alternative terms were called into use, is referred to by Rabbi Epstein, in the introduction to his first volume, by the terms *beki'ut*, wide knowledge, and *sevarah*, logical analysis. On its elementary level these terms, and their various substitutes, distinguish between a broad but often superficial knowledge and a deep but often narrow knowledge of Talmud. In Lithuania, under the impact of the spread of the Brisker method, the pendulum had swung in favor of depth—the honing of logical analysis, even to the relative neglect of parts of the normative talmudic literature.

On its face, Rabbi Epstein's introduction views this tendency favorably. "The essence of knowledge of the Torah is not in breadth and in the form of things, but in logical analysis and the understanding of things." He continues:

> If one has mastered the details of a single law, but not its logical basis, not the feel of the thing, we cannot say that he lacks part of the thing. He lacks the whole thing, since the essence of the matter is the logic of the matter. Consequently, even he who has studied all six orders of the Talmud, if he has not accustomed himself to the methods of logical analysis, is to be called ignorant; while he who has studied but a single tractate, in which he has worked intensively to accustom himself to and to acquire logical analysis, is to be called a sage.[85]

At the end of the introduction he turns from logical analysis to breadth. "Anyone with understanding will know, of course, that with logical analysis alone one will not enter the sanctuary. Without breadth, one's knowledge of Torah will be of no effect."[86]

Now, with his ending, Rabbi Epstein has not let in the back door what he wished to close out at the front. Nor has he simply paid his respects to a time-honored goal of talmudic study and universal knowledge. He has, rather, completed the Slobodka understanding of logical analysis—an understanding according to which breadth of knowledge serves the interests of logical analysis. For Rabbi Epstein, as for Harry Wolfson, breadth of knowledge, universal interest, *is* logical analysis. Solid knowledge of every author and commentator, of every text, even remotely linked to the subject of one's interest—Talmud or philosophy—inevitably provides instances of logical and critical information—the term, the critical distinction, or the corroboration needed, respectively, to understand, to conceptualize, or to affirm a reconceiving of the problematic text at hand. In their books, both the rabbi and the professor repeatedly solve problems by pulling in some distant, seemingly irrelevant source that, upon examination, provides just the required insight. For Rabbi Epstein the distant material may be from the *midreshei halakhah* or the *Tosefta*, extratalmudic material virtually ignored in the Lithuanian context. For Wolfson the distant material may be a forgotten or minor Greek or Arabic text called upon to illuminate a perplexity in Crescas or Maimonides. Logical analysis, as we have seen, already entails a textual and not a purely conceptual orientation for the rabbi and the professor. The two further imbed their use of the critico-conceptual method in text by probing any and every text, however overtly remote, for any and all aid, terminological, commentatorial, or logical; for, to them, expansive intellectual curiosity nurtured compressive conceptual analysis. On the first page of his first volume, Wolfson set the tone for all that was to come:

> . . . just as one cannot treat of the new life that appeared in Europe during the Middle Ages as merely the result of the individual exploits of heroes, or of the eloquence of preachers, or of the inventive fancy of courtiers, so one cannot treat of the development of mediaeval philosophic thought as a mere interplay of abstract concepts. There is an earthly basis to the development of philosophic problems in the Middle Ages—and that is language and text.[87]

IV.

Wolfson learned the centrality of text in Slobodka; the centrality of language, in Scranton and Cambridge. Wolfson, his research technique reflective of Slobodka in all its specificity and detail, transposed the locale and transformed the use of that technique until it became repercussive, in all its range and foci, only outside the world of Slobodka. It became possible at a university to be so explicit about a technique so phenomenologically Jewish, so rooted in nonacademic scholarship, because it became so obvious how unlinked Wolfson had become to the traditional social and intellectual context in which he had first learned it.

Claims of belief, of text, or of lifestyle that one has ostensibly rejected, but that still prick at one's conscience, cannot be described placidly, grandly, with that ease and confidence with which Wolfson always described "the Talmudic hypothetico-deductive method of text interpretation." It became his intellectual patrimony precisely because he was thoroughly beyond any philosophical commitment to its natural matrix.

And yet, for all of Wolfson's distance from the Orthodoxy of Slobodka and the Zionist-Hebrew surge of early twentieth-century Boston, for all of his thorough and sustained loyalty to Harvard specifically and to the discourse of academic, objective scholarship generally, he was rife with partisan commitment, in spite of himself. Cloaking himself in every imaginable cloak of scholarship—in ascetic self-denial for the sake of life in the library, morning, noon, and night; in submergence in language for the sake of deciphering musty manuscripts and secondary literature in Hebrew, Greek, Latin, Arabic, Aramaic, French, Spanish, Italian, Dutch, German, and English; in interest in and impotent absence of preference for a single one of the views of hundreds of Greek, Jewish, Christian, and Islamic philosophers for the sake of breadth and objectivity—with cloak upon cloak, withal Harry Austryn Wolfson remained the partisan.

To be certain about the precise locale and nature of this partisanship, we must inquire into what lies beneath the surface of Wolfson's personal dedication and formal allegiance to the canons of scholarship—into his dry, wry, irreverent wit ("the three theories of the origin of the human soul held by various religious philosophers . . . in plain English may be described, respectively, as the theory of custom-made souls, the theory of ready-made souls, and the theory of second-hand souls").[88] This wit, formally a vestige of Wolfson's early literary experiments, may be seen as a safety valve, an outlet, for the tension of living in the contradiction of maintaining that only Scriptural philosophy is authentic, and of simultaneously rejecting the demands of any Scripture in one's personal life or belief. Scholarship in philosophy so disembodied that it betrays no evidence of any philosophic stance reveals an emptiness of soul that can only engender deep doubt or ambivalence about the ultimate value of the enterprise, and banter as flight from anguish is not uncommon. Even so, in a post-Freudian age generally and with reference to the man who activated "the unfolding of latent processes of reasoning" especially, one may ask, was Wolfson's wit mask, not mirror? Was there a philosophic commitment beneath his playful irreverence, which intermittently squeezed through the seemingly impenetrable facade of massive scholarship? Or, was his wit itself the telling Freudian slip?

It may well be that irony and a spirit of puckishness helped [Wolfson] to survive a conflict which can be savage (banter as flight from anguish is not uncommon) when memory leads to longing and intellect leads to a different persuasion. "You see," [Gershom] Scholem reports that Wolfson said to him during a visit, "nobody will ever know whether I believe anything or not."[89]

Nobody, one suspects, including Wolfson himself. For if sixty-two years of intensive study and exposition of philosophic texts could not even unconsciously squeeze a personal philosophic hint into print, then the answer to the question—was there belief beneath irreverance, commitment beneath inhibition?—is, it is likely, no.

And yet, Wolfson was not a disembodied spirit. The fundamental presuppositions of his entire "Structure and Growth of Philosophic Systems from Plato to Spinoza" bespeak partisanship, if not in personal belief, then in existential structure. An irreducible, East European *shtetl* ethnocentricity permeated Wolfson's major claims: that Scripture, delivered originally by Jews, was the be-all and end-all in philosophic truth-seeking, and that it was two Jews, Philo and Spinoza, who did everything fundamental in the history of real—that is, Scriptural—philosophy; the one Jew set Scriptural philosophy on its feet, the other Jew swept it from its feet.[90] The further Wolfson tried to flee from the world of the East European *shtetl* generally and from Slobodka specifically, the more clear it became how closely he reflected both. It is true that the Judaism that Wolfson claimed to have influenced the entire Western world—Jewish, Christian, Moslem—could not influence one man, Wolfson himself. And yet, from the Slobodkan contours of his research procedure to the ethnocentricity of his conception and periodization of philosophy—from the most specific to the most general of his concerns—he gave voice, partisan voice, to his own background. Its religious, social, and nationalistic settings—Orthodoxy, ethnicity, and Zionism—he transposed and transformed, respectively, into the neutral, the universal, and the international canons of scholarship.

Wolfson's anguish of transition left a truly absolute silence about self because he pushed to their farthest extremes the two fundamental poles he tried to bridge: Hebrew Scripture—matrix of religion and peoplehood—and universal scholarship—matrix of humanity and the humanities. Like Isaac Hutner (Chapter Four), another son of Slobodka, another master of self-concealment, Harry Austryn Wolfson guarded a privacy never to be pierced even by the closest of associates and students. Unlike

Isaac Hutner, whose loneliness was entwined with his complex understanding of how tradition gave him succor and support, Wolfson and his loneliness were entwined with the secret of how tradition had failed him, and of how he had failed it. He was divided from both man and God: an absolute, physical, and metaphysical aloneness. "What's the most important verse in the Bible?" Wolfson asked his cousin, Harry Austryn Savitz, shortly before he died. Savitz replied (following the ancient sage, Hillel and Elder), "Love your neighbor as yourself." "No," said Wolfson, "[Genesis 2:18] 'It is not good for man to be alone.' "[91]

CHAPTER FOUR

Rabbi Isaac Hutner

"Not that any of us could write it, but if each major disciple of the Rosh Yeshiva were to write a book about him, each would write a different book."
Disciple of Rabbi Isaac Hutner, "the Rosh Yeshiva"—dean of Chaim Berlin talmudic academy

"Regardless of what you hear quoted in my name, do not believe it unless I have told it to you personally."
Disciple, quoting Rabbi Hutner

Genesis describes Adam as having been "born" as an adult, created as a fully developed, mature being. Rabbinic commentary observes that Adam was born circumcised—a ritual, in Jewish tradition, symbolizing need for rectification, but, in the case of Adam, born without need of circumcision, a symbol of completion.[1] In encountering Rabbi Isaac Hutner (1906–1980), it is as if the accounts of creation in Genesis and in rabbinic commentary were devised as metaphors for him. For example, one opens Rabbi Hutner's letters, glancing at those written when he was sixteen.[2] Here, there writes neither a child nor a teenager, but an adult, and in every sense. Ideas are fully developed and often original; sense of self is complete but without the self-consciousness of youth; the Hebrew is remarkable for its crystalline clarity, for its rootedness in biblical metaphor, and, no less, for its control of modern Hebrew, giving the stern, austere biblical metaphor a suppleness and shading not endemic to it. One rereads the date on the letter: surely there has been a mistake. A sixteen-year-old does not write this way. But there is no mistake. Isaac Hutner was born circumcised.

As his thought worked its way into print, as his personality left an unerasable imprint on disciples, rebellious or loyal, Rabbi Hutner performed a striking feat: he learned from a wide array of intellectual types and national styles without becoming confused or diffuse. He remained always in control, learning and appropriating entire systems of thought and style yet transmuting them such that although their individual identities were clearly recognizable in him, they nonetheless constituted parts of something larger.

Rabbi Hutner embodied a problem: How can contrary, even contradictory systems of thought and life mesh without eclectic blending, or oscillation between poles? If the answer cannot be logical, it can be phenomenological: the complex and straightforward "Varshever Illui" (Warsaw prodigy) himself, born in 1906, soon to become a renowned Talmudist; and poet, and philosopher; and pietist, and egoist; and intellectual, and humorist; and private person, and public persona; and lover of Zion, and anti-Zionist; and personally liberal, and programmatically conservative; and devotee of the towering opponent of Hasidism, the Vilna Gaon, and practitioner of Hasidism itself. Rabbi Hutner once commented autobiographically on a rabbinic midrash on Adam: "Adam, it says, was created from earth gathered from all over the world. I, too, am a gathering point: from Poland, from Lithuania, from Riga, from Germany, from *Eretz Yisrael* [the Land of Israel], from the United States."[3]

A panorama of influences, impinging on radical autonomy, entailed still another pair of contrary impulses: self-revelation and self-concealment. Revelation of self was possible because there was so much colorful and diverse baggage that Rabbi Hutner could set forth, layer after layer, without ever reaching the bottom layer. This he could guard from intrusive eyes. Captivating friendliness went hand in hand with unstated but clear prohibition of excessive familiarity with his person, such that the more one knew him, the less one knew. Similarly, the more one probes his writings—all of which he structured in both form and content with a clear definitiveness—the less certain one is of the ultimate perspective of the constellations of thought therein. Rabbi Hutner, like all transition figures, is an enigma. In his case the quandary is deepened because we know so much about him.

I.

From his early youth Isaac Hutner kept diaries and maintained an active and diverse correspondence. Self-reflection, first in relation to his own aspirations and to his self-chosen separation from his parents, and then in relation to his numerous travels and studies, was his lodestar. He entered school—a yeshiva in Lomza, Poland—apparently for the first time when he was fifteen. His first studies away from home launched a thirteen-year odyssey that saw him in close contact with virtually all of the major intellectual centers and mentors in the worlds of Talmud study, piety (the Musar movement), and Hasidism. Mere recitation of the itinerary, in its geographical diversity and rotation between lengthy and short pauses, gives evidence of the breadth, the urgency, and the discipline of his quest. After his brief stay in Lomza he returned to Warsaw (one-half year, until 1921); then to the Musar yeshiva in Slobodka, Lithuania (three and a half years, until 1925); then to Slobodka's branch in Hebron, Palestine (four years, until 1929); then back to Warsaw (briefly, 1929); then to the University of Berlin (four months, 1929); then to Warsaw (one year, until 1930); then to Hebron and Jerusalem (three-quarters of a year, until 1931); then to Kovno, Lithuania, to write his prodigious work on naziriteship (one year, until 1932); then, for the last time, to Warsaw (one year, until 1933), where he married; then to Palestine (one year, until 1934); then to New York City (1934, until settling in Israel, late 1970s).[4]

"Slobodka"—after Warsaw, the first and lengthiest stop on the itinerary—was as much a concept and a person as it was an institution. A single wooden building across the Niemen River in a small suburb of Kovno, Lithuania, Slobodka was a wellspring of brilliance, graduating more world-renowned Talmud scholars in the first quarter of the twentieth century than all other similar institutions combined, and molding the research method of the nonconformist, Harry Austryn Wolfson. Behind the intellectual brilliance stood Rabbi Moses Mordechai Epstein, but this was but part of the pulse in Slobodka. Wolfson was an anomaly in Slobodka in the sense that he drew his major inspiration from Rabbi Epstein. For most of the prodigies there, Talmud study—central as it was—drew its motivation and coloration from Rabbi Epstein's collaborator. The uniqueness of Slobodka was the idea of intellectual piety as embodied in "the Elder of Slobodka"—the academy's founder and mentor for nearly fifty years—Rabbi Nathan Zvi Finkel.

Secretive in the extreme, self-sufficient even earlier in life than was Isaac Hutner, the Elder, an orphan, appeared as if from nowhere at the of his integration of antireligious, socialist Zionism into a mystical worldview in which harmony was conceived as the temporary, if positive, inclusion of opposites on the path to perfection.[13] The controversial side of Rabbi Kuk dominated Rabbi Hutner's attitude toward him years later, but as a young man his predominant interest was in learning from him. The dominant note then was high esteem and admiration. In many ways Rabbi Kuk was the Elder's opposite, notwithstanding Rabbi Kuk's own roots in the Musar movement[14] and reputation as a pietist of the highest rank—an 'ish kadosh, a holy man. The Elder was personally closed, writing nothing, teaching through the power of insight into others, while Rabbi Kuk was personally open, spilling forth in lectures and writings that welled up so spontaneously that, for some years, he wrote only in pencil, unable even momentarily to interrupt the flow of inspiration to dip the premodern pen into the inkwell. If the Elder addressed the whole person, restricting the flow of knowledge in accord with the powers of receptivity of the addressee, Rabbi Kuk addressed the heart and the mind, unleashing torrents of discourse woven from the entire range of Jewish thought: law, lore, philosophy, poetry, mysticism, pietism, homiletics, exegesis. The Elder was a pedagogue; Rabbi Kuk, an intellectual. Rabbi Hutner sought to combine the two, to become the two.

For Rabbi Hutner the personal, pietistic orientation of the Elder was necessary, but not sufficient. Rabbi Hutner's intellectual curiosity required validation, and it was Rabbi Kuk who provided it, bringing him to an unrestricted confrontation with Jewish mysticism and philosophy on their own terms. From Rabbi Kuk, Rabbi Hutner acquired breadth of knowledge, from the Elder, an awareness of the value in revealing it selectively; from Rabbi Kuk, legitimization of intellectual quest, from the Elder, the need to channel and sometimes limit another's quest. Rabbi Kuk taught the young Hutner fearlessness in intellectual search; the Elder, wisdom in intellectual transmission. Rabbi Kuk taught the need for loyalty to one's vision and aspirations; the Elder, the need for legerdemain in making available one's intellectual integrity. Rabbi Kuk embodied ever-expanding horizons; the Elder, self-restraint in nurturing the limited horizons in most people. In Rabbi Kuk Rabbi Hutner witnessed self-revelation, in the Elder, self-concealment, and he appreciated both.

II.

The Elder and Rabbi Kuk planted seeds in fertile soil, but sprouts were not immediately forthcoming. Rabbi Hutner wished his seedbed to body forth a greater diversity than the complements of piety and thought, and not one sprout could blossom until each root was in place. Still to be nurtured was the ground of the enterprise, talmudic study; still to be designed were a number of hues among the flowers, such as critical scholarship and Polish hasidic thought; and, most important, still to be decided was the ultimate location of the garden.

After eight years in Lithuania and Palestine, Rabbi Hutner returned home for the first time in 1929, at the age of twenty-three. The reunion with parents was poignant, but the overriding tone in his letters seems not to be genuine tenderness but awareness of the pain that the long absence of a son—and the lack of opportunity to observe a ripening talmudic scholar—brought to people, parents, a generation his senior.[15] Ever solicitous of their feelings, he was only too aware of how much his journeys of body and soul had transformed him. In letters his family has chosen to publish, there is no reference to his siblings (his official biography mentions them not at all).

Whatever the precise complex of his family relations, and notwithstanding his developing penchant for self-concealment, his capacity for friendship and his depth of identification with the stopping points along his odyssey—his self-revelation—were pronounced. A few weeks after arriving home in Warsaw, he set out for Berlin, writing at that time to a friend in Hebron:

> These leave-takings [from, for example, parents in 1921, Slobodka in 1925, Hebron in 1929, parents, again, in 1929] have overtaken me just a little too much. But what can I do? This is my nature. Every place where I arrive, even as but a passing guest, I take root at once; I become a citizen in the land, in the environment. Naturally that makes the parting seven times more difficult. Am I, then, to be counted among the righteous, who lack tranquility in both this world and the next? I begin to feel a little bit proud.[16]

In Berlin were contemporaries of Rabbi Hutner on their own odysseys, young Orthodox prodigies of a kind whom he could hardly have expected to encounter in Palestine; and there were mentors whose syntheses were different from those of both the Elder and Rabbi Kuk, and whom he had good reason to suspect would open their doors to him. There was, for example, Rabbi Jehiel Jacob Weinberg, Ph.D., then forty-four, a pre-World War I student in Slobodka who had become its first graduate to seek a doctorate (at the University of Giessen), who was among the first to bring a Lithuanian approach to Talmud study to the West; and who now was rector of the Rabbinical Seminary for Orthodox Judaism, an explicitly cross-cultural enterprise.[17] Weinberg was a practitioner of what then occupied a central place on the agenda of critical Jewish scholarship, the editing of critical editions of seminal Jewish texts by collation of manuscripts and philological expertise. Two other former Slobodka students, Saul Lieberman and Harry Austryn Wolfson, were doing this, respectively, in talmudic and medieval philosophic texts (*Al ha-Yerushalmi* [*On the Talmud of the Land of Israel*] and *Crescas' Critique of Aristotle*, both published in 1929).

Rector Weinberg was working in the history of Jewish law. We may suppose that in Rabbi Hutner's visits with the rector, this kind of scholarship was discussed. A few years later we find young Hutner independently taking pains to secure a manuscript of Hillel of Verona's thirteenth-century commentary of *Sifra*᾽, a rabbinic work on Leviticus of roughly the same authority as Mishnah. The manuscript was written in Italian script, which Rabbi Hutner taught himself by comparing passages from the Talmud quoted in the manuscript with the Talmud itself, until he was able "to study it as easily as a printed book."[18] His goal was to write a commentary on Hillel of Verona's work in order to open up study of *Sifra*᾽.

He began work on the Italian commentary in 1934, during his last stay in Palestine, and devoted his first years in the United States to completing it. Only one small section was published, however, in 1938.[19] It was one of the last of the few items that he allowed to be published under his own name, until he officially broke his silence in 1964. In setting out for Berlin in 1929, he had translated Orthodox then-athiest then-Zionist then-Diaspora nationalist then-again-Orthodox Nathan Birnbaum's *Eternal People* from German to Hebrew as a self-written letter of introduction. When word of the translation was leaked to a Hebrew journal he refused to let it be published, eventually relenting, typically, to allow part of it to be published anonymously.[20]

To be accepted in the East European world of talmudic scholarship—"East European" signifying a metonymy for insulated, intensive Talmud study in Eastern Europe, Palestine, or the United States—as Rabbi Hutner always was, it was impolitic to be associated with literary or scholarly endeavors. Early in his career, it seems to me, he made the conscious decision neither to limit the breadth of his interests nor to pursue them any more openly than his keen sense of their tolerability among his colleagues told him was possible. In this, Rabbi Hutner was unlike Joseph Baer Soloveitchik (Chapter Five), whom Rabbi Hutner first met in Berlin and who was so different from him, notwithstanding their similar urge to twin intensive talmudic studies with extratalmudic perspectives. Rabbi Soloveitchik never concealed his extratalmudic, philosophic interests—a stance that aggravated his already natural penchant for loneliness by overtly setting him apart from that community of first-level East European talmudic scholars who should have been his natural circle. Rabbi Hutner, through public concealment of his broad interests, did gain acceptance in his natural circle, but at a price: a different kind of self-induced loneliness. He would become a lonely eminence because of a sweep and grasp that he could rarely share.

For the same reasons that he would hesitate to reveal his literary and scholarly endeavors, he would be unhesitant in revealing his talmudic abilities. It was to this task—not critical scholarship—that he turned upon his return to Warsaw from Berlin. He did not begin at once. A customary, twofold gesture—waiting, absorbing, maturing; and quick movement, sudden initiative—preceded *Torat ha-Nazir (Law of the Nazirite)*. Its germination found him studying a year in Warsaw, then another nine months in Palestine, whereupon he returned, full circle, to the Slobodka yeshiva in Lithuania, promptly and intensively to undertake a work that would reflect the erudition of a scholar beyond his years. People had known him to study for nearly twenty-four hours without stop. That is apparently what he did now, learning tractate *Nazir*, setting down both analyses and original interpretations, completing the work in no more than half a year! So unfailing was his certitude that he sent every few pages to the printers as soon as they were finished, not even waiting until the entire manuscript was finished to ensure that all sections correlated.[21] Various proofs were sent to internationally renowned Talmud scholars with a request for a formal approbation. Enthusiastic replies were readily forthcoming.[22]

The book marked a turning point. Isaac Hutner would marry soon after it was published, securing not just his lifelong partner but steady financial support from his in-laws in order to allow him to develop his intellectual interests freely, unburdened by practical considerations.[23] In no small measure this was the result of the stature that the book both conferred and confirmed. Isaac Hutner would become "Rabbi"—teacher—setting his sights less on how and what to absorb from others, more on how and what to transmit to others. It was this reorientation that entailed his most radical uprooting—an uprooting, as he said, always for the sake of growth.

> And so [he wrote in 1934] I am now on my way to America. Here I am, on the ship, sailing to New York. In these last years, I have been swept by the flux of events in my life, wave after wave, journey after journey,

migration upon migration, and have known no rest. All these journeys, migrations, travels, all that probing—inside and outside of myself— . . . were nothing other than the result of an inner urge disturbing my peace, consuming me with its flame, beating my back with a thousand hammers and grabbing my head by its tails—goading me to find the way *to myself by myself*. I must create even the first stalks with my own hands.[24]

As a comprehensive retrospective, unifying and conceptualizing his dense and differentiated itinerary into a single period of search, this reflection identifies one unmalleable quality that stood out even at the journey's beginning: independence. If Europe and Palestine were most fertile ground for independence as a student, the United States would be most fertile ground for independence as a teacher, a rabbi. "I must concede that had I not been in the United States all these years—had I remained in the Holy Land—life there would not have allowed me that nonalignment [*i-hizdahut*] so essential to my spirit. . . ."[25]

Independence, in the sense of guarding the essential self, the bottommost ego, from the insistent demand for transformation: a term not to be cherished by pietists, but to be taken for granted in much of Hasidism. If in the Elder's Musar Rabbi Hutner observed self-concealment, self-scrutiny, self-sacrifice, and growth and tranquility—all of which he sought to embody—he saw all this after his formative years in Warsaw, "formative" because, by sixteen, he was beyond his years. Although his paternal heritage derived from the Lithuanian pocket within the predominantly hasidic, religious sector of Jewish Warsaw, he knew the larger hasidic community of his birth. His maternal heritage was hasidic. The attractive traits of the Elder's Musar he could locate in the iconoclastic, Polish hasidic eddy of Kotsk, with which an uncle was associated. He studied in the Gerer *shtibl* in Warsaw. He absorbed Hasidism's dominant view that the ego, though not to be left untended, was not to be transformed, either. Whether hasidic ethos shaped Rabbi Hutner, or merely confirmed prior inclinations, we cannot know. We do know that he was able to reconcile a Musar stress on criticizing the ego and a hasidic stress on nurturing it.

The Musar practice of self-scrutiny presumed an essential psychological health, an ability to step outside the self and view it objectively, to analyze and criticize it without destroying it. However, with the passage of the generations, thought Rabbi Hutner, the presumption of essential psychological health no longer held; people had weakened. It became necessary to build ego, to foster self-regard—self-confidence and self-trust—to restore the rung of being with which the Musar sensibility had begun and from which it ascended. Implicit in all of Rabbi Hutner's writings is a clear message of encouragement: Man can achieve. Man is great. While in Slobodka this concept (*gadlut ha-adam*) had represented the foundation of pietistic devotion, the state from which an essentially healthy person could transform himself; in Rabbi Hutner's thought the concept represented the culmination, the essence of psychological health, which itself required much effort to attain. Rabbi Hutner himself spared no effort in fostering his own foundation of essential health or self-regard. His letters are unified by the pronoun "I" and the adjective "my." He set forth the significance of these ubiquities most clearly in a letter in 1933.

> I am now becoming steeped in studies. . . . Study in its various guises absorbs me, and yet I know that the essence of my personality is the life of my soul and not the life of my mind. . . . For me to live a life of the soul means to live a life of soul-creativity. For myself, I cannot imagine any realm of life of the spirit to be without creativity. But this is the rub: I am not able to be creative in the life of the soul without first taking important strides—creative ones—in study and *mada'*. And so, I am stuck between the insistent claims of the soul, which penetrate to my depths, and between the command of my personality to overcome these claims temporarily, [as I pursue my studies] to build for greater soul-creativity at a later time.[26]

The soul—the ego—was to be trained to perform acts of righteousness and tasks of holiness, to be nurtured and channeled, not changed. And at bottom, the twenty-eight-year-old groom who set out for America, manuscript of Hillel of Verona in hand, was now to use, not change, his ego to build an institutional-intellectual world of a kind never before seen there.

III.

America unleashes zest, all the more so for a person who possesses it to begin with and especially if he senses that America will do just that. Already within a year after his arrival Rabbi Hutner was delivering addresses in English. His appearance was modern: no East European, long black rabbinical caftan, and no beard. It would be three to four decades before American rabbinical academies (yeshivas) produced their own deans; earlier ones were European transplants—with the exception of Rabbi Hutner. To all outward appearances—dress, language, easy camaraderie with American ways of thinking and the American street urchins who became some of his first students—he was the first American yeshiva dean. Energetic, financially secure, something of a bon vivant, his personal tapestry, which already interwove whole schools of thought, was further recast. His adjustment to America proceeded so rapidly that it entailed recoil from America. It was as if he had leaped over the sequential, prototypical achievements of an immigrant generation and its offspring—a first generation's struggle for survival and a second generation's adjustment and desire for acceptance—and moved directly into a third generation's assumption of acceptance and the right to be critical. For if Rabbi Hutner learned rapidly to fit in, he also consciously developed an authoritarian style at variance with the American ethos.

The style, if personally rooted, was also contextual. Amid a second generation of rapidly assimilating Jews who spurned what he called "the honor of Torah" *(kevod ha-Torah)*, such honor could be instilled by insisting strictly that honor be paid to a person, a rabbi—himself—who, through knowledge of Torah and its vast talmudic commentary, embodied it.[27] Rabbi Hutner was not to be addressed except in the third person ("the Rosh Yeshiva"), not to be taken leave of by turning one's back and leaving, but by walking backwards out the office door (so as not to turn one's back on Torah), and, most important, not to be challenged once he had reached decisions on matters of communal policy, of yeshiva administration, of personal guidance, of intellectual formulation.

Personal and contextual, all this also constituted a reversal: If young Isaac Hutner made it a habit to seek mentors and to accept the submission of discipleship, the mentor Rabbi Hutner expected a parallel submission from his own disciples. Sometimes he sounded almost Nietzschean: "The single refuge in 'the tangible' is this: the Personality. The Person, Man: it is he who is Fact; the Tangible; Reality. One personality can revitalize a generation's majestic life, suffusing it with the light of Torah—such a personality being weightier than innumerable ideas, speeches, intellectual creations."[28] At the core of such a personality was the power not of manipulation, but of self. In Rabbi Hutner's case the power was not just intellectual and literary, but pedagogical and personal. If some were repelled by his carefully cultivated sense of distance, others learned that this did not preclude accessibility, good conversation, humor—friendship—and show of emotion. In personal conversation he would tell jokes and would entrance with grace and charm. He would give hours to counseling, sing tunes from Italian opera in informal attire, or ask his driver to stop suddenly in the mountains so that he could put to poetry a spiritual inspiration that had overcome him. He would sign letters, "with joyful tears of love,"[29] or write, after his visit to the grave of Rabbi Judah Loew (Maharal, c. 1526—1609), in Prague:

> When tears well up into weeping, we know why we weep. My tears at this moment, however, surely and surely did not well up now. My tears are old and venerable now, having gathered in the subsoil of the soul now and over time, in their own time. Hidden tears, the soul itself hid them by placing a concealing rock over the entrance to the well of the soul. Across time—their own time—there gathered types of tears, different tears. In this hidden spot of tears there are those of "My eyes dropped streams of water for not having kept your Torah" and of "Extend grace to me, wretched am I"—tears of sharing the sorrows of men, of pitying an orphaned generation, of yearning for the countenance of parents and teachers whom I was privileged to view once upon a time, of yearning for the higher light in blessed hours of engagement with the secrets of Torah, of reciting the *Song of Songs* from out of a mighty sense of their loftiness—tears flowing as water libations upon the altar, the altar of love of God, tears of exaltation. All these types of tears, sentenced to hiding across ages, across years, now coalesced into one unity beneath the concealing rock, and behold! When my fingers just grazed Maharal's tombstone, the concealing rock on my breast split to smithereens and my tears came gushing, like a waterfall cascading downward between clefts in the rock.[30]

In the encounter with America, in which the implications of Rabbi Hutner's intricate intellectual baggage were to be pulled and tugged into kaleidoscopic diversity, it was Maharal who came to be a model. Rabbi Hutner became devoted to his writings, as both expositor and appropriator. The most protean figure in medieval Jewish thought, unclassifiable in his range of interests, Maharal wove them into his own unique blend, undissolvable into its component parts. These, according to contemporary enthusiasts, embraced not only Jewish law, lore, philosophy, mysticism, ethics, educational theory, and homiletics, but even a theory of relativity that marked him as Albert Einstein's most serious precursor.[31] Rabbi Hutner's attachment to Maharal grew as his own development in America underwent seemingly diametrically opposed transformations.[32]

Institutionally Rabbi Hutner took root in a talmudic academy, Mesivta Rabbi Chaim Berlin, beginning in 1936. For a brief period, he also served as principal of Yeshiva Rabbi Jacob Joseph high school. Mesivta Chaim Berlin, which he headed for over four decades, and which, in 1956, expanded to include a *kolel*, or advanced center for married students (named after two of Maharal's books), was vintage in Lithuanian orientation—an extension of Slobodka and Hebron. However, even as Rabbi Hutner grew into the archetypical Lithuanian yeshiva dean—beginning his beard in 1941, assuming the title "Rosh Yeshiva," delivering lectures in Talmud—he planted the seeds of an opposite growth that flowered, decades later, alongside the Lithuanian tradition. In dress he eventually adopted the Polish hasidic garb of his native Warsaw—tall, round, wholly fur hat *(spodik)* for Sabbath and holidays, flowing black robe, prayer belt *(gartel)*—even as he came increasingly to adopt certain customs of Hasidism's arch opponent, the Vilna Gaon.[33]

The synthesis had a Hutnerian logic. The devotion to the Vilna Gaon was grounded in his achievement, unprecedented in centuries, of mastery of the entirety of Jewish legal and kabbalistic traditions, together with a marked (if instrumental) interest in math, sciences, and textual studies.[34] The devotion to Hasidism was grounded in a post-Holocaust commitment to perpetuating the unassimilatory stance of that segment of Jewry least easily swayed by Western narcissisms in pursuit of goods and glory.

If the synthesis had its logic, it could also have met sociological needs. Why did Rabbi Kuk's picture, hung yearly in Rabbi Hutner's *sukkah*, come down some years after his arrival in America? Was it because Rabbi Hutner deferred to the majority, anti-Kuk opinion of the "Torah community" (as he deferred to Rabbi Aaron Kotler; below), because Rabbi Hutner changed his mind on Rabbi Kuk, or because Rabbi Hutner believed that Rabbi Kuk's thought, while intrinsically valuable, was unsuitable for his generation? Why were Rabbi Hutner's writings, with rare exception, published anonymously up to 1964? Was it because they represented personal teachings, delivered in the privacy of his classes (to which no outsiders were admitted), shaped for the specificity of an induplicable classroom atmosphere? Or, was it because of other reasons?[35]

The constant ferment in Rabbi Hunter entailed a periodic reorientation not only toward mentors, such as Rabbi Kuk, but also toward contemporaries and students. On the one hand, a disciple could write (on the occasion of the posthumous publication of Rabbi Hutner's letters):

> The outpouring of love in these letters, the delicacy with which he gave the sharpest of reproofs, the passionate pleas with which he provided encouragement, the lucidity and authoritativeness with which he clarified fundamentals of belief, the insistence on being kept informed of the most mundane details of the lives of *talmidim* [students or disciples], his inquiring after the welfare of a correspondent's spouse, reminds us dramatically of

our own individual contacts with the Rosh Yeshiva. Who can forget the quite extraordinary interest with which he devoted himself to the personal concerns of the *talmidim* of his study hall? These letters bring to mind the Rosh Yeshiva being prepared again and again to spend hours on end in conversation with an individual young yeshiva student, probing, searching, healing and uplifting. . . . They recall for us the Rosh Yeshiva as the master craftsman engaged in fashioning—out of the crudest clay—nothing less than the noblest form of creation, the *talmid chacham* [Talmud scholar].[36]

And yet, although his yeshiva succeeded in inculcating a sense of both devoted discipleship and personal autonomy, there were periodic house cleanings. Students or disciples, some of long standing, suddenly were no longer to be seen in the yeshiva. If given to good humor, friendship, and emotional sharing of a disciple's burdens, Rabbi Hutner also elicited hostility or repudiation. He could be abrasive in admonition, high-handed in asserting his independence of monied or competing intellectual interests, disdainful of publicity agents of even Orthodox organizations, and forceful in branding insubordination among students. For a variety of reasons, many of his closest disciples would not send their children to Mesivta Chaim Berlin.[37] Some in attendance at Mesivta Chaim Berlin or in its circle left of their own accord to become, for example, a prominent antitraditional Holocaust theologian (Richard Rubenstein),[38] a noted academic-critical scholar of Talmud (David Weiss Halivni), or a foremost student of Rabbi Soloveitchik (Aharon Lichtenstein).

Those who left Mesivta Chaim Berlin—and, presumably, those whom Rabbi Hutner forced to leave—pained him precisely because he was usually effective in winning fierce loyalty. This loyalty derived in part from his students' gratitude for the extent and effectiveness of the time he devoted to them—for his drawing them out, identifying their strengths, giving them confidence. The diversity and influence of his many students—his enduring legacy as a pedagogue—is doubly remarkable for the inhospitable soil—secular, economically declining Brownsville—whence it originally sprang.

IV.

Rabbi Hutner's relationship with contemporaries also generated tensions. Rabbi Soloveitchik, for example, spoke at an early dedication of Mesivta Chaim Berlin, and at least as late as 1939 these two Lithuanian titans corresponded in talmudic matters.[39] There was also an old connection to the Soloveitchik family, stemming from Rabbi Soloveitchik's father having asked young Isaac Hutner to keep an eye on his youngest son, back in Eastern Europe. However, as the views of Rabbis Hutner and Soloveitchik on philosophical and public matters developed, they came to differ sharply.

On the question of whether secular knowledge has a place in sacred studies, Rabbi Soloveitchik's position is clearly affirmative. For him, secular knowledge must be studied openly, analyzed explicitly, and then synthesized with the pertinent teachings of Jewish sacred literature. If, in the synthesis, Torah remains dominant, its coloration takes on a contemporary, Western hue, which represents the actualization of the Divine word for the present generation. In Chapter Five we shall examine Rabbi Soloveitchik's synthesis of talmudic and neo-Kantian epistemology.

Rabbi Hutner rejected synthesis but not secular study, at least for a select few. The unexceptional Talmud student would be unable to cope with intellectual challenges to tradition that Western philosophy, historiography, and other branches of learning pose. For Rabbi Hutner himself, secular study was less central than for Rabbi Soloveitchik. First, Rabbi Hutner conceived Jewish sacred literature itself to be more inclusive than did Rabbi Soloveitchik. For example, Rabbi Hutner subsumed under the rubric of "Torah" the psychological and pietistic teachings that the Musar movement harnessed, while Rabbi Soloveitchik did not. Then, with regard to knowledge that both categorized as secular, they conceived it differently. To Rabbi Hutner's unitive mind, secular study identified a domain of the sacred within itself, a procedure that amounted to Torah's reclaiming what rightfully belonged to it; for Torah, said Rabbi Hutner, was the sovereign source of all that is sacred. Hence he saw neither a moral nor a technical justification for the citation of secular sources in his writings. To Rabbi Soloveitchik's categorizing mind, secular knowledge, even if subject to the sovereignty of Torah, retained an intrinsic value. Hence, he cites it freely and extensively.

On the public question of whether Orthodox participation in pluralistic umbrella groups such as the Synagogue Council of America conferred legitimacy on Conservative and Reform Judaism's representatives in these groups, Rabbi Hutner opposed Orthodox participation while Rabbi Soloveitchik took a different stand.[40] To Rabbi Hutner, it was impossible to separate legitimate, common interests from conferring legitimacy on heterodox coworkers. To Rabbi Soloveitchik, such categorization was possible. The Lubavitcher Rebbe, Rabbi Menahem Schneerson (born 1902), who also opposes Orthodox participation in umbrella groups, still met with Rabbi Hutner's opposition—and also against a background of earlier friendship. From Rabbi Schneerson's arrival in America in 1941 until he became the Lubavitcher Rebbe in 1950, he and Rabbi Hutner maintained an intimate ḥavruta, or fixed time for joint study. Decades later, when Rabbi Hutner lay on his deathbed, the Lubavitcher Rebbe had his physician phone from the United States to Israel regularly to inquire about Rabbi Hutner's condition. But all this could not obscure a clear breach. Rabbi Hutner relentlessly sustained a biting critique of the Lubavitcher movement on a number of grounds.[41]

All three prodigies who met in Berlin in 1929—Joseph B. Soloveitchik, Isaac Hutner, Menahem Schneerson—sustained a self-image so powerful and a certitude so unqualified that there could be no room for even delicate criticism among them as they each developed mutually exclusive kingdoms, so to speak: modern, secular-talmudic philosophic synthesis for Rabbi Soloveitchik; a worldwide hasidic movement for the Lubavitcher Rebbe; and an elite, talmudic-pietistic training center for Rabbi Hutner. In their divergence, the larger problem they embody is the elusiveness of an affirmative definition of modern Orthodox Judaism. There was no disagreement, however, on what it was not. Rabbi Hutner demonstrated this most poignantly, going beyond biting disagreement, to definitive rebuke, in his attitude toward Abraham Joshua Heschel.

Heschel, who taught at the Conservative movement's Jewish Theological Seminary of America for twenty-seven years, was literally Rabbi Hutner's contemporary, as both were born in Warsaw, a year apart. One of Rabbi Hutner's students in the late 1970s cited an interpretation of Heschel, without citing it in his name, to which Rabbi Hutner responded, "You read that in Heschel!"—and (atypically) slapped the student across the face.

The opinionated Rabbi Hutner had read whom he took to be an unacceptable interpreter of Judaism. Heschel fit no single religious, secular, or academic category within modern Judaism. No one of his titles—"rabbi," "doctor," "professor"—fit him. He was always, simply, "Abraham Joshua Heschel," a creation unto himself. Rabbi Hutner rejected this. It was not Heschel's affiliation with the Conservative movement *per se* that repelled Rabbi Hutner. For if, in Rabbi Soloveitchik and the Lubavitcher Rebbe, Rabbi Hutner perceived competing conceptions of Orthodoxy, in Professor Saul Lieberman (1898–1983)—a critical scholar of Talmud at the same Jewish Theological Seminary—Rabbi Hutner observed a greater, yet not unbridgeable, distance. Given what he took to be their common doctrinal links (forged in Slobodka), Rabbi Hutner offered Professor Lieberman a position at Mesivta Chaim Berlin, which was turned down. The irony is derived from Rabbi Hutner's consistent, fierce opposition to any Orthodox association, on the institutional level, with the Conservative movement—the dean of whose rabbinical school Professor Lieberman later became.

Rabbi Hutner's continual ferment entailed an uncharacteristic submission to the authority of two figures—an approximation of his stance as a student in Europe, when he searched out mentors. One of the two represented an extension of Rabbi Hutner's past; the other, a deviation from it. The first, Rabbi Aaron Kotler (1892-1962), was the "*ari shebaḥavurah*," "the lion of the pack," the most talented, loyal extension of the talmudic scholarship and intensity of pietistic purpose of Slobodka. In matters of high policy, such as whether to open a college in which secular studies would be sanctioned, Rabbi Hutner bent to Rabbi Kotler's will (the school was not opened).[42] A far different figure, the Hungarian anti-Zionist Satmar Rebbe (Rabbi Joel Teitelbaum, 1888–1980), was, said Rabbi Hutner, royalty; and one honors royalty. Rabbi Hutner explained with reference to the midrash that states that Noah once was late in feeding the two lions in his Ark, and was clawed. Noah humbled himself in the service of his zoo: why did he deserve to be clawed? Because, said Rabbi Hutner, these were the last lions. One does not neglect the honor of a last, majestic leader of undifferentiated, communally cohesive, pre-Holocaust East European Jewry. It delighted the protean Rabbi Hutner when representatives of two diametrically opposite faces of Orthodoxy—the arch Zionist Rabbi Kuk's son, Rabbi Zvi Judah, and the arch anti-Zionist Satmar ally Rabbi Amram Blau—once met uncomfortably in Rabbi Hutner's waiting room. Both sought counsel from the same person. That Rabbi Hutner grew apart from Rabbi Kuk's Zionist views is clear. That he retained the highest regard for his person and his erudition is also clear. How he squared that regard with his emergent homage to the Satmar Rebbe is an issue he never addressed. Did the dialectical tensions in his multihued prism find a welcome anchor, a stream of pure light, in monochromatic Satmar Hasidism? Or did the meeting of the two opponents in his waiting room signify that Rabbi Hutner had tugged their perspectives into a unity?

V.

To unify perspectives: This is the burden of Rabbi Hutner's thought, whose scope transcends traditional topics of Jewish thought. In his corpus, gathered in eight volumes of *Paḥad Yitzhak* (1951–1982),[43] Rabbi Hutner sought to integrate opposites beyond well-known pairings such as reason and emotion, or autonomy and theonomy, stretching into unbroken ground, conjoining the likes of naive and informed faith, abstract and parabolic expression, and laughter and seriousness.[44] It was not that traditional pairings did not occupy him; they suffuse his writings throughout. The dialectic between Halakhah and Aggadah—Jewish law and lore, finely calibrated legal discussion and unrestrained magical, anecdotal, and imaginative discussion—for example, was in Rabbi Hutner's writings no dialectic at all. So thoroughly did he harmonize law and lore that only by consulting the source listings in the appendices to his expositions in *Paḥad Yitzhak* is it possible to separate the one from the other. In neither tone nor content can they be extricated from the unifying matrix into which he cast them. To Rabbi Hutner, as to Rabbis Israel Salanter and Joseph B. Soloveitchik, law and lore are mutually illuminating; interpenetrating and completing each other. The difference between Rabbi Hutner on the one hand and Rabbis Salanter and Soloveitchik on the other is that only Rabbi Hutner undertook thoroughly to set forth the interrelation of law and lore. Not the occasional, sharp ray of luminous insight of Rabbi Salanter, nor the more sustained yet occasional essays of Rabbi Soloveitchik, but volume upon volume of discourse, ranging across the whole of talmudic law and lore, consitituted Rabbi Hutner's agenda. For him the entire Talmud comprised not two legitimate but different and discrete types of discourse, and still less a regrettably stale marriage of adjacencies who dwelled together but could not warm each other's consciousness. The Talmud was a felicitous juxtaposition of apparent discrepancies—law and lore—the perception of whose deeper interrelationship awaited only the proper intellectual and spiritual sensibility to bring it forth.

If the source listings of Rabbi Hutner's discourses reveal overtly the integration of law and lore, these listings reveal covertly an integration no less significant: the blending of philosophy and kabbalah with law. Covertly: A statement of Rabbi Hutner will, for example, take as its fulcrum a stock philosophical concept—such as the distinction between the unknowability of God's essence and the knowability of his activities—with no reference to any philosophic source. The reference will be to a seemingly tangential, legal source, which draws the distinction in a legal context, without philosophic elaboration.[45] One who brings no prior philosophic knowledge to the statement will not notice the mask but, under the impression that he is studying law, will learn philosophy. One who does bring prior knowledge will, under the impress of Rabbi Hutner's analysis, observe the limits of law, philosophy, and kabbalah dilate, reaching into each other in hitherto unnoticed ways and to a hitherto unnoticed extent. All this is covert. Substantively the reader perceives the multifaceted topic without the mediation of any technical terms, but formally it is like reading in a hall of mirrors—you think you see one thing, but really see another—like reading (in the language of Rabbi Hutner himself) the secret Torah (*nistar*) in the language of the revealed Torah (*nigleh*)[46]—and one never knows whether one has comprehended all the allusions.

The use of halakhic terminology to argue implicitly for the interpenetration of Jewish law, lore, philosophy, and kabbalah is one of two ways that Rabbi Hutner subsumes these disciplines under the one rubric of Halakhah. The other way is the style of his "Statements," or *ma'amarim*, as he entitled his discourses with characteristic definitiveness (and also because he first presented them orally, the written statement being a reformulation of lecture notes). These statements follow no usual style of philosophical, logical, or imaginative reasoning; they are, rather, "battlefields," to use the traditional halakhic term for halakhic exposition, oral and written. All that Rabbi Hutner sets forth, in any area, is done in the form of purely halakhic analysis. Halakhic sources are marshalled; contradictions or other problems in the sources are set on the table; additional halakhic sources (or other sources; parts of Maharal, for example) with little or no apparent relevance are expounded and illuminated such that the glimmerings of a solution to the original problems begin to flicker; and, finally, an original thrust of thought brings all sources (both originally cited and subsequently expounded) into unforseen harmony. Such, in general, is halakhic analysis, used by Rabbi Hutner throughout, most fully in his longer discourses. Such is the irreducibility of the Lithuanian Talmud student in all of Rabbi Hutner's formal, published writings.

Less prominent problematic pairings in the history of Jewish thought occupy Rabbi Hutner as much as the pivotal modern issue of the Halakhah and its complements and contraries. I have chosen a short selection to illustrate the Hutnerian blend because only a lengthy exposition could demonstrate it fully, as he does, in lengthy statements. With reference to Maimonides' commentary to Mishnah, Rabbi Hutner discusses the pairing of the natural and the demonic (the material and immaterial), and of man and the world. Maimonides writes that demons have no reality, but, comments Rabbi Hutner,

> in several instances statements of the talmudic sages point to the reality of demons. The way to explain the seeming discrepancy is with reference to *'Avot de-Rabbi Natan*, which states (chapter 31) that all that exists in the

world finds an analogue in man. And the opposite is also true: all that exists in man finds an analogue in the world. Now, in the mind of man there exists the power of imagination, with which man can sketch a reality that in fact does not exist in the world. It is a reality only by the power of imagination. Since this kind of power exists in man, it certainly has a creaturely analogue in the world—the creatures whom we call demons. That is to say, demons are reality-nonreality. Proof: When we speak about something as a figment of the imagination, we mean that such a thing has no reality. However, to the researcher in human psychology at the moment of his examination of the inner workings of the mind of man, this imagination is reality, apodictically. And so, Maimonides has written well that demons have no existence in reality, but this in no way contradicts all of the talmudic passages pointing to the reality of demons.[47]

Just as man has an imagination, so does nature. Just as man's imagination is real to him, nature's imagination is real to it (or, if the imagination of the world is to be a concept without sense, then so is the imagination of man, and this is unthinkable). Therefore, just as man is subject to the imaginary world he creates, the world is subject to the demonic world it unleashes. On the plane of reality–nonreality, the natural and the demonic—the material and immaterial—meet.

This worldview reflects not simply an Enlightenment assumption of continuity between man and nature (of "natural law" in man and society), but finds its deeper roots in ancient interpretations of the Platonic logos,[48] one of which is reflected in an ancient midrashic tradition. "The Holy One, Blessed be He, looked in the Torah and created the world"[49]—the Torah, blueprint for human living, is the blueprint for nature. But if man and nature are uniplanar, their real-nonreal creations—imagination and demons—need not necessarily be equivalent in value. Elsewhere Rabbi Hutner elaborates on Rabbi Israel Salanter's imperative to transfigure human imagination.[50] What this implies for the ultimate reality and malleability of the demonic remains unknown, for if Rabbi Hutner left volumes of thought, he also left suggestive, unfinished notebooks, from which the citation above is taken. If unfinished, his notebooks, no less than his finished work, illustrate the range of constituent elements in his aspiration to unity. Rabbi Hutner works with Jewish legal sources, but the upshot is more than strictly halakhic. It is kabbalistic, psychological, philosophical, homiletical. A unique blend has been created.

The blend impels the reductionist temptation to express Rabbi Hutner's thought in categories of Western philosophy or modern Jewish thought. Behind the temptation is the difficulty of classifying thought, such as Rabbi Hutner's (and Abraham Joshua Heschel's), which controls an entire range of sources—halakhic, mystical, philosophical, homiletical, pietistic, poetic, exegetical. The temptation itself is to regard Rabbi Hutner's use of these sources as but the clothing of an essence, a clothing that can be stripped to reveal the essence. Rabbi Hutner's use of an array of sources, however, is not merely a mode of expression. It is his mind, his pith, his being.[51] To abstract him, to pry him loose from his sources, is to eviscerate him. Rabbi Hutner's mask was to use one kind of Jewish source to hide another, but not to hide a doctrine unlinked to the Jewish sources at all. To succumb to the temptation to see Rabbi Hutner this way is merely to concede the difficulty of evaluating a fresh claim about the authoritativeness and the unity of all traditional Jewish sources, a claim that would render obsolete familiar distinctions between philosopher and mystic, *ba' al Musar* and *ḥasid*, halakhist and poet, commentator and original interpreter.

The medium of Rabbi Hutner's essays, no less than the substance, betokens a melding of opposites. Rabbi Hutner's use of Judaism's appointed times—Sabbath and holidays—as the medium through which to explicate Judaism's beliefs represents a confluence of two streams in the Jewish approach to dogma. In the most fertile period of the drawing up of dogmas of Judaism—the medieval period—the debate over whether Judaism had dogmas, and, if it did, over what they were, was confined to Iberian Jews, to thinkers working under the attack or the stimulus of Christian or Islamic theology and philosophy.[52] East European Jewry, with the single exception of Yom Tov Lippman Muhlhausen, implicitly took a phenomenological approach: Jewish consciousness was to be constituted from the living of Jewish law and lore, not from discussion of beliefs upon which law and lore rest. The living of Judaism is readily differentiated according to its special times, Sabbath and holidays, while the discussion of Judaism is readily differentiated according to its doctrines. The blending of the phenomenological and the doctrinal in Judaism is readily achieved by classifying each of Judaism's beliefs as a lesson taught by each aspect of its special times.

In bringing together the phenomenological and the doctrinal, Rabbi Hutner is unique only in the rigor he brings to the task. The rubric itself, though traceable to Isaac Arama of the fifteenth century,[53] has emerged in the last half-century as a popular form.[54] The breakdown of the insulation of East European Jewry and its derivatives, and the vitality it has brought to rationalist West European Jewry and its derivatives,[55] have led to the Sabbath-holiday frame for discussion of Jewish belief. Nowhere is the cross-fertilization it represents put to firmer use than in Rabbi Hutner's eight-volume *Paḥad Yitzhak*, with one volume devoted to Passover, Pentecost, New Year, Day of Atonement, Sabbath and Tabernacles, Chanukah, Purim, and letters and other writings. As with the sources and the substance of Rabbi Hutner's thought, its Sabbath-holiday medium reflected his being. His statements on the Jewish beliefs, expressed in the frame of each Jewish special time, were delivered during that time. This scheduling was intentional. The atmosphere of the given holiday would assure the statement about it the stamp of authenticity.[56]

VI.

"I speak poetry, and they want to hear prose!" Rabbi Hutner once lamented. A pithy remark, pregnant with meaning—with humor, irony, a sense of self-worth, of style, of imperfect acceptance, imperfect understanding on the part of his audience. Rabbi Hutner formed deep attachments, not just to places and ideas. By humor or by intellect, by confidence stemming from ability or by an exotic touch stemming from nonconformity, he charmed, taught, forged bonds of relationship that left close associates unable to function for weeks after his death. And yet, "they" wanted to hear prose: with many he did not communicate. Attraction and repulsion—the strands of others' relation to him—were the strands of his own relation to an enduring pulsation, from his youth to his deathbed: the Land of Israel, *Eretz Yisrael*. Attraction—of the world for him, and to him—and repulsion—of the world by him, and for him—underlay his complex personality. As he encountered the world, as it encountered him, the enduring dialectic came to especially poignant expression in his relation to the Land of Israel. He left it so often, returned to it so insistently.

> I remember how a lyrical exaltation formed in and around me in preparing to go up to the Land of Israel the first time. All of my personal, written reflections and letters to friends and comrades at the time constituted nothing other than one exuberant and majestic outpouring. And truth to tell, all of my ascents to the Land of Israel—the second time, the third time—were events of the soul, root-and-branch, mighty in value, momentous in result.[57]

These early ascents, as a student, were problematic. They were too placid, too perfect. The Talmud: "The Holy One, blessed be He, gave three precious gifts to Israel, all through suffering: Torah, the Land of Israel, and the world-to-come."[58] Without suffering there is no acquisition in the Land of Israel. Suffering, said Rabbi Hutner, is required, not optional. Suffering, if absent during the young Isaac Hutner's student years in the Land, descended upon him during his descents, or departures, from it.

> I am rooted in the Land of Israel. It is this ground from which I draw nurture. And now, as I am about to leave this Land I bear the pain not just of a tree stripped of its roots but of a tree uprooted whole. The pain is double: the absence of nurture, and roots dragged along after a tree, everywhere it goes . . . The pain of departure presses, presses, to the point of depression. I only hope to God that He give me the merit to return, soon.[59]

For a year or two after his arrival in the United States he still wrote to friends in Palestine that he hoped, expected, to see them soon, and at the moment of departure in 1934 he hoped that his return would entail suffering, since "in the Land of Israel I was and in it I dwelled and at it I looked, but an acquisition in it I did not acquire. When I return to it this time it will be in suffering and I shall taste a new taste, that of acquisition. With black fire on white fire these words blaze in my blood . . ."[60]

If young Hutner departed in uncharacteristic monolithic passion, he returned, decades later, with typical dialectic vitality, trying to articulate the twinning of tangible and intangible objects of sanctification (land and time), of each day and the End of Days, and of rejection and return: "Abraham our Father did not merit his high ranking, in its essence, until after he ascended to the Land of Israel *for the second time:* 'And Abraham went up from Egypt.'"[61]

On his last return dialectic vitality did not resonate in the exposed, raw, geographically and socially ubiquitous extremes of the Middle East. These were no longer the days of the Elder and of Rabbi Kuk—and of Rabbi Joseph Hayyim Sonnenfeld, the staunchest ideological opponent of Rabbi Kuk; of Rabbi Abraham Dov Ber Kahane Shapiro, the rabbi and talmudic author of Kovno; of Rabbi Menahem Ziemba, the scholar and martyr of Warsaw and its ghetto; of Rabbi Solomon Eliezer Alfandari, the centenarian mystic and rabbinical judge of Constantinople, Damascus, Safed, and Jerusalem; of Rabbi Isser Zalman Meltzer, scholarly father-in-law of Rabbi Aaron Kotler. The days of carefree absorption from all of these teachers,[62] days of undistracted integration of all their intents and purposes, were long behind Rabbi Hutner. Old, seasoned, suffering, escaped from Palestinian terrorists (who held him, with others, on a hijacked airplane for a month in Jordan), and entrapped in a sapping lawsuit (over rights to a yeshiva), Rabbi Hutner with his subtle correlations could not take root in the Land of Israel so readily, so effectively, as he once had. And yet, it is difficult to assess his last decade. His controlling metaphor then was planting, as opposed to building.[63] Building can be rushed; natural seeding cannot. It must proceed in its own time. Perhaps we simply do not know what Rabbi Hutner was attempting. Perhaps he was not granted the time to husband a last dialectic. As Maimonides said of God, as Rabbi Jacob Kaminecki (colleague of Rabbi Hutner) said of the Elder of Slobodka,[64] so may we say of Rabbi Isaac Hutner himself, "To know him one would have to be him."

CHAPTER FIVE

Rabbi Joseph Baer Soloveitchik

"I am held captive . . . From my youth I was taught to hold in my feelings, not to show anything of my emotional world. My father and master, may his memory be a blessing, used to say: 'The holier a feeling—the more intimate a feeling—the more it requires hiding in the depths.' . . . Never once did I have the privilege of being kissed by him."

From 1941 to 1985 Rabbi Joseph Baer Soloveitchik (born 1903) lectured in talmudic law and lore four to seven times weekly, to both scholars and laymen, in both New York and Boston, his lectures not infrequently lasting two-and-a-half to four hours (one student from the 1930s recalls him lecturing without stop for eight hours). Teaching what he labels an exoteric religious literature, embodying the majesty of what he calls the "king-teacher," devoted to expounding not just the folios or phrases or words but the "letters (*otiyyot*) of the Torah,"[1] Rabbi Soloveitchik has been a public persona for over half a century—and here the contradictions begin.

An advocate of inner reticence of the kind that permeated Rabbi Israel Salanter, Rabbi Soloveitchik spills forth in lectures and writings the most intimate of thoughts, expressing, for example, feelings toward his wife, conflicts with family, and anguished struggles with God. Ever ready to lecture, quite reluctant to publish—the opposite pattern of Harry Austryn

Wolfson—the literary style of Rabbi Soloveitchik is formally the opposite of Wolfson's, more profoundly just like it: formally an opposite in its unsystematic, rush-of-thought, impassioned push from first word to last; profoundly a parallel to the Wolfson oeuvre in its disclosure of the innermost psychological stance of the author. The stance is complex and not easily classifiable, like that of Rabbi Isaac Hutner, who is in many ways Rabbi Soloveitchik's clone: born but three years apart, both educated in the critico-conceptual Lithuanian talmudic dialectic, both interested in obtaining a secular education at the same time, together in Berlin (1929), immigrants to the United States within two years of each other, and quickly adaptable to the language and mores of America.[2] Yet substantively Rabbis Hutner and Soloveitchik could not have been more different. Rabbi Hutner was enigmatic because he wished to shield his self, and did. Rabbi Soloveitchik is enigmatic despite his failure to shield his self, although he wished he could. Beneath the Hutnerian conundrum was a complexity arising from an integration of multiple influences. Beneath the Soloveitchikian disclosure is a complexity arising from a confusion of influences, clashing and unintegrated. The upshot of Rabbi Soloveitchik's life and thought is the impossibility of harmony in life or thought, neither the living harmony of oscillation between struggle and tranquility, nor even the intellectual harmony of dialectic balance between polar concepts.

A pedagogic master at laying plain abstruse, contradictory, and interlocking talmudic texts, Rabbi Soloveitchik has written about the supremacy, the stability, and the serenity of "Halakhic Man"—the talmudic scholar par excellence—with such an evident, raw sensitivity to the unstable subjectivity of what he takes to be the competing "Religious Man" that only oxymoron and paradox can do Rabbi Soloveitchik justice: he is a passionate lover of intellect, a revelatory advocate of reticence, a bookbound talmudic lecturer given to effusive praise of science and secular pursuits, and the list, as we shall see, runs on. It is reducible to no simple pattern of conflict, let alone to rational system, and represents the cynosure of conflcting personality characteristics and intellectual commitments in his ancestral heritage.

I.

The Soloveitchik family was one of the oldest continuing lines of talmudic scholarship and rabbinical leadership in Eastern Europe. The first identifiable Soloveitchik was Joseph Ha-Levi Soloveitchik, communal leader in Kovno, Lithuania, in the mid-eighteenth century. One of his two grandsons, Moses, became rabbi of Kovno, and Joseph Ha-Levi's great-grandson, also named Joseph Ha-Levi, linked the Soloveitchik name to the vintage Lithuanian talmudic tradition of the Vilna Gaon by marrying a daughter of the Gaon's preeminent disciple, Hayyim of Volozhin (teacher of Rabbi Joseph Zundel Salanter). From this marriage there issued a many-branched family tree of scholars, rabbis, yeshiva deans, and communal leaders.[3] Now, after the death of Hayyim of Volozhin (1821), his renowned yeshiva was headed by his son, Isaac, upon whose death Isaac's son-in-law took over until his own untimely death a few years later.[4]

At that time, in 1849, the second Joseph Ha-Levi Soloveitchik's grandson (Hayyim of Volozhin's great-grandson) arrived in Volozhin to assume the duties of co-dean of the yeshiva. This man, a preeminent talmudic scholar, represented the one strain that would reappear in his descendant, and is, appropriately enough, his namesake, Joseph Baer Soloveitchik (1820–1897). Dynamic, sharp-witted, respecter of no person in argument, he clashed with his co-dean, Naphtali Zvi Judah Berlin ("Netziv"), a modest, patient, moderate scholar.[5] They presented their dispute to independent scholars, who decided in favor of Rabbi Berlin,[6] in whom the other strain in the present Rabbi Soloveitchik would wend its way into his lineage.

Years after the Soloveitchik-Berlin dispute, Rabbi Joseph Baer Soloveitchik gave his son, Hayyim Soloveitchik, in marriage to Rabbi Berlin's granddaughter. The present Rabbi Joseph Baer Soloveitchik is Rabbi Hayyim Soloveitchik's grandson, who, in his contact with his grandfather, had access to both the Soloveitchik and the Berlin styles and strains of thinking. On the Soloveitchik side the young Joseph Baer Soloveitchik witnessed fierce intellectual independence, innovative critico-conceptual talmudic technique, constant even if undiplomatic honesty, and coolness or outright hostility to Zionism and secular studies. On the Berlin side young Soloveitchik witnessed active support of Zionism, sympathy to secular studies, resort to broad (not just conceptually pungent) learning, and low-keyed, consensus-building leadership. Although some of these elements predominate in Rabbi Soloveitchik at the expense of others, none is omitted; and, more important, a meshing or harmonization of his manifold family tradition is absent. Joseph Baer Soloveitchik, Rabbi Hayyim Soloveitchik's most intellectually talented grandson, is both perpetuator and confounder of a protean heritage.

Born in 1903 to Rabbi Moses Soloveitchik (Rabbi Hayyim's son), Joseph Baer Soloveitchik grew to manhood in a household whose supreme value was intellection and in which secular studies were, on the surface, both superfluous and anathema. For twelve years his father educated him rigorously in the critico-conceptual talmudic method of his grandfather, but his mother—herself from a family attuned to the differentiated, Rabbi Berlin orientation—surreptitiously introduced her son to Hebrew, Russian, and Scandanavian literature. Primarily at the urging of his mother he received a secular education in his latter teens under private tutors and then, when he was twenty-two, enrolled in the University of Berlin[7]—a transition that, because of his unusual talmudic talent, reverberated as a shock and a betrayal in most of the Soloveitchik side of the family. Prior to university, then, Joseph Baer Soloveitchik never went to school. Inherent tendencies to solitariness and absence of peer contact and interaction combined with bruised family relations and coming, radical intellectual departures to form a tumultous, torn, often terrifyingly powerful personality from whom system and order are unrealistic expectation.

Rabbi Soloveitchik arrived in Berlin at a propitious moment. In the span of a few years, "Berlin" would take its place alongside "Slobodka" as a concept, a seedbed of quest for young talmudic scholars. No less than for followers or fellow travelers of Martin Buber or Gershom Scholem, of Erich Muehsam or Else Lasker-Schueler, of Albert Einstein or Max Planck, of Alfred Hugenberg or Adolf Hitler, for Orthodox Jews "Berlin" would become a metonymy—a symbol of encounter with Western philosophy, literature, or critical historical inquiry. In the 1920s there converged in Berlin a cluster of intellectuals, all but one in their twenties: from Rituva, Lithuania, came Joseph Zev Lipovitz in 1923; from Haslovitz, Lithuania, came Joseph Baer Soloveitchik in 1925; from Warsaw, Poland, came Abraham Joshua Heschel in 1927; from Yekaterinoslov (now Dnepropetrovsk), USSR, came Menahem Schneerson in 1929; from Warsaw, Poland, came Isaac Hutner in 1929; earlier Jehiel J. Weinberg and Abraham Elijah Kaplan had arrived from Slobodka.

Not only the cravings of marginal Jews located Weimar Germany at the center of cross-cultural quest. In its own way, the movement of the Orthodox intellectuals entailed a particularly perplexing suffering—not assimilated German Jews' centrifugally focused pain of rejection, burden of acceptance, or shock of betrayal by the culture they had so devotedly sought to nourish,[8] but centripetally focused suffering—the struggle to correlate a discrete and complex religious tradition, proudly affirmed, with ideas that challenged its validity. Not even Philo of Alexandria or Maimonides and Judah ha-Levi of medieval Hispanic-Jewish synthesis had embodied so sudden and drastic a shift from an indigenous, affectively as well as religiously enveloping Orthodoxy to the heart of Gentile culture, as did these iconoclasts. Save Abraham Joshua Heschel, Rabbi Soloveitchik remained in Berlin longer than any of them.

Just as the concept of Slobodka took root in charismatic personalities—the Elder of Slobodka and Rabbi Moses Mordechai Epstein—so did the concept of Berlin. Rabbi Hayyim Heller, born in Bialystock, Lithuania, in 1878, rabbi in Lomza, Poland, by 1910, conversant in Hebrew, Yiddish, German, Arabic, and Aramaic, publisher of a critical edition of Maimonides' Arabic work, *Book of the Commandments* (1914)—this scholarly, quiet, inarticulate, short man was an unlikely role model. He moved to Berlin in 1917 to pursue his researches, and in 1922 opened a unique institute for the advanced talmudic scholars then arriving in Berlin, most of whom studied at its university. By 1929 he was gone, off to New York,[9] then Palestine, then Chicago, and again New York. Rabbi Heller compelled respect solely by virtue of his combination of Lithuanian talmudic learning and critical historical scholarship. Unlike the Elder of Slobodka or Rabbi Moses Mordechai Epstein, Rabbi Heller nurtured not implicit or latent encounter with secular study but explicit and open confrontation. He both fostered and cushioned his students' struggle, impelled cross-cultural research and reflection, and softened their effects. Such was his impact on the young Soloveitchik that decades later, when both were in New York, and when Rabbi Soloveitchik was at the height of his powers, deferring to no one, he would rise for an hour or so to render lucid the awkwardly formed remarks of a sitting Rabbi Heller addressing an audience. Talmudic titan turned tame translator out of deference to his guide.[10]

Rabbi Soloveitchik arrived in Berlin *"mushlam"* (complete), a colleague of that period later commented.[11] The reference was to knowledge of the entire Babylonian Talmud, sixty-three volumes, 5,894 folio pages of alternately intricate and imaginative, elliptical and expansive, free-association legal and homiletic discourse. The young scholar's reputation was based on no published work, in accord with both the designation and pedagogic frame of the Talmud as "oral law."

Of the two main classifications of Jewish sacred literature—Scripture, "written law," and talmudic commentary, "oral law"—the latter is the far more voluminous of the two, usually transmitted as its name implies, orally. In a venerable practice stretching back through modern and medieval Europe, North Africa, and the Near East to ancient Babylonia and Palestine, scholars typically memorized long tracts of talmudic material and analyzed them orally in the presence of disciples, who, once they were trained, were expected to do the same for a coming generation of students.

The oral law, paradoxically, was constantly reduced to writing—crystallized in multivolume works such as the Talmud itself (c. 450), the Code of Maimonides (1180), and the Code of Rabbi Joseph Karo (1565)—yet each new epoch-making formulation was added to the repertoire that a preeminent scholar would commit to memory and convey in lectures. Scholars also put to writing thousands of volumes of responsa (replies to inquiries seeking the guidance of Jewish law), of commentary on individual talmudic texts, and of other forms of critical investigation, yet writing and publishing rarely established reputations. These more often derived from evidence of erudition displayed in conversation or in teaching. It was not uncommon for a talmudic author who published a first-rate work to be overshadowed by another scholar whose superior reputation was acquired strictly through discourse with disciples and peers. The Vilna Gaon was the towering authority in his lifetime even though none of his writings was published when he was alive, in the eighteenth century. Similarly, strictly by the evidence of discourse, Rabbi Soloveitchik's reputation was already well established as he entered adulthood, an object of respect by a father who was parsimonious in praise and by a grandfather who had died when his grandson was only fifteen, but who already then accorded him special regard. (It is said that young Soloveitchik climbed out the window of the study hall to preclude embarassing his grandfather, who would rise before him out of respect for his learning.)

In Berlin against the wishes of his father and the aspirations of his grandfather, the breach between him and those whose appraisal he valued most highly was doubly difficult because it was anything but complete. If Rabbi Soloveitchik's original intentions in majoring in philosophy are irretrievable, the philosophic bent of his subsequent writings indicates that in his study of Greek, Latin, and German philosophy he sought not an alternative worldview of Judaism, but tools for subjecting certain philosophic questions, especially epistemological ones, to dogmatic criticism, and for thereby establishing the autonomy of Judaism in general and of Halakhah in particular. He sought to translate to philosophic terminology the worldview implicit in the analytical methods and assumptions of his progenitors' critico-conceptual method,[12] but he did so only by failing to follow the analysis ruthlessly to its logical conclusion—ruthlessly, for such a conclusion would have been untenable for a practitioner of halakhic study. Both a biting epistemological formulation of "halakhic man" and a web of contradictions following in its wake frame Rabbi Soloveitchik's first major essay, "Halakhic Man" (*'Ish ha-Halakhah*). This reflects the primary focus of his concerns at the University of Berlin: Hermann Cohen's epistemology, the subject of his doctoral dissertation.[13]

Two matters are immediately noticeable in "Halakhic Man": first, its date of publication, 1944, a full twelve years after he left the university; and second, its homiletical essence, notwithstanding the learned references, wide philosophic range, and technical terminology. The two matters are interrelated. Because of Rabbi Soloveitchik's philosophic training, and because he published little, his students expected for decades that a comprehensive and systematic work that would tie together the lose ends in the available work was yet to come. The issue of *Tradition* (Spring, 1965) that published his second major essay, "The Lonely Man of Faith," announced that a major work by Rabbi Soloveitchik on the possibility of a formal philosophy of Halakhah would be forthcoming.[14] It still has not appeared. Consequently, instead of looking to future publications to resolve outright inconsistencies and contradictory embryonic tangents, translation of his Hebrew works or transcriptions of his lectures become the occasion retrospectively to read system and "classical" status back into earlier works or lectures that, at the time of origin, did not stimulate such claims.[15]

With the additional publication of Rabbi Soloveitchik's writings since 1944—three major essays, a number of shorter essays and eulogies, as well as volumes of lectures transcribed and edited by followers[16]—the cumulative effect has been not to cast Rabbi Soloveitchik in the role of systematic theologian or methodological philosopher, but to reaffirm the characteristics evident in his essay of 1944. In it he appears as a serious, anguished, religious personality, standing under the specter of a God whom he conceives to be always commanding but now fascinatingly present, now terrifyingly absent. Seeing himself as seizing and seized by a magnetic, continuously fluctuating relation with God, Rabbi Soloveitchik can, at bottom, do nothing other than give a thoughtful and learned turn to the infinitely varied emotions that this relationship imposes. In his case, thought is linked intimately to life. With a formally awkward yet vivid and evocative literary power to etch his emotions into print, Rabbi Soloveitchik attempts to transfer the special persuasiveness of the spoken word, evident in the talmudic realm, onto the page and into the realm of Jewish thought. In attempting such a transfer, he is following in a long tradition of seminal Jewish thinkers, from Philo to Judah ha-Levi to the Baal Shem Tov, who were given to unsystematic, respectively allegorical, philosophic, and mystical forms of expression. For Rabbi Soloveitchik, philosophically informed homiletics, with its allowance for continuity and innovation, emotional confession and rigorous argument, dramatic repetition and anecdotal flashes of insight, has proven to be the most effective way of expressing the complex blending of thought and experience that shapes his talmudic-philosophic orientation.

The preponderant impression conveyed by Rabbi Soloveitchik's writings is that from the beginning his thinking, like his life, was stamped by elemental conflicts so powerful that they would recur over and over in variation, mutation, or repetition of the original form, but never in any clear pattern of development. Rabbi Soloveitchik is too volatile to be confined to system. A thinker living in an unusually intensive and demanding relation with God cannot express that relationship except under the impact of its unanswerable mysteries, its fluctuating delights and disappointments, and all of the shifts in perspective that these entail. "Creation springs from primordial chaos, religious profundity springs from spiritual conflict," said Rabbi Soloveitchik in 1945. "The Jewish ideal of the religious personality is not the harmonious individual determined by the principle of equilibrium, but the torn soul and the shattered spirit that oscillate between God and the world. In his substrata of spiritual existence, the *homo religiosus* endures constantly the diastrophic forces of mental upheaval and psychic collision."[17] The search for consistency and order in Rabbi Soloveitchik is not simply doomed; it belies the animating ground of this thinking.

II.

"Halakhic man," begins Rabbi Soloveitchik in his early major essay of that name, is unique. "All the frames of reference constructed by the philosophers and psychologists of religion . . . cannot accomodate halakhic man as far as his reaction to empirical reality is concerned."[18] Halakhic man is to be wholly distinguished from "religious man," who is wracked by fluid, subjective, contradictory, "frenzied, raging, stormy"[19] torments of consciousness in yearning for transcendence, and partially distinguished from "cognitive man," who seeks to uncover the fixed, the objective, and the ordered imbedded in the cosmos. Religious man is subjective and seeks to flee the cosmos; cognitive man is objective and seeks to understand the cosmos. In the opening pages of "Halakhic Man," Rabbi Soloveitchik writes that halakhic man is compounded of both religious and cognitive man, but not a hybrid; that halakhic man unifies the two types, as if in chemical reaction, into a "radiant, holy personality";[20] and that in accordance with the original depth of the split within halakhic man between his opposing religious and cognitive strands is the completeness of the eventual union. What unfolds in "Halakhic Man," however, is something quite different: descriptions and embellishments not of union, not of halakhic man in the "consummate splendor" of his "fusion,"[21] but of the opposite, of the splits, contradictions, and conflicts of halakhic man. His ultimate unification is asserted on page 4, then never heard from again; his antitheses and disharmony are elaborated over the next 160 pages.

We may see in the dichotomy between religious and cognitive man a dichotomy between what Rabbi Soloveitchik is and what he would like to be. Religious man—torn, fraught with contradiction—is what he is; congnitive man—deliberate, rational—is what he would like to be. Rabbi Soloveitchik, to be sure, is deliberate and rational. His consuming interest in talmudic study and teaching testifies to deep attachment to intellection. But his cognitive side is but part of a larger whole, residing in a stormy internal world of "torments and upheaval,"[22] "anxiety, anguish and tension."[23] Rabbi Soloveitchik's continuing disavowals of the indistinct, inchoate, sweeping emotions of religious man, of his "ontological pessimism"[24]—a chafing against existence in pining for higher transcendental worlds—strikes the reader as sheer irony. He who fulminates against a "subjective religiousity comprised of spiritual moods, of emotions and affections"[25] understands it so intimately, expresses it so searingly! Some lines after he denounces it, willy-nilly he announces his approval of "spiritual ecstasy and exaltation, when our entire existence thirsts for the living God."[26]

If praise of intellection within an irrepressible seedbed of emotion is paradox, it is, in Rabbi Soloveitchik's case, double paradox, for ultimately the origin of his rapturous descriptions of religious man is his intellect. His stormy, internal world that runs counter to his cognitive side is rooted in cognition itself. The recurring outbursts of identification with the passionate and contradictory moods of religious man occur against a background of a certain emotional death—of a lecturer whose perpetually haunting tone erects a partition between lecturer and listener, a partition whose opaqueness grows in direct proportion to the intimacy of the details of personal life he reveals;[27] of a person without contact with peers in childhood and youth, and without intimate friendship in adulthood ("comrades and acquaintances . . . do not alleviate the passional experience of loneliness which trails me constantly");[28] of a Talmudist temperamentally comfortable with making hypothetical distinctions, temperamentally uncomfortable with making practical decisions.[29]

In Harry Austryn Wolfson (Chapter Three), emotional attenuation received no psychological compensation, only acute imagination and expression. Wolfson—unmarried, fatherless, distant, without faith—could see emotion but not touch it. In Rabbi Soloveitchik—married, a father, distant, inflamed with faith—emotional attenuation receives the compensation of forceful intellect of a peculiar kind. It is an intellect that negates emotion and subjective religiosity so powerfully that they rebound; emotion and subjective religiosity so finely attune their negator (the intellect) to them that intellect comes to possess them, in a sense. In Rabbi Soloveitchik, there is an oddly textured suffusing of emotion downward from the head rather than upward from the gut. Thus, he writes, halakhic man "does not struggle with his evil impulses,"[30] but in his mind, in his writings and lectures, Rabbi Soloveitchik struggles openly with them. In such a state, his passionate love of talmudic teaching and distinction making is not just nature or nurture but the very salvation from the fluid, raging, intellective imaginations and emotions. The intellect must be pressed into service with particular force because the intellect is, by peculiar transfer, the seat of contending, unworthy emotion.

How Rabbi Soloveitchik's constellation of raging emotions, encased in a volcanic mind, took root in his home is revealed in an autobiographical passage, touching and telling:

> I am held captive . . .
> From my youth I was taught to hold in my feelings, not to show anything of my emotional world. My father and master, may his memory be a blessing, used to say:
>
>> The holier a feeling—the more intimate a feeling—the more it requires hiding in the depths . . . If all goes well, if a person's heart is full of joy and happiness, let him reveal his feelings to God, in the innermost part of the soul—there, let him give thanks to Him, let him let go, with abandon. But he must not show his feelings to any person, lest that person cast an unsympathetic glance and desecrate the holy of holies. And if the opposite—if it does not go well, forfend, if a person is existentially in straits, in the bowels of suffering and torments—. . . let him confess before the Master of Worlds, . . . but no one else must enter the holy of holies lest he desecrate by his indifference the holiness of the mute suffering pressing on the person. . . .

My father, may his memory be a blessing, practiced what he preached. Never once did I have the privilege of being kissed by him. When he took leave of me he would shake my hand and say, "Go in peace, and may God keep you." An outsider, witness to the moment and hearing the formulaic farewell, would wonder, would stammer, "Dry, Brisker coldness . . ." . . . That outsider, mocking the Brisker indifference, saw only the outside . . . of my father and master's personality, and did not perceive the insides—the holy of holies—draped with mercy and kindness, with love, tender and fierce, for his children.[31]

"Never once did I have the privilege of being kissed by him." In Rabbi Moses Soloveitchik's ambience, emotion could never be granted full autonomy. It had to be imploded; it was for God, not for man. Denied the human outlet but actively sustained in relation to God, emotion in Rabbi Joseph B. Soloveitchik became at once alive and filtered, blocked, speaking from behind a veil. "I am a captive."

We may now approach the question of why Rabbi Soloveitchik cannot consistently translate the epistemological assumptions of his progenitors' and his own critico-conceptual talmudic method in terms of Hermann Cohen's neo-Kantianism. For Cohen, thought produced itself out of itself, without the occasion, or secondary aid, of sensation. For the Soloveitchikian, Brisker talmudic method, purely hypothetical distinctions for resolving contradictory talmudic sources produce themselves out of the mind, without the aid of anything inherent in the sources (the Kantian analogue to sensation). In Hermann Cohen's epistemology the Brisker method found a philosophic underpinning, which, as we have seen in our discussion of Harry Austryn Wolfson's adaptation of Rabbi Moses Mordechai Epstein's semi-Brisker method, need not constitute the only way of putting talmudic methodology in philosophical terms (Chapter Three).

Wolfson and Epstein modified talmudic distinction making in a more strictly Kantian fashion, rendering it responsive to the nuances (the "sensation") of the material it dissected, but Rabbi Soloveitchik could not proceed so straightforwardly. Although he, too, felt the need to modify the Brisker method, he could not do so by altering the method itself. To have altered the method would have run counter not only to his patrimonial heritage but also to his own enthusiastic adoption of it and his emergent philosophical investment in recasting it in Cohenian-epistemological terms. He modified it, then, by overturning it altogether—by admitting alien elements of subjectivity and practicality into a supposedly purely idealist frame, in which Cohenian "thought" and his own creative distinction making constituted everything—while denying that he had overturned it at all.

In Rabbi Soloveitchik's modification of Cohen's neo-Kantianism, it proceeded as if no modification were being made. On the one hand, Rabbi Soloveitchik could not, in fact, translate halakhic man's method of knowing Talmud into Hermann Cohen's method of knowing ideas because halakhic man's very analyses entailed rendering practical decisions in the real, nonideal world of factory, bedroom, farm, and banquet hall. One could not plausibly render the subject matter of talmudic sources entirely conceptual. And yet, on the other hand, Rabbi Soloveitchik had to, for to treat them as they were in their fullness would cast him inexorably into his forbidden world of subjective mood, passion, and frenzy.

What he closed out at the front door, however, he admitted through the back. He conceded the validity of his forbidden world since his very models of the ideal Jew, of halakhic men such as the founder of the Brisker method, the compassionate and communally active Rabbi Hayyim Soloveitchik,[32] were complex, conveying the notion that the ideal Jew knows God not simply with his mind. Inconsistently, Rabbi Soloveitchik proceeds to push his view—the critico-conceptual halakhic practitioner as embodiment of a Jewish dogmatic epistemology—to its logical conclusion. He reduces the Talmud scholar to a one-dimensional, intellectual phenomenon—a mind who, after the manner of Cohenian epistemology, can be certain of the existence only of his own mind and its creations, such as hypothetical distinctions applied to contradictory talmudic texts. At the same time, he flinches from this conclusion by illuminating emotional and subjective sides to halakhic man. Halakhic man was not merely a neo-Kantian, Cohenian creator of concepts, not least because of the imaginative and emotional promptings of Rabbi Soloveitchik's own intellect, which of course run at crosscurrents with its analytical penchant and purpose.

Out of this tangle of discrepancies there flows Rabbi Soloveitchik's contradictory juxtaposition of pure idealism and subjective desire, of pure thought and practical life. On the side of idealism, Rabbi Soloveitchik insists that "halakhic man is not particularly concerned about the possibility of actualizing the norm in the concrete world. He wishes to mint an ideal, normative coin"; that "the theoretical Halakhah, not the practical decision, the ideal creation, not the empirical one, represent the longing of halakhic man." But then, Rabbi Soloveitchik describes "halakhic man's most fervent desire [as] the perfection of the world under the dominion of righteousness and loving-kindness—the realization of the a priori, ideal creation, whose name is Torah (or Halakhah), in the realm of concrete life."[33] Despite himself, Rabbi Soloveitchik is not just idealist but empiricist, not just neo-Kantian but Kantian, not just steeped in intellectual creation but bound by the domain of its realization.

III.

This crosshatch of ideas and impulses sheds much of its complexity in Rabbi Soloveitchik's later writings. As soon as one year after the publication of "Halakhic Man," he unabashedly characterizes the Jewish ideal of the religious personality in terms of the subjective "religious man" whom he so strenuously and unsuccessfully attempted to suppress in "Halakhic Man."[34] In Rabbi Soloveitchik's second major essay, "The Lonely Man of Faith" (1965), he explicitly describes his thought as subjective and riddled with irresolvable conflicts. At the opening of "The Lonely Man," a lonely man confesses:

> I have no problem-solving thoughts. I do not intend to suggest a new method of remedying the human situation which I am about to describe; neither do I believe that it can be remedied at all. The role of the man of faith, whose religious experience is fraught with inner conflicts and incongruities, who oscillates between ecstasy in God's companionship and despair when he feels abandoned by God, and who is torn asunder by the heightened contrast between self-appreciation and abnegation, has been a difficult one since the times of Abraham and Moses. It would be presumptuous of me to attempt to convert the passional antinomic faith-experience into a eudaemonic-harmonious one, while the Biblical knights of faith lived heroically with this very tragic and paradoxical experience.
>
> All I want is to follow the advice given by Elihu the son of Berachel of old who said, "I will speak that I may find relief"; for there is a redemptive quality for an agitated mind in the spoken word and a tormented soul finds peace in confessing.[35]

The relation of "The Lonely Man" to "Halakhic Man" is itself fraught with confict and incongruity since the basic personality types in the later essay neither develop nor modify the earlier types of halakhic, religious, and cognitive man. In 1965 Rabbi Soloveitchik writes of two conflicting types of people embodied by Adam in the first and second creation stories: "Adam I" and "Adam II." Adam I is superficial, pragmatic, a man of the world, conquerer of diseases and builder of bridges. He is "majestic" and his watchword is dignity. Adam II is profound, purposive, a man of the spirit, nurturer of prayer and builder of true community. He is "covenantal" and his watchword is redemption. Adam I is secular and can work only in instrumental association with others to accomplish his worldly goals. Adam II is spiritual and can work only in intrinsic association with himself and with God to surpass his loneliness, but he yearns also for an interpersonal transcendence of loneliness and draws near to him like-minded spirits. In their quest to transcend loneliness by doing the same thing—by establishing contact with God through prayer, and by advancing moral and ethical goals—they form the "covenantal community."

The tasks of both Adam I and Adam II are divinely mandated but cannot be integrated. Man in his two irreducible aspects is perpetually doomed to oscillate between two intrinsically valuable, distinct poles. Here, as in "Halakhic Man," the unity of two typological ideals—the "majestic" and the "covenantal" communities—is asserted; but, also as in "Halakhic Man," this unity is beyond human reach. In "The Lonely Man" Rabbi Soloveitchik does explain how Adam I and Adam II can unite, and in this he moves closer to a resolution of dialectic tension than in "Halakhic Man," but what he gives with the right hand he takes away with the left. Unity between Adam I and Adam II *is* possible—" 'When we therefore find them also engaged in ruling others, in increasing their property and endeavoring to obtain possession of wealth and honor, we see in this fact a proof that when they were occupied in these things their bodily limbs were at work while their heart and mind never moved away from the name of God' "[36]—but the people who achieved this degree of perfection were four: Abraham, Isaac, Jacob, and Moses. No one else ever did or ever will.

As if to highlight his deep-seated awareness of and frustration over the impossibility of unifying typological ideals, Rabbi Soloveitchik's third major essay is shot through with thirst for unification of opposites. The window to the special poignance and pain of this essay is opened by locating its position in the Soloveitchikian corpus. Published in 1978, "U-Vikashtem mi-Sham" ("And from There You Shall Seek" [Deuteronomy 4:29]) was substantively begun thirty years earlier. With the original draft of "U-Vikashtem mi-Sham" unavailable, we cannot know precisely how the article developed into final form, but its basic thrust reflects Rabbi Soloveitchik's state in the late 1940s. His yearning for unification of typological elements in the human personality, which dominates the essay, follows shortly after his assertion of the impossibility of such unification, implicitly in *Halakhic Man* (1944) and explicitly in his essay of 1945, when he said that spiritual disharmony was the Jewish ideal of the religious personality. As the reality of the schisms in his own personality set in, his thirst for unification engaged his vision with searing—and ephemeral—yearning, like a resplendent burst of a flame just before it goes out. Never before and never again does Rabbi Soloveitchik address the question of unification so extensively or positively. He describes unity between man and nature, man and society, and man and God (through man's participation in the Divine intellect as revealed in Halakhah).

It is not mere extrapolation from currents of his thought or splits in his personality that leads to the characterization of "U-Vikashtem mi-Sham" as a "period piece"—a reflection of and reaction to his stark delineation of fissures in his thought and in himself. Imbedded in the essay itself is Rabbi Soloveitchik's dichotomy between what he is and what he would like to be: between his passionate subjectivity and equally passionate (and unrealistic) assertion of the possibility of its objectification; between his absolute loneliness, his severance from normal human contact, and his description of cathartic communication; between his actual emotional stuntedness and his imagining of emotional fullness. Rabbi Soloveitchik telescopes all this into the denouement of a remembrance of his early relationship with his father (the remembrance cited in the epigraph and body of this chapter stands eerily as its complement and reinforcement).

In "U-Vikashtem mi-Sham," Rabbi Soloveitchik describes himself in his youth as "lonely, isolated, in fear of the world," with only one friend—a book, Maimonides' Code, as taught by his father. Following a moving description of his father's struggle to comprehend Maimonides, Rabbi Soloveitchik relates that with the passage of years he acquired several other "friends"—books of other preeminent medieval Talmud scholars. With great pathos he relates that these friends—his only friends—reach across the centuries and "kiss him on the forehead." His own father will not kiss him! Books do! He is kissed only from across centuries, only by living words of deceased scholars, and only when these words are properly deciphered. His emotion is vicarious, cerebral, wrapped up with study, with the exercise of intellect; again, he is painfully separated from a living friend and from society—the very objects he describes, with great philosophic care, as susceptible to unification. For Rabbi Soloveitchik, unification is all theory and yearning; disharmony is the reality, and the pain.[37]

Several other essays of Rabbi Soloveitchik, long and short, project inventive and illuminating models of religious personality types—the intellectual and the emotional, the slow and the spontaneous, the absolutional and the cathartic repentant personalities, for example—[38]but the thrust is always the same: philosophically informed homilies etching unintegrated paradigms of personality.

There is one exception, and here, too, dating is pivotal. Rabbi Soloveitchik's fourth major essay, *The Halakhic Mind: An Essay in Jewish Tradition and Modern Thought*, was published in 1986 but written in 1944[39]—the same year as the publication of "Halakhic Man." We may assume that "Halakhic Man" was written earlier because it was already published by 1944. As the prior essay, "Halakhic Man" sought to achieve by way of philosophic rigor what *The Halakhic Mind* did in fact achieve. *The Halakhic Mind* occupies a unique place in the Soloveitchikian corpus. Unlike Rabbi Soloveitchik's other non-halakhic writings, *The Halakhic Mind* is philosophically rigorous and tautly argued, not given to digression or confession, nor to homiletics. It is the fulfillment of the Soloveitchikian philosophic promise. The immense, scientifically informed philosophic learning indicated in some of his other writings is, in *The Halakhic Mind*, neither incidental nor illustrative. It is of the essence. Yet, notwithstanding the rigor and learning, *The Halakhic Mind* highlights the fundamental cleavages of Rabbi Soloveitchik. The essay provides the final verification of what had to be extrapolated from his earlier published work.

The essay begins with a synoptic review of the recent history of philosophy, focusing on modern science's stripping modern philosophy of its autonomy. To restore this autonomy, Rabbi Soloveitchik constructs an argument for what he terms "epistemological pluralism." The argument's axis: "Reason itself leads the physicist, psychologist, philosopher, and *homo religiosus* to a pluralism of viewpoints. The heterogeneity of knowledge [is based] upon the plurality of the objective orders they encounter."[40] With the autonomy of philosophy reestablished, the autonomy of religious philosophy is likewise reestablished, both generally and specifically. Generally: "By accepting pluralistic interpretations of reality, philosophy released the *homo religiosus* from his fetters and encouraged him to interpret the polychromic and polyphonic appearances impinging upon him."[41] Specifically: "The *homo religiosus* . . . is not the naive believer who, when confronted with reality, turns to mysticism and non-rationality. He substitutes neither belief for knowledge nor faith for critical reasoning; no less than the philosopher himself, he is an enthusiastic practitioner of the cognitive act."[42]

Rabbi Soloveitchik now reaches the crux: How critical—better, how exclusive—is the cognitive act to the *homo religiosus*' interpretation of reality? The answer is that cognition is of the very essence; as such, it rescues the *homo religiosus* from the inferiority of subjectivity: "The *homo religiosus* must regain his position in the cognitive realm. He is no longer the emotional creature, swayed by abstruse sentiments and ephemeral feelings. He is a cognitive type, desiring both to understand and interpret . . . Indeed, the urge for *noesis* is of the very essence of religion."[43]

With cognition of Reality as the goal of religious life, Rabbi Soloveitchik defines cognition as if to define away his own inescapable passions. As cognition objectifies the subjective religious consciousness, cognition discovers that subjectivity is so inaccessible—literally, infinitely inaccessible—that it is not worth trifling with.

> We delve persistently in the enigmatic, subjective mists. Yet, however far the regressive movement continues, we are never quite able to fathom subjectivity. What we call subjectivity is only a surface reproduction which still needs exploration. An infinite regression takes place along the stationary track left behind the objectifying "logos." . . . The starting point in any analysis of subjectivity must be the objective order. It is impossible to gain any insight into the subjective stream unless we have previously acquired objective aspects.[44]

Whereupon, Rabbi Soloveitchik's critique of subjectivity becomes a veritable rout. Religious subjectivity is self-absorbing, turning one *away* from God; subjectivity leads to the renunciation of ethical authority and moral awareness; subjectivity is esoteric, and in religion esotericism is "decadence."[45]

Despite his sustained attack on subjectivity, Rabbi Soloveitchik, in the end, again admits through the back door what he closed out at the front. Subjectivity, as a *cause* of an objective religious act, is disallowed—its analysis is subject to infinite regress—but as the "trail left behind the religious 'logos,'" subjectivity is inevitable.[46] That trail, of course, is different for each religious practitioner. That trail, once again, touches Rabbi Soloveitchik most deeply, and in two ways. First, his entire essay, as an extreme, unrelenting attack on subjectivity, ironically highlights its continuing power and persuasiveness for him. Second, he allows his acute sensitivity to subjective religion to push phraseologically through the rigorous argumentation against it. Example: "The *homo religiosus*, oscillating between sin and remorse, flight from and return to God . . . "[47] Or: " . . . to have analyzed the deepest strata of the religious consciousness and to have examined the God-thirsty soul with all its conflicting emotions and paradoxical sentiments."[48]

Such language, common in "Halakhic Man" of 1944 and the essay of 1945, is conspicuous for its rarity in *The Halakhic Mind*. Squeezed between two essays whose tone and substance characterize Rabbi Soloveitchik for the next four decades, *The Halakhic Mind* is his best attempt to argue philosophically for what he could not carry forth phenomenologically. *The Halakhic Mind* is structurally the reverse of "And from There You Shall Seek." In the latter, dating from the late 1940s, he gave one last effort to unifying opposites before throwing the effort to the winds; in the former, in 1944, he attempted to negate the existence of opposites by promoting the objective logos as the only legitimate object of analysis by religious philosophy. Here, too, the effort was doomed, for opposites—the inescapable power of Rabbi Soloveitchik's subjective, if mental, passion and objective, if passionate, analysis of the halakhic norm—dominated his maturity.

IV.

Brisk. Berlin. Boston. In Brisk Rabbi Soloveitchik received his training in Talmud; in Berlin he subjected its epistemology to philosophical analysis; in Boston he lives out the problematic talmudic-philosophic synthesis. But the move from Berlin to Boston entailed more than intellectual creativity and disquietude. The tradition from Brisk was subjected not just to unsettled philosophic analysis but also to an ambivalent Zionist critique. What Hermann Cohen was to Rabbi Soloveitchik's adaptation of the intellectual heritage of Brisk, Rabbi N. Z. J. Berlin ("Netziv") and his son were to Rabbi Soloveitchik's adaptation of its social heritage. Cohen and the Berlins were the conduits through which constituent elements of the Brisker heritage received the stamp of modification at Rabbi Soloveitchik's hand.

The early rise of Zionism proceeded in three stages: the emergence in the nineteenth century of precursors of Theodor Herzl, such dissimilar thinkers as Moses Hess and Judah Alkalai; then "proto-Zionism," *Ḥibbat Zion* activity in Eastern Europe from the Russian pogroms of 1881 to the first Zionist Congress of 1897; [49] and, finally, Zionism under Herzl, from the first Zionist Congress to his death in 1904.[50] Rabbi Hayyim Soloveitchik (died 1918) observed the growth of the movement from the scattered *Ḥibbat Zion* activity well before 1897 to a well-organized if small movement, into the twentieth century. He concluded that Zionism was emerging as the central danger to the autonomy of East European Jewish communities under the rule of Halakhah—as a competing ideology that threatened to dissolve a social fabric already attenuated by Enlightenment, persecution, and emigration.[51]

Rabbi Hayyim Soloveitchik's mentor and wife's grandfather, however, was favorably disposed to Zionism. Netziv supported *Hibbat Zion* from its beginning, was a counseling member of its executive, and made plans to emigrate to Palestine. A Zionist "cell" developed in his Volozhin yeshiva. He opposed it only because it was illegal and threatened to bring down the wrath of the Tsar on the yeshiva, and because he felt that students ought to devote themselves fully to studies.[52] Netziv died in 1893, before Zionism acquired institutional solidity. His son by his second wife, Meir Bar Ilan (1880–1949)—Rabbi Joseph B. Soloveitchik's great-uncle—became a forceful leader of Mizrachi, the religious wing of Zionism's twentieth-century institutional bedrock, the World Zionist Organization.[53] Rabbi Soloveitchik's father, too, was sympathetic to Zionism, and unlike other children and grandchildren of Rabbi Hayyim Soloveitchik,[54] both Moses and Joseph Baer Soloveitchik cast their allegiance with Netziv, Bar Ilan, and Mizrachi.[55] Since 1946 Rabbi Joseph Baer Soloveitchik has served as honorary president of the Religious Zionists of America and is now honorary president of the Mizrachi-Hapoel Mizrachi World Organization.

This orientation generated another conflict not only with his family but within himself. Just as his approach to the Brisker critico-conceptual method entailed idiosyncratic, internal conflicts, so did his adoption of the Netziv–Bar Ilan Zionist commitment. Initially, he sought to "fulfill" *(le-hagshim)* his Zionism by seeking the chief rabbinate of Tel Aviv in 1935, but lost out to an older man, Moses Avigdor Amiel (1883–1946).[56] Then he involved himself in the non-Zionist, Orthodox Agudah circle by, for example, delivering its eulogy in America for Agudah's world leader, Rabbi Hayyim Ozer Grodzinski, in 1941. Rabbi Soloveitchik's aspiration to leadership found its final configuration in allegiance to and ultimate ambivalence over the religious Zionist, Mizrachi circle. Since the mid-1940s, he has both praised Zionism effusively[57] and played little role in it personally, both stood as titular head of Zionism's religious wing and refused to accept an offer to become Israel's Ashkenazi chief rabbi (in 1959),[58] both lent his prestige to Zionism—Israeli prime ministers, presidents, and chief rabbis paid their homage to him in Boston—and refused to visit Israel. In double contrast, Rabbi Isaac Hutner was intellectually unsympathetic to Zionism but emotionally bound to Zion; he spent much of his youth and old age there and wrote about it with consuming passion. Rabbi Soloveitchik, on the other hand, is intellectually sympathetic to

Zionism but emotionally bound to it only in his eerie, intellectual way. He has spent virtually no time in Zion and places his passion elsewhere. Rabbi Hutner, suspicious of Zionist revival as a social and political development, pledged his personal allegiance to the Land of Israel. Rabbi Soloveitchik, ardent welcomer of the State of Israel, pledges his personal allegiance to the Diaspora.

Rabbi Soloveitchik must have sensed early on that he would be unable to transmit his complex synthesis in its fullness. It would be persuasive in neither Brisk nor Berlin. For although he saw himself as sufficiently rooted in tradition to recast Jewish nationalism and Western idealist and existential philosophy in light of tradition, he was a renegade to Brisk and an anomoly in Berlin, especially on the eve of Hitler's rise, when he left Berlin for Boston (1932). From 1932 to 1941 he taught in Boston, founding the Maimonides School and an advanced talmudic institute, Heichal Rabbenu Hayyim Ha-Levi, named after his grandfather. Upon his father's death in 1941, he replaced him as lecturer in Talmud at Yeshiva University in New York City. For the next forty-four years, he commuted from Boston to New York to teach three to four days weekly. Through lectures in both Boston and New York he trained generations of rabbis and built respect for talmudic-philosophic synthesis—respect, but not understanding, nor actualization. His synthesis is forbiddingly idiosyncratic, quirky, rooted in the lineaments of his own influences and personality; and it requires a depth of talmudic and Western learning, and of personal religious imagination, that only an elite can hope to acquire. The ironic indicator of his failure to mold students in the frame of his synthesis is the collective split personality of his disciples: there are Soloveitchikian disciples in talmudic learning and Soloveitchikian disciples in Jewish thought, but only rarely are they the same people. The two groups have little to do with each other, in some cases do not even know of the existence of the other.[59]

Each group is convinced that it knows the "real" Rabbi Soloveitchik, for he has trained most of his Talmudists so narrowly that they presume that "real" religious thought can only be produced by a method of Talmud-like rigorous logic—surely not by passionate subjectivity and confession—and he has communicated his religious thought only outside of his Talmud classes, so that most of his philosophic and theological following presumes that an existentialist thinker cannot really take seriously a fixed, intricate, legal–religious system—Halakhah. Rabbi Soloveitchik confounds this presumption by his absorbing interest in Talmud, more subtly by his perception of existential categories in normative behavioral prescriptions, still more subtly by the genuine humility and piety with which he imbues his own observance of those prescriptions. To Rabbi Soloveitchik, subjectivity does not coexist alongside objective religious law but is generated and nourished by it. In a vintage passage, Rabbi Soloveitchik notes that Maimonides, the seminal medieval Jewish scholar (1135-1204), regarded prayer as ordained by the Hebrew Bible *(midorayyta')*, while Nahmanides, another authoritative medieval Talmudist (1194-1270), cited a number of sources to demonstrate that prayer is ordained only by rabbinic enactment *(miderabbanan)*.[60] Rabbi Soloveitchik grinds this legal debate on sources and precedents into a lens that refracts divergent, respectively existential and nonexistential worldviews.

Nahmanides, notes Rabbi Soloveitchik, concedes that in time of communal distress prayer is ordained on the highest (the biblical) authority.[61] This comment leads Rabbi Soloveitchik to postulate a hypothetical distinction that reconciles Maimonides' and Nahmanides' views.

> Both [Maimonides and Nahmanides] regarded prayer as meaningful only if it is derived from a sense of *tzarah* (crisis). They differ in their understanding of the word. Maimonides regarded daily life itself as being existentially in straights, inducing in the sensitive person feelings of despair, a brooding sense of life's meaninglessness, absurdity, lack of fulfillment. . . . Real prayer is derived from loneliness, helplessness, and sense of dependence. Thus, Maimonides [by regarding *daily* prayer as obligatory on the highest—the biblical—authority] regarded all life as a "depth crisis."[62]

To Nahmanides, however, life itself is not ontologically in crisis. That is why, in his view, prayer is biblically obligatory only when distress imposes itself from without, arising

> independently of man. . . . One need not be a reflective, introspective or a brooding type to perceive this crisis; the simplest person experiences it, whether it be poverty, illness, famine, war, or death . . . it is a crisis which can be shared with others, through empathy and sympathy.
>
> The "depth crisis" of Maimonides, however, is an inner, personal, clandestine, and undefined crisis which is not readily manifest to the eye. . . . This type of crisis cannot be attributed to man's stupidity, negligence or incompetence, as can the "surface crisis" [of Nahmanides]. The "depth crisis" [of Maimonides] is clearly beyond solution; it is an existential reality, a

condition of human existence. It will be felt more poignantly by persons of greater intelligence and imaginative perception; the wiser and more sensitive one is, the greater the crisis. It is rooted in man's essence, his metaphysical origin. It is existential, not social, political, or economic.[63]

How does one decide the final, "Torah" view on whether life is perpetually or only intermittently in crisis—whether Maimonides or Nahmanides is right? Rabbi Soloveitchik simply declares:

> The Torah bids man actively to combat . . . superficial, external crises. The ills of poverty, disease, and war are debilitating and impair our spiritual freedom. The Torah, however, encourages man to submit to and embrace the experience of the "depth crisis." Thereby does man truly grasp the reality of his condition and become stirred to great heights of the spirit. For this "depth crisis," there is no solution except [daily] prayer. "Surface crisis" can be overcome; the existential crisis can only be met by prayer.[64]

The implications of this passage are many: Jewish thought does not derive primarily from philosophic, Musar, kabbalistic, or homiletical works, but from Jewish law itself; the method of deriving thought is the same as deriving law, namely, the reconciliation of contradictory halakhic sources by the framing of a hypothetical distinction (here, between daily life as crisis, or not); conceptual analysis supersedes historical reality (Maimonides did not philosophize in terms of Nahmanides, still less about life as depth crisis, since Maimonides died when Nahmanides was a child, and as an advocate of both the adequacy and supremacy of intellect, Maimonides was not an existentialist);[65] normative religious-legal obligations, such as the recitation of fixed texts of prayer at fixed times, do not stifle the individuation of emotion and experience, but sustain and channel it; and, finally, "Torah" is equated with that view—Maimonides' "depth crisis"—that is compatible with Rabbi Soloveitchik's own inclinations, which he vented straight-forwardly in his post-1940s essays.

In Rabbi Soloveitchik's insistence on placing his personal inclinations as the controlling nexus of his thinking and teaching, we reach the final, most essential reason for his inability to found a movement of talmudic-philosophic disciples. Whether as Brisker practitioner of self-cultivated distance prior to his wife's death, or as embarrassingly open, public confessor of personal life after her death (1967),[66] Rabbi Soloveitchik himself always dominates Rabbi Soloveitchik the teacher. The self-control, the contraction and hiding of self at which Rabbis Hutner and Israel Salanter were so adept, and which enabled them to see the needs and take the time to nurture the individuality of potential disciples, is attenuated in Rabbi Soloveitchik. It requires great ego to suppress ego, and if the ego of Rabbi Soloveitchik is ever-present, at least in part this is because of its weakness, its lacking in that paradoxical self-regard required to squash self-regard. By the side of his forceful personality is genuine fragility, and enigma.[67]

The comparison between Rabbi Israel and Rabbi Soloveitchik is poignant and difficult, not least because Rabbi Soloveitchik draws it implicitly himself, and does so with revealing hostility and carelessness with historical fact. In "Halakhic Man," he characterizes Rabbi Israel's Musar movement "in its early years . . . in Kovno and Slobodka" as ridden with fear, melancholy, self-negation, consciousness of sin, and self-lacerating torment. To balance this picture, Rabbi Soloveitchik observes that "in all truth and fairness it should be emphasized that when the Musar movement reached a state of maturity in the [Slobodka] Yeshiva Knesset Israel under the directorship of [the Elder of Slobodka] R. Nathan Zvi Finkel . . . it assumed an entirely different form. . . . "[68] Now, there never was any Musar movement presence in Slobodka except for that under the directorship of the Elder of Slobodka,[69] so that the supposed self-lacerating torment and other unworthy traits that Rabbi Soloveitchik opposes could only have permeated the very yeshiva that he praises.

The historical confusion betrays a deeper malady, signaled by the portrait of Musar as given excessively to self-negation, to "an atmosphere in which man loses his spiritual shield, his sense of power, confidence, and strength and becomes utterly sensitive and responsive, [engaging in] a monologue about death, the nihility of this world, its emptiness and ugliness."[70] The hostility here is the projection of those very themes and formulations that permeate Rabbi Soloveitchik's own corpus onto the Musar movement. Musar is subject to excess in struggling to balance two poles, head and heart, intellect and instinct: the power and confidence in studying Talmud and interpreting it creatively, and the sensitivity and latent melancholy in probing motivation and instinct, and making them pure. The Musar struggle constituted a particularly threatening challenge to Rabbi Soloveitchik since his own intellectualization of heart—of fear, melancholy, and self-negation, of "wretchedness," "torment," and "psychic collision"—stand as concession of failure to mount the twofold, dialectical challenge of bringing head and heart into relation. To the Musar movement, the ideal character of that relation is harmony;[71] the movement's task is assessed by how successfully it integrates the two poles, avoiding a slippage toward the one or the other.[72] To Rabbi Soloveitchik, there can be no relation between head and heart, for he has eviscerated the task of integration by intellectualizing instinct. All is in the head ("Halakhic man does not struggle with his evil impulses, nor does he clash with the tempter, [he is] not subject to the whispered proffer of desire").[73] Accordingly, Rabbi Soloveitchik's largest threat and easiest target become one and the same: a truly dialectical, Musar aspiration that, in the nature of things, can periodically slip toward the heart.

In face of this Musar slippage, Rabbi Soloveitchik projects his flight from reality, his "perspective directed toward the transcendent,"[74] onto Musar, concluding, also against historical fact, that "this whole mood posed a profound contradiction to the Halakhah and would undermine its very foundations."[75] Against fact: the early Musar master most given to slipping toward a "monologue about death" was its greatest halakhic expositor—Rabbi Isaac Blazer, author of *Peri Yitzhak*.[76] And the advocates of a perspective that is said to have lost its sense of power had the power to discipline itself, to restrain itself, in order to instill confidence and strength in enough disciples to raise up a Musar movement.[77] In struggling to live in the two worlds of head and heart, the best of the Musar disciples mustered the power of heart to suppress it, creating the space in which a disciple felt the freedom to grow in association with the mentor. The excesses to which the Musar dialectic were subject—and they bent toward the head, not just the heart, especially in Slobodka[78]—were less important than the fact of dialectic; and Rabbi Soloveitchik's nondialectical vessel, cognition, in which his critique of Musar excess is carried out, is more important than the subtlety of the critique.

Rabbi Israel went to Eastern Europe, including Berlin, sixty years before Rabbi Soloveitchik.[79] The first preeminent East European Talmudist to do this, Rabbi Israel studied law, medicine, sciences, and other disciplines.[80] This informal curriculum was sufficient to make him realize that the challenge it presented to a normative behavior and belief system, such as Halakhah, could only be either ignored or met selectively. And if the latter, then the transitional Orthodox Jew would pick and choose between the claims of secular study and life, and preserve a naive Jewish affirmation within the self-consciousness that the process of selection entailed. Rabbi Soloveitchik's linguistic and critical training in Western learning far surpassed Rabbi Israel's, and this may have been a snare. It may have persuaded Rabbi Soloveitchik that the key to the preservation of tradition in encounter with nontraditional learning was knowledge alone, and that he could selectively appropriate Western learning with a profundity that the relatively untrained Rabbi Israel could not.

"Kant would not have understood my grandfather!" exclaims Rabbi Soloveitchik in lectures. It is a telling comment, revealing not simply a conviction about the intellectual acuity of his forbear, nor yet a philosophic critique about the difference between strict Kantianism and the neo-Kantian, talmudic method of his grandfather. The comment betokens an ambivalence about the value of what Rabbi Soloveitchik learned in Berlin, no less than his hostility to Rabbi Israel Salanter betokens an ambivalence about an East European precursor who, too, sought to move from the hearth of pure Talmud study to widen (perhaps the better word is, to deepen) horizons. The penultimate paradox in Rabbi Soloveitchik is his ultimate uncertainty about the propriety of his highly intellective, talmudic-philosophic quest, by the side of his unbending reliance on the intellect to judge, to embody, and to sustain the correctness of the data of experience, human and Divine. The ultimate paradox in Rabbi Soloveitchik is his intellectual life (uncertainty and certainty alike)—a life he extended for years with heroic dedication, transcending extreme physical weakness to teach Talmud at Yeshiva University until his energy gave out in late 1985—by the side of his striking personal piety. This is the piety that moved me, back in 1965, the piety that leaves one of his closest disciples less with the memory of illuminating lectures, more with the image of Rabbi Soloveitchik beatifically reciting *hallel* at the seder table.

CHAPTER SIX
_____

Professor Abraham Joshua Heschel

"I received the gifts of
elasticity in adapting to
contradictory conditions."

Joseph Baer Soloveitchik is a masterful teacher, an occasional and awkward writer. Abraham Joshua Heschel was a masterful writer, an occasional and awkward teacher. Isaac Hutner was a native of Warsaw who absorbed hasidic thought but bent it to conform to the outward forms of rational, controlled, talmudic expression. Abraham Joshua Heschel was a native of Warsaw who absorbed talmudic method but bent it to conform to the outward forms of imaginative, emotional, hasidic expression. Harry Austryn Wolfson was an East European who was surprisingly successful at the heart of an elite, American, academic culture but never quite felt at home there. Abraham Joshua Heschel was an East European who was surprisingly at home at the heart of American religious and political culture but never quite felt successful there. Israel Salanter was a Lithuanian rationalist who infused talmudic study and halakhic ritual with emotion and an introspective feeling tone. Abraham Joshua Heschel was a Polish mystic who imbued hasidic study and custom with logic and an outreaching feeling tone. Joseph Zev Lipovitz (Chapter Seven), following his desire, went from Lithuania to Berlin to live in Palestine, although there was little field for his talents there. Abraham Joshua Heschel went from

Poland to Berlin to the United States, against his desire to live in Palestine, since there was little field for his talents there.

In crossing his cultural, political, and religious lines, Abraham Joshua Heschel combined so many words of discourse that of mid-twentieth-century transition figures from Eastern Europe only Rabbi Isaac Hutner matched him in complexity. The two also resembled each other in the opacity that underlay a compelling clarity. Their dazzling marshalling of sources from the entire spectrum of Jewish intellectual creativity—poetry, law, lore, mysticism, ethics, homiletics, philosophy, exegesis—served to shield the inner vortex whence they sprang. In illuminating all four major periods of Jewish thought—biblical, rabbinic, medieval, and modern—Heschel led his readers ultimately to a mirror: the confrontation with the essential Heschel was really his way of turning the reader back to constituent elements in the reader's own image.

In teaching, he produced the same effect in a roundabout way. Sitting there, reading his notes (often drafts or finished manuscripts of his books), or ruminating out loud from the recesses of his own research or spiritual life at that moment, Heschel in a sense taught nothing—no transmittal of an organized body of knowledge, no inculcation of facts and data necessary to their conceptual or creative shaping. It was personal shaping of material that occupied Heschel in the classroom, such that a student could gain from the experience only by putting aside his own questions or concerns, stepping into Heschel's world. Since Heschel's text or thinking-out-loud stood between him and student needs, the student was left to make his own connection between the world of Heschel that he was compelled to enter and the world of his own that he had left behind. The drawing of that connection would necessarily entail a heightened confrontation with self, for the world of Heschel was elusive. One could hardly appropriate from it. With all of Heschel's emphasis on "soul" (*neshamah*), it was never clear just where or what his was. In Rabbi Hutner's case, his own inner pivot was clear to him, if not to others. In Heschel's case, the inner pivot seemed ever vague, emanating immensely powerful light from worlds now lost, as if from a distant star whose observer cannot be certain whether the source of the light even exists.

If Wolfson's scholarly and Soloveitchik's personal styles merge in their disclosure of the author's fundamental psychological stance, Heschel's poetic and Hutner's discursive styles merge in the obfuscation of that stance. This, too, is the case with the elliptical Israel Salanter, though one suspects that in his case the obfuscation was a veil for humility, for he raised up disciples who claimed to have responded to his essence. In

Heschel's case, his closest students inevitably turn vague when asked to identify the sense in which they are disciples, and, in fact, most recoil at the word. Heschel was a mysterious inspiration of awesome proportion, but neither a clear nor a substantive guide. He could not be, for he knew what he was for, what treasures he held, what deficiencies he beheld, but not who he was.

I.

The problem lay in those circumstances of Heschel's youth that led him to encounter a wide range of types of Jewish spirituality without having to fix himself firmly within any one or combination of them. He was born in Warsaw, in 1907, to the Peltzovizner Rebbe, Rabbi Moses Mordechai Heschel, and to Rebeccah Reisel Heschel[1]—twin sister of the Novominsker Rebbe, Rabbi Alter Israel Simon Perlow (1874–1933). Abraham Joshua Heschel, in accordance with the dynastic tradition that had implanted itself in Polish Hasidism for over half a century, was expected to grow to take his father's place upon his death. From birth, the child (namesake of a founder of Polish Hasidism, the rabbi of Apt, died 1825), would be a rebbe-in-training.

But when the child was eight, his father died.[2] On the face, nothing changed. Abraham Joshua Heschel still occupied a special place, sitting next to his uncle, the Novominsker Rebbe, during *tishn*—the hasidic ceremonial meals of singing, of *Toyrah*, of eating from the rebbe's food. Young Heschel remained a dutiful and indeed dazzling pupil—following ceremony, studying Talmud, entering the mysteries of the kabbalah. He could, as later opined by his brother-in-law, the Kapitchenitzer Rebbe (1888–1967, also a namesake of the rabbi of Apt), "save Hasidism" with his already evident spiritual sensibility and intellectual aptitude. He needed a suitable match—the proper anchoring—for the task. His uncle, the Novominsker Rebbe, proposed his daughter. The two dynasties would be cemented, the young genius put on his way. But Reisel Heschel objected on the grounds that her son, then about fourteen, was too young to marry. Heschel, the story goes, was ready for any eventuality. He prepared a two-hour *derashah*, or learned discourse, for delivery should the match be finalized.[3] It was not, and the institutional substitute of mother and uncle for father-and-rebbe could not hold him. Whether it was immanent intellectual or spiritual strivings, or lack of paternal or avuncular guidance, that predominated in setting Heschel loose, it is clear that his childhood robbed him of the hasidic structure to keep him within it. There would never be an anchoring. By the time he was seventeen, with his enrollment in the secular Yiddish gymnasium in Vilna, he left traditional hasidic society forever. To much of his family he would become a scandal.

And yet, Heschel was hasidic to the core—and yet, he was not. He was: In his maternal and paternal ancestry were five major and several other important figures in the history of Hasidism. In his career he suffused theological and impressionistic tracts with hasidic teaching and tonality. In his last two works he declared his rootedness in two hasidic figures, the fervent founder of Hasidism, Israel Baal Shem Tov, and the movement's rebel and iconoclast, the brooding, forbidding Menahem Mendel—the Kotsker Rebbe.[4] Hasidic to the core, Heschel was nonetheless elsewhere—everywhere. He came to range widely, to set forth disparate doctrines and personality types sympathetically. He aspired to do justice to all, for the essential dynamic within his youth was twofold: the absorption of one thrust, Hasidism, by the side of an unbudgeable insistence on freedom to wander elsewhere—everywhere. Emblematic of his unique, elastic dynamic was young Heschel, dressed in hasidic garb, sitting in his family garret, out of sight but not out of hearing of his mother, chanting Polish and Latin declensions to talmudic singsong.[5] His mother thought he was studying Talmud; his freedom, uncompromised, exercised itself at cross purpose to maternal—and social—expectation. In one of his last two works, Heschel unwittingly explained:

> The Kotsker [whose presence entered my life when I was eight] restricted me, debunked cherished attitudes. From the Baal Shem [whose heritage I received through my father, who died when I was eight,] I received the gifts of elasticity in adapting to contradictory conditions.[6]

The debunking of cherished attitudes—of conformance to family expectation—amounted to a restriction of the familial, hasidic heritage. But through the gifts of elasticity Heschel accommodated his rebellion—adapted to contradictory conditions—especially since this process, as part of his exercise of freedom, he slyly hid from his mother. When Heschel left home, then, the disappointment and shock of his family took their coloration from the absence of any evident reason for his departure. His break was salient because it appeared illogical. Since his absorption of intellectual, Polish Hasidism seemed to be organic and whole, his expression of radically new interests seemed to be betrayal.[7]

This set a pattern for Heschel's life.

He would come to absorb the program of the Hebraists,[8] the Yiddishists,[9] the Reform,[10] Conservative,[11] and Orthodox Jews,[12] the Zionists,[13] and the "science of Judaism" scholars,[14] yet he was never counted exclusively among a single one of these groups though he was part of all of them. The elemental dynamic in Heschel's youth—a strange freedom, throwing off the yoke of an ancestral tradition while yet embodying its content—left him appearing organically reflective of a tradition or program to all who were outside it, but strangely—slightly and saliently—transgressive of a tradition or program to all who were inside it.

There was no central figure in Heschel's life to whom he submitted, even if incompletely, or against whom he rebelled, even if posthumously. There was no Moses Soloveitchik—a commanding, venerated father who, notwithstanding his inability to halt his son Joseph Baer's rebellion, served as a standard against which personal decision and intellectual program were to be measured, even if in rejection. There was no Elder of Slobodka—an insightful, penetrating mentor who understood and shaped some of the deepest yearnings of his disciple Isaac Hutner, even if this was admitted only after the Elder's death. Since Heschel never rejected a father or father figure, or their teachings, he carried them forth as if he did not adapt them in transition from hasidic court to university to non-Orthodox rabbinical schools. Since Heschel never accepted a mentor and a searing reading of his soul, he carried on without the existential decision of marking himself either as the perpetuator of a specific Jewish spiritual or intellectual tradition, or as the founder of a new synthesis. Synthesis connotes fresh interlinking of creeds, deeds, or the inward spiritual tonalities underlying them. Heschel forged no such new Jewish identity. Rather, he continually added to his Polish hasidic genesis. He added depth, creativity, expressiveness, erudition, and daring, but no organizing principle—no controlling vision—appeared either openly or by hint. His vision was everywhere. And so, paradoxically, in Heschel's own eyes he never existentially left home. His spiritual peregrinations were always self-conceived as a process of expansion, of actualization and differentiation of an inner unity, bereft of tension, without contradiction. His periods of critical examination and self-doubt never ended in fundamental change of direction, of revamping of intellectual or social program, but in enlargement of perspective. The new did not modify the old, but was joined to it.

In his trek from Warsaw to Vilna to Berlin, then to Cincinnati and

New York, there were three types (and periods) of expansion. The first was philosophical, in Berlin; the last was social, in New York. The second, intervening development, preponderantly in Cincinnati, was decisive. This was Heschel's response to the Holocaust, which affected his work as a critical mass, giving the power to expand and energize the enlarged perspective he had derived from his mystical unifications, philosophical reflections, and philological researches.

Underlying Heschel's expansion in all its guises was thought about written expression in theory and practice: what language can and ought to do, and how one can make it do that. Accordingly, the first evidence of Heschel's divergence from family expectation was his surreptitious study of Polish and Latin, and his first identity expansion upon leaving home in 1924, at seventeen, was his joining "Young Vilna," a new group of Yiddish writers.[15] Heschel's initial publications (after some youthful talmudic novellae) were Yiddish poems.[16] The title of his first collection of poetry is emblematic of all that would occupy Heschel philosophically until the end of his days, particularly in its implied interpenetration of two ontologically distinct, but not disjunct, foci: *God's Ineffable Name: Man.*[17]

In 1927 Heschel entered the University of Berlin, studying German, classical languages, and all five branches of philosophy. He cross-enrolled at the Hochschule fuer die Wissenschaft des Judentums,[18] the Reform rabbinical seminary, while also maintaining relations with Rabbi Hayyim Heller, mentor of Rabbi Soloveitchik.[19] The formal blurring of lines would become typically Heschelian. The substantive expansion in Heschel during his seven years at the university was twofold: the development of criteria for both the use and the transcendence of philosophy; and the manufacture of a model, from Jewish history, for the mentor he never had. An article Heschel published in 1953 is build around a memoir of his years at the university.

> I came with great hunger to the University of Berlin to study philosophy. I looked for the meaning of existence. Erudite and profound scholars gave courses in logic, epistemology, esthetics, ethics and metaphysics. They opened the gates of the history of philosophy. I was exposed to the austere discipline of unremitting inquiry and self-criticism. I communed with the thinkers of the past who knew how to meet intellectual adversity with fortitude, and learned to dedicate myself to the examination of basic premises at the risk of failure.
>
> What were the trends of thought to which I was exposed at the university?[20]

Heschel answers by listing only one trend: Kant. And Heschel proceeds by describing what amounts to a parody of reality—reality as seen by the professors of Kant, as contradicted by all that Heschel "knew" of reality from his childhood and youth.[21] I use the word "knew" literally, for, unlike Rabbi Soloveitchik, Heschel objected to Kant on ontological grounds, not epistemological ones; and he objected wholly, not partially. Rabbi Soloveitchik's pre-Berlin baggage, consisting as it did (in part) of passion for talmudic distinction making, could accomodate Kant by pushing him to an extreme, Cohenian idealism. To Rabbi Soloveitchik, Kant was problematic because he did not go far enough in according the mind the supreme and exclusive role of creator of reality. To Heschel, Kant was problematic in whatever direction he could be pushed because the very skepticism that Kant attempted to overcome was unwarranted. To Heschel, the problem of knowing "the thing in itself" was no problem; and the Kantian solution—"symbolic knowledge . . . knowledge in the form of categories [that,] in the last analysis, are only representational constructions for the purpose of apperceiving what is given"[22]—was itself a problem. The "thing in itself," to Heschel, was God Himself, and *"if God is a symbol, He is a fiction.* But if God is *real*, then He is able to express His will unambiguously."[23] And more: man is able to know God unambiguously, for man is ontologically built to do so.

The burden of Heschel's thought is to translate the reality of his Warsaw youth, his sacred life-with-God, into post-Kantian, theological argument, which proceeds as follows. Man's proper assessment of his own being grants him simultaneously knowledge of himself, knowledge of God, and knowledge of reality. Ultimately, man knows himself because he knows unambiguously the will of God that is addressed to him ("I am commanded, therefore I am"[24]), but Heschel begins with man, not with God. He begins with categories of ontological, that is, universal, perception, such as *wonder, awe,* and *radical amazement.*

> [He] begins in this world, with that part of men and women left untouched by the critique of the Enlightenment: emotions and responses. He reaches into the inner life and looks for those elements which, present and accepted in a this-worldly framework, speak of the next world and testify to God, to the image of God impressed upon man and women. People exhibit the capacity for wonder . . . How so? It means that not everything can be explained. The opposite of religion is taking things for granted. Wonder is a 'form of thinking,' an act that goes beyond knowledge.[25]

The Hebrew Bible, the sacred deed, and nature elicit wonder.[26] Nature, for example, commands attention for its ability to be exploited, enjoyed, or *accepted in awe*.[27] To be in *awe* of nature is to perceive its *sublimity*, that which all things ultimately stand for, the allusion of things to a meaning greater than themselves.[28] The meaning beyond the awesomeness of nature divides in two seemingly opposite directions. First, man, as he is in awe of something outside himself, reaches back to himself, *radically amazed* not only in relation to what he sees "but also to the very act of seeing as well as to our own selves, to the selves that see and are amazed at their ability to see."[29] Second, man, as he is in awe of something outside himself, reaches beyond that something to the *ineffable*, to something "objective which cannot be conceived by the mind or captured by imagination or feeling."[30] In turning from the sublimity of nature both back to himself and beyond sublimity, man does not create the ineffable, he encounters it.[31] Man, radically amazed at his ability to perceive and to reason, and knowing the independence of his self-reflecting soul from the content of his perceptions and reasonings,[32] knows the independence of God, a reality separate from the subjective content of man's descriptions of that to which the sublime alludes. *Mystery* "is not a synonym for the unknown but rather a name for a meaning which stands in relation to God."[33] The relation is commandment; the meaning is the certainty of both my and God's existence. "I am commanded, therefore I am."

Beginning with universal categories of perception, Heschel ends with the specific modality of Jewish theology, of the revealed Torah law, commandment. He moved "from the shared experience of ordinary people to the distinctive truth" of Judaism.[34]

With his philosophical critique of Kant, such as it is, Heschel expanded his consciousness without modifying its essential nature. He now had absorbed this Western, "austere discipline of unremitting inquiry and self-criticism," but in such a way as to leave his own phenomenology of God-consciousness untouched. Accordingly, his doctoral dissertation, completed in 1934 and published in 1936 as *Die Prophetie*, described the Prophets' consciousness from the postulate that their consciousness of God was real, irreducible to any other phenomenon.[35] Although Heschel had established the postulate that would govern his theological works in English, some fifteen and twenty years hence, he had not established their direction and rhetorical edge: from the universal to the particular. In Berlin Heschel's struggle was not to save man's soul with the aid of Judaism, but to save his own soul as it navigated the new and difficult paths of logic, epistemology, esthetics, ethics, and metaphysics. It would take the Holocaust to wrench Heschel's anti-Kantian philosophic assertions from intermittent rumination, Jewish phenomenology, and personal solution to the sustained reflection, human ontology, and universal solution of his later works. Meanwhile a mentor, a guide in his quest for the personal solution, emerged.

In 1935 the young Abraham Joshua Heschel—he was twenty-eight at the time—went to visit the publisher Erich Reiss at his home in Berlin in order to discuss the manuscript of a friend. Reiss, a cultivated and perceptive person . . . , was so impressed by the young scholar that he immediately asked him to write a book. Heschel, surprised and delighted, accepted the offer and in a relatively short time completed [his] biography of Maimonides.[36]

II.

Rabbi Soloveitchik's Maimonides is primarily the halakhist, author of the Code (*Mishneh Torah*), glossed by Rabad—the critical spur to critico-conceptual, talmudic analysis[37]—and secondarily the philosopher, author of *Guide of the Perplexed*. Heschel's Maimonides was the whole man, halakhist, philosopher, persecuted wanderer, medical healer, master Hebrew stylist, communal leader, solitary teacher. Maimonides, surmises one of Heschel's students, was Heschel's model.[38] Heschel's biography of Maimonides testifies to a depth of appreciation surpassing scholarly interest, for if Heschel produced *Maimonides* shortly after having been invited to write a book, the book gives evidence of long comtemplation of the entire Maimonidean corpus and epoch. Maimonides' *Commentary on the Mishnah*, Code, *Guide of the Perplexed*, his letters and treatises, the issues and personalities of his time, the political conditions in Spain, North Africa, Palestine, and Egypt, as well as the pertinent secondary literature, had all percolated through Heschel's mind. Clearly Maimonides had been on his mind; and, what Heschel illuminates in Maimonides he illuminates in himself. Our method, here, of discerning in Heschel's appropriation from the works of his model an emulation of the totality of his life is put to vigorous use by Heschel himself, in *Maimonides*.

Heschel reads Maimonides' kinship to the first codification of rabbinic law, the Mishnah, as kinship also for its compiler. Of the compiler of the Mishnah, Judah ha-Nasi, Heschel writes that "not since Moses had learning and authority been so thoroughly blended in one man," and of the

Mishnah itself, "no other [talmudic] work was spiritually so close to [Maimonides] in form, language, and diction. . . . "[39] Judah ha-Nasi, in short, "with a tremendous and unparalleled talent, served as the model for young Maimonides,"[40] the greatest embodiment of Jewish learning and authority in a millenium. And so, Maimonides' first major work was a commentary on Judah ha-Nasi's major work, the Mishnah. Commentary linked commentator to the author of the text commented upon. And so it was with Heschel. His *Maimonides* linked him to Maimonides himself.[41] Maimonides, with a tremendous and unparalleled talent, served as the model for the young Heschel, whose first major work was on Maimonides. What Maimonides loved in Judah ha-Nasi, Heschel loved in Maimonides: Maimonides [*Heschel*] "had a deep intellectual affinity for" the Mishnah [*the Commentary on the Mishnah*], "which excelled in its terseness and purity of style, in its precision and its arrangement according to certain aspects."[42] Up and down *Maimonides*, lines, sentences, or paragraphs jump at the reader for their obvious dual illumination, their description of author as well as of subject.

> Maimonides seems to have had no passion for immediate public instruction. His need to teach was fulfilled in written form, not in oral lecturing. He loved direct instruction, but apparently only to a single person, not to a group of listeners. He saw his special mission not in founding an academy but in writing books. Apparently his soul, given the thoughtful length of its inspirations, found expression in the silence of the written word, avoiding the haste, frailty, and sketchiness of speech.[43]

One need merely substitute "Heschel" for the first word in this paragraph to obtain a precise summary of Heschel's career.

We have here but the first example of the subtle inversion of time that governs the peculiar relationship between living disciple and deceased model. In the usual case, when living disciple attaches himself to living mentor, the illumination that mentor will transmit to disciple in the unfolding of time can only be anticipated by the disciple at the inception of the relationship. With a deceased model, however, the unfolding of his life is laid out before the disciple. The model becomes not simply someone whom the disciple emulates, but someone whose greatness is, though palpably evident, also unfathomable. It is unfathomable because the disciple lacks knowledge of when and how the characteristics and the spirit of the model will emerge or resonate in his own life, even as his very link to the model is his attraction to these characteristics and this spirit. The disciple carries the model in his mind in order that the mysterious greatness of the model can unfold in time in his own life. Consequently, if the model is portrayed at the beginning of the quest, as Heschel portrayed Maimonides, the disciple sets forth what, in retrospect, may leap at us from the pages as eerie premonitions of what, in fact, transpired in the disciple's own life. That Heschel may have projected from his own expectations into the life of Maimonides is just the point: it was Maimonides, not someone else, who elicited within Heschel sufficient expectation-identification to generate projection from self to model. Let us examine a few of these remarkable expectation-identifications of Heschel's life and work as set down in *Maimonides*.

Illustrating Maimonides'—and his own—full length, mature work, Heschel reflects: " 'An independent work offers solid tenets, with no objections or justifications and no demonstrations, such as Rabbi Judah the Holy did in the Mishnah.' "[44] The opposite approach—rejected by Maimonides, by Heschel—cites, " 'along with fixed tenets, . . . the possible arguments against them and the refutations, as well as the objection to each thesis and the proof that this is true and that false, this evident and that not evident.' "[45] Heschel rarely digressed from his tenets to treat possible refutations or to offer justifications. He rarely answered critics or even cited them; he anticipated them, thoroughly distilling from out of his wide learning his own conclusions in exegesis and in content, theologically, philosophically, and psychologically. "Maimonides [Heschel] did not want to convince, he wanted to be conclusive."[46] Steeped in sources, loyally reflecting yet also perceiving new meanings in them, Maimonides'—Heschel's—conclusive works revealed "balance of independence and fidelity, of originality and authority[: they were works] of intellectual art."[47] "The equilibrium of his soul permeates the style of [the] work."[48] *His* soul: whose soul? Either Maimonides' or Heschel's. Both.

Maimonides lived to sixty-nine, Heschel to sixty-five. In the last fourteen years of Maimonides' life,

> the passion for scholarly labor, dominating him since his youth, was replaced by a different motive. . . . At the height of his life, he turned from metaphysics to medicine, from contemplation to practice . . . from knowledge to imitation of God. God was not only the object of knowledge. He was the Model one should follow. His works, the creatures of the world which He guides in Providence, replaced abstract conceptions which constitute a spiritual act through intellectual knowledge of God. The observation of and absorption in concrete events replaced abstract viewing.[49]

In the last ten years of Heschel's life, the passion for scholarly labor, dominating him since his youth, was supplemented by a different motive: the observation of and absorption in concrete events, such as the struggle for Soviet Jewry, for rights for American Blacks, for extrication of America from Vietnam, for ecumenical dialogue, for Israel. At the height of his life, Heschel turned from artistry to activism, from works of intellectual art—from abstract viewing—to active service of His works, the creatures of the world which He guides in Providence—to imitation of God.

The transformation of Maimonides' life was triggered by tragedy, one kind following upon the other, culminating in the drowning of his beloved brother, raised in Maimonides' lap, Maimonides' pupil and breadwinner, and sole remaining link to his family. "My only joy was to see him."[50] Compelled to make a living, and to support his brother's family, Maimonides became a physician. And out of his lengthy mourning came a reevaluation of his view of evil, and a corresponding calming of personality. Evil, concluded Maimonides, is delusion, privation, interstices of good and solely real Being. "This exposé robbed disaster of its strength,"[51] and freed the soul from anxiety.

> Metaphysical knowledge produced what the doctrines of virtue and spiritual therapy were unable to do. The crisis invaded Maimonides's existence like a thunderstorm; but then . . . he became more balanced . . . and his mind achieved an early transfiguration, blending the lucidity of old age and the colorfulness of maturity, stillness and warmth, the remoteness of ideas and the proximity of objects, renunciation and desire, shaping self-control and quiet resistance into unique human wealth. He overcame suffering.[52]

III.

Heschel overcame the Holocaust, in an act of early and immense transfiguration, enabling him to write, with lucidity and colorfulness, stillness and warmth, of the unique wealth of East European Jewry—and of the meaning of its destruction—even before the destruction was complete. Already in 1938 Heschel was speaking publicly on the destruction then unfolding.[53] By 1944 he had formulated his response, and by January 1945, even before the official German surrender five months later, he had moved beyond response to memorialization: "The Eastern European Era in Jewish History,"[54] later expanded to *The Earth is the Lord's: The Inner World of the Jew in East Europe*.[55] Critics have searched Heschel's later, mature works for overt theological commentary on the Holocaust, and wondered at its absence in the broad spectrum of his intellectual concerns. In fact, the Holocaust was absent only explicitly. It had generated a Copernican revolution in Heschel's perspective; the reversal animated all that he wrote after 1944, date of his highly compressed essay, "The Meaning of This War."[56]

"Emblazoned over the gates of the world in which we live is the escutcheon of the demons," opens "The Meaning of This War."[57] The meaning of the war is to be located in the context of "the gates of the world," not only the gates of the Jewish people. The analysis that follows the opening sentence moves from universal to particular—the reverse of Heschel's solution to his intellectual quandary upon first opening up from hasidic Warsaw to philosophic Berlin. The meaning of the war is that "*we* have trifled with the name of God."[58] *We:* now mankind is Heschel's audience. "We did not sink into the pit in 1939, or even in 1933. We had descended into it generations ago, and the snakes have set their venom into the bloodstream of *humanity,* gradually paralyzing *us,* numbing nerve after nerve, dulling *our* minds, darkening *our* vision."[59] The solution to the war must be the solution of man. The solution of the Jew must proceed in alliance with the solution of man, "for evil is indivisible."[60] Granted, for the martyred there was no alliance, in fact or in hope.

> What was in the minds of our martyred brothers in Poland in their last hours? They died with disdain and scorn for the civilization in which the killing of civilians could become a carnival of fun. . . . A messenger recently came and conveyed the following message from all the European Jews who are being slaughtered in the hell of Poland: "We, Jews, despise all those who live in safety and do nothing to save us."[61]

But the survivors are not the martyrs. The task of survivors is disdain for neither man nor God. "God will return to us when we shall be willing to let Him in—into our banks and factories, into our Congress and clubs, into our homes and theaters. For God is everywhere or nowhere, the Father of all men or no man, concerned about everything or nothing."[62] This is no mere disembodied, universal panegyric. It is the meaning to be extracted from the Holocaust itself: "The martyrdom of millions in this very hour demands that we consecrate ourselves to the fulfillment of God's dream of salvation."[63] And the *we* here is Israel. Heschel continues:

> Israel did not accept the Torah of their own free will. When Israel

approached Sinai, God lifted up the mountain and held it over their heads saying: "Either you accept the Torah or be crushed beneath the mountain." The mountain of history is over our heads again. Shall we renew the covenant with God?[64]

The spur to renewal of the covenant is not simply Sinai, but "the mountain of history," the burden of mankind. And the renewal itself is the salvation of mankind. Accordingly, whenever Heschel henceforth addressed himself intellectually or practically to a quandary of mankind, he was responding to the Holocaust and overcoming its suffering.

As Maimonides, Heschel's model, overcame suffering, such that an equilibrium of soul permeated the style of his work, so too, with Heschel; although in Heschel's case it is difficult to ascertain how extensively equilibrium ever departed.[65] The Holocaust reversed the direction of his concerns, but not their impetus. After the Holocaust, Heschel wrote in order to save man—and hence also the Jew—with his ontologically normative God-consciousness; while before the Holocaust, Heschel studied and wrote to save himself by assuring himself of the ontological validity of his own God-consciousness. The Holocaust, then, expanded Heschel's own consciousness of the preciousness and the cosmic importance of his Polish hasidic heritage, but did not alter it intrinsically. The Holocaust required no fundamental reorientation toward God; the crux of the issue was whether *man* would seek to renew the covenant that God, with such enormity, had compelled him to confront. The challenge was quantitative in its enormity; not qualitative, in its essence. The rhetorical edge, not the essential doctrine, shifted in Heschel's thought, for no contradiction, no cleavage, rent him into pre-Holocaust and post-Holocaust halves. The question as to the definition of Heschel's own crux, or essential self, remained unanswered by the crisis of the destruction of his world. If, in his own mind, he had never left his world even as he did leave it, physically, in 1924, then, in his own mind, he never left it, even as it did leave him physically, in 1940 to 1945.

Heschel's aspirations in the wake of the Holocaust came to expression in two fields, different but linked. First there was his reconstruction of the spirituality, and of the spiritual implications, of the "hidden light of the East-European period"[66] in Jewish history. Then there was the construction, for all people, of the physical conditions that constituted prerequisites for attaining the spiritual light. The reconstruction of East European Jewish spirituality took the form of studies of hasidic masters,[67] and of his evocative memoir, *The Earth is the Lord's*. The unfolding of the implications of this spirituality took the form of full-fledged theological works, grounded in his philosophically validated post-Kantian approach. These works were penned separately for man—*Man is Not Alone: A Philosophy of Religion*—and for Jew—*God in Search of Man: A Philosophy of Judaism*.[68] The construction of the prerequisites for the theological life took the form of vanguard positions of leadership in four social movements (two of universal and two of Jewish scope) and in a school of thought bridging the universal and the particular—the resolve of ecumenical negotiation and dialogue. The unifying endeavor in all of this was Heschel's translation and expansion of his doctoral thesis, *Die Prophetie* (1936).[69] Scholarly or practical, his post-Holocaust aspirations led to, resonated in, or flowed from *The Prophets* (1962).[70] Heschel's Hebrew prophet became the revealer of resplendent light in the Jewish spirit, the embodiment of the fundamental human norm of God-consciousness, and the vanguard leader for social change and universal reconciliation. Preceding the republication of *Die Prophetie* were Heschel's studies of the spirit; flowing from *The Prophets* was his social and ecumenical activism.[71] These immanent strivings unfolded against the background of American life in the 1950s and 1960s in a way that transformed Heschel from obscure scholar in Berlin and Cincinnati to public figure in New York.

Heschel had been plucked from the fire of Europe in 1940 by Julian Morgenstern, president of Hebrew Union College. Heschel taught there, in Cincinnati, until 1945, and gathered his first disciples. The most devoted followed him to the Jewish Theological Seminary, in New York, at which he would become Professor of Jewish Ethics and Mysticism until his death in 1972.[72] Assiduous in mastering English and productive in research, Heschel wrote three volumes in rapid succession in the early 1950s and another two by 1955.[73] As the fifties drew to a close Heschel turned to preparation of *The Prophets*. It was a propitious choice, for the fifties harbored two thrusts. With the end of the Korean war in 1953, and especially after the United States Senate's censure of Joseph McCarthy in 1954, there was surface placidity and confidence, political apathy and excitement over nonpolitical developments, such as the rapid growth of television, highways, and jet air travel. But there was also the fall of Dien Bien Phu, the beginning of America's involvement in Vietnam, and *Brown v. Board of Education*, the catalyst of the civil right movement. If happy and placid, the Eisenhower years also "incubated not only the problems, but the abundance, the vitality, the passion that exploded in the tormented sixties."[74] The fifties nurtured cultural fixtures of the sixties, men like Herbert Marcuse, Allen Ginsberg, and Paul Goodman, who, as dissidents hostile to the happy spirit of the age, were "the minor themes [that became] major, the aberration [that served] as a carrier to the next generation... 'the new shoots of life springing up and slowly bursting the foundations.' "[75]

In American religious life, Heschel was a new shoot. His post-Holocaust sense of the need of man to surge toward salvation dovetailed with his sense of the direction of the next generation. His twofold, political and theological aspiration could find nurture in the double passion that emerged in the sixties—the search for social justice and the quest for personal authenticity.[76] Heschel's twofold concern meshed also with the emergent self-acceptance in the American Jewish community. What American Jewry assumed by the 1970s, what was given a decisive thrust by "Black is beautiful" and by the Zionist outpouring in the aftermath of Israel's stunning victory in the Six Day War of 1967, was first stirring when Heschel published his philosophy of Judaism, *God in Search of Man*, in 1955. It was Heschel who explained, out of the sources of Judaism, the reasoning of Jewish particularity to a culture beginning to question the legitimacy of the melting pot, to tolerate ethnic diversity, to create conditions for Jewish self-acceptance.[77] The special resonance in Heschel's particularistic emphasis derived from his attempt not to justify Jewish insulation from Gentiles, but to explain to Jews and Gentiles alike how a Judaism with the strength of its specificity could nurture salvation for all.[78] The Prophets were the vortex. In Heschel's eyes, Jew and Gentile, politics and theology, artistry and activism, all took root in the legacy of the biblical Prophets.

> Instead of showing us a way through the elegant mansions of the mind, the prophets take us to the slums. . . . Prophecy is the voice that God has lent to the silent agony, a voice to the plundered poor, to the profaned riches of the world. It is a form of living, a crossing point of God and man. God is raging in the prophet's words. . . . The prophet's use of emotional and imaginative language, concrete in diction, rhythmical in movement, artistic in form, marks his style as poetic. Yet it is not the sort of poetry that takes its origin, to use Wordsworth's phrase, "from emotion recollected in tranquility." Far from reflecting a state of inner harmony or poise, its style is charged with agitation, anguish, and a spirit of nonacceptance. . . . The prophet knew that religion could distort what the Lord demanded of man, that priests themselves had committed perjury by bearing false witness, condoning violence, tolerating hatred, calling for ceremonies instead of bursting forth with wrath and indignation at cruelty, deceit, idolatry, and

violence. . . . the purpose of prophecy is to conquer callousness, to change the inner man as well as to revolutionize history.[79]

To revolutionize history. One could not call Prophets small in self-image. Nor Heschel. In ecumenical negotiation with two Popes and several cardinals (1960–1965), he sought to remake the Catholic image of the Jew into a being of grandeur, with rights of conscience and freedom from guilt.[80] In a seminal call to action (1963), he sought to unleash an American Jewish struggle on behalf of Soviet Jewry.[81] In addresses and demonstrations (1963–1965), he sought to dramatize the plight of Blacks, which simply dramatized "the fact that the entire system of our civilization finds itself in a grave crisis."[82] In speechmaking, pamphleteering, and succoring of imprisoned civil disobedients (1966–1972), he sought to influence clergy and laymen to bring their influence to bear on American administrations doing battle in Vietnam.[83] In the aftermath of the Six Day War (1969), with its disappointment with dialogue, its reflection of feeble Christian support for Israel,[84] Heschel sought to establish the Jewish right to "space," to Israel, in *Israel: An Echo of Eternity*.[85]

The relation of idea to action in Heschel was dialectical. Idea prompted action,[86] response to Holocaust roused revolutionary activity, but the activity itself roused an accretion of ideas. Again, Heschel expanded. In *The Sabbath: Its Meaning for Modern Man* (1951),[87] the controlling idea was *time*, the sanctification of the human consciousness by obedience to rituals of desire and renunciation—of positive and negative commandments of Torah—which built a palace in time, which made the passage of time holy, in the Sabbath. Salvation was to be located in training one's consciousness to step into the climate of God's consecration of time. In *Israel: An Echo of Eternity*, space was added to time. Salvation was now also to be located in directing one's technology to build a just society of Jews upon God's holy land, a spatial activity providing the purest vessel for the consecration of time. "The six days of war must receive their ultimate meaning from the seventh day, which is peace and celebration."[88]

IV.

As it happened, Heschel's double program of politics and theology played itself out in the American context, but it might not have happened this way. Heschel was unhappy at The Hebrew Union College because he was ritually and theologically out of place at this American

Reform stronghold, but when he shifted to the Conservative Jewish Theological Seminary, he was unhappy there, too. His role as a teacher, and in the institution generally,[89] was far less than befit his stature. Heschel yearned for Palestine.[90] His major scholarly investigation, on the talmudic sages' understanding of revelation, was written in Hebrew.[91] The first volume of the work that was to be his credential for the scholars of Jerusalem appeared the same year as the work, *The Prophets*, that anchored his theological and charismatic development in New York. One wonders whether Heschel would have departed for Israel even if a position had opened for him in Israel. As it was, "there was no field for his abilities in the Palestine of that day,"[92] as Heschel wrote about Maimonides, and, it turned out, himself. Heschel's theology of ancient Judaism exhibited all of his strengths, which, to scholars in Jerusalem and elsewhere, were weaknesses: a pithy, rich, allusion-laden Hebrew, at once easy and learned; a kind of backing into the central theme, a presentation of lengthy introductory material, to set mood, to give context, to persuade of the importance of the topic, even to summarize conclusions; a breadth of knowledge and instinct for the substantive jugular, often to the neglect of technical analysis, of a textual, philological, and historical nature; and, finally, what one sympathetic critic called Heschel's Jewish thinking, in contradistinction to reflective thinking about religion and Judaism.[93] By the time the second volume appeared (1965), Heschel was busy on another work, this time in Yiddish, which was at once uncharacteristically idiosyncratic and typically prescient, responsive to coming social change.

The two volume *Kotsk: The Struggle for Integrity* (1973)[94]—a study of the teachers, the life, and the thought of Hasidism's atypical rebbe, Menahem Mendel of Kotsk (1787–1859)—bristles with conundra. It is written in Yiddish, yet presumes the same unfamiliarity with the topic, on the part of the reader, as Heschel's English books. It is as if a Yiddish reading audience brought no special sensibility to the topic—as if the study were written for the translator. But Heschel needed no translator; he could have penned the work in English himself. He wrote that only in Yiddish could he capture Kotsk,[95] yet his volumes assume little of the special intimacy to be expected in a work capturing the native feel of a phenomenon. Was the work to be Heschel's monument to the vanished world of his youth? If so, it was monumental only in its language, for it bodies forth neither nostalgia nor commemoration, but Heschel's own fate as an American avatar of protest.

As the sixties waned, Heschel and other white prompters of protest "were pushed aside as the . . . movements grew more fragmented, violent, and divided along racial lines."[96] The bond between the hopes in Heschel's prophetic vision and the revolutionary impulse within the sixties is highlighted by Heschel's alienation from the sixties as they broke down.

The sixties, reminiscent of the Italian Renaissance, were an era in which preachers of extraordinary talent emerged against a background of religious corruption and renewal; creativity, in the religious sphere, was nurtured less in renunciation of tradition than in obedience to what were deemed its true dimensions; learning and culture burgeoned not to buttress scholarship but to enliven the mind and the senses—"discovery was delightful and system its enemy."[97] Heschel could fix himself in the glow of the future, could summon his post-Holocaust horror of man's aptitude for evil in order to wrench salvation from the bursting foundations of an old world gasping in racism and war. The sixties suited Heschel; they demanded less a firm identity than a commitment to transforming it.

With the failure of apocalyptic moral rhetoric, Heschel's sense of leadership, like that of other mentors of protest, plummeted. The work on the Kotsker Rebbe, especially in its comparison of Kotsk and Kierkegaard in the book's English adaptation,[98] provided the means to recapture the momentum. The book reflects an in-turning, not the in-turning of the late sixties, not an embrace of untaxed emotion and intellect, of self-interest, evasion, or paralysis, not an abandonment of political causes—but an introspective effort to find the true way to their fulfilment. Heschel yearned to prolong the sixties' progress to salvation, and Kotsk (and Kierkegaard) provided the intellectual justification. They taught how to perceive the texture of mendacity interwoven in social protest, how to learn to sustain one's vision and keep nerves intact in a time of disillusionment and distrust. The goal, Heschel's Kotsker said, "was not in finding the Truth but, rather, in an honest search for it."[99] The legacy of Kotsk and Kierkegaard was "not a set of final tenets but a limitless challenge."[100]

A correlative of a limitless future is an indistinct present. One realm of evidence of inner distinctness is the erotic. The erotic is paradoxical, the most universal, undifferentiated human passion, and, in its most acute actualization, the most particular, individuated of all human acts. With the erotic, one stamps a segment of one's innermost character.

A sign of Heschel's essential indistinctness is his attitude toward the erotic. In Heschel's large, extraordinarily wide-ranging corpus, the erotic is nearly absent, conspicuously so. Maimonides, we are told, was crushed by the death of his brother, grieved by the death of his father.[101] Of his response to the death (and life) of his wife(s),[102] we are told nothing, save that Maimonides cannot laud highly enough Aristotle's idea that "the sense of touch is our disgrace."[103] The Sabbath, we are told on the basis of numerous learned references to rabbinic and kabbalistic sources, is a delight to body as well as to soul, metaphorically a bride and a queen, its celebration like a wedding.[104] Of the rabbinic references to the suitability of this sacred time for marital relations,[105] we are told nothing. The ancient theology and the contemporary philosophy of Judaism, we are told (in 1,222 pages),[106] is to be discussed with serious reference to purity and halakhic observance, to "the self" and "the art of being." Of the selfhood or the concepts arising out of the observance of the laws of family purity (*hilkhot niddah*, the halakhic patterns of female purification and of the timing of sexual relations between wife and husband), we are told nothing.

This lacuna is no contemporary sexist disfiguration. It is a deficiency in the halakhic sensibility, to which Heschel was committed; and the deficiency cannot be from ignorance, for Heschel moves with breathtaking range over all arenas of Jewish thought and sensibility. And yet, in *Who is Man?*, Heschel writes nothing about man in relation to woman.[107] In *The Insecurity of Freedom: Essays on Human Existence*, the closest reference to erotic existence is a mention of childbirth, as a metaphor for the nurture of the "seed of insight."[108] In *Kotsk: The Struggle for Integrity*, deviations in halakhic observance attributed to the Kotsker Rebbe or his disciples are cited—and elaborated and reiterated; except for deviations in the laws of family purity, mentioned briefly, baldly, without explanation.[109] It is as if the subject should be a source of embarrassment.

Heschel cites the Kotsker Rebbe's twenty-five year period of celibacy, and the negotiations leading to his second marriage, turning on the question as to whether he would agree to have children.[110] This, to my knowledge, is one of only three serious references to the erotic in Heschel's entire corpus, and it turns on a celibacy not sanctioned by Jewish law.[111] Another reference, in *Theology of Ancient Judaism*, discusses Moses' celibacy in strictly theological terms (was Moses celibate of his own accord, or was he commanded to be so by God), uncharacteristically ignoring the substance of the issue, the relation between asceticism and revelation.[112] In footnotes thereon, the topic in midrash that fascinates Heschel foreshadows his discussion of Kotsk: Did Moses separate from his wife only at times of divine revelation, or for forty continuous years? And should Moses have rejoined his wife to beget more children? In a one-line reference in a chapter entitled "The Pleasures of This World," also in *Theology of Ancient Judaism*, Heschel writes: "A certain one of the bodily pleasures seemed to Rabbi Eliezer ben Hyrcanus as 'one coerced by a demon.' "[113] The talmudic source is *Nedarim* 20b, on which page different views of sexuality are recorded, none of which Heschel quotes or elaborates.

Heschel's corpus from beginning to end mirrors a reciprocal relationship between subject and author, text and response. On both levels, the erotic appears either not at all, or with reference to extreme asceticism. It is as if Heschel, who idealized Moses Maimonides and wrote of his thirst to be the first to attain prophecy in over a millenium,[114] aspired to imitate the chief prophet, Moses himself, Jewish sacred literature's epitome of the being who could empty himself of self before the Glory of God, and thereby become the receptacle of the entire Jewish tradition. As much as possible by a human, Moses embodied and integrated all that there was in Jewish life and thought.

In Heschel's life and thought, there was no evident tension. He was a prism, an instrument through which all passed, a refraction of the claims of hasidic passion and talmudic ratiocination, of the poetry of Young Vilna and the scholarship of Berlin, of the evil of Holocaust and the goodness of God, of the abstraction of philosophy and the activism of the prophets; of inquiry and faith, theology and anthropology; of Hebrew and Yiddish, English and German; of the uniqueness of Israel and the holiness of the Black, the Catholic, the Asian, of all people. Heschel was a prism, not a source, not a root or irreducible ground of being and thought. Heschel the orphan was his own creation, and that creation was a receptacle. It gathered spiritual light as if from the numberless hues on the color wheel, but in the clash of color there was no real dissonance.

To be in tension is to be pulled in opposite directions. Rabbi Soloveitchik is pulled between intellect and emotion, self-revelation and self-concealment, the objectivity of Halakhah and the subjectivity of his own existence. Rabbi Hutner was pulled, Rabbi Israel was pulled, each in his own way, but each wrought harmony out of the tension, or could identify the harmony to which he aspired. Heschel was not pulled. He was not torn by opposites, but coexisted with opposites.[115] He suffered personal disappointments in his career at the Jewish Theological Seminary, he did not succeed in his political-theological program as he would have liked, but this was in the circumstances of life, not in the essence of being. Disjunctive on its face, the closest analogue to Heschel is Harry Austryn Wolfson. Heschel's life was laden with exhortation, his writings were laden with critical judgment, evaluation, and sophisticated sermonic calls to action and belief—all that was absent in Wolfson. Yet, in Heschel, all was reflected—mysticism and rationalism, scholarship and activism, theology and philosophy, poetry and law—because in Heschel there were no criteria for distinguishing between the one and the other, as in Wolfson there were no criteria for distinguishing between Jewish, Christian, or Moslem "Scriptural philosophy." To Heschel, all streams of the Jewish spirit were legitimate, equal in value. There was no way to pronounce the one lesser and the other greater. Wolfson was committed to nothing, Heschel, to everything—a momentous difference, to be certain—but there is an underlying common denominator: the absence of a solidifying center or field, of a governing point or criterion of fundamental concern and identity. Wolfson was committed to nothing—and everything; Heschel, to everything—and nothing. In one sense it is all the same—the sense excluded from Heschel's volume, *Who is Man?* This question Heschel answered. The real question, unanswered, is, *who is a man?*

CHAPTER SEVEN

Rabbi Joseph Zev Lipovitz

"Although it is true that in order to understand the essence of Jewish history one must first know the world, even this kind of comprehensive knowledge cannot acquit the historian who aspires to investigate Jewish history of the need for personal identification with the soul of the chosen people."

If ever in modern Jewish history there has been a seedbed for the bridging of cultures, it is in the land of the "ingathering of exiles" *(kibbutz galuyyot)*. The uniqueness of Palestine (and Israel), however, lies not in its high rate of cultural transition. The ubiquity and the speed of transition there have a distorting effect, analogous to the increase in mass, and slowdown in time, as velocity accelerates toward the speed of light. The distortion in Palestine derives from both the geometrically disproportionate rise in Jewish immigration upon the British assumption of the League of Nations Mandate (1922)—the increase in mass—and the slow-motion adaptation of Jewish agencies in and out of Palestine to the unprecedented challenges cascading down upon them. Never was the opportunity for cross-cultural interaction greater in modern Jewish history than with the crystallization of Palestinian Zionism; and never was the delicate intellectual and social task more sidetracked and frustrated than by the bureaucratic, military, and economic labyrinth of a society pressed to found itself as if from nothing.

The response to the twofold challenge of latent cultural richness and life-sapping disorder was a bifurcation of the transition experience. Palestine is the land of extremism—the birthplace of monotheism, the birthplace of terrorism. All is sharply defined, sharply divided, including transition. Its one path in Palestine is an individual tranquility, a capacity to embody the binding of cultures by transcending the daily, bureaucratic raking of the flesh, by rising above in a concentrated attempt to tie together colliding influences brought to, and nurtured by, Palestinian Jewish society. This was the path of Rabbi Joseph Zev Lipovitz, and it is the path on which we shall concentrate. The other path is a social effort, an intense attempt to embody the bridging of cultures by steering the burgeoning bureaucracy so that it serves all parts of the kaleidoscopic ingathering. This was the path of the likes of Henrietta Szold and David Ben Gurion. It was a path that bequeathed less than a ripened intellectual response to the cross-cultural discontinuities launched in a society of immigrants.

The first path was that of the saint; the second, that of the politician and social worker. For the first, as time slowed down, the mind settled, the richness of thought deepened. For the second, as the mass of the body politic increased, the mind agitated, until only impossible choices presented themselves. From the first path there emerged mature thought that, however, had little practical consequence. From the second path there emerged practical policy that, however, could not solidify itself in rich intellectual contribution. Palestine, then, presented a peculiarly troublesome challenge to transition figures from Eastern Europe, even as it nurtured a peculiarly complex cross-cultural response. For the latter, we turn to the example of Rabbi Lipovitz, a thinker who, typically, arrived in Palestine with rich intellectual baggage already intact. He was a disciple of both the Elder of Slobodka and Rabbi Hayyim Heller, a product of many worlds—Musar piety, academic inquiry, and Lithuanian talmudism—and creator of still another world in Palestine.

I.

The study of Rabbi Joseph Zev Lipovitz (1889–1962) presents special difficulties and entails unyielding gaps.[1] If other transition figures from Eastern Europe hid, romanticized, or simply blocked out their late adolescence, Rabbi Lipovitz left no clues, not even the inverse clues of denial or distortion, about his life in general. Among the transition figures in our survey, we know the least about Rabbi Lipovitz, at least in the conventional sense. If Rabbi Israel left a few letters, Rabbi Lipovitz left none. If Harry Austryn Wolfson was silent about himself in his last forty-five years of publications, Rabbi Lipovitz was silent about himself from birth to death. If Rabbi Hutner and Abraham Joshua Heschel maintained a personal reserve that nonetheless silhouetted their inner quandaries, Rabbi Lipovitz's reserve was undifferentiated. If Rabbi Soloveitchik speaks and writes passionately of mind and soul in such a way as to illuminate his own life, Rabbi Lipovitz's passion illuminated his mind and soul, but not his life. He was too much the disciple of the Elder of Slobodka to reveal himself, yet, in spite of this restraint, and also like the Elder, he escaped the deformations of Harry Austryn Wolfson by knowing his own mind, and knowing it unashamedly. Unlike the Elder, Rabbi Lipovitz knew his mind unselfconsciously and put it to a full and rich expression, to an unfiltered, unstrategized revelation of innermost conviction.

On an unconventional plane, then, Rabbi Lipovitz revealed himself in a way not comparable to any of the transition figures with whom we have dealt. Least known, least read, Rabbi Lipovitz nevertheless constitutes a key to the ultimate possibilities of the transition experience from Eastern Europe.

He brought together diverse strands of twentieth-century Jewish thought with unlabored grace and harmony, such that his writings are free of the complex strategies of Rabbis Salanter, Hutner, and Heschel, the searing confessions of Rabbi Soloveitchik, and the stringent constrictions of Harry Austryn Wolfson. Rabbi Lipovitz naturally set forth the soul of his mind, and the mind of his soul. Palestine's political and military battles carve from the one extreme of transition in Palestine, that of Henrietta Szold and David Ben Gurion, a supreme social agitation; they carve from the other extreme, that of Joseph Zev Lipovitz, a supreme serenity. From both, they carve straightforwardness. It is as if the rebirth of the hard and responsive land of the Bible resuscitated also its rhythms: the contortions of Judges and Kings, and the lucidities of Prophets, coping with backsliders. As the soul of Prophets, about whose lives we know so little, are revealed with transparent clarity through their writings, so is the soul of Joseph Zev Lipovitz.

To the best of our knowledge, Rabbi Lipovitz gave no thought to writing prior to his sixties. Unlike all of the other figures in this book, he had no career, in a professional sense. He held no academic, rabbinic, or political position, led no social or intellectual movement, and came close to being a figure of purely posthumous reputation. Such is often the way of Palestine. There, gifted individuals, who are denied by fate the notice of peers, absorb, distill, and freshly and profoundly integrate truths within this or the other domain—from sociology to Jewish law, from psychology to Jewish thought. The absence of opportunity to pursue their interests in a professional framework turns them back upon their own resources. These, supplemented by ready access to specialized libraries and by countless informal opportunities for collegial discourse, create scholars-in-the-rough, in pursuit of truth for its own sake. In the nature of things, from out of this pool of self-made inquirers there emerge a few who are rounded and original. Such, in brief, describes the soil from which sprang the three volumes of Rabbi Lipovitz's *The Heritage of Joseph (Naḥalat Yosef)*, essays on literary, philosophic, and theological themes, and his commentary on the *Scroll of Ruth*, the only work of Rabbi Lipovitz published in his lifetime. (There is a fourth volume of *Naḥalat Yosef*, on Halakhah.) If conditions in Palestine brought his thinking to fruition, the foundations were laid in both Eastern and Western Europe.

Joseph Zev Lipovitz was born in 1889 in a small town near Bialystock, Poland, to parents who were Kotsker hasidim. When Joseph was sixteen or seventeen he learned of the Slobodka yeshiva from students passing through town. His gifts in both intellect and sensibility became clear soon after he enrolled in Slobodka. Its dean, Rabbi Moses Mordechai Epstein, asked young Lipovitz to take his place in delivering the daily lecture for the local talmudic study circle *(ḥevrah Shas)* when he was detained elsewhere. An internationally renowned talmudic scholar, Rabbi Meir Simhah of Dvinsk (author of *'Or Sameaḥ*), visited Slobodka in 1912, met Lipovitz, and generously praised his learning. Rabbi Epstein wanted him to become his son-in-law, but the Elder of Slobodka discouraged the match apparently because he thought that Lipovitz lacked in administrative skill. Perhaps the Elder, knowing the naturalness of Lipovitz's expression, thought that Lipovitz lacked the capacity for intellectual self-concealment, in accord with which the Elder nurtured the individual powers within his best students.

Rabbi Lipovitz married a woman of indistinguished lineage in 1912, settled in Rituva, Lithuania, and opened a leather store. For the most part his wife ran the store, while he taught Talmud (without pay) in a yeshiva he had founded. Each year he returned to Slobodka for the high holidays and for the month prior. Between 1922 and 1924 he studied for one-and-a-half years under Rabbi Hayyim Heller in Berlin, and at the

University of Berlin, to which he commuted periodically from Lithuania. Notwithstanding the paucity of details, there emerges a picture of a couple not wishing to earn a living from pedagogy and study, and of a man already in his thirties still wishing to widen his intellectual horizons. In 1924 the Lipovitzes closed their business, went up to Palestine, and settled in Tel Aviv.

At that time two Slobodka graduates, Rabbis Abraham E. Kaplan and Jehiel J. Weinberg, were the first to teach Talmud in the critico-conceptual manner in German, in Berlin, while Rabbi Lipovitz became one of the first to do so in Hebrew, in Tel Aviv. He was a Judah ha-Levi Zionist, dedicated to the upbuilding of Jewish Palestine and to the renaissance of the holy tongue. He would teach in Hebrew, not Yiddish—a first sign of his harmonistic penchant. He would adapt Musar to a Zionist, or sociological, analysis. Now, in Slobodka Musar, as in all Musar schools derived from Rabbi Israel, the focus of pietistic attention had invariably been the individual. Rabbi Isaac Hutner found this constricting for its inability to meet nonpietistic disciplines in Jewish thought on their own terms. Rabbi Lipovitz found it constricting for its inability to consider the community as more than the sum of its individuals. Musar thought had removed itself from a sociological perspective. Society, said Musar, would achieve perfection as the sum total of perfected individuals. Musar thought had been neither Zionist nor anti-Zionist, but pre-Zionist, its psychological focus laid down before modern Zionism arose. With the rise of proto-Zionism in 1881 and Zionism in 1897, the Musar movement neither condemned nor condoned them. The Musar mind did not absorb Zionism's consideration of Jewish fate in national terms.

Rabbi Lipovitz transferred Slobodka's pietistic criterion of Judaism from the individual to the communal frame. This transferral, however, was transitional, that is, it remained rooted in two traditions. His embrace of the sociologico-communal preserved his individual, psychologico-pietistic perspective. Rabbi Lipovitz did not transmute the pietism of Slobodka but refined and enlarged it. By way of illustration, in Rabbi Lipovitz's extensive discussions of biblical figures, individual spiritual failings and conquests reflect the subtle layers of personal decision and fate, and, simultaneously, the pervasive fruits and flaws of communal character. His writings are unique among Musar commentary in their perception of biblical figures as irreducibly individual, and simultaneously reflective of communal character. To Rabbi Lipovitz the psychological (Musar) and the sociological (Zionist) turn of mind were interanimative.

Rabbi Lipovitz taught the Slobodka talmudic method in Hebrew, then, not as a necessary accomodation to Hebraic Tel Aviv, but in order to become a channel through which the individuated piety of the talmudic culture of Slobodka could flow into the communal culture of the Zionist enterprise. After ten years of teaching, in 1935 Rabbi Lipovitz resigned for health reasons, whereupon he and his wife opened a modest hotel-restaurant (a *"pensiyyon"*) in the living room and porch of their small home, near the Mediterranean. For the next twenty-seven years the Lipovitzes fashioned an anomolous intellectual setting. Buoyed and bound by necessity, their restaurant became an informal talmudic gathering place in Tel Aviv, then effervescent, coarse, and confident. Laborers, yeshiva deans, literary figures, factory owners, young and old, weak and hearty, occupied the Lipovitzes, she bringing the food, he bringing the discourse. Rabbi Lipovitz transformed the subjects of discussion into a lens through which to refract lessons in Bible and Talmud and their myriad commentaries and supercommentaries. Visitors recall: "Nothing was foreign to him"; "his thirst for knowledge was unquenchable"; "he spoke to those living 'in the world' "; "he made biblical figures come alive."

Visitors also recall both Lipovitzes in demand as counselors to the troubled. One may speculate that their own trials in coping with childlessness abetted in becoming trusted confidants. On Sabbaths and holidays Rabbi Lipovitz volunteered to lecture, often in four or five synagogues on a single holy day. Later, he also volunteered to administer the finances of the Ponavitch yeshiva, the largest in Israel, in nearby Benei Berak. For over a quarter of a century, then, the Lipovitzes were quiet recreational, intellectual, psychological, and financial resources, wholly outside the framework of professional rabbinic and academic centers.

When a few disciples, particularly Rabbi Hayyim Zev Finkel (grandson of the Elder of Slobodka), witnessed Rabbi Lipovitz's health deteriorate, they pressed him to write, before it was too late. He was then in his sixties, confined to home. Since no Lipovitz children would be left behind, disciples felt a special urgency in securing something from their teacher to be left behind; they recorded each of his lectures, delivered in his home. One series of talks, on the *Scroll of Ruth*, was transcribed in time for Abraham Kariv, an Israeli author, to edit it, and for Rabbi Lipovitz to put it into final form before he died in 1962. When his wife eulogized him, she characterized his orphans as "words of the talmudic sages he left unglossed." Baylah Lipovitz died in 1978 after having sold her possessions, down to her wedding ring, to finance the publication of her husband's works. Except for the commentary on *Ruth*, these are unedited transcriptions of the lectures recorded in the last years of his life.

II.

Much was recorded, and every scrap of extant lecture notes was printed. The results range from truncated, one-page essays, barely begun, to fully realized monographs, fifty pages long. Then there is the commentary on *Ruth*. It is more developed than fragmentary, anthologized, or specialized modern commentaries on *Ruth*. It is more than an interweaving of rabbinic sources episodically fleshing out the narrative, more than a random selection of the abundant talmudic and post-talmudic commentaries, and more than a philological or historical inquiry into isolated problems in the text. It is a sustained psychological interpretation of the personalities in the book—a subtle probing of motivation, of inner conflict, and of moral decision, aided by talmudic commentary—within a larger interpretation of these personalities as typologies of faith and rebellion, of persecution and redemption, in Jewish history. Microcosm—the individual development of character and of powers of soul—intertwine with macrocosm—the collective fate and destiny of the Jewish people. In *Ruth*, the dominant note is comprehensiveness: the individual in conjunction with history, the subtle stain or sheen on personal piety in conjunction with analysis of destiny, the synthesis and symbiosis of the individual quest for (or fall from) spiritual ascent in conjunction with the collective advancement toward (or delay of) national redemption.

The uneven quality of the Lipovitz corpus has its advantages. With access to the corpus in all stages of its production, we can measure the balance between conscious crafting and unselfconscious, natural flow. The upshot of this measurement is a unity in tone, a consistency of unselfreflective naivete within the shortest fragments and lengthiest essays. Rabbi Lipovitz's writings reveal extensive ponderings of Jewish lore (*midrash*, *aggadah*, and *derush*), of the Hebrew pietistic literature, of Jewish philosophy and poetry, as well as of German historiography and idealistic philosophy, political theory, and biblical criticism, higher and lower.

Unlike Rabbi Hutner's *Paḥad Yitzhak*, Rabbi Lipovitz's *Naḥalat Yosef* hides none of this; unlike Rabbi Soloveitchik's essays, *Naḥalat Yosef* projects none of this saliently; and unlike Abraham Joshua Heschel's corpus, *Naḥalat Yosef* makes no effort to transform all this in light of Judaism. Rabbi Lipovitz so thoroughly absorbed, dissected, and selectively incorporated his sources—religious and secular—that the final product gives no evidence of Hutnerian camouflage, Soloveitchikian struggle, or Heschelian craftsmanship. He had no need to disguise secular reading, to prove its legitimacy, or to be self-reflective about it. He had no need to strategize, to design lectures for a desired audience (although even some of his most densely argued essays illustrate points with reference to "the common man"—a reflection of some of his immediate audience, the simpler of the restaurant patrons). In essence, the Lipovitz writings constitute the ruminations of an inquisitive soul at ease with all facets of its knowledge, content to give its muse free rein in shaping fresh statements on a wide range of subjects, from the purpose of the Jewish historian to the nature of prophecy, from the character of the biblical Ruth to the nature of Jewish political sovereignty.

To say that philosophic and political ideas are not consciously salient in Rabbi Lipovitz's writings is not the same as to say that he absorbed them from a climate of opinion. Rabbi Hutner's mentor, Rabbi Abraham Isaac Kuk, was a twentieth-century Palestinian transition figure whose writings also reveal an unselfconscious reflection of Western ideas, but scholars must guess at his Western sources. They assume that Rabbi Kuk himself probably did not read them, that they passed to him through intangible channels—the "spirit" or "climate" of the age. Unlike Rabbi Kuk, Rabbi Lipovitz was introduced to a bibliography and a scholarly agenda under Rabbi Hayyim Heller, and at the University of Berlin, which served as a source of topical interest and methodological challenge throughout his life.

Rabbi Lipovitz met the most difficult challenge facing the twentieth-century transition figures who emerged from the worlds of intensive piety and talmudic learning. The ultimate difficulty in the modernization of the East European talmudic ambience was not to develop a *Weltanschauung* informed by Western ideas, but to do so without allowing intellectual inquiry to transform a living relationship with tradition into a self-reflective enterprise. The challenge was to absorb new knowledge without disturbing spiritual naivete. Rabbi Hutner grasped the issue when he sought to integrate, in his terms, "naive faith" and "sophisticated faith." The fact that he formulated the issue indicates that he had distanced himself from naive faith (as he confessed). Rabbi Lipovitz did not formulate the issue. He both advanced beyond Rabbi Soloveitchik and fell behind Rabbi Hutner. He advanced beyond Rabbi Soloveitchik in his integration of naive faith with new knowledge. He fell behind Rabbi Hutner in being sufficiently untouched at the core of his pietistic serenity so as not to have to defend, explicitly or implicitly, his synthesizing. In this, he realized the aspiration of Rabbi Israel Salanter to grow in devotion and in intellect within a seedbed of unselfconscious tranquility.

Palestine both abetted and retarded Rabbi Lipovitz's aspiration. Palestine helped in presenting material and social challenges so overwhelming and ubiquitous that the only way to cope was with transcending forbearance. Paradoxically, intense and inescapable problems settled the mind. Save great agitation, there was no choice. Palestine hindered in preventing the settled mind from either moving within or creating an academic or pietistic center of influence that would give intellectual integrity *cum* authentic serenity a social resonance. The paradoxes abound: social problems catalyzed personal tranquility; while serene approaches to social problems—the integration of both the sociological challenge of the new Yishuv, and the intellectual challenge of Western philosophy and historiography with the piety of traditional, Musar Judaism—led to social isolation.

Palestine is replete with idiosyncratic solutions to labyrinthine problems. The irony is that even when idiosyncrasy, such as Joseph Zev Lipovitz's unfinished theology of Judaism, contained within it the seeds of social redemption, it could not reach beyond itself. Such is the beauty and quandary of a society replete with self-made scholars, intellectuals, and artists. Without benefit of exposure in another society, they tend to cancel each other out, the one unable to gain clear ascendance over the other. On the one hand, this was the substratum that conditioned Rabbi Lipovitz's obscurity. On the other hand, it is little more than a quarter century since his death—the slimmest passage in a seemingly ageless history given to almost rhythmic resurrection of commentaries that become staples of the Jewish intellectual tradition.

Conclusion

One travels from Boston to Martha's Vineyard, from Jerusalem to Netanya, Denver to Aspen, or Zurich to Grindelwald (the urban reader may substitute his own international vacation spot in the general proximity of his city). On vacation in that spot, one is transported by the stream of languages and national customs from the fixity of daily burden to a floating yet momentarily real world, churning fantasies in the imagination. One comes to feel a universe of discourse or custom different from one's own. Perhaps one enters a brief conversation with inhabitants of a faraway place, hears new music, views strange art, or even makes a foreign friend. One "grows," reaches beyond oneself, realizes ambitions. Vicariously, one becomes a transition figure.

The journey of transition figures from Eastern Europe was no vacation because there was no turning back. Their penetration of a second culture was accompanied by linguistic tools and by a special perceptivity and sensibility, which moved ambition beyond vicarious fulfillment to daily burden. In turning the fantasia of fleeting cross-cultural encounter to a lifetime agenda, the East European transition figures created their own world, unfathomable to visitors from their native and new worlds alike. What can be grasped vicariously and momentarily in the balm of a vacation is different from the crystallization of the cross-cultural position. This is carefully built up and differentiated into a sophisticated psychological, political, or philosophical reality that, if beginning with a momentary cross-cultural insight or encounter, very likely transmutes it. Accordingly, and ironically, the transition figures from Eastern Europe were not actually a part of their adopted culture, notwithstanding their creation of a following that, in many cases, successfully dominated it.

To this rule there are exceptions. Harry Austryn Wolfson, with his extreme solitude and Yiddish accent, may in some ultimate sense have recoiled at his total public identification with Harvard and with the academic study of philosophy—but a total and unqualified public loyalty it was. The contrasting predominant nonconformity is typified by Rabbis Joseph Baer Soloveitchik and Isaac Hutner. Abstemious in personal habit, contemptuous of self-advertisement, especially through the media, and trenchant in criticism of sexual, acquisitional, and other drives nurtured by print and broadcast journalism, the Lithuanian-American Talmudists set themselves apart from their country of naturalized citizenship. Their very success in dominating, through their students, thousands of Orthodox synagogues, communal organizations, or specialized Jewish agencies in the United States stemmed tactically from a deep-rooted indifference to American ways. Having renounced early in life the controlling judgment of peers, in fierce assertion of intellectual and occupational independence, they acquired the habit of steering by their own lights. For their synthesis to have resonated, it had to have been because of grace as well as will. With all the fine calibrations that guided their search, with all the considered strategizing built into their antennae, so to speak, their will to communicate had self-imposed limits. The boundaries of an inner gyroscope were never to be transgressed. If their message was to find listeners, then the potential listeners would have to find it, indeed, would have to fight for the right to hear it. In a critical sense, the transition phenomenon is as much a study in the receptivities of a culture as it is of those who sought to address them. Accordingly, there was the resonance of Rabbis Solovetchik and Hutner, and the idiosyncrasy of Rabbi Joseph Zev Lipovitz.

Now, Abraham Joshua Heschel carefully nurtured his public image, making every tactical effort not to set himself apart. Even pious Rabbi Israel Salanter, who consciously fled from acclaim, advanced several ideas, all ahead of their time, for exploiting new media for the dissemination of Judaic culture. It would be insensitive to the peculiar psychology of East European transition, however, to regard Heschel or Rabbi Israel as essentially divergent from Rabbis Soloveitchik, Hutner, and Lipovitz, who spurned the media. What Heschel and Rabbi Israel sought was not celebrity—a public preening for its own sake—but notoriety—a way of calling attention to a program that otherwise could not succeed. For Rabbi Israel, notoriety was necessary, and distasteful; for Heschel, it was necessary but not distasteful. For both, as well as for Harry Austryn Wolfson and Rabbis Soloveitchik, Hutner, and Lipovitz, fame was never confused with success. Behind the variation in tactics toward media among transition figures was an essential apartness. If anything, the links of Heschel and Rabbi Israel to media only highlighted their nonconformity, since, for them, publicity was a means to an end, not an end to itself.

Nonconformity is an unexpected appellative in association with such staunch Orthodox figures as Rabbis Salanter, Hutner, Soloveitchik, and Lipovitz. "Orthodox transition figure" is oxymoronic, alerting the observer to a peculiar, but not inconsistent, linkage. The association of Orthodoxy and nonconformity takes its peculiarity from the circumstances of East European Jewish history, which shielded most of the guardians of Orthodoxy from Western intellectual influences for an inordinate length of time. As Heschel movingly argued in *The Earth is the Lord's,* the inner world of the East European Jew was so thoroughly sealed off from Christianity and its secularized, cultural outgrowths that it was East European Judaism, in the pre-Holocaust centuries, that most closely approximated a purely Jewish phenomenology. For East European Orthodoxy, then, an attempt to build psychological or philosophical bridges beyond its confines seemed especially jarring. However, the task was not inherently contradictory, and not simply because of earlier models of cross-cultural encounter in Spanish, Italian, and Alexandrian periods of Jewish history.

The ultimate consistency of transition figures from Eastern Europe is to be measured substantively, in terms of the rigor and the richness of their synthesis of psychology, philosophy, politics, or theology with Judaism. The issue is complicated by both the terminological masks that these transition figures adopted and by the personal filter that sustained their thinking. Beyond specific judgments (already set forth in detail in earlier chapters), it is critical to recall that the transition figures treated in this book were selected from among the most Jewishly erudite, natively intelligent thinkers of the past two centuries. Ultimate failings or weaknesses in their respective syntheses bring one up against a wall: One cannot argue that others were more fit for the task. Just those individuals who were most talented undertook to link Judaism to its contemporary world. If one observes serious differences of opinion among transition figures—even among Orthodox ones—then the final substantive issue is whether even a supremely learned, fully informed normative Judaism must sustain pluralism—tolerance of contradiction—on some level.

Rabbi Israel Salanter, and his second-generation disciple the Elder of Slobodka, addressed the issue explicitly. The pinnacle of Rabbi Israel's ethics was, in his own words, "a thing and its opposite." One should seek honor for others, but reject it for oneself; one should seek material welfare for others, but not for oneself. The Elder pushed this principle, which in Rabbi Israel's corpus was explicitly ethical and only implicitly theological, openly into theology. As recorded in this book's epigraph, the ways of God Himself are polar. Man, in his polarity, imitates God. Here, one subsumes Orthodoxy, but also reaches beyond it, to an all-inclusive Judaic structure, both explaining pluralism within Judaism, at its most particular, Orthodox boundary, and setting Judaism off against its daughter religion and predominant competitor—Christianity—at its most universal boundary.

With regard to Orthodoxy, the ways of God, being paradoxical, subsume even within Orthodoxy a Jewish pluralism not of fundamental belief or practice, but of attitude, of supererogatory ethics, and of feeling tone. With regard to Christendom, in relation to whose belief system or larger, Western cultural context the Orthodox transition figures had to erect or limit their bridge, paradox becomes a fundamental demarcation. Its field in Judaism is both distinct from and smaller than a similar demarcation in Christianity itself.

Christianity cannot imagine existence without a final reconciliation of opposites.

> God expresses his Goodness most fully in the union between God and man in Christ. This union achieves a final reconciliation of opposites. In the God-man . . . one sees the primal first joined to the last of all, the eternal joined with the temporal, the most simple with the most composite, the most actual with the most suffering and altered, the most immense with the littlest, and the perfectly one with the individual composed and distinguished from all others. God's Goodness, revealed in the Incarnation, is even more manifest when one considers especially Christ's Passion, . . . for here one sees God united with the nadir of existence. . . . Christ on the cross, then, transcends all contradictions, . . . the Passion is "the book wherein contrary propositions are reconciled" . . . Christ is the coincidence of opposites in whom God and redeemed man, that which is All and that which by nature is nothing, become one.[1]

Notwithstanding Christian ethics and Jewish conceptions of afterlife, a fundamental dividing point between mother and daughter religion is the ability to live with contradiction. Christianity, spurning contradiction, moves beyond this world by making available eternal reconciliation even within this world. Judaism stays with this world, eyes fixed on unending worldly tasks, living with contradictions. Such are the ways of God Himself, says the Elder of Slobodka. And even his spiritual progenitor, Rabbi Israel Salanter, and his spiritual disciple, Rabbi Joseph Zev Lipovitz, who both held perfect harmony to be the highest psychological-religious ideal, could not conceive that idea to be static, unable to be made still more perfect (again, a contradiction) through constant struggle against social and personal sources of anxiety. It is in view of this willingness to live with struggle, to bear contradiction, that one understands plurality among Orthodox transition figures specifically, and the Jewish penchant to cross cultural lines generally.

I cite Christianity not simply as a familiar, illustrative metaphor, for in bearing contradictions Jewish transition figures are subject to temptation, to slippage toward the one or the other side of a contradiction. One notes, for example, the characterization of Heschel's Judaism as incarnational theology without Incarnation. Heschel's personal and theological resonance among Christian theologians and scholars, Protestant and Catholic—the "commanding presence," or sacred charisma, that they associated with Heschel—and Heschel's own overt cultivation of a Christian audience, all bespoke his inclination toward the spiritual side of the spiritual-material polarity at the heart of Judaism. Heschel's attitude toward sexuality—alternatively, unequivocally negative, a passion to be sublimated in religion, or a metaphor for love between God and the Jewish people—fit more readily into a Catholic sensibility than, say, Rabbi Soloveitchik's avowed affirmation of the Jewish husband's sexual obligations, of the laws of family purity, and of the raging passions of man and women.

Similarly, disagreements on ecumenicism between Heschel and Rabbi Soloveitchik were more than doctrinal. They reflect differing evaluations of how far Judaism could go in transcending the contradictions of human existence without forsaking the material-spiritual polarity of Judaism. Heschel's positive views on ecumenicism, and Rabbis Soloveitchik's and Hutner's negative views, really amounted to a debate on whether Jewish-Christian dialogue could, by its very aspiration to a final, humanly initiated, this-world reconciliation, be a Jewish enterprise. Wolfson, of course, was willing to eviscerate Judaism to effect a reconciliation with Christianity, but even Heschel, who was far more subtle and Jewishly proud than Wolfson, grasped the essence: For ecumenicism to work, not just Christianity but Judaism would have to change. This, Rabbis Salanter, Hutner, Soloveitchik, and Lipovitz were unwilling to consider.

The temptation of escaping contradiction into a monochromatic existence did not escape Rabbi Soloveitchik. For him, the temptation was Kant (whom Heschel simply circumvented). As tempted as Heschel was by the spiritual stress of Christianity, Rabbi Soloveitchik was tempted by the intellectual stress of neo-Kantianism, in which thought, producing itself out of itself, was the pivot of existence. For both Heschel and Rabbi Soloveitchik, the underlying temptation was the same: the search for a less textured, less contradictory and burdensome existence. The evidence available to the observer, never fully privy to the inner workings of the soul, suggests that their search failed. Their rootedness in Judaism could not be uprooted. The burden of participating in two worlds could not propel even Wolfson, let alone Heschel and Rabbi Soloveitchik, into a culturally unidimensional existence. Rabbis Salanter, Hutner, and Lipovitz adopted a different strategy—more subtle, more Jewish—and the temptation did not arise. Their strategy took the form of a dynamic equilibrium, a struggle for integrity amidst the study of tranquility. Dynamic equilibrium, conceived simultaneously as a psychologically healthy state of being, a theologically mandated connection to God, an ethically sound way to human service, and an intellectually compelling way to enlightenment, amounted to a Jewish struggle so consuming that the temptation to escape from contradiction was obviated, the need for a final grace was fully retained, and the experience of a partial grace was ever-present.

For transition figures, language was something like graphology. The figurative squiggles and angles told as much as the substance. We penetrate the facade of a transition figure's highly conscious style by examining the contours of the facade itself. We need not actually penetrate it, for in understanding the strategy it served—was it seductive? contrived? opaque?—we actually reach beneath the facade to a level of understanding more profound than the conscious level of thought that it was intended to obscure.

Both Rabbi Israel and Abraham Joshua Heschel wrote to persuade. As much as they were the considered conclusions of scholarship, the writings of both men were rhetorical experiments in eliciting personal response. Rabbi Israel failed because he was a poor stylist. Heschel was an incomparably better stylist. "So compelling are his sentences that a paragraph literally chokes from wealth," wrote one of Heschel's disciples.[2] Intended as a compliment, the characterization is an apt formulation of Heschel's reader's problem. Choking (figuratively, of course), the reader of Heschel is overwhelmed, knowing that he has confronted great epigrammatic profundity, but unable to weave his way through relentless waves of meaning and implication, let alone to place their constituent parts into the structure of thought of which they were—or were they?—latently integral parts. Rabbi Israel, on the other hand, without grace of expression, had the grace of clarity, once his learned, obscure references were unraveled and his double entendres were fit into their carefully constructed double level of simultaneous discourse. In both Rabbi Israel's and Heschel's cases, the rhetorical approach succeeded, if at all, only with disciples who were sufficiently attuned to the master to decipher all of the allusions. The attempt to communicate from the inner travail of bicultural discovery offered little solace to the communicators, if the communication was intended to work a catharsis. Precisely their sophistication complicated all attempts to communicate.

Now, Harry Austryn Wolfson was clear and cadenced, unable to be *mis*understood by anyone reasonably disciplined in reading philosophy. He, too, labored hard to craft his style, but not in order to communicate for catharsis, or to persuade. His style derived its uniqueness from its full and integral connection to his personality. In his case, an initial clue to the inextricable link between person and expression was the unity in tone and form between early and late academic expositions, spanning a period of forty-five years. The tone encased in even Wolfson's shortest fragments (his catchy two-word phrases, such as "faint echoes," his ubiquitous and mundane "and," "or," and "out of," and his prepositional verbs, such as "tagged on," "trotted out," "trudged through") is irreproducible because the stance behind the style—the personality of the writer—was inaccessible. The connection between style and personality in Wolfson turned on the opaqueness of both.

Most ironically, Wolfson's compelling clarity hid Wolfson himself far more effectively than Rabbi Israel's or Heschel's passionate, problematic rhetoric. By scraping away at Rabbi Israel and at Heschel, one reaches their heart. To scrape at Wolfson is impossible: the surface is as smooth (and clear) as a fine diamond finely polished. Similarly, Rabbi Hutner's compelling clarity blocks all channels to Rabbi Hutner himself. The difference between Rabbi Hutner and Harry Wolfson is that Wolfson's writings were unlabored, while Rabbi Hutner's were contrived. The difference is critical. Wolfson could write with perfection because knowledge and style were all that he had. Rabbi Hutner had incomparably more, in substance, in wisdom. All this could be hidden only with an iron discipline, a ruthless suppression of rhetoric and confession, of essay and poetry (in, at least, the writings he chose to publish). Such comprehensive suppression could only succeed with an exclusively conscious style. It had to be contrived for fear that otherwise the reader could penetrate through to its author. Wolfson's style could be natural, for there was nothing underneath it that he had to hide.

Rabbi Soloveitchik's style is neither contrived nor polished nor obscurely rhetorical. It is passionate, arresting in its lack of polish, in its raw power and clarity. His mask is his derivation of emotional power from his mind—the intellectualization of emotion and experience. The reader confronts a man of immense sensitivity; the listener witnesses a man of immense distance; the student is privy to an almost pathetic inability to act on that sensitivity. Like other transition figures from Eastern Europe, Rabbi Soloveitchik tried to conceal himself with his style. Only Rabbi Lipovitz was different. We know frustratingly little about his life, whether by accident or by his own intent. Be that as it may, he opened himself fully and easily in the lectures that became his writings. In these, he gave no evidence of disguising himself, wittingly or unwittingly.

We are left, ultimately, with the impossibility of dividing between writer and work, life and thought, personal and published impression. Transition figures from Eastern Europe were not transition thinkers. Transition figures were larger than their thought, or, better, their thought was smaller than they. Their thought was but part of them, colored by their totality, not just by their mind.

The study of these transition figures in their totality is an exercise in both inspiration and frustration. These people beckon ordinary mortals from behind an enormous sensibility and an enormous knowledge. They beckon us to stretch our own imaginative and intellectual capacities beyond seemingly intractable limits. At the same time, these transition figures betray foibles and failures with poignance and obviousness that call out for instant, and, of course, impossible solution. To study transition is to confront life constantly in a state of heightened awareness, of ceaseless questioning of first principles, and of an endless variety of masks for both—masks that, on occasion, and in varying degrees, are stripped away for privileged disciples. This book has attempted to strip away those masks, to provide the insight of the disciple alongside the sober analysis of the scholar. With perspective from both inside and outside, we can choose intelligently how intensively we might wish to respond to the example of life lived to its limits, how extensively we might wish to risk the living of Jewish life beyond its indigenous limits.

NOTES AND BIBLIOGRPAHY

NOTES

1. Introduction

1. Bernard Septimus, *Hispano-Jewish Culture in Transition: The Career and Controversies of Ramah* (Cambridge, Massachusetts, and London: Harvard University Press, 1982); Carle E. Schorske, "Politics in a New Key: An Austrian Trio," *Fin-de-Siecle Vienna: Politics and Culture* (New York: Vintage Books, 1981), 146–75, esp. 152, 158–9, 163 [on Theodor Herzl]; Allon Gal, *Brandeis of Boston* (Cambridge: Harvard University Press, 1980).

Other works that adumbrate the concept of transition as used in this book include Frank E. Talmage, "Narbona: Exile," in *David Kimhi: The Man and the Commentaries* (Cambridge, Massachusetts, and London: Harvard University Press, 1975); Daniel M. Swetschinski, "The Portuguese Jews of Seventeenth-Century Amsterdam: Cultural Continuity and Adaptation," in Frances Malino and Phyllis Cohen Albert, eds., *Essay in Modern Jewish History: A Tribute to Ben Halpern* (New York: Herzl Press, and London and Toronto: Associated University Presses, 1982); Yosef Hayim Yerushalmi, *From Spanish Court to Italian Ghetto: Isaac Cardoso, A Study in Seventeenth-Century Marranism and Jewish Apologetics* (New York: Columbia University Press, 1971; rpt., Seattle and London: University of Washington Press, 1981).

2. Septimus, *Hispano-Jewish Culture*, 3.

3. Robert Wohl, *The Generation of 1914* (Cambridge: Harvard University Press, 1979), 131–32.

4. There is an extensive literature on Freud, Einstein, and other prominent Jews that argues for their rootedness in Judaism, "Jewishness," or Jewish nationalism. An essential problem in assessing the Freuds and Einsteins as Jews is in choosing the standard by which to measure.

Freud's commentators measure his Jewishness as over against the self-hating or apostate Jew. Against them, Freud's Jewishness seems salient. The commentators claim Freud for the Jewish people because he stood up against anti-Semitism, suffered in delayed professorial advancement on account of anti-Semitism, had Jewish friends and associates, particularly in B'nai B'rith, and occasionally expressed mild support for Zionism.

On a different level, commentators claim Freudian psychoanalysis for Judaism. Ernst Simon argues that Freud's theories, personality, and analytical method correspond to Judaism's rational-talmudic tradition. David Bakan argues that

Freud's theories, personality, and analytical method correspond to Judaism's irrational-kabbalistic tradition. John Murray Cuddihy, Philip Rieff, and others argue that Freud's theories, personality, and analytical method embody an archtypical Jewish character that, though bereft of talmudic, kabbalistic, or other Jewish ideational content, is not simply *as* Jewish as Jewish doctrines, ceremonies, and the like, but even more so. Peter Loewenberg, Marthe Robert, Sigmund Diamond, and others also approach Freud's Jewishness with mutually exclusive, reductionist, or speculative results.

Much of this critical secondary literature is serious and sustained, but, because of the near absence of primary evidence, is inevitably inferential, sometimes extremely so. For example, Diamond sees Freud as unabashedly assertive as a Jew by explaining Freud's comment on a novel that should have aroused Freud the Jew, but did not, only by positing that Freud did not seem to have read the novel that he ostensibly said that he had!

My presupposition is that for Judaism to be significant, in whatever sense, it must be at least an abiding and conscious concern. On the best available primary evidence, it seems that to Freud himself, Jewishness was hardly a concern or a conundrum. Save *Moses and Monotheism* (an ingenious but Jewishly uninformed work), Freud wrote virtually nothing about Judaism and gave no evidence of an abiding interest in Jewish theological, ceremonial, historiographical, or nationalistic matters. His Jewishness was not central to either his personal psychic or professional psychoanalytic life. His Jewish allegiances and antipathies, if intensified during intermittent periods of anti-Semitism, varied little throughout his life. His pride in being Jewish, aversion to Jewish ritual, mild and sometimes repressed Zionism (see Loewenberg), and high concentration of Jewish friends and associates were typical of a self-respecting, early twentieth-century Central European Jew whose preponderant assimilation entailed a sometimes conscious, sometimes unconscious ambivalence about Jewishness, which was but a small segment of a larger movement of consciousness.

The hollowness of Freud's Jewishness is most readily limned if measured in relation to the Jewishness of a comparable transition figure. Israel Salanter, for example, explictly, consciously, and extensively tried to link the investigation of the unconscious, and of both the sources of and the solutions to conflicts between psychology and religion, in talmudic and midrashic norms of thought and action—a consciously cross-cultural approach profoundly alien to Freud, who, in essence, was separated from Judaism.

The following is an illustrative sampling of the literature on Freud as a Jew:

Ernst Simon, "Sigmund Freud, the Jew," *Leo Baeck Institute Yearbook*, vol. 2 (1957); David Bakan, *Sigmund Freud and the Jewish Mystical Tradition* (Boston: Beacon Press, 1975); John Murray Cuddihy, *The Ordeal of Civility: Freud, Marx, Levi-Strauss, and the Jewish Struggle with Modernity* (New York: Basic Books, 1974; rpt. Boston: Beacon Press, 1987); Philip Rieff, *Freud: The Mind of the Moralist* (New York, 1959); Peter Loewenberg, "A Hidden Zionist Theme in Freud's 'My Son, the Myops. . . .' Dream," *Journal of the History of Ideas*, vol.

XXXI, no. 1 (January–March, 1970), esp. 131; Marthe Robert, *From Oedipus to Moses: Freud's Jewish Identity*, trans. by Ralph Manheim (Garden City: Anchor Books, 1976); Sigmund Diamond, "Sigmund Freud, His Jewishness, and Scientific Method: The Seen and the Unseen as Evidence," *Journal of the History of Ideas*, vol. XLIII, no. 4 (October–December, 1982). For the debate on Freud's response to anti-Semitism, see Bakan, *Freud and Mystical Tradition*, 27–29, 151–55; Ronald W. Clark, *Freud: The Man and the Cause* (New York: Random House, 1980), 488–89, 492–93, 520–24 (cf. also 5–13, 27, 30, 32, 84, 95, 215, 242–43, 252, 297, 504); Dennis B. Klein, *Jewish Origins of the Psychoanalytic Movement* (New York: Praeger, 1981), 48–62, 70–73, 96; and Frank J. Sulloway, *Freud, Biologist of the Mind: Beyond the Psychoanalytic Legend* (New York: Basic Books, 1979), 6, 423 (cf. also 7, 137 in note). See my review of Klein, *Jewish Origins*, in *The American Historical Review*, vol. 89, no. 2 (April, 1984), 408–409.

5. Einstein's commentators measure his Zionism, adopted when he was about forty, as over against his active renunciation of his Jewish identity before then. Against that, Einstein's Zionism seems salient. Yet, to Einstein himself, his Zionism was relatively insignificant, even if placed against his official renunciation of affiliation with the Jewish community in 1895, and his strictly pragmatic reassumption of that identity, in 1910, when membership in a "church" was an Austro-Hungarian prerequisite for his becoming a professor at the German University in Prague.

Einstein's Zionism was essentially an embodiment of his universal social convictions—a pragmatic way of coping with "undignified assimilationist cravings" and discrimination against Jews, particularly East European Jewish students in Western Europe. Einstein's adoption of Zionism rarely altered his daily routine as a research scientist, did not change his attitude to Judaism in particular or religion in general, did not spur him to join the official Jewish community in Berlin (after he left the German University in Prague), did not deepen his understanding of Jewish sources, did not induce him to accept the Presidency of Israel, and did not restrain him from harshly criticizing the Zionist movement even as Hitler seized power. Einstein's role as a Zionist was more important to the Zionists than to Einstein, who, in essence, was separated from Judaism.

An illustrative sampling of the literature on Einstein as a Jew:

Phillip Frank, *Einstein: His Life and Times*, trans. by George Rosen (New York: Alfred A. Knopf, 1947), 4, 5, 7, 9, 15, 17, 23, 79, 151–53, 182–83, 284–87; Banish Hoffmann and Helen Dukas, *Albert Einstein: Creator and Rebel* (New York: Hart-Davis, 1973), 16, 18, 94–95, 143–44, 147, 237, 239; idem, eds., *Albert Einstein: The Human Side* (Princeton: Princeton University Press, 1979), 60–66; Yitzhak Navon, "On Einstein and the Presidency of Israel," Fritz Stern, "Einstein's Germany," and Uriel Tal, "Jewish and Universal Social Ethics in the Life and Thought of Albert Einstein," in Gerald Holton and Yehuda Elkana, eds., *Albert Einstein: Historical and Cultural Perspectives* (Princeton: Princeton University Press, 1982); Paul A. Schlipp, *Albert Einstein: Philosopher-Scientist* (La Salle, Illinois: Opent Court, 1969–1970), 3–5. Quote, A. Einstein, *About Zionism*:

Letters and Speeches, trans., intro. by Leon Simon (London: Soncino Press, 1930), 30 (see also 23–24, 28–29, 36–38, 42, 44–46, 52–53, 56–59).
  5. See Chapter Two.
  6. See Chapter Three.
  7. See Chapter Four.
  8. See Chapter Five.
  9. Dov Katz, "ʿAl ha-Rav ha-Meḥabber Ztz'l" [On Rabbi Lipovitz, Author of *Naḥalat Yosef*], in Joseph Z. Lipovitz, *Naḥalat Yosef* [The Heritage of Joseph], vol. 1 (Tel Aviv, 1966).
  10. See Chapter Six.
  11. Dov Katz, *Tenuʿat ha-Musar: Toldotehah, ʾIshehah, ve-Shitotehah*, vol. 1 (Jerusalem: Abraham Zioni, 5th rev. ed., 1969), trans. in 2 vols. by Leonard Oschry, *The Musar Movement: Its History, Leading Personalities and Doctrines*, vol. 1 (Tel Aviv: Orly, 1975), 184–85, 197–202, 205. See also Chapter Eight.
  12. Wolfson's wizardry with languages is evident throughout his writings. On Wolfson's English, see Chapter Eight, and Judah Goldin, "On the Sleuth of Slobodka and the Cortez of Kabbalah," *American Scholar* (Summer, 1980), 391–95, 398–400.
  13. On Hutner's Hebrew, see Chapters Four, Eight. He kept his knowledge of Italian, physics, and calculus secret, it becoming known through his private discussions with disciples who were pursuing these disciplines in undergraduate or graduate school, and through similarly obscure means.
  Aaron Lichtenstein, "Joseph Soloveitchik," in Simon Novek, ed., *Great Jewish Thinkers of the Twentieth Century*, vol. 3 (Washington: B'nai B'rith Department of Adult Jewish Education, 1963), 284–87; Emanuel Feldman, "Reflections of the Rav: Lessons in Jewish Thought," *Tradition*, vol. 19, no. 1 (Summer, 1981), 84–87, rpt. idem, *The Biblical Echo: Reflections on Bible, Jews, and Judaism* (Hoboken: Ktav Publishing House, 1986). See also Chapter Eight.
  15. Edward K. Kaplan, "Language and Reality in Abraham J. Heschel's Philosophy of Religion," *Journal of the American Academy of Religion*, vol. XLI, no. 1 (March, 1973); Abraham Joshua Heschel, *Between God and Man: An Interpretation of Judaism*, ed. Fritz Rothschild (New York: The Free Press, rev. ed., 1975). See also Chapter Eight.
  16. See Chapters Seven, Eight; Hillel Goldberg, *Israel Salanter: Text, Structure, Idea—The Ethics and Theology of an Early Psychologist of the Unconscious* (New York: Ktav Publishing House, 1982), Bibliography IV.
  17. Isaac Blazer, ed. and contributor, *ʾOr Yisrael* (Vilna, 1900), 30, 44, 124; Katz, *The Musar Movement*, vol. 1, 180–86; Ezriel Carlebach, "R. Yisrael mi-Salant" [Rabbi Israel of Salant], *Sefer ha-Demuyyot* (Tel Aviv, 1959); Hillel Goldberg, "An Early Psychologist of the Unconscious," *Journal of the History of Ideas*, vol. XLII, no. 2 (April–June, 1982).
  18. Leo W. Schwarz, *Wolfson of Harvard: Portrait of a Scholar* (Philadelphia: Jewish Publication Society of America, 1978), 11–21.
  19. See Chapter Four.

20. Lichtenstein, "Joseph Soloveitchik."
21. See Chapter Six.
22. Ibid.
23. See Chapter Four, and Isaac Hunter, *Paḥad Yitzhak:* ʾ*Iggerot u-Khetavim* [*Paḥad Yitzhak*: Letters and Writings] (Jerusalem and Brooklyn: Gur Aryeh Institute for Advanced Jewish Scholarship, 1981), esp. 251–332.
24. Goldin, "On the Sleuth of Slobodka," 402–04.
25. Blazer, ʾ*Or Yisrael*, 31, 124; 111.
26. Omission: Katz, "ʿAl ha-Rav."
27. Goldberg, *Israel Salanter*, 6–8, 12, 155–57; Katz, *The Musar Movement*, vol. 1, 318–32; Blazer, ʾ*Or Yisrael*, 63; Israel Salanter, ʾ*Iggerot u-Mikhtavim* [Letters and Epistles], ed. Shraga Wilman (Brooklyn, 1970), 61, 66.
28. Goldin, "On the Sleuth of Slobodka," 400.
29. Anonymous [Rabbi Hutner's family], "Zikhronot" [Memories], in Joseph Buxbaum, ed., *Sefer ha-Zikkaron le-Maran Baʿal ha-Paḥad Yitzhak Ztzʾl* (Jerusalem: Machon Yerushalayim, and Brooklyn: Gur Aryeh Institute for Advanced Jewish Scholarship, 1984).
30. Contrast, for example, the absence of kabbalistic motifs and terminology in early Soloveitchikian reflections on prayer ("Prayer as Dialogue," 1950; "The Lonely Man of Faith," 1965) with the kabbalistic motifs and sources in "Redemption, Prayer, Talmud Torah" (1973). Similar developments can be traced throughout earlier and later writings of Soloveitchik. Cited articles appear, respectively, in Abraham R. Besdin, ed., *Reflections of the Rav: Lessons in Jewish Thought Adapted from Lectures of Rabbi Joseph B. Soloveitchik* (Jerusalem: World Zionist Organization, 1979); *Tradition*, vol. 17, no. 2 (Spring, 1978).
31. Hillel Goldberg, "Abraham Joshua Heschel and His Times," *Midstream*, vol. XXVIII, no. 6 (June–July, 1982), 41–42; below, Chapter Six, IV.

2. RABBI ISRAEL SALANTER

1. Ezriel Carlebach, "R. Yisrael mi-Salant" [Rabbi Israel of Salant], *Sefer ha-Demuyyot* (Tel Aviv, 1959).
2. The preponderant scholarly opinion places Rabbi Israel's birthplace in Zagory, Lithuania (though Steinschneider says it was in Telshe), and his birthdate as Nov. 3, 1810 (though Steinschneider and Katz say it was earlier). The sources are gathered and analyzed by Menahem G. Glenn, *Israel Salanter: Religious-Ethical Thinker* (New York: Bloch Publishing Co., 1953), 168 notes 2, 3; and by Dov Katz, *Tenuʿat ha-Musar*, vol. 1 (Jerusalem: Abraham Zioni, 5th rev. ed., 1969), trans. in 2 vols. by Leonard Oschry, *The Musar Movement: Its History, Leading Personalities and Doctrines*, vol. 1 (Tel Aviv: Orly, 1975), 181 notes 3, 4. All references to the first volume of Katz's five-volume work will be to Oschry's translation, except when the translation is deficient, when the reference will be to the Hebrew volume. Only the first volume of Katz's work has been translated.

The most complete family tree of Rabbi Israel remains that in *The Jewish Encyclopedia* (New York and London: Funk and Wagnalls Co., 1904), vol. 8, p. 96.

3. *Hagahot ben Aryeh* [Aryeh's Son's Glosses], standard editions; Commentary on *Ha-ʿIttur* and Responsa of Alfasi, unpublished ms. (*The Musar Movement*, vol. 1, p. 182 note 5).

4. Eliezer Rivlin, *Ha-Zaddik R. Yosef Zundel mi-Salant ve-Rabbotav* [The Righteous Rabbi Joseph Zundel of Salant, and His Teachers] (Jerusalem: Gross Bros., 1926), 3, 4.

5. Ibid., 5, 6; Israel Salanter, Introduction, in Israel Salanter, ed., *Tevunah* [Understanding] (Memel: August Stobbe, 1861), 3 (rpt. of all issues of *Tevunah*, unedited, in *Sheloshah Sefarim* [New York: Grossman's Publishing House, 1965], and in seventeen other editions, emended and slightly edited, listed in Hillel Goldberg, *Israel Salanter: Text, Structure, Idea—The Ethics and Theology of an Early Psychologist of the Unconscious* [New York: Ktav Publishing House, 1982], 313–14); Letter of Naphtali Amsterdam, interpolated in Isaac Blazer, "Netivot ʾOr" [Paths of Light], in Isaac Blazer, ed., *ʾOr Yisrael* (Vilna, 1900), 123 col. 2.

6. Rivlin, *Ha-Zaddik R. Yosef Zundel*, 12–16; Letter of Naphtali Amsterdam, 122 col. 2–123 col. 1; Blazer, "Netivot ʾOr," 124 col. 2.

7. Isaac Blazer, "Shaʾarei ʾOr" [Gates of Light], *ʾOr Yisrael*, 31 col. 2; Letter of Naphtali Amsterdam, 124 col. 1.

8. "Ethical Literature," *Encyclopedia Judaica* (Jerusalem: Keter, 1971), vol. 6; Hillel Goldberg, "Israel Salanter and *ʾOrḥot Zaddikim*: Restructuring Musar Literature," *Tradition* vol. 23, no. 4 (Summer, 1988).

9. See note 7.

10. Marriage: Katz, *The Musar Movement*, 186; Blazer, "Netivot ʾOr," 109 col. 2, 113 col. 2. Study: *The Musar Movement*, 186-87; "Netivot ʾOr," 110 col. 2–111 col. 1. Contact with mentor: *Tevunah*, 3; Blazer, "Shaʾarei ʾOr," 31 col. 2, "Netivot ʾOr," 110; Letter of Naphtali Amsterdam, 124 col. 1.

11. Blazer, "Netivot ʾOr," 111.

12. Rivlin, *Ha-Zaddik R. Yosef Zundel*, 7–8.

13. Jehiel J. Weinberg, "Tenuʿat ha-Musar" and "Baʿalei ha-Musar" [The Musar Movement and Musar Personalities], *Seridei ʾEsh*, vol. 4 (Jerusalem: Mosad Harav Kook, 1969), trans. and slightly abridged by Leo Jung and Howard Levine, "The 'Mussar' Movement and Lithuanian Jewry," in Leo Jung, ed., *Men of the Spirit* (New York: Kymson Publishing Co., 1964), 228–30.

14. Prior to the invitation, Rabbi Israel considered other positions through which to reveal himself: *maggid*, preacher, and *mashgiaḥ*, counselor to yeshiva students. Preaching, however, seemed to Rabbi Israel not to enable permanent influence, and counseling seemed to be an insufficiently respected position from which to launch a movement of ethical and spiritual renewal. To Rabbi Israel, the offer of yeshiva dean overcame both drawbacks. See Katz, *The Musar Movement*, vol. 1, 191–96; and Immanuel Etkes, *R. Yisrael Salanter ve-Reshitah shel Tenuʿat ha-Musar* [Rabbi Israel Salanter and the Beginning of the Musar Move-

ment] (Jerusalem: The Magnes Press, 1982), 87–89. Rabbi Israel's letter of appointment is reprinted in H. N. M. Steinschneider, ʿIr Vilna [The City of Vilna] (Vilna, 1900), 128–29 note 3. Economic considerations—the apparent collapse of the small business of Rabbi Israel's wife, Esther Feige—contributed to the move to Vilna. See Blazer, "Netivot ʾOr," 109 col. 2.

15. Katz, *The Musar Movement*, 201–06; Weinberg, "The 'Mussar' Movement," 232–33. Although Rabbi Israel left the position of yeshiva dean not long (about a year) after assuming it, it established his reputation as a scholar. His institutional base in Vilna became an academy he established in a small Vilna suburb, Zaritche. On Rabbi Israel's departure from Rameiles yeshiva, see Etkes, *R. Yisrael Salanter*, 89–92.

16. On opposition to Rabbi Israel and the Musar movement, see Dov Katz, *Pulmus ha-Musar* [Polemics over the Musar Movement] (Jerusalem: Abraham Zioni, 1972); Etkes, *R. Yisrael Salanter*, 208–14. On the opposition of the Soloveitchik family, see Chapter Five. For Rabbi Israel's innovative justification of study by women (refined character and personality traits, unlike knowledge of Torah, are demanded equally from male and female by the Torah itself; hence, the study of everything related to piety and ethics is equally obligatory on male and female), see letter 3, paragraphs 1, 2, Blazer, ʾ*Or Yisrael*, 44. This position is adopted by subsequent Musar disciples. See Simhah Zisl Ziv, *Kitvei ha-Sava mi-Kelem: Pinkas ha-Kabbalot* [Writings of the Elder of Kelm: Diary of Resolutions] (Benei Berak: Sifsei Chachamim, 1984) 35 in note; Abraham Grodzinski, *Torat Avraham* [The Teachings of Abraham] (Benei Berak: Kolel Torat Avraham, 1978), 267 in note.

17. Eight untitled homilies in Shneur Zalman Hirshowitz, ed., ʾ*EvenYisrael* [Rock of Israel] (Warsaw, 1883), 5–38; five letters in Blazer, ʾ*Or Yisrael*, 41–47.

18. Goldberg, *Israel Salanter*, Part Five, I, 155–56, Part Five, IV, 193–96; idem, "Israel Salanter's Suspended Conversation," *Tradition*, vol. 22, no. 3 (Fall, 1986).

19. Harry Austryn Wolfson, *The Philosophy of Spinoza: Unfolding the Latent Processes of His Reasoning* (Cambridge, Massachusetts, and London: Harvard University Press, 1934; rpt., 2 vols. in one, n.d.), vol. 1, pp. 23, 22.

20. Goldberg, *Israel Salanter*, Part Two, II, 53.

21. Quotation is a composite of letter 1, paragraph 5, and letter 2, paragraph 2, Blazer, ʾ*Or Yisrael*, 42.

22. Letter 1, paragraph 2, Blazer, ʾ*Or Yisrael*, 42.

23. Letter 1, paragraph 3, ibid.; Goldberg, *Israel Salanter*, Part Two, II:1, 21–22.

24. Letter 4, paragraph 2, Blazer, ʾ*Or Yisrael*, 46.

25. Letter 3, paragraph 9, ibid., 45.

26. *Psalms* 51:10.

27. Goldberg, *Israel Salanter*, Part Two, II:2a, 28–36; cf. Part Four, IV:1, 132–35.

28. Baruch Epstein, *Mekor Barukh* [Baruch's Sources] (New York, 1954), vol.

2, 1012; *Ha-Shaḥar*, VI, 230a; Katz, *The Musar Movement*, vol. 1, 208–16; Isaac Lipkin [Rabbi Israel's son], "Mi-Derakhav u-Feʿulotav shel Maran ʾOr Yisrael mi-Salant] Zts'l" [On the Demeanor and Deeds of Our Master, the Light of Israel from Salant], *Tevunah* [same name as, different journal from, Rabbi Israel's *Tevunah*] (1941), no. 7 (Nisan), 74–76; Jacob Mark, *Gedoylim fun Unzere Tseyt* (New York, 1927), trans. by Samuel Haggai, *Bi-Meḥitzatam shel Gedolei ha-Dor* [In the Sanctum of the Generation's Greats] (Jerusalem: Gevil, 1958), 68; Samuel Rosenfeld, *R. Yisrael Salanter* (Warsaw, 1911), 17. Steinschneider, *ʿIr Vilna*, 51; Weinberg, "The 'Mussar' Movement," 234.

All sources, except Mark, agree that Rabbi Israel ruled that it was *obligatory* to eat on Yom Kippur. All sources, without exception, agree minimally that Rabbi Israel ruled that it was *permissible* to eat, and all sources, with the sole exception of Lipkin, agree that Rabbi Israel's ruling provoked opposition among the rabbis. All sources, except Mark and Lipkin, say that Rabbi Israel himself ate; Mark says he did not and Lipkin does not say one way or the other. In spreading Rabbi Israel's name, the incident triggered the imagination of Hebrew writer David Frischman, whose short story dramatized the incident. "Sheloshah she-ʾAkhlu" [Three Who Ate], *Kol Kitvei David Frishman*, vol. 1 (Warsaw and New York, 1929).

29. Levi Obschinski, *Toledot ha-Yehudim be-Kurland* [History of the Jews in Courland] (Vilna, 1912), 61. On Uvarov, see Cynthia H. Whittaker, *The Origins of Modern Russian Education: An Intellectual Biography of Count Sergei Uvarov* (Dekalb: Northern Illinois University Press, 1984).

30. On Rabbi Israel's objections to the seminary's curriculum and purposes, see Emil Benjamin, *R. Jsrael Lipkin Salant: Sein Leben und Werken* (Berlin, 1899), 10; Jacob Lipschitz, *Zikhron Yaakov* [Jacob's Memoirs], vol. 3 (Kovno, 1930), 132, 177; Obschinski, ibid., 61–62. On the history of the seminary, see Y. Slutsky, "Bet ha-Midrash le-Rabbanim be-Vilna" [The Rabbinical Seminary in Vilna], *He-ʿAvar*, vol. 7 (1960). Rabbi Israel's objections to the curriculum (Benjamin, Lipschitz), while real, were overshadowed by an ultimate fear (Obschinski), namely, that the seminary was intended to foster apostasy. Some students did convert, and teachers who were apostates were maintained. In 1873, the seminary was closed. See Katz, *The Musar Movement*, 225–26.

Rabbi Israel must have felt tainted by his association with the seminary since he left Vilna days after the offer to head it. See Obchinski, ibid., 61–62.

31. The destructive inclination in the maskilic agenda is summarized by David Roskies, *Against the Apocalypse: Responses to Catastrophe in Modern Jewish Culture* (Cambridge, Massachusetts, and London: Harvard University Press, 1984), 57:

> The levity of this literary face-off between Mendl Lefin and Levi Yitskhok should not obscure the radical nature of the maskilic agenda: the maskilim accepted non-Jewish thought and mores as at least equal in authority to the teachings and practices of Jewish tradition, and they threw their weight behind the fundamental reform of Jewish life in line with

Western ideas of progress. When tsarist rule was imposed upon the majority of eastern European Jews following the dismemberment of Poland at the end of the eighteenth century, the stakes in this contest rose significantly. The draft decree of 1827, dreaded for so long, was the first great test of collective will, and as the Jewish polity reeled under the blows, the maskilim, for the most part, stood by and applauded.

In and of itself, the draft would have met with resistance on the part of a people who had no stake in Russian society, let alone in its military enterprise. Because minors were drafted into Cantonist battalions (special military training units) followed by a full, twenty-five-year term of service when they reached majority, the period 1827–1855 was the most divisive in the history of Russian Jewry in the nineteenth century, reaching a crescendo of anarchy in the last three years of Tsar Nicholas' rule. Nicholas, a great believer in the military as an agency of social control, in the case of the Jews was additionally motivated by missionary zeal. Of the estimated 70,000 Jews conscripted during this period, about 50,000 were minors, many under twelve years of age when they were caught, and at least half of this latter group were forcibly baptized.

Roskies is based on Michael Stanislawski, *Tsar Nicholas I and the Jews: The Transformation of Jewish Society in Russia 1825–1855* (Philadelphia: Jewish Publication Society of America, 1983), chapters 1, 5.

32. Mark, *Be-Meḥitzatam shel Gedolei ha-Dor*, 73.

33. On Rabbi Israel in Kovno, see Katz, *The Musar Movement*, 228–45; Etkes, *R. Yisrael Salanter*, 191–214.

34. Katz, *The Musar Movement*, 213.

35. Weinberg, "The 'Mussar' Movement," 234.

36. Letter 3, paragraph 2, p. 44, letter 2, paragraph 8, p. 42, letter 4, paragraph 1, p. 45, Blazer, *ʾOr Yisrael*; homily 6, paragraph 5, p. 26, homily 2, paragraph 6, p. 8, Hirshowitz, *ʾEven Yisrael*.

37. Letter 3, paragraph 9, p. 45, letter 2, paragraph 3, p. 43, letter 3, paragraph 5, p. 44, letter 5, paragraph 4, p. 47, letter 1, paragraph 3, p. 42, letter 4, paragraph 2, p. 46, Blazer, *ʾOr Yisrael*.

38. Esp. "Maʾamar be-ʿInyan Ḥizzuk Lomedei Torateinu ha-Kedoshah" [Statement on Encouraging Students of Our Holy Torah], in *ʿEtz Peri*, ed. anonymous [Nathan Zvi Finkel; Katz, *Tenuʿat ha-Musar* (The Musar Movement), vol. 3 (Tel Aviv: Abraham Zioni, 1967), 26] (Vilna, 1881); Goldberg, *Israel Salanter*, Part Four, II, Part Five, II.

39. Weinberg, "The 'Mussar' Movement," 249.

40. On Isaac Blazer, see Hillel Goldberg, *The Fire Within: The Living Heritage of the Musar Movement* (New York: Mesorah Publications, 1987), 85–93; Katz, *Tenuʿat ha-Musar* [The Musar Movement], vol. 2 (Tel Aviv: Abraham Zioni, 1954), 220–73; Weinberg, ibid., 247–53; Hayyim Ephraim Zaitchik, *Ha-Meʾorot ha-Gedolim* (Jerusalem: fourth rev. ed., 1969), retold from the Hebrew by Ester van Handel, *Sparks of Musar* (Jerusalem: Feldheim Publishers, 1985), 85–99. Blazer's

ethical thought: "Kokhevei ᵓOr" [Stars of Light], in Blazer, ᵓOr Yisrael, 125–84; Kokhevei ᵓOr (Jerusalem, 1974). Confrontation with Rabbi Soloveitchik: Weinberg, ibid., 251–52; Joseph B. Soloveitchik, " ᵓIsh ha-Halakhah," Talpiot, vols. 3, 4 (1944), trans. by Lawrence Kaplan, Halakhic Man (Philadelphia: Jewish Publication Society of America, 1983), 74–76.

41. On Naphtali Amsterdam, see Goldberg, The Fire Within, 93–100; Katz, Tenuʿat ha-Musar, vol. 2, 274–302; Weinberg, "The 'Mussar' Movement," 253–71; Handel, Sparks of Musar, 101–110. Amsterdam's ethical thought: Letters in Kokhevi ᵓOr, ibid., 208–48; "Yesod ha-Teshuvah" [Foundation of Repentance], vol. 1, "Zavaᵓah" [Last Will and Testament], vol. 2, ᵓOr ha-Musar (Poland: Central Student Organization of Yeshivot Novorodock; rpt. Benei Berak: Ḥokhmah u-Musar, 1966); "Ha-Sekhel veha-Ḥush" [The Intellect and the Senses], vol. 1, "Ḥeshbon ha-Nefesh" [Accounting of the Soul], vol. 2, ᵓOr ha-Musar (Ostrov: Student Organization of Yeshivat Bet Yosef; rpt. Benei Berak: Ḥokhmah u-Musar, 1966).

42. On Simhah Zisl Ziv, see Goldberg, The Fire Within, 63–78; Katz, Tenuʾat ha-Musar, vol. 2, 26–219; Handel, Sparks of Musar, 61–84; Ziv's ethical thought: Ḥokhmah u-Musar [Wisdom and Musar], vol. 1 (New York, 1957), vol. 2 (New York, 1964); ᵓOr Rashaz [The Light of Rabbi Simhah Zisl] 5 vols. (Jerusalem, 1960–1965; Kitvei ha-Sava mi-Kelem: Pinkas ha-Kabbalot.

43. On Joseph Jozel Hurvitz, see Goldberg, The Fire Within, 129–153; Katz, Tenuʿat ha-Musar [The Musar Movement], vol. 4 (Jerusalem: Abraham Zioni, 1957), 179–351; Handel, Sparks of Musar, 111–50; Hillel Goldberg, Encyclopedia Judaica Yearbook Supplement (Jerusalem: Keter Publishing House, 1982), 317–18. Hurvitz's ethical thought: Madregat ha-ᵓAdam [The Stature of Man] (New York: The Foundation for the Advancement of Torah and Ethics of the Central Yeshiva "Beth Joseph," 1947; rpt., emended by Moshe Yemini [Jerusalem, 1970]), last chapter trans. by Shraga Silverstein, To Turn the Many to Righteousness (Jerusalem and New York: Feldheim Publishers, 1970). A biographical novel of Hurvitz is David Zaritsky Gesher Zar [Narrow Bridge], 2 vols. (Benei Berak: Netzah, 1968). Other novels and short stories on Hurvitz and his Novorodock school of Musar are Samuel Ben Artzi, Shivti [I Sit Eternally in the Study of Torah] (Jerusalem: Kiryat Sepher, 1967); Ben Zion Gershuni, Bi-Metzudah ha-Perusah [In the Citadel of a Slice of Bread] (Jerusalem: Mosad Harav Kook, 1962); Chaim Grade, Tsemakh Atlas, 2 vols. (New York, 1967), trans. by Curt Leviant, The Yeshiva, vol. 1, 1976, vol. 2, 1977 (Indianapolis and New York: The Bobbs-Merrill Co.); "Mein Krig mit Hersh Rasseyner," Yiddisher Kemfer, vol. 32, no. 923 (Erev Rosh Hashanah, 5712 [1951]), trans. and abridged, "My Quarrel with Hersh Rasseyner," in Irving Howe and Eliezer Greenberg, eds., A Treasury of Yiddish Stories (New York: Fawcett, 1968); Musernikes (poems) [Musarniks] (Vilna, 1939; rpt., 1938 recension, Grade, Dorot [New York, 1945]).

44. Katz, The Musar Movement, 237–40; Etkes, R. Yisrael Salanter, 196–208.

45. On Shraga and Golda Frank, see Katz, Tenuʿat ha-Musar, vol. 1, p. 317, vol. 3, pp. 37–40; Yedael Meltzer, Be-Derekh ʿEtz Ḥayyim [In the Way of the

Tree of Life] (Jerusalem: Arzei ha-Ḥen, 1986), vol. 1, pp. 59-81; Chaim Shapiro, "Torah Pioneers," *Jewish Observer*, vol. X, no. 2 (June, 1974).

46. Stanislawski, *Tsar Nicholas I and the Jews*, chapter 4.
47. Mark, *Bi-Meḥitzatam shel Gedolei ha-Dor*, 78.
48. "The rapid advance of Jewish social and cultural integration in early nineteenth-century Germany was only sporadically accompanied by efforts at theoretical and practical religious reform. The gap between a broadened professional spectrum and a heightened sense of European cultural identity on the one hand and a basically unchanged Judaism on the other was perceived as onerous, especially by those who were personally the most alienated from traditional Judaism but still desired to remain within the Jewish community. Their greater penetration into gentile circles made them especially self-conscious regarding the non-Jewish perception of Judaism, and hence also of themselves as associated with it. These feelings were not limited to embarrassment about the lack of decorum in Jewish worship services. They extended to the fundamentals of the faith and especially to the Talmud as the underlying authority for traditional Judaism."

One line extending from this burden led to radical Reform or apostasy. Another line, thought Rabbi Israel, could lead to reacceptance of faith and rejection of thirst for acceptance by Gentiles. Aspects of Rabbi Israel's program were overtly sensitive to this thirst; see below. Quotation: Michael A. Meyer, "Alienated Intellectuals in the Camp of Religious Reform: The Frankfurt Reformfreunde, 1842-1845," *AJS* [Association for Jewish Studies] *Review*, vol. 6 (1981), 66.

49. Of his letters from this period (1858-1883) that bear a date and location, no two from the same city bear a date over any two consecutive years. See Shraga Wilman, ed., *'Iggerot u-Mikhtavim* [Letters and Epistles] (Brooklyn, 1970). An exception to his travels was one (and perhaps a second) two-year period; see below.
50. Wilman, ibid.
51. Benjamin, *R. Jsrael Lipkin Salant*.
52. Letter of Rabbi Israel's chief disciple, Simḥah Zisl Ziv, cited in Katz, *Tenu'at ha-Musar*, vol. 1, p. 331:

> Let none of those who knew Reb Yisrael in his last years think that they really knew him. . . . The truth is that even in his younger years Reb Yisrael's conception of holiness included extreme self-concealment. My knowledge on this point is completely certain. Even when Reb Yisrael was active in public matters he never revealed more than that which the occasion required, whether in Torah or piety. However . . . whoever knew Reb Yisrael at the end of his days knew him not at all, regardless of what he might imagine. We who knew Reb Yisrael from earlier years, when he was publicly active, knew that we could know him . . . only through an exacting process of clarification. Similarly, we would hear a statement from him, interpret it in our own way, and then, several years later, it became known to us from him that a different point inhered in the statement—a point that would occur to virtually no one. This happened countless times. . . . Even

with my scanty knowledge of Reb Yisrael, several long pages would not suffice to recount a few of his wondrous ways. My intention here is simply to inform those who knew him at the end of his days that they can easily deceive themselves into believing that they knew him, and thus fall into the category of those who don't know that they don't know.

53. Benjamin, R. *Jsrael Lipkin Salant*, 27–29; Naphtali Ehrmann, in *Israelit*, no. 21–22 (1883); Mark, *Bi-Meḥitzatam shel Gedolei ha-Dor*, 82–84. Cf. Tuvia Preschel, "Rabbi Yisrael Salanter ve-Tirgum ha-Shas le-Sefat ʾEver" [Rabbi Israel Salanter and the Translation of the Talmud to Hebrew], *Ha-Doʾar*, no. 53 (1974). See also Katz, *The Musar Movement*, 272–74.

54. On Rabbi Israel in Paris, see: Benjamin, ibid., 19; Blazer, "Netivot ʾOr," 122; Katz, *The Musar Movement*, 319-26; Mark, *Bi-Meḥitzatam shel Gedolei ha-Dor;* 83–84; Wilman, ʾ*Iggerot u-Mikhtavim*, letter 49, p. 63, letter 50a, p. 64, letter 53, p. 66; *Ha-Maggid* (1882), 276.

55. Emissaries and brief trips: Katz, *The Musar Movement*, 254, 259, 260. Two year stay in Vilna, around 1870: Katz, ibid., 261.

56. *Tevunah*, 96 col. 1, 4 col. 1; cf. Goldberg, *Israel Salanter*, 127–28.

57. "Maʾamar," ʾ*Etz Peri*, paragraph 20, pp. 22–24, paragraph 20b, p. 25, paragraph 21, p. 26 col. 2; cf. Wilman, ʾ*Iggerot u-Mikhtavim*, letter 45 (1879), p. 60.

58. Mark, *Bi-Meḥitzatam shel Gedolei ha-Dor*, 81, writes that he knew a brother of Rabbi Israel who suffered the same symptoms; and Sarah Elka Horowitz, Rabbi Israel's daughter-in-law, writes that Rabbi Israel's son, Aryeh Leib Horowitz, suffered similarly. See Aryeh Leib Horowitz, *Ḥayyei Aryeh* [The Life of Aryeh] (Vilna, 1907), 3.

59. Katz, *The Musar Movement*, 312–15; Mark, *Bi-Meḥitzatam*, 89–90; *Ha-Maggid* (1865), nos. 7, 11; *Ha-Shaḥar*, vol. 6, p. 538; *He-ʾAsif* (1865), 259.

60. Katz, *The Musar Movement*, 262.

61. Blazer, "Netivot ʾOr," 115, 119, 120; Epstein, *Mekor Barukh*, vol. 4, p. 1800; Katz, ibid., 151–52, 174–75, 183–85; Abraham Isaac Kuk, "Kedosh Yisrael" [Holiness of Israel], *Shaʾarei Zion*, vol. 13, nos. 3–5 (1933), 16; Mark, *Bi-Meḥitzatam shel Gedolei ha-Dor*, 79.

62. Harry Austryn Wolfson, *The Philosophy of the Kalam* (Cambridge, Massachusetts, and London: Harvard University Press, 1976), 70–71.

63. Wilman, ʾ*Iggerot u-Mikhtavim*, letter 62 (1883), 70. Perhaps the term was passed to Agudath Israel through Dr. Solomon Ehrmann, a world Agudah leader who was the son of Rabbi Dr. Naphtali Ehrmann, a confidant of Rabbi Israel in Germany. See Katz, *The Musar Movement*, 319–20 note 5.

64. Goldberg, *Israel Salanter*, Part Four, III.

65. Katz, *The Musar Movement*, 262–72; idem, *Tenuʾat ha-Musar*, vol. 2, pp. 228–229; Shaul Stampfer, *Shalosh Yeshivot Litaʾiot be-Meʾah ha-19* [Three Lithuanian Yeshivot in the Nineteenth Century] (The Hebrew University of Jersualem: Ph.D. dissertation, 1981), 139–52.

66. Goldberg, *Israel Salanter*, 22, 48–49, 108–12, 138–39.

67. Hirshowitz, ʾ*Even Yisrael*, homily 7, p. 32 (cf. also homily 4, pp. 16, 21), cited in Goldberg, ibid., 244–45. See also Goldberg, ibid., Part Two, III, and Part Five, III.
68. This phenomenon has recently begun to be studied. See Janet O'Dea Aviad, *Return to Judaism: Religious Renewal in Israel* (Chicago and London: The University of Chicago Press, 1983).
69. Katz, *Tenuʿat ha-Musar*, vol. 1, pp. 373–74. This and the following four stories are slightly abridged.
70. Zaitchik, *Ha-Meʾorot ha-Gedolim*, 82–83.
71. Weinberg, "The 'Mussar' Movement," 251.
72. Ibid., 258.
73. Katz, *The Musar Movement*, 252; Abraham Joshua Heschel, *The Earth is the Lord's: The Inner World of the Jew in East Europe* (New York: Harper Torchbooks, 1966), 21.

3. Professor Harry Austryn Wolfson

1. H. A. Wolfson, "Escaping Judaism," *Menorah Journal*, vol. 7, no. 3 (August, 1921), 167. This article was published in two parts. The present citation is from the second part, hereafter "Escaping Judaism, II."
2. Ibid.
3. Letter to Isadore Singer, on twenty-fifth anniversary of *Jewish Encyclopedia*; cited in Leo W. Schwarz, *Wolfson of Harvard: Portrait of a Scholar* (Philadelphia: Jewish Publication Society of America, 1978), 84.
4. Schwarz, ibid., 6.
5. Wolfson: Ostrin, Grodno, Slonim, Bialystock, Kovno, Slobodka, Vilna, and Ossining, New York City, and Scranton; Schwarz, ibid., 6, 11–18. Salanter: see Chapter Two.
6. Wolfson: Schwarz, ibid.: study, 23–40; analysis of community, see below; socializing, 74–79, 83; Europe, 41–58; Army, 63–66. Salanter: see Chapter Two.
7. "After the appearance of *Crescas* in 1929 his life appears to have passed into a more eremitical phase. He had thought of marriage, and his friends had urged it on him. . . . But his energies were absorbed and expended in his work. The longing for family life became more and more deeply buried, and by force of circumstance and character he made the hard adjustment to being a bachelor. His study became his home, his books and students his children. . . . Far from being a hermit, he was nonetheless a solitary man, and his books are the offspring of his solitude. Endowed with tremendous energy and rich talents, he had a strain of self-absorption." Schwarz, ibid., 83, 232.
8. Lewis S. Feuer, "Recollections of Harry Austryn Wolfson," *American Jewish Archives*, vol. XXVIII, no. 1 (April, 1976), 40–41:

> Wolfson never married. From 1912 to 1925, he said, he could not afford to be married. There was one woman whom he vaguely courted, but he

said "we used to fight all the time," and he did not regret it that their association ended. Also he did not like the idea, he said, of having to come home at a definite time. There was a librarian, a Gentile woman, who was extremely helpful to Wolfson while he was writing his *Philosophy of Spinoza*, and he remarked to me that he was thinking of inviting her out. I doubt whether he ever did. He was once perturbed when an old friend of his at Salem divorced his wife and then, finally, shrugged his shoulders. I could not help feeling that he had a basic mistrust of all human relationships. "Friends," he used to say, "like you so long as you are good company." Somewhere and sometime he had felt so rejected that he hesitated ever to commit his feelings fully.

Pp. 37–38:

One political incident . . . survives in my memory with the poignancy of a recalled divergence of friends. In the spring of 1934 the small group at Harvard of communist, socialist, and fellow-traveler students decided to join with the national student organizations in calling the first one-hour "peace strike." On the appointed day near the hour, several of us who were to speak gathered outside the Robbins Library at Emerson Hall. Wolfson happened to be there; he knew what was pending from the large crowd which was gathering in front of the Widener Library where the meeting was to take place. Wolfson approached me in full view and hearing of my fellow-radicals. He pleaded with me not to be one of the speakers. "You are making a mistake. This will do no good. You will be hurting yourself for no purpose. There are other ways to do things. Please don't do it. I tell you, I know, you are wrong." It cast a certain pall over the radical circle—this voice, earnest, and speaking with its experience so different from ours . . . I refused to follow his advice, and Wolfson, head bent to the side, as if he was always half-averting his glance from the world, or half-hiding, or looking upon reality with an angular perspective peculiar to his people of outsiders, left sadly. He seemed always to recognize that limit where determinist forces exceeded the power of the individual will.

9. Morton Smith, presentation of a citation to Wolfson by the Tarbut Foundation, New York, 1962 (cited in Schwarz, *Wolfson of Harvard*, 122): "No other man I have known has been so much concerned by purely intellectual problems, so determined to discover the solutions, so excited by the hunt and so delighted by the capture."

10. Feuer, "Recollections," 41–42; Schwarz, ibid., 219.

11. In understanding the phenomenology of the Musar movement, literary and anthropological analysis must combine, for the image of the Musar personality and of the spirituality peculiar to the Musar movement that one would predict or imagine on the basis of literary remains are often at odds with the results of direct observation and analysis. Accordingly, doctrine, memoir, and analysis are all necessary to understand the Slobodka school.

The tone and substance of Slobodka doctrine are best preserved in Nathan

Zvi Finkel, *Siḥot ha-Sava mi-Slobodka* [Intimate Addresses of the Elder of Slobodka], ed. Zvi Kaplan (Tel Aviv: Abraham Zioni, 1955); Joseph Zev Lipovitz, ed., "Naḥpesah Derakheinu" [Let Us Search Our Ways], in idem, *Naḥalat Yosef ʾal ha-Torah*, vol. 2 (Tel Aviv, 1972); Nathan Zvi Finkel, *ʾOr ha-Zafun* [The Hidden Light], ed. Dov Katz, vol. 1 (1958; rpt. Jerusalem: E. Hoffman and Z. Weinrib, 1978), 227–84. See also Finkel, *ʾOr ha-Zafun*, ed. Katz, vol. 2 (Jerusalem: Committee for Publication of the Addresses of the Elder of Slobodka, 1968), vol. 3 (2nd ed. Jerusalem: E. Hoffman and Z. Weinrib, 1978).

Memoir: Ezriel Carlebach, "Musar. Notizen zur Geschichte einer Bewegung," *Jarbuch der Judisch-Literarischen Gesellschaft* (Frankfurt a. M., 1931–32); M. Gerz [Gershon Movshovich], *Musarnikes: Tipn un Geshtaltn* [Musarniks: Types and Images] (Riga, 1936), chapters 1, 2, trans. Lucy Dawidowicz, "The Old Man of Slobodka," in idem, ed. and Introduction, *The Golden Tradition: Jewish Life and Thought in Eastern Europe* (New York, Chicago, San Francisco: Holt, Rinehart, and Winston, 1967); Hillel Goldberg [memoirs of Slobodka graduate Jacob Moses Lesin], "From Berkeley to Jerusalem," *Midstream*, vol. XXVIII, no. 6 (June-July, 1982), rpt. *Jewish Action*, vol. 46, no. 2 (Spring, 1986), and "Slobodka Musar," in idem, *The Fire Within: The Living Heritage of the Musar Movement* (New York: Mesorah Publications, 1987); Dov Katz, *Tenuʿat ha-Musar* [The Musar Movement], vol. 3 (Tel Aviv: Abraham Zioni, rev. ed., 1967), 208–316; see also below, note 15.

Analysis: Katz, *Tenuʿat ha-Musar*, 17-207; Shaul Stampfer, *Shalosh Yeshivot Litaʾiot be-Meʾah ha-19* [Three Lithuanian Yeshivot in the Nineteenth Century] (The Hebrew University of Jerusalem: Ph.D. dissertation, 1981); Goldberg, "Slobodka Musar."

12. Katz, *Tenuʿat ha-Musar*, 43–54; idem, *Pulmus ha-Musar* [Polemics over the Musar Movement] (Jerusalem: Abraham Zioni, 1972), chapter 7. The relationship between Slobodka and Knesset Bet Yitzhak and other facts about the two yeshivot are garbled by Schwarz, *Wolfson of Harvard*, 12–13.

13. Interview with H. A. Wolfson, August, 1972 (Boston).

14. Schwarz, *Wolfson of Harvard*, 14.

15. Hillel Goldberg, "The Mute Radiance of Eliyahu Sobel," *Intermountain Jewish News*, vol. 70, no. 25 (June 24, 1983), rpt. *Jewish Tradition*, vol. 32, no. 4 (April, 1987).

16. Schwarz, *Wolfson of Harvard*, 14–18; Feuer, "Recollections," 26.

17. Schwarz, *Wolfson of Harvard*, 18; Feuer, "Recollections," 26: "He walked through the halls of the Scranton High School always courteous, with a reflective smile, albeit elusive to fellow students and teachers alike. . . ."

18. Schwarz, *Wolfson of Harvard*, 20–21; Feuer, "Recollections," 26–27.

19. H. A. Wolfson, "Hebrew Studies at Harvard," *Ha-Yom* (Elul 4, 5669 [September, 1909]); "The Menorah Society at Harvard," *Ha-Yom* (Elul 24, 5669 [September, 1909]); "The American Trend in Hebrew Literature," *Ha-Yom* (Av 22, 5669 [August, 1909]); Review of *Encyclopaedia Britannica*, *Ha-Deror*, vol. 1, no. 2 (September 8, 1911); "Before the Tent of Temurah," *Ha-Deror*, vol. 1,

no. 6 (October 6, 1911). Earlier, Wolfson had published one Hebrew poem, "Ha-Dim'a" [The Tear] in *Ha-Le'om* (Sept. 4, 1908), three pieces in *High School Impressions*, a journal published by Scranton's high schools; and articles and poems in a mimeographed Hebrew journal, *Ha-Zeman*, which Wolfson edited in Slobodka (Schwarz, *Wolfson of Harvard*, 13, 21).

20. Bluebook, on Lessing's *Laocoön*, 1910–1911, written for George Santayana, Houghton Library archives, Harvard University; cited in Schwarz, *Wolfson of Harvard*, 35.

21. Judah Goldin, "On the Sleuth of Slobodka and the Cortez of Kabbalah," *American Scholar* (Summer, 1980), 398.

22. Wolfson, "Escaping Judaism, II," 157.

23. Schwarz, *Wolfson of Harvard*, 25, 27, 33–39.

24. Wolfson's Zionist activity usually expressed itself in Hebrew writing. In Slobodka he had joined a Zionist society, and edited and contributed to a mimeographed Hebrew journal (Schwarz, ibid., 13). In Scranton he joined a Zionist club and published his first Hebrew poem (Schwarz, 20–21). At Harvard he joined a Hebrew literary club (1908), attended a Zionist meeting at which he began a relationship with Reubin Brainin, Hebrew editor and biographer (1909), delivered a paper as a sophomore to a conference of faculty and graduate students on "A Comparative Study of the Structure of Biblical and Modern Hebrew" (1909), and was elected secretary of the Boston delegation to the 11th Zionist Congress in Vienna, while he was on his Sheldon Traveling Scholarship (1913), and where he renewed acquaintance with Brainin (Schwarz, 24, 28, 45). He associated with the founders of the Intercollegiate Menorah Association (Schwarz, 25–27), published a Hebrew article on the Association (above, note 19), played a leading role at its dinners, and wrote for its journal (see below).

25. See Warren Zev Harvey's analysis of the essay, "Hebraism and Western Philosophy in H. A. Wolfson's Theory of History," *Immanuel*, no. 14 (Fall, 1982), 78–81. Wolfson's essay is "Maimonides and Halevi: A Study in Typical Jewish Attitudes towards Greek Philosophy in the Middle Ages," *Jewish Quarterly Review* n.s., vol. 2, no. 3 (1912); rpt. H.A. Wolfson, *Studies in the History of Philosophy and Religion*, eds. Isadore Twersky and George H. Williams, vol. 2 (Cambridge, Massachusetts, and London: Harvard University Press, 1977). The essay was awarded the Harvard Menorah Society's $100 prize "for the best essay by an undergraduate on a subject connected with the work and achievements of the Jewish people." The contest was judged by a faculty committee appointed by Harvard President Charles Elliot; the grant was provided by Jacob H. Schiff. See Schwarz, *Wolfson of Harvard*, 37.

26. Caption to photo-inset of Wolfson in his "Jewish Students in European Universities," *Menorah Journal*, vol. 1, no. 1 (January, 1915), 26. This article was published in two parts. The present information is from the first part, hereafter "Jewish Students, I."

27. George Santayana, marginal notes to Wolfson essay in bluebook (above, note 20), cited in Schwarz, *Wolfson of Harvard*, 36. There was a strain of similarity between Wolfson and Santayana, all of whose courses Wolfson took. Something

akin to what Santayana saw in Wolfson, Walter Lippmann saw in Santayana. Santayana's critique applied, perhaps, as much to himself as to his student; perhaps the two were attracted to each other not just intellectually but temperamentally.

Lippmann, who entered Harvard in 1906, two years before Wolfson, described Santayana in those years: "You feel at times that his ability to see the world steady and whole is a kind of tragic barrier between him and the common hopes of ordinary men. It's as if he saw all forest and no trees. . . . There is something of the pathetic loneliness of the spectator about him. You wish he would jump on the stage and take part in the show. Then you realize that he wouldn't be the author of *The Life of Reason* if he did. For it is a fact that a man can't see the play and be in it too."

Lippmann's biographer, Ronald Steel, said that this description, "perceptive in its judgment," was as "revealing of the student [Lippmann] as of the teacher [Santayana]." What Santayana saw in Wolfson, Lippmann saw in Santayana, and what Lippmann saw in Santayana, Steel sees in Lippmann. Lippmann, cited by Ronald Steel, *Walter Lippmann and the American Century* (Boston: Little, Brown, 1980), 21–22; Steel, 21. On Santayana, see John McCormick, *George Santayana: A Biography* (New York: Knopf, 1987).

28. Wolfson, "Escaping Judaism, II," 160.

29. Stearns described Wolfson in his autobiographical work, *The Street I Know* (New York: Lee Furman, Inc., 1935), 79. Feuer, "Recollections," 28:

> Stearns moved to Greenwich Village to undertake a literary career, and later years saw him enveloped in personal tragedy and decline. Wolfson used to visit Stearns at his McDougall Street apartment, and they would sit up to the early hours of the morning while Stearns narrated all the details of his love affairs. Wolfson recalled how one night several years later Stearns told him despairingly of his wife's death. Wolfson was an entranced listener to the stories of a world of which he was never a part. Always he retained something of the spectator's stance, valuing the confidences of his friends, but somehow ever mindful of the evanescence of human relations. I have never heard anyone talk with such warmth in so many instances of how "we were great friends," but no one I have ever known kept the basic essence of himself so aloof from the strains of such relations.

30. Feuer, "Recollections," 30. See also Schwarz, *Wolfson of Harvard*, 39–40.

31. "Jewish Students, I," 27, 28, 32.

32. H. A. Wolfson, "Jewish Students in European Universities," *Menorah Journal*, vol. 1, no. 2 (April, 1915), 107–108.

33. Ibid., 110.

34. H. A. Wolfson, "Pomegranates," *Menorah Journal*, vol. 4, no. 1 (February, 1918) and vol. 4, no. 3 (June, 1918). All quotations are from vol. 4, no. 1.

The editors at *Menorah Journal* wished to distance themselves from this acidulous piece. Against Wolfson's wishes, they insisted on prefacing it with a disclaimer and a motto. The disclaimer read:

Editors' Note.—The boldness of some of the *ex cathedra* views expressed by our anonymous contributor in the following paragraphs makes it desirable to remind our readers again that THE MENORAH JOURNAL is an open forum (or arena, if you choose) for the expression of opinions to which neither THE JOURNAL nor the Intercollegiate Menorah Association is in any way committed.

The motto, stretched in italic below the title and above the disclaimer, read:
"*Pomegranates are eaten raw, their acid juice being most refreshing.*"
—*Jewish Encycl.*, X, 122.

The editors insisted on retaining the motto's nonliteral translation, with its reference to acid, while Wolfson unsuccessfully insisted on the literal translation, "Pomegranates, likewise, set the teeth on edge." The editors welcomed Wolfson's resort to a pseudonym (though they revealed the author's name three years later; vol. 7, no. 2, p. 71). See Schwarz, *Wolfson of Harvard*, 60–61.

Nowhere is Schwarz's pious homage to Wolfson more in evidence than regarding "Pomegranates," about which Schwarz writes, "[Wolfson] never gores down his adversaries," then quotes the two most innocent of the article's thirteen sections, and finally refers to the article as "acidulous," leaving the reader of *Wolfson of Harvard* to wonder why.

35. "Pomegranates," 16.
36. Ibid., 20.
37. Feuer, "Recollections," 28: "When Wolfson came to Harvard, Kallen was a fledgling Ph.D. who was giving courses as a lecturer in philosophy, and meeting sections as well. Kallen took this immigrant boy under his protective wing: he corrected Wolfson's English grammar, and removed the Yiddishisms from his essays. He appreciated the poems which Wolfson wrote in Hebrew, poems filled with a nationalistic fervor, and translated several of them into English." One of Kallen's translations was published as "The Arch of Titus," *Menorah Journal*, vol. 1, no. 4 (October, 1915), front piece, 201 ("Done into English by H. M. K. from the Hebrew of H. A. W. Original and translation read at a dinner of the Harvard Menorah Society"). See also Schwarz, *Wolfson of Harvard*, 27–28; cf. 74, 156, 203.
38. "Pomegranates," 21.
39. Ibid., 22.
40. Ibid., 23.
41. *Menorah Journal*, vol. 7, no. 1 (February, 1921).
42. "Escaping Judaism," *Menorah Journal*, vol. 7, no. 2 (June, 1921), 71; hereafter, "Escaping Judaism, I."
43. Ibid., 73.
44. Ibid., 80–81.
45. "Escaping Judaism, II," 161, 166.
46. "Escaping Judaism, I," 74, 76–81; "Escaping Judaism, II," 165, 167–168.
47. In a rare and brief foray into these issues at a later time, Wolfson's position remained unchanged. See H. A. Wolfson, "Our Survival in the Modern World," *The Hebrew Union College Monthly*, vol. 34 (Chanuko [sic], 1946). See also H.

A. Wolfson, F. T. Lewis, "The Kosher Code," *Science* (August 23, 1940), 174 col. 2, 175 col. 2.

48. "Escaping Judaism, II," 168.

49. H. A. Wolfson, *The Philosophy of the Church Fathers: Faith, Trinity, Incarnation* (Cambridge, Massachusetts, and London: 3rd rev. ed., 1970), ix–x.

50. "Escaping Judaism, II," 167.

51. Ibid.

52. Over the conflict between admission examinations to a great university and Yom Kippur, Wolfson wrote (ibid.): "Many a Jew in the community where the university is located feels sorely aggrieved at this repeated refusal [of the university to make an accommodation], but I confess that I could never work up any indignation over it." I am presuming that the university to which Wolfson refers is Harvard because it would seem natural for him to be most familiar and responsive to conditions in his own institution and community, and because I cannot locate evidence of this kind of conflict at other "great universities" in recent studies. See Dan A. Oren, *Joining the Club: A History of Jews and Yale* (New Haven and London: Yale University Press, 1985), Part II, esp. 98, on which Oren indicates that students were not penalized for missing classes on the Jewish high holy days at about the time Wolfson wrote; and Marcia Graham Synnott, *The Half–Opened Door: Discrimination and Admissions at Harvard, Yale, and Princeton, 1900–1970* (Westport and London: Greenwood Press, 1979).

When Harvard President Abbott L. Lowell proposed that Wolfson serve on a faculty committee to deal with Lowell's proposal for a *numerus clausus* for Jews, in 1922, Wolfson agreed. What construction is to be put on Wolfson's service? Feuer is severe:

> Distinguished Jews were chagrined by the choice of Wolfson. And, indeed, Lowell had chosen Wolfson because he had heard from the anthropologist Alfred Tozzer of Wolfson's opinion that too many Jews were trying to go to Harvard.

Synnott's research, more informed and nuanced than Feuer's, concludes that Wolfson did speak on behalf of Jewish students while serving on the faculty committee but, given Wolfson's motivations, the severity of Feuer must remain unchanged. At some points in the selection and work of the committee, Wolfson did advise against a quota, but only because Jewish students were fully capable of assimilating Harvard norms and becoming essentially indistinguishable from its other students. To Wolfson, maximum Jewish affirmation for Jewish students at Harvard was for them to walk together in the College Yard. Wolfson addressed proponents of restriction:

> You assume that Jewish students coming to the University bring with them ideals and loyalties different from those of other students, that they are still to go through the so-called process of assimilation and be made over into good Americans, that assimilation is not complete until no two Jews are ever seen to walk together in the College Yard, and that the assimilation of Jews beyond a certain percentage is impossible.

Wolfson opposed "the development of a distinctive Jewish group" within Harvard, though he wanted to promote "among Jewish students a more accurate and more intelligent understanding of things Jewish." Lewis S. Feuer, "The Professionalization of Philosophy" [review of Bruce Kuklick, *The Rise of American Philosophy: Cambridge, Massachusetts, 1860–1930*], *The Chronicle of Higher Education*, vol. XVI, no. 2 (March, 1978); Wolfson, cited in Synnott, 67, 87.

53. During the celebration of Harvard's tercentenary in the fall of 1936, the *Boston American*
> carried an article saying that Harvard University was deliberately offending Jewish scholars by having one of its sessions on Saturday. The reporters came to Wolfson for a statement obviously hoping that a sensational issue might be provoked. Then, as Wolfson described it, a prophetic inspiration, *ruaḥ nevu'ah*, descended upon him. "Not at all," said Wolfson to the reporters, "not at all is Harvard offending the Jewish scholars. Quite the opposite. Harvard has arranged that the Jewish scholars shall have a religious service at the Semitic Museum in the morning before the sessions begin." It was all manufactured of pure imaginative cloth. . . . Of course, Wolfson himself almost never went to religious services. But this time, he got together a *minyan* composed of a dozen friends . . . and they duly conducted their Sabbath service in the Semitic Museum."

Feuer, "Recollections," 33–34.

54. Ibid., 33: "Wolfson had an abiding loyalty to Harvard University. He was on occasion active to bring his word to bear to help particular individuals secure appointment or promotion, but he never took public stands on issues, whether it was the *numerus clausus* which Lowell proposed, or Harvard's virtual failure to welcome any refugee professors during the Nazi era. He went out of his way to prevent any embarrassment for Harvard University." Wolfson was privately anguished by the Holocaust. See William G. Braude, "Harry Wolfson as Mentor," *Rhode Island Jewish Historical Notes*, vol. 7, no. 1 (November, 1975), 142–43; Feuer, ibid., 43.

Whence the wellspring of Wolfson's loyalty to Harvard?
> Wolfson will never be understood unless one recognizes immediately and plainspokenly that he fell in love with Harvard. He fell in love with it in 1908, and that love affair endured till the day he died, September 19, 1974. He left to Harvard his books and the bulk of his modest estate. . . . Though he could talk of [the] quaintness [of Jewish life in Lithuania], its devout spirit, he was always aware of the contrasting "spaciousness," the freedom, the liberty, the let-live in a land where there was still a regrettable prejudice against Jews but no pogroms. . . . Inevitably that very bright Jewish young man contrasted his life in the small Lithuanian village with the orderliness and tranquillity of Harvard—its self-confidence, its atmosphere of learning, and the presence of resources for learning Greek, Latin, Arabic, English, modern European languages, and historical-philological disciplines. Unless we recover the intoxication he felt, we will fail to understand Wolfson's temptation. . . .

Goldin, "On the Sleuth of Slobodka," 395.

55. Feuer, "The Professionalization of Philosophy."

56. Schwarz, *Wolfson of Harvard*, 69. Schwarz dates the conversation to after Wolfson's return from the Army. He was discharged January 13, 1919.

57. H. A. Wolfson, *The Philosophy of Spinoza: Unfolding the Latent Processes of His Reasoning* (Cambridge, Massachusetts, and London: Harvard University Press, 1934; rpt., 2 vols. in one, n. d.), vol. 2, p. 351.

58. Ibid., vol. 1, p. 23.

59. *Crescas' Critique of Aristotle: Problems of Aristotle's Physics in Jewish and Arabic Philosophy* (Cambridge: Harvard University Press, 1929; rpt. 1971); *Spinoza* (1934); *Philo: Foundations of Religious Philosophy in Judaism, Christianity and Islam*, 2 vols. (Cambridge: Harvard University Press, 1947; 4th rev. ed., 1968); *Church Fathers* (1956); *The Philosophy of the Kalam* (Cambridge, Massachusetts, and London: Harvard University Press, 1976). See also H. A. Wolfson, *Repercussions of the Kalam in Jewish Philosophy* (Cambridge, Massachusetts, and London: Harvard University Press, 1979) [originally part of *Kalam*, but, in its final form, without a final editing by Wolfson—without, for instance, transitional paragraphs, summations, or introductory sentences; see vi–vii].

60. *Spinoza*, vol. 2, pp. 351–52.

61. See note 49.

Wolfson's suppleness regarding Christianity was more than tactical, if less than apostatizing. Feuer, "Recollections," 46:

> Wolfson . . . as he told me was once asked, in his years as an annual instructor, by the Harvard department whether he would be willing to take a post at some small college, and if so, whether he would join the local church. Wolfson replied that provided there was no Jewish synagogue or temple in the neighborhood, he would be quite willing to attend services at the local church. Indeed, like his imagined Spinoza, from time to time he conducted the services and gave the sermons in the little chapel of his beloved Divinity Hall.

Schwarz, *Wolfson of Harvard*, 33, writes that Wolfson, as an undergraduate, pinned on his wall a colored reproduction of Jesus. This was not (said Wolfson) because he was "paying homage to the founder of Christianity; he was fascinated by the power of his eyes, which seemed to open whenever he looked at the picture." Other pictures, of other figures, do not give the same effect?

In "Escaping Judaism, II," 155–65, Wolfson dwells at length on the present attraction of Christianity for Jews. However, he illustrates this thesis only with respect to Jews of the early nineteenth century or earlier, to European fictional characters a half century old, or older, to contemporary, unidentified "Jewish youth" or "Jewish friends," who, too, may have been fictional, and to fictional creations of his own. For example, Wolfson writes about "a Jewish boy who once lived a lonesome life in a great city who was attracted to the revival meetings of 'militant Christianity'" because "to lose oneself in the multitude, body and soul, is one of the elemental human passions." In other words, Wolfson's attraction to Christianity was social. And yet also, "the question as to what we intend to do with Jesus has become so urgent as to demand an answer." The answer? A rejection of Jesus not on doctrinal grounds, but only because he does not fit the pattern of the Jewish "national hero," and because he did not influence the history of Jewish thought.

Again, in "How the Jews Will Reclaim Jesus" (Introductory Essay in Joseph Jacobs, ed., *Jesus as Others Saw Him* [New York: Bernard G. Richards, 1925]), Wolfson writes as if he were living in Emancipation Germany. "In everything that guides our life and determines our view thereof, we have become Christianized . . . if not in the theological sense of a savior at least in the historical sense of a civilizer." Doctrinal differences between the ethical teachings of Jesus and those of the rabbis amount to "fine-spun speculations . . . expended upon subtle distinctions." The teachings of Jesus were rejected by the rabbis on strictly technical grounds—they were collected and published "before any official collection of the Tannaim was allowed to be publicly circulated in writing" and hence declared "unauthorized." It becomes simply a matter of time, then, for Jewish scholars in "free and unhampered conditions in a Jewish environment" to reclaim the teachings of the "Shammaite, Rabbi Jesus."

Projecting the social and ethical attraction of Christianity onto American Jewish life, Wolfson gives no evidence of the urgency of that attraction for anyone besides himself.

62. *Spinoza*, vol. 1, vii.
63. Ibid.
64. Schwarz, *Wolfson of Harvard*, 12.
65. Moses Mordechai Epstein, *Levush Mordekhai* [on *Bava Kamma*] (Warsaw, 1901; rpt. Jerusalem: Yeshivat Ḥevron, 1957), hereafter *Levush: Bava Kamma*. Subsequent volumes: On *Bava Metzi'a* (Jerusalem, 1929); on *Zevaḥim, Menaḥot* (Jerusalem, 1937); *Responsa* (Jerusalem, 1946); on *Yevamot, Gittin* (Jerusalem, 1948); on *Ketubot, Shabbat* (Jerusalem, 1969).
66. Epstein, *Levush: Bava Kamma*, 6.
67. Wolfson, *Philo*, vol. 1, p. 107.
68. Wolfson, *Crescas*, 25–27. Shorter formulations of Wolfson's method are in *Spinoza*, vol. 1, pp. 20–31, esp. 24; *Philo*, vol. 1, pp. 105–107; *Church Fathers*, vi–vii; *Kalam*, 72.
69. Isadore Twersky, *Rabad of Posquières: A Twelfth-Century Talmudist* (Cambridge: Harvard University Press, 1962), 65 note 112.
70. My positive characterization of the Brisker method is grounded in the writings of Hayyim Soloveitchik. The earlier, negative characterization—in terms of imposed methodological restrictions—is grounded in the contrast between the Brisker method and that of *Levush Mordekhai*—the Slobodka method. On the Slobodka method, see next note. On the Brisker method, see Hayyim Soloveitchik, *Ḥiddushei Rabbenu Hayyim ha-Levi: Ḥiddushim u-Vi'urim 'al ha-Rambam* [The Talmudic Investigations of Our Master Rabbi Hayyim, the Levite: Interpretations and Clarifications of Maimonides' *Mishneh Torah*] (Brisk, 1936); and

S. Y. Zevin, *'Ishim ve-Shitot* [Modern Talmudic Personalities and Methods] (Jerusalem: Bet Hillel, 1979), 45–78.

71. This method remains consistent throughout all volumes of *Levush Mordekhai* (listed in note 65). I am indebted to the analysis of Zevin, *'Ishim ve-Shitot*, 279–91.

72. Zevin, ibid., 289.

73. The type and the ubiquitousness of repetition in Wolfson's writings is the most prominent continuing influence of Wolfson's early interest in the structure of Hebrew (including biblical) literature (above, note 24). We cite but one biblical and one Wolfsonian passage from thousands of possible instances. Genesis 1:7 reads, "And God made the sky, and he divided between the waters which were underneath the sky and between the waters which were above the sky, and it was so." Note the repetition of the phrase: *between the waters which were*. The verse could have read: ". . . and He divided between the waters which were underneath and above the sky." The plenitude of the biblical phraseology creates a clarity, a cadence, and a balance retained by Wolfson so extensively that one locates it by opening his works almost at random. An example: "When God by His own good will decided to create this world of ours, He first, out of the ideas which had been in His thought from eternity, constructed an 'intelligible world,' and this intelligible world He placed in the Logos, which had likewise existed previously from eternity in His thought." Note the repetition of the phrase: *and this intelligible world*. The sentence could have read: "When God by His own good will decided to create this world of ours, He first, out of the ideas which had been in His thought from eternity, constructed an 'intelligible world,' which He placed in the Logos, which had likewise existed previously from eternity in His thought." See H. A. Wolfson, "Extradeical and Intradeical Interpretations of Platonic Ideas," *Religious Philosophy: A Group of Essays* (Cambridge: Harvard University Press, 1961), 31.

74. *Crescas*, 100–102, and notes thereon, 579–90.

75. *Kalam*, 112–13.

76. *Crescas*, 99–113.

77. Wolfson, *Religious Philosophy*; idem, Twersky and Williams, eds., *Studies*, vol. 2; idem, Twersky and Williams, eds., *Studies in the History of Philosophy and Religion*, vol. 1 (Cambridge: Harvard University Press, 1973).

78. *Kalam*, viii.

79. Schwarz, *Wolfson of Harvard*, 224.

80. Wolfson, *Philo*, vol. 1, p. v.

81. Wolfson's restructuring of the periodization of philosophy began in the aftermath of his work on Spinoza, which was followed by the two-volume work on Philo. Wolfson's series title, "Structure and Growth of Philosophic Systems from Plato to Spinoza," first appears in *Philo*, and his conception of his reperiodization also first appears in *Philo* (vol. 1, v–viii; vols. 1–2, concluding part of each chapter ["Conclusion, Influence, Anticipation"]; vol. 2, chapter 14); then in

Church Fathers, v–ix, 80–101; *Religious Philosophy*, v; and *Kalam*, 73–79, 720–39. See also Schwarz, *Wolfson of Harvard*, 137.

82. On Wolfson's view of Greek (pre-Philonic) and modern (post-Spinozan) philosophy as, respectively, precursory and repetitive, see "Philo Judaeus," *The Encyclopedia of Philosophy* (New York: Macmillan, 1967) and "Greek Philosophy in Philo and the Church Fathers," Arnold Toynbee, ed., *The Crucible of Christianity* (New York: World Publishing Co., and London: Thames and Hudson, 1969), both rpt. Twersky, Williams, eds., *Studies*, vol. 1; and three essays in *Religious Philosophy*, "The Philonic God of Revelation and His Later-Day Deniers," esp. 25–26, "Causality and Freedom in Descartes, Leibniz, and Hume," esp. 216, and "Spinoza and the Religion of the Past," esp. 269.

83. Several examples are collected and summarized by Zevin, *'Ishim ve-Shitot*, 280–86.

84. *Spinoza*, vol. 1, p. 27. When Wolfson attaches to this method the following sentence, "Here, again, most of these new distinctions, aspects, and interpretations were invented *ad hoc*. . . . ," he does not mean that they were invented in Brisker fashion, out of pure thought, but in the Slobodkan fashion, in conjunction with reconceiving the text. The *ad hoc* character of these distinctions, aspects, and interpretations, which arose from the reconceived text, refers merely to the initial absence of any search for parallel, corroborating distinctions that inhered in related philosophic texts. As Wolfson put it, he reconceived the use of a term, the statement of an idea or view of Spinoza "merely for the purpose of solving a certain problem, and the evidence corroborating [the reconception] was discovered afterwards" (27–28).

85. *Levush: Bava Kamma*, 6.

86. Ibid.

87. Preface, *Crescas*, vii.

88. "Spinoza and the Religion of the Past," 257. Other examples of Wolfson's wit: four essays in *Religious Philosophy*, "The Philonic God of Revelation," 26; "Extradeical and Intradeical Interpretations," 67; "Immortality and Resurrection in the Philosophy of the Church Fathers," 101–103; "Causality and Freedom," 215; review of James Moffat, *The Old Testament: A New Translation*, in *Boston Sunday Post* (Dec. 14, 1924), partial rpt. Schwarz, *Wolfson of Harvard*, 70–71; "Spinoza's Mechanism, Attributes, and Panpsychism," *Philosophical Review*, vol. 46, no. 3 (May, 1937), 309, rpt. Twersky, Williams, eds., *Studies*, vol. 2, p. 595; "Some Guiding Principles in Determining Spinoza's Medieval Sources," *Jewish Quarterly Review* n.s., vol. 27, no. 4 (1937), 333, rpt. *Studies*, vol. 2, p. 577; Schwarz, *Wolfson of Harvard*, 61.

89. Goldin, "On the Sleuth of Slobodka," 402. Wolfson's statement referred to his "Sermonette: The Professed Atheist and the Verbal Theist," *Religious Philosophy*. Indicative of the obscurity that Wolfson generated about his religious belief is the inability of commentators to locate any passages in Wolfson's oeuvre that are explicit enough to compel an explicit characterization of his position. One encounters, instead, supposedly knowing allusions. See, for example, Gerson D.

Cohen, "The Legacy of Philo," *Menorah Journal*, vol. 49, nos. 1–2 (Autumn–Winter, 1962), 151: "The upshot of [Wolfson's] critique is to put before the modern man an either-or decision. What Wolfson himself would have modern man decide he does not say, but it is not too hard to guess." See Also Mark Jay Mirsky, *My Search for the Messiah: Studies and Wanderings in Israel and America* (New York: Macmillan, 1977), 68.

90. See note 81, and Arthur Hyman, "Harry Austryn Wolfson 1887–1974," *Jewish Book Annual*, vol. 33 (1975–1976), 143–44; Leon Wieseltier, "Philosophy, Religion, and Harry Wolfson," *Commentary*, vol. 61, no. 4 (April, 1976), 61–62.

91. Lewis H. Weinstein, "Epilogue," in Schwarz, *Wolfson of Harvard*, 255.

4. RABBI ISRAEL HUTNER

1. *'Avot de-Rabbi Natan* (minor tractate, Babylonian Talmud, standard editions, end of fourth division), chapter 2; trans. Judah Goldin, *The Fathers according to Rabbi Nathan* (New Haven: Yale University Press, 1955), 23.

2. Anonymous [Rabbi Hutner's family], *"Zikhronot"* [Memories], in Joseph Buxbaum, ed., *Sefer ha-Zikkaron le-Maran Ba'al ha-Paḥad Yitzhak Ztz'l* (Jerusalem: Machon Yerushalayim, and Brooklyn: Gur Aryeh Institute for Advanced Jewish Scholarship, 1984), 5 (letter dated Nisan 2, 5682 [1922]), 8 (letter dated Rosh Hashanah eve, 5682 [1922]), 9–10 (letter dated Tishrei 7, 5683 [1922]), 10 (letter dated 5723 [1923]).

"Zikhronot" is a 128-page biographical essay divided into two parts: a chronological review of Rabbi Hutner's life (3–66), and an analysis of his thought and spiritual character (67–130). Even though the essay is a personal remembrance. and deletes important material, it is a primary source for its letters and diary notations, and for certain biographical information and oral statements of Rabbi Hutner, published nowhere else.

3. *"Zikhronot,"* 79 (oral tradition).

4. *"Zikhronot,"* 3–27.

5. On Slobodka, see Chapter Three (Wolfson), note 11.

6. Introduction, *'Etz Peri* (Vilna, 1881); for identification of the Elder as author, see Dov Katz, *Tenu'at ha-Musar* [The Musar Movement], vol. 3 (Tel Aviv: Abraham Zioni, rev. ed., 1967), 26. It was in this anthology that Rabbi Israel Salanter published his clearest and maturest formulation of unconscious psychological forces.

7. Katz, *Tenu'at ha-Musar*, 212.

8. Ibid., 37.

9. Ibid., 280–81, 306–307.

10. Isaac Hutner, *Paḥad Yitzhak; 'Iggerot u-Khetavim [Paḥad Yitzhak:* Letters and Writings] (Jerusalem and Brooklyn: Gur Aryeh Institute for Advanced Jewish Scholarship, 1981), letter 159 (Nisan 11, 5687 [1927]), p. 251; letter 153 (Av 10, 5687 [1927]), p. 253.

Paḥad Yitzhak, the series title of Rabbi Hutner's writings, has several layers of meaning. *Paḥad* denotes both dread and awe, representing in turn both fear of Divine punishment and awe at the Divine majesty. All this is the *paḥad* of Isaac *(Yitzhak)* Hutner. The series title hints, however, at something more: not only the transcendent gaze and experience *of* Isaac, but also the sense that his disciple-readers must ascribe all this *to* Isaac. The series title is not only inherently twofold, denoting Divine punishment and Divine majesty, but rhetorically a double entendre, a statement about both the attitude of Isaac himself and the attitude of others toward him. As we shall indicate below, part of Rabbi Hutner's style was authoritarian.

11. Ibid., letter 159; "Greater the righteous," *Ḥullin* 7b.

12. Biography on Kuk: Jacob Agus, *Banner of Jerusalem* (New York: Bloch Publishing Co., 1946); Zvi Yaron, "Introduction: Toward a Biography of Rabbi Kuk" [Hebrew] (and literature cited therein), *Mishnato shel ha-Rav Kuk* (Jerusalem: World Zionist Organization, 1974); Moses Zvi Neriyah, compiler, *Ḥayyei ha-Reʾiyah. ʾOrḥotav ve-Haguto* [The Life of Rabbi Abraham Isaac ha-Kohen (Kuk): His Ways and His Thought] (Tel Aviv: Moriah, 1983).

13. I owe this formulation to Kuk scholar Jerome Gelman.

14. On Rabbi Kuk's personal and intellectual links to the Musar movement, see Agus, *Banner of Jerusalem*, 13–16; Hillel Goldberg, *Israel Salanter: Text, Structure, Idea—The Ethics and Theology of an Early Psychologist of the Unconscious* (New York: Ktav Publishing House, 1982), 281 note 166; and Abraham Isaac Kuk, "Kedosh Yisraelʾ" [Israel (Salanter) the Holy], *Shaʿarei Zion*, vol. 13, nos. 3–5 (Kislev–Shevat, 5693 [1933]), 17–19.

Zvi Judah Kuk (Rabbi Kuk's son) does not confirm Agus's contention that Rabbi Kuk observed formal mourning rites for Rabbi Israel Salanter upon his death in 1883, but does confirm the general picture of Rabbi Kuk's early appreciation of Musar doctrine and personalities (interview with Zvi Judah Kuk, July, 1977, Jerusalem).

15. "Zikhronot," 7–8 (letter dated Summer, 5682 [1922]), 8 (letter dated Rosh Hashanah eve, 5682 [1922]); 8 (letter of father, dated Yom Kippur eve, 5683 [1922]), 8 (letter dated Elul, 5683 [1923]), 8–9 (letter dated Tammuz, 5684 [1924]), 11 (letter dated Nisan 10, 5685 [1925], 17; Hutner, *ʾIggerot u-Khetavim*, letter 165 (Adar 12, 5689 [1929]), pp. 276–77. Rabbi Hutner's first book is dedicated to his parents "with love and admiration"; see note 22.

16. "Zikhronot," 17 (letter, 1929).

17. Biography on Weinberg: Eliezer Berkovits, "Rabbi Yechiel Yakob Weinberg Ztsʾl: My Teacher and Master," *Tradition*, vol. 8, no. 2 (Summer, 1966); Samuel Atlas, "Ha-Gaʾon Rabbi Yehiel Yaakov Weinberg Ztsʾl: Kavvim li-Demuto [The Gaon Jehiel J. Weinberg: Elements of a Portrait]," *Sinai*, vol. 58, nos. 4–6 (1966); Gavriel Hayyim Cohen, "*Devarim le-Zikhro shel Haraha"g Dr. Yehiel Yaakov Weinberg Ztsʾl* [Words in Memory of the Gaon, Rabbi Dr. Jehiel J. Weinberg], and Moses Stern, "*ʾIsh ʾEshkolot*" [Multifaceted Personality], *Deʿot*,

no. 31 (Winter-Spring, 1966). Weinberg's writings have been collected in *Seridei)Esh* [Remnants of a Conflagration], 4 vols. (Jerusalem: Mosad Harav Kuk, 1961–1966; rpt. in 2 vols., 1977); and *)Et)Aḥai)Anokhi Mevakkesh: Rashei Perakim le-Hiddabberut bein Palgei ha-Yahadut* [I am my Brother's Keeper: Outlines toward a Dialogue between the Factions of Judaism] (Benei Berak: Netzaḥ, 1966). On the continuing relationship between Weinberg and Hutner, see *Seridei)Esh*, vol. 3, #64. On the relationship between Weinberg's successor Abraham Eliyahu Kaplan, and Hutner, see Moses Zvi Neriyah, *Bi-Sedeh ha Re(iyah: (Al Demuto ve-Darko ve-(Al Ne(emanei Ruḥo shel Mara(de-)Ar(a) de-Yisra)el* [In the Field of Rabbi Abraham Isaac ha-Kohen (Kuk): Portrait, Path, and Those Faithful to the Spirit of the Master of the Land of Israel] (Kfar Haroeh, 1987), 431.

18. "Zikhronot," 26 (undated letter, c. 1934).

19. Isaac Hutner, *Kuntres (Osef ha-Halakhot ha-Meḥudashot ha-Nimtza)ot be-Sifra))Asher Lo) Ba) Zikhran be-Talmud Bavli* [Monograph Collection of the Derived Laws Found in *Sifra)*, unmentioned in the Babylonian Talmud]. This and Hutner's commentary on Hillel of Verona's commentary were reprinted as appendices to vol. 2 of Shachne Koleditsky's critical edition of and commentary on Hillel of Verona's commentary, *Sifra) de-Vei Rav, Torat Kohanim*, 2 vols, (Jerusalem, 1961). The commentary was printed anonymously. On identification of Hutner as author of this anonymous appendix, see Hutner, *)Iggerot u-Khetavim*, letters 177, 191.

20. "Zikhronot," 17, and diary notation cited there.

21. "Zikhronot," 12, 25 (letter, c. Nisan, 5693 [1933]), 19–20 (diary notation); 20.

22. Hayyim Ozer Grodzinski, Abraham Isaac Kuk, Abraham Dovber Kahane Shapira, in Isaac Hutner, *Torat ha-Nazir* (Kovno, 1932), unnumbered front pages. Rabbi Grodzinski, the venerable rabbi of Vilna, referred to young Hutner as one of the generation's greats *(gedolei Torah)*, and wrote that even though it was his custom not to respond to requests for approbrations, in this case he would make an exception. Rabbi Kuk referred to young Hutner as a genius *(ga)on)*, and his book as the product of a fully ripened mind *(da(at zekenim)*. Rabbi Shapira referred to him as a sage and a genius. Rabbi Hutner's letter to Rabbi Kuk requesting the approbation appears in Neriyah, *Bi-Sedeh ha-Re(iyah*, 421.

23. "Zikhronot," 23–25.

24. "Zikhronot," 26 (diary notation).

25. "Zikhronot," 79 (oral tradition). The original impetus to emigrate to America may have originated in Rabbi Hutner's encounter with the American contingent studying in the Slobodka branch in Hebron. Perhaps through this contingent he glimpsed the possibilities for iconoclastic educational work. See the special appreciation that he allotted to these American students, murdered in the Arab pogrom in Hebron, 1929, in his essay in the memorial volume for the victims. He took note of the Americans' special sacrifice and special mission—to teach "Torah and fear of God" to American Jewish youth. Did his decision to emigrate

to the United States partially originate in a desire to take up the task of the martyred? See Isaac Hutner, "Mi-Maʿamakim" [From the Depths], Sefer Zikkaron li-Kedoshei Yeshivat Ḥevron "Keneset Yisrael" (Jerusalem: Ḥever Talmidim mi-Yeshivat Ḥevron, 1930); rpt. ʾIggerot u-Khetavim, letter 166, p. 259.

26. ʾIggerot u-Khetavim, letter 174 (Elul 28, 5693 [1933]), p. 267. Since Rabbi Hutner studied science and math, it is plausible that madaʿ in this passage refers to secular studies, especially since the passage earlier refers to "study in its various guises."

27. Binyomin Ben Chaim [pseudonym], "The Sefer Torah of the Azoroh: Rav Yitzhak Hutner Zts'l," *Jewish Women's Outlook* (January–February, 1981), 9.

28. "Zikhronot," 91 (diary notation, 1934); cf. similar remarks delivered in 1974, in "Zikhronot," 91.

29. ʾIggerot u-Khetavim, letter 233 (Shevat 6, 5719 [1959]), p. 312.

30. "Zikhronot," 62 (1974). Rabbi Hutner's emotional responsiveness and poetic soul pervade his writings. For a few of many possible examples, see "Zikhronot," 16–17 (letter, c. 1927), 43 (oral tradition, 1956), 60 (oral tradition, 1972), 77–78, 102 (poems and songs composed by Hutner, undated and 1954, respectively); ʾIggerot u-Khetavim, letter 171 (Nisan, 5690 [1930]), p. 263, letter 252 (1968), pp. 323–24; *Paḥad Yitzhak: Ḥanukkah* (Brooklyn, 1953), 38.

31. On Maharal, see Byron L. Sherwin, *Mystical Theology and Social Dissent: The Life and Works of Judah Loew of Prague* (Rutherford, N.J.: Farleigh Dickenson University Press and Associated University Presses, 1982); Theodor Dreyfus, *Dieu parle aux hommes: la révelation selon le Maharal de Prague* (Paris: C. Klincksieck, 1969); Andre Neher, *Le Puits de l'Exil; la théologie dialectique du Maharal de Prague* (Paris: A. Michel, 1966); Aaron F. Kleinberger, *Ha-Maḥashavah ha-Pedagogit shel ha-Maharal mi-Prag* [The Educational Thought of the Maharal of Prague] (Jerusalem: Magnes Press, 1962); Gershom Scholem, *Zur Kabbala und ihrer Symbolik* (Frankfurt am Main: Suhrkamp, 1977), 209–59; Ben Zion Bokser, *From the World of the Cabbalah: The Philosophy of Rabbi Judah Loew of Prague* (New York: Philosophical Library, 1954); Aaron Mauskopf, *Religious Philosophy of the Maharal of Prague* (Brooklyn: Hammer Publishing Co., 1949). See also Johanan Cohen-Yashar, *Bibliografyah Shimmushit shel Kitvei ha-Maharal mi-Prag* [Select Bibliography of the Writings of the Maharal of Prague] (Jerusalem, 1967).

On Maharal as precursor of relativity, see Judah Loew (Maharal), *The Book of Divine Power, Introductions: On the Diverse Aspects and Levels of Reality*, trans., annotated, illustrated Shlomo Mallin, in collaboration with Aryeh Carmell (Jerusalem and New York: Feldheim, 1975).

32. According to Neriyah (*Bi-Sedeh ha-Reʾiyah*, 432), it was Rabbi Kuk who opened up Maharal for Rabbi Hutner.

33. Institutional career: "Zikhronot," 30–31, 35, 43. Hasidic development (*gartel*, mid-1950s; *spodik*, mid-1970s): "Sefer Torah of the Azoroh," 9. Attachment to Vilna Gaon: "Zikhronot," 37, 49, 76.

A product of this synthesis is "Torah Lives and Sings: Twelve Original Melodies music originating in American yeshiva or hasidic circles. The record jacket attributes the composition of the twelve melodies to *yeshiva* origin: Mesivta Chaim Berlin students' natural accompaniment of Talmud study with song. The emphasis on song in Mesivta Chaim Berlin reflects a *hasidic* penchant: the reaching beyond informal talmudic singsong to emphasis on song and its formalization in a record.

34. On the Gaon's secular interests, see Emmanuel Etkes, "Ha-Gra veha-Haskalah—Tadmit u-Metziʾut" [The Vilna Gaon and Enlightenment—Image and Reality] in Etkes and Y. Salmon, eds., *Studies in the History of Jewish Society in the Middle Ages and in the Modern Period* (Jerusalem: Magnes Press, 1980); Nahum Glatzer, "The Beginnings of Modern Jewish Studies," in Alexander Altmann, ed., *Studies in Nineteenth-Century Jewish Intellectual History* (Cambridge: Harvard University Press, 1964), 28–31; Jacob Dienstag, "Ha-ʾIm Hitnagged ha-Gra le-Mishnato ha-Filosofit shel ha-Rambam?" [Did the Vilna Gaon Oppose the Philosophic Teaching of Maimonides?], *Talpiot*, vol. 4, nos. 1–2 (1949).

On the Gaon and Rabbi Hutner, see the latter's statement, *Zikhronot*, 76.

35. Of the primary sources on Hutner not published by his family, one of the most revealing is a letter he wrote in 1962 to Rabbi Kuk's son, Rabbi Zvi Judah. On the one hand, Rabbi Hutner is effusive in his admiration of Rabbi A. I. Kuk. Rabbi Hutner declares that he considers himself a disciple of Rabbi Kuk in a far more authentic sense than others who claim to be disciples. Clearly, at least as late as 1962, Rabbi Hutner's attitude to Rabbi Kuk was positive. On the other hand, he writes that his recent trip to Israel occasioned a "renewal" of his sense of discipleship. Clearly, between his departure from Palestine in the early 1930s and his first trip back in 1962, his sense of discipleship had declined or become dormant. The letter, 28 Elul (September, 1962), is in Neriyah, *Bi-Sedeh ha-Reʾiyah*, 437. See idem, 425, for an example of Rabbi Hutner's praise of Rabbi Kuk at the time his picture hung in Rabbi Hutner's *sukkah*.

Many of Rabbi Hutner's students are firmly convinced that there was nothing unusual or calculated about their mentor's refusal, for years, to attach his name to his writings. One student said: "Everybody knew that the Rosh Yeshiva wrote them. The message was simply that if you did not hear the *maʾamar* directly from the Rosh Yeshiva, you did not get the whole thing. These *maʾamarim* were whole productions—the way he sat down, the way he took off his glasses, the build-up and denoument of the issues at hand. You had to have been there to get the full import."

The comment explains why the *maʾamarim* were published anonymously, but not why they were subsequently published with Rabbi Hutner's name. Also, the comment presumes that a very wide circle—"everybody"—knew Rabbi Hutner altogether, let alone his articles. The fact is that a penchant for secrecy was part of Rabbi Hutner's style. This came through in every interview I conducted with his disciples and others close to him. What personal, pedagogical, sociological, or other reasons underlay this penchant in relation to the anonymous publication of his articles, I do not know. On the anonymity and subsequent identification in 1964 of Rabbi Hutner's writings: Introduction, *Paḥad Yitzhak: Ḥannukah*

[Chanukah] (Brooklyn: Gur Aryeh Institute for Advanced Jewish Scholarship, 1964).

36. Yisrael Mayer Kirzner, "By the Writing Desk of the Master: Reflections on Pachad Yitzhok: Igaros Ukesavim," *Jewish Observer*, vol. XV, no. 10 (December, 1981), 12. I have translated some Hebrew terms in this citation, and omitted others.

37. Because of various dislocations—"purges" and physical relocations—Mesivta Chaim Berlin went through a weak period during the mid- and late 1960s, just the time when children of Rabbi Hutner's first disciples reached the age for advanced yeshiva education. One objective reason for parental refusal to send children to Mesivta Chaim Berlin may have been its lack of an organized curriculum. Beyond objective reasons for some disciples' refusal to send their children to Chaim Berlin stood, perhaps, ambivalences: over whether a parent wished to subject his child to the complex emotional burden of the inevitable relationship, within Chaim Berlin, with Rabbi Hutner; over whether a certain hostility on the part of the parent overrode his personal relationship with Rabbi Hutner and appreciation of the latter's educational ability; and over whether a parent wished his child to attend a yeshiva that permitted secular studies in college.

The single time that Rabbi Hutner publicly addressed a contemporary issue—Holocaust theology—his position elicited wide argument and even some denunciation. In an Orthodox society that reveres its scholar-leaders (*gedolei Torah*), the only way to express hostility in print is through issues. Personal response accounted for some of the disagreement that greeted Rabbi Hutner. See his "Holocaust," rendered into English by Chaim Feuerman and Yaakov Feitman, *Jewish Observer*, vol. XII, no. 8 (October, 1977); letters, and Yaakov Feitman, "Reviewing a Shiur: Rabbi Hutner's 'Holocaust' Seminar," *Jewish Observer*, vol. XII, no. 10 (January, 1978); Lawrence Kaplan, "Rabbi Isaac Hutner's 'Daat Torah Perspective' on the Holocaust: A Critical Analysis," *Tradition*, vol. 18, no. 3 (Fall, 1980).

38. For Rubenstein's relationship to Hutner, See Richard Rubenstein, *Power Struggle* (New York: Charles Scribner's Sons, 1974), 98–118. "[Rabbi Hutner] was certainly the most authoritative yet humane interpreter of what I regarded as God's law I had ever met. Twenty-five years later, a part of me still regrets that I could not permanently remain his disciple. I know that he cannot be happy with the direction my career has taken. Nevertheless, of all my religious teachers, I retain the greatest respect for him" (101).

39. Correspondence: Buxbaum. *Sefer ha-Zikkaron*, 221–27.

In presentations of Jewish thought, Rabbis Hutner and Soloveitchik sometimes follow an almost identical line of argument, citing the same sources, raising the same questions, and resolving them in a similar way. See Joseph B. Soloveitchik, "*Ish ha-Halakhah*," *Talpiot*, vol. 1, nos. 3–4 (1944), trans. Lawrence Kaplan, *Halakhic Man* (Philadelphia: Jewish Publication Society of America, 1983), 110–13; Isaac Hutner, *Paḥad Yitzhak, Yom ha-Kippurim* [Day of Atonement] (Brooklyn: Gur Aryeh Institute for Advanced Jewish Scholarship, 1978), 27:1.

In the absence of evidence indicating direct influence, in the one direction or the other, disciples of either rabbi might set form claims for priority of discovery. Recent research has demonstrated the fruitlessness of such claims in various contexts. On the simultaneous and independent discovery of the calculus, see A. Rupert Hall, *Philosophers at War: The Quarrel between Newton and Leibniz* (New York: Cambridge University Press, 1980). See also Robert K. Merton, "Resistance to the Systematic Study of Multiple Discoveries in Science," *European Journal of Sociology*, vol. 4, no. 4 (1963).

40. According to Louis (Eliezer Zalman) Bernstein, Rabbi Soloveitchik seemed genuinely in favor of such participation, but he backed down under pressure from Orthodox rabbis such as Rabbi Hutner in order to preserve the unity of American Orthodoxy. No copy of Rabbi Soloveitchik's *heter* (halachic permission) to participate in the Synagogue Council of America—a *heter* upon which much subsequent division and debate in American Orthodoxy was based—is known to exist. This has given rise to an opposite claim: Rabbi Soloveitchik would have approved the *issur* (halakhic prohibition) against participation in the Synagogue Council of America had he been included in the process of its formulation, Rabbi Yitzhak Hutner being one of its signators, Rabbi Aaron Kotler being its moving spirit. For Rabbi Soloveitchik, lack of concrete evidence for his positions, or taking a stand and then changing it, is not unusual.

Hutner's position: *"Zikhronot,"* 39–42; Soloveitchik's position: Eliezer Zalman Bernstein, *"Ha-Rav ve-Histadrut ha-Rabbanim"* [Rabbi Soloveitchik, and the Rabbinical Council of America], in Saul Israeli, Norman Lamm, Yitzhak Rafael, eds., *Jubilee Volume in Honor of Moreinu Hagaon Rabbi Joseph B. Soloveitchik, Shelita* (Jerusalem: Mosad Harav Kuk, and New York: Yeshiva University, 1984), vol. 1, pp. 23–25.

41. Rabbi Hutner's opposition to Lubavitch came to expression with colorful asperity. For example (interview with Saul [pseudonym], January, 1985, Jerusalem):

> I was a student at Mesivta Chaim Berlin for only half a year, and had not spoken to Rabbi Hutner in about twenty years. I phoned him in New York, saying only "hello," to which he responded, "Hello, Saul, how are you?" He knew my voice! He had this habit of making appointments at strange times, so we met at 2:10 p.m., Sunday afternoon. I told him that I had come to New York to pick up my children from a summer camp—a Lubavitch camp. Whereupon he suddenly turned his whole body around in his chair, his back facing me, and just sat there in blazing anger, glaring into space for what seemed to be an eternity. He must have been silent for two minutes. I was dumbfounded. Then he said, "Saul, you come to see me once in twenty years, and all you can tell me is that you send your children to a *Lubavitch* camp? There aren't enough *other* camps?" He said that my children would return home saying that the Lubavitcher Rebbe was the Messiah, that Lubavitch would ruin my children.

Rabbi Hutner was opposed to the personality cult built up around the Lubavitcher Rebbe, and to the public projection of both the Rebbe and the Lubavitch movement, by the movement, through public media—print and broadcast journalism, books, film, and the like.

42. William B. Helmreich, *The World of the Yeshiva: An Intimate Portrait of Orthodox Jewry* (New York: The Free Press, 1982), 46–47, 50.

43. All volumes of *Paḥad Yitzhak* are regularly reprinted (and sold only through Mesivta Chaim Berlin). Initial publication dates for some of the volumes (listed in "Zikhronot," 47, and beginning in 1951) signify first publication of chapters about individual holidays. These chapters were collated in separate volumes devoted to a single holiday except for Sabbath and Tabernacles, which are printed together, and except for the final volume, the posthumous collection of letters. As it now stands, *Paḥad Yitzhak* (Brooklyn: Gur Aryeh Institute for Advanced Jewish Scholarship) consists of separate volumes on Passover (1984), Pentecost (1983), New Year (1974), Day of Atonement (1978), Purim (1966), Chanukah (1964), Sabbath and Tabernacles (1982), and Letters and Writings (1981). The series title, *Paḥad Yitzhak*, was first introduced in 1964; see Introduction, *Paḥad Yitzhak: Ḥanukkah* [Chanukah] (1964). On the name see above, note 10.

44. Reason and emotion: "Zikhronot," 67 (oral tradition, undated), and *Paḥad Yitzhak* throughout.

Autonomy and theonomy: "Zikhronot," 72 (diary notation, 1973); *Paḥad Yitzhak: Yom ha-Kippurim* [Day of Atonement], statement 18; cf. Léon Ashkenazi, "Un Enseignement sur le 'Chabatt,' " *Tenth Anniversary Souvenir Journal, Gur Aryeh Institute* (Brooklyn, 1966); Steven S. Schwarzschild, "An Introduction to the Thought of R. Isaac Hutner," *Modern Judaism*, vol. 5, no. 3 (October, 1985).

Naive and informed faith (*ʾemunah peshutah* and *gadlut*): "Zikhronot," 70 (diary notations, 1933, 1937), 71 (diary notations, 1935, 1953, 1973).

Abstract and parabolic expression: "Zikhronot," 73–74 (diary notations, 1925 and undated, respectively); *Paḥad Yitzhak: Pesaḥ* [Passover], cited in "Zikhronot," 73; *Paḥad Yitzhak: Shabbat, Kuntres Reshimot* [Sabbath, appendix] 1:2–7. Quandaries of language occupy Rabbi Hutner throughout *Paḥad Yitzhak*. See, for example, *Paḥad Yitzhak: Shavuʿot* [Pentecost] 4, *Shabbat* [Sabbath] 3:3, for a discussion of the ambiguities inherent in the use of secular Hebrew terminology for sacred purposes; cf. Alan Mintz, "Mordecai Zev Feierberg and the Reveries of Redemption," *Association for Jewish Studies Review*, vol. 2 (1977), 171–72, on the inevitable simultaneity of meanings in the Hebrew of classical sources as it is pressed to modern uses.

The "unpacking" of Rabbi Hutner's philosophic position on, for example, autonomy and theonomy, is complicated by his insistence on grounding his discourse in terms such as the imaginative language of midrash and aggadah. Rabbi Hutner's advancement over Slobodka Musar is his concretization of abstract discourse about the "greatness of man" *(gadlut ha-adam)*, but the ultimate point of his use of nonabstract discourse is his unitive aspiration itself, manifesting itself in this instance in the aspiration to unify different modes of discourse, the abstract and the parabolic. His use of parabolic and imaginative sources, then, is not simply an inherited form of discourse, or a pedagogic tool, as Schwarzschild argues (cited above, this note).

Laughter and seriousness: "Zikhronot," 124–29, on relation of joy (simḥah) to life. To several disciples, Rabbi Hutner was one of the most humorous people they ever knew.

45. Paḥad Yitzhak: Shabbat [Sabbath] 13:3, citing Rashba, Responsa, vol. 5, #52.

46. "Zikhronot," 76 (oral tradition, undated).

47. "Zikhronot," 74 (diary notation, undated); Maimonides, Commentary on the Mishnah, ʿAvodah Zarah 4.

48. Harry Austryn Wolfson, "Extradeical and Intradeical Interpretations of Platonic Ideas," Religious Philosophy: A Group of Essays (Cambridge: Harvard University Press, 1961), 28–38.

49. Bereshit Rabbah 1:1.

50. Paḥad Yitzhak: Pesaḥ [Passover] 70:4–12, esp. 10, 12.

51. See above, note 44, "abstract and parabolic expression."

52. Menahem Kellner, "Dogmas in Medieval Jewish Thought: A Bibliographical Survey," Studies in Bibliography and Booklore (1984), 20.

53. Isaac Arama, ʿAkedat Yitzhak [The Binding of Isaac] (Salonica, 1552; rpt. Pressberg, 1849, New York, 1960). See Sara Heller-Wilensky, R. Yitzhak Arama u-Mishnato [Rabbi Isaac Arama and His Thought] (Jerusalem: Mosad Bialik, 1956).

54. Authors have used this rubric, and anthologies have structured the writings of authors who did not use it in accord with it. Examples of the former: S. Y. Zevin, Ha-Moʿadim ba-Halakhah [The Jewish Holidays in Jewish Law] (Jerusalem: Mosad Harav Kuk, 1954); Moses Sternbuch, Moʿadim u-Zemanim ha-Shalem [Jewish Holidays and Special Times: The Complete Works], 9 vols. (Benei Berak: Netivot ha-Torah veha-Ḥesed, rev. ed., 1981). Examples of the latter: Moses Ibgi, ed., Ḥokhmat ha-Matzpun [The Wisdom of the Conscience], vol. 5 (Jewish Holidays according to the Disciples of Israel Salanter) (Nice, 1979); Moses Zvi Neriyah, ed., Moʿadei Hareʾiyah; Ḥaggim u-Zemanim be-Haguto u-veʾOraḥ Ḥayyav [Jewish Holy Days according to Rabbi Abraham Isaac ha-Kohen Kuk: Holidays and Special Times in His Thought and Life] (Jerusalem: Moriah, 1982).

55. The insulation of East European Jewry broke down during World War I with the movement of the German army eastward. This brought German Jewish soldiers into contact with Polish Jewry, and, more broadly, held open East European Jewry for a brief period to visitors from the West. Neo-Kantian Hermann Cohen's Jewish revision of his position, for example, was partially spurred by an eye-opening visit to the East, earlier in 1914. After the war, mutual cross-fertilization manifested itself in the attendance of both West Europeans in East European yeshivas, and East Europeans in West European rabbinical seminaries, such as Rabbi Hayyim Heller's institute in Berlin. Of the thirty-eight students enrolled in 1924 at the Rabbinical Seminary for Orthodox Judaism in Berlin (which Dr. Jehiel J. Weinberg later headed), twenty-two were East Europeans (Isi Jacob

Eisner, "Reminiscences of the Berlin Rabbinical Seminary," *Leo Baeck Institute Yearbook* [1967], 41). On the other hand, American, West European, Australian, and South African Orthodox rabbinical students gravitated to East European yeshivas. In the Mir yeshiva in the 1930s, for example, about one quarter of the student body was of non-Polish origin: forty Americans, thirty Germans, six Austrians, three Frenchmen, one Swede, one Dane, eight Englishmen, two South Africans, four Belgians, three Irishmen, two Scots, and two Canadians (Cyril Domb, ed., *Memories of Kopul Rosen* [London, 1970], 56; see also Alexander Carlebach, *Adass Yeshurun of Cologne* [Belfast, 1964], 121–25). On Hermann Cohen, see Samuel Hugo Bergman, *Faith and Reason: Modern Jewish Thought* (New York: Schocken Books, 1963), 43–44.

56. *"Zikhronot,"* 77. Part of the atmosphere was song, which, in his view, rendered the mind better able to absorb his statements.

57. *"Zikhronot,"* 11 (diary notation, c. 1935).

58. *Berakhot* 5a.

59. *"Zikhronot,"* 19 (diary notation, c. 1931).

60. *"Zikhronot,"* 26–27; 27 (diary notation, c. 1935).

61. *"Zikhronot,"* 53 (diary notation, c. 1970).

62. *"Zikhronot,"* 16, 17, 20 note 82.

63. "Sefer Torah of the Azoroh," 8. See also Pinchas Stolper, "The Great Planter—Ha-Gaon Rav Yitschok Hutner Z'tl," *Jewish Press* (Dec. 4, 1981).

64. Interview with Rabbi Jacob Kaminecki, May 1984 (Monsey, New York).

5. Rabbi Joseph B. Soloveitchik

1. Exoteric religious literature: Joseph B. Soloveitchik, ")Ish ha-Halakhah," *Talpiot*, vol. 1, nos. 3–4 (1944), trans. Lawrence Kaplan, *Halakhic Man* (Philadelphia: Jewish Publication Society of America, 1983), 42, 44. Hebrew rpt. Pinchas Peli, ed., *Be-Sod ha-Yaḥid veha-Yaḥad* (Jerusalem: Orot, 1976), and Joseph B. Soloveitchik, *)Ish ha-Halakhah—Galui ve-Nistar* (Jerusalem: World Zionist Organization, 1979).

"King-teacher": Joseph B. Soloveitchik, "A Eulogy for the Talner Rebbe," *Boston Advocate* (June 22, 29, 1972), rpt. with corrections and elaborations, Joseph Epstein, ed., *Shi'urei Harav: A Conspectus of the Public Lectures of Rabbi Joseph B. Soloveitchik* (New York: Hamevaser, Student Publication of Jewish Studies Divisions of Yeshiva University, 1974), 22–26.

"Letters (*)otiyyot*) of the Torah": Epstein, *Shi'urei Harav*, 23.

2. Biography on Soloveitchik is Aaron Lichtenstein, "Joseph Soloveitchik," in Simon Noveck, ed., *Great Jewish Thinkers of the Twentieth Century*, vol. 3 (Washington: B'nai B'rith Department of Adult Jewish Education, 1963); Charles S. Liebman, "Orthodoxy in American Jewish Life," *American Jewish Yearbook*, vol. 66 (New York: American Jewish Committee, and Philadelphia: Jewish Publication Society of America, 1965), 53, 64, 87–88; idem, "The Training of American Rabbis," *American Jewish Yearbook*, vol. 69 (1968), 69–70; "Joseph Baer Solov-

eitchik," *Encyclopedia Judaica* (Jerusalem: Keter Publishing House, 1971), vol. 15.

3. Chaim Karlinsky, *Ha-Rishon le-Shoshelet Brisk: Toledot Ḥayyav u-Faʿalav shel ha-Gaon Rabbi Yosef Dov ber ha-Levi Soloveitchik Ztz'l* [First in the Geneological Chain of Brisk: The Gaon Rabbi Yoseph Ber Soloveitchik, His Life, Times, and Activities] (Jerusalem: Machon Yerushalayim, 1984), 37–70; "Soloveitchik," *Encyclopedia Judaica*.

4. Shaul Stampfer, *Shalosh Yeshivot Litaʾiot be-Meʾah ha-19* [Three Lithuanian Yeshivot in the Nineteenth Century] (The Hebrew University of Jerusalem: Ph.D. dissertation, 1981), 37–39.

5. Biography on Joseph Baer Soloveitchik: Karlinsky, *Rishon le–Shoshelet Brisk*, 5–37, 71–482. Biography on Netziv: Meir Bar Ilan, *Rabban shel Yisraʾel* [Rabbi of Israel] (New York, 1943); Joseph Litvin, "Naphtali Tzevi Berlin (The Netziv)," Leo Jung, ed., *Men of the Spirit* (New York: Kymson Publishing Co., 1964); Karlinsky, *Rishon le-Shoshelet Brisk*, index.

6. Stampfer, *Shalosh Yeshivot*, 39–47; Litvin, "Berlin," 290–91.

7. Lichtenstein, "Joseph Soloveitchik," 282–84; interview with Lichtenstein, Soloveitchik's son-in-law, January, 1982 (Jerusalem).

8. Peter Gay, *Freud, Jews and Other Germans: Masters and Victims in Modernist Culture* (Oxford: Oxford University Press, 1979); Frederic V. Grunfeld, *Prophets without Honor: A Background to Freud, Kafka, Einstein and Their World* (New York: Holt, Rinehart, and Winston, 1979); Donald L. Niewyk, *The Jews in Weimar Germany* (Baton Rouge: Louisiana State University Press, 1980); Gershom Scholem, "Against the Myth of the German-Jewish Dialogue" and "Once More: The German-Jewish Dialogue," *On Jews and Judaism in Crisis: Selected Essays* (New York: Schocken Books, 1976).

9. Biography on Hayyim Heller: Hillel Seidman, in S. Federbush, ed., *Ḥokhmat Yisraʾel be-Maʿarav ʾEropah*, vol. 2 (Jerusalem and Tel Aviv: Ogen, 1963); Tuvia Preschel, *ʾOr Hamizraḥ*, vol. 9 (1962), 74–76, vol. 10 (1963), 52; Karlinsky, *Rishon le-Shoshelet Brisk*.

10. Soloveitchik's reverential eulogy of Heller is in *Ha-Doʾar*, vol. 40 (1961), rpt. *Shanah be-Shanah* (Jerusalem: Heichal Shlomo, 1970), and as "Peleitat Sofreihem" [Remnant of the Scribes], in Peli, *Be-Sod ha-Yaḥid veha-Yaḥad*, 255–94, trans. and abridged Shalom Carmy, "A Eulogy for R. Hayyim Heller," in Epstein, *Shiʿurei Harav*.

11. Interview with Mordechai Feuerstein, March, 1982 (Jerusalem), citing Alexander Altmann. The halakhic authority, rabbi of Kovno, Abraham Dov ber Kahane Shapira, wrote about the young Soloveitchik baldly: "In each and every contemporary halakhic debate, the law is to be decided in accordance with his view" *(ha-halakhah kamoto be-khol makom)*. Shapira's letter is cited in Moses Soloveitchik's letter, " ʾAv Meʿid ʿal Beno" [A Father Testifies about His Son], Shaul Israeli, Norman Lamm, Yitzhak Raphael, eds., *Jubilee Volume in Honor of Moreinu Hagaon Rabbi Joseph B. Soloveitchik Shelita*, 2 vols. (Jerusalem: Mosad Harav Kuk, and New York: Yeshiva University, 1984), unnumbered pages at end of vol. 1.

12. Besides the analysis of *Halakhic Man* below, see Lichtenstein, "Joseph Soloveitchik," 284–85, and Joseph B. Soloveitchik, "Mah Dodekh mi-Dod [What is Your Beloved-Uncle More Than Another Beloved-Uncle], in Peli, *Be-Sod ha-Yaḥid veha-Yaḥad*, 213, 220–28.

13. Josef Solowiejczyk, *Das reine Denken und die Seinskonstituierung bei Hermann Cohen* (Berlin: Reuther & Reichard, 1932), 113 pp.

14. Unnumbered end page; see also 51 in note (vol. 7, no. 2).

15. Pinchas Peli, "ʾAharit Davar" [Epilogue], ʿAl ha-Teshuvah (Jerusalem: World Zionist Organization, 1975), 315–52, trans., "Repentant Man—A High Level in Rabbi Soloveitchik's Typology of Man," *Tradition*, vol. 18, no. 2 (Summer, 1980), 135–59; Lawrence Kaplan, "Translator's Preface," *Halakhic Man*, xi. See Eugene Borowitz, "The Typological Theology of Rabbi Joseph B. Soloveitchik," *Judaism*, vol. 15, no. 2 (Spring, 1966), rpt. idem, *A New Jewish Theology in the Making* (Philadelphia: The Westminster Press, 1968).

16. The three major essays are "The Lonely Man of Faith," *Tradition*, vol. 7, no. 2 (Summer, 1965); "U-Vikashtem mi-Sham" [And from There You Shall Seek], *Hadorom*, vol. 47 (1978), rpt. Soloveitchik, *ʾIsh ha-Halakhah—Galui ve-Nistar; The Halakhic Mind: An Essay on Jewish Tradition and Modern Thought* (New York: The Free Press, 1986); see also "Confrontation," *Tradition*, vol. 6, no. 2 (Spring-Summer, 1964). As indicated below (III), *The Halakhic Mind* is a temporary exception to the generalization that now follows.

The shorter essays and eulogies thus far collected appear in Epstein, *Shiʿurei Harav* (1974); Peli, *Be-Sod ha-Yaḥid veha-Yaḥad* (1976); and Joseph B. Soloveitchik, *Five Addresses* [Delivered to Conventions of the Mizrachi Religious Zionist Movement during the Period 1962–1967], trans. S. M. Lehrman, A. H. Rabinowitz [from Yiddish? Hebrew?] (Jerusalem: Tal Orot Institute, 1983).

Transcribed lectures are Pinchas Peli, ed., ʿAl ha-Teshuvah (Jerusalem: World Zionist Organization, 1975), trans., *On Repentance* (Jerusalem: Orot, 1980); Abraham R. Besdin, ed., *Reflections of the Rav: Lessons in Jewish Thought adapted from Lectures of Rabbi Joseph B. Soloveitchik* (Jerusalem: World Zionist Organization, 1979).

Some halakhic discourses have been collected in Joseph B. Soloveitchik, *Kovetz Ḥiddushei Torah* (Jerusalem: Machon Yerushalayim, n.d.); idem, *Shiʿurim le-Zekher Abba Mari Z'l* (Jerusalem: Machon Yerushalayim, 1983); idem, *Kuntres be-ʿInyan Yom ha-Kippurim* (Jerusalem: n.p., 1986).

17. Joseph B. Soloveitchik, "Sacred and Profane: *Kodesh* and *Chol* in World Perspectives," *Gesher*, vol. 3, no. 1 (New York: Student Organization of Yeshiva University, 1966), 7. This essay was written in 1945.

18. Kaplan, *Halakhic Man*, 17.

19. Ibid., 141.

20. Ibid., 4.

21. Ibid.

22. Ibid., 141.

23. Ibid.

24. Ibid., 61.
25. Ibid., 58.
26. Ibid.
27. Perhaps an orator of Rabbi Soloveitchik's eloquence has not elicited an evocative account of his popular lectures because of his withdrawal into a personal world, his sharing of insight and knowledge from out of a diaphanous cocoon: one can see through it, but not move through it. One can be moved by the haunting cadences but not identify with them. Of the two reports cited here, the first is the more successful since its context is a weekly, medium level Talmud lecture open to the public. The second—a valiant and detailed attempt—falls flat; its context is the nonhalakhic, aggadic ruminations of Rabbi Soloveitchik's weekly Saturday evening lectures in Boston. See Morris Laub, "Tuesday Evenings with the Rav," *Congress Bi-Weekly* (Nov. 12, 1971), and Mark Jay Mirsky, *My Search for the Messiah: Studies and Wanderings in Israel and America* (New York: Macmillan Publishing Co., 1977), 69–93. See also Edward B. Fiske, "Rabbi's Rabbi Keeps the Law up to Date," *New York Times* (June 23, 1972); Emanuel Feldman, "Reflections of the Rav: Lessons in Jewish Thought," *Tradition*, vol. 19, no. 1 (Summer, 1981), 84–87, rpt. idem, *The Biblical Echo: Reflections on Bible, Jews and Judaism* (Hoboken: Ktav Publishing House, 1986).

The intellectual techniques, as opposed to the affective sense, of Rabbi Soloveitchik's talks are ably described by Norman Lamm, "Notes of An Unrepentant Darshan," Baruch A. Poupko, ed., *Sermon Anthology of the Rabbinical Council of America* (New York: Rabbinical Council Press, 1986), 9–10.

28. "The Lonely Man of Faith," 6.
29. Although the halakhic authority in Kovno pronounced Rabbi Soloveitchik to be capable of rendering halakhic decisions (above, note 11), Rabbi Soloveitchik's forte has always been theoretical Talmud—the elucidation of the reasoning behind differing points of view, not their resolution in practical decision. In an unpublished halakhic responsum integrating philosophic argument and halakhic acumen on the question of whether an interfaith, collegiate chapel is permissible, Rabbi Soloveitchik added a postscript: "I would greatly appreciate it if you would keep the context of this letter confidential. Please do not show it to anyone except those persons who are directly concerned with the matter." The number of Rabbi Soloveitchik's responsa that he has chosen to publish is extremely small. Halakhic man, according to Rabbi Soloveitchik (*Halakhic Man*, 91), "cannot be cowed by anyone. He knows no fear of flesh and blood." But Rabbi Soloveitchik has been fearful of practical Halakhah. It would require him to stretch beyond subjective philosophic musings, to build the legitimacy of an integrated, philosophic-talmudic approach into the Halakhah itself. This—the logical conclusion of his intellectual position and life's work—he has not done. It is as if, despite all, despite the University of Berlin and Yeshiva University, he were always conscious of grandfather Rabbi Hayyim Soloveitchik standing over his shoulder, sternly signaling disapproval.

A carbon copy of the unpublished responsum—four-and-a-half pages, single-

space typewritten, dated Dec. 6, 1950—is in my possession.
Published responsa include: Ten-part series, *Tog Morgen Journal*, Nov. 15, 19, 22, 29, 1954, Dec. 13, 20, 29, 1954, Jan. 3, 10, 17, 1955; Letter to Benjamin Lapidus, *Conservative Judaism*, vol. 11, no. 1 (1956); Letter to Editor, *Cantorial Council of America Bulletin*, vol. 4, no. 1 (1965).
Summaries of and excerpts from Rabbi Soloveitchik's responsa are found in Louis Bernstein, *Challenge and Mission: The Emergence of the English Speaking Orthodox Rabbinate* (New York: Shengold Publishers, 1982), rpt. and abridged in *Jubilee Volume in Honor of Rabbi Soloveitchik*.

30. Kaplan, *Halakhic Man*, 65.
31. Joseph B. Soloveitchik, "Be-Seter uve-Galui" [Concealed and Revealed], in Peli, *Be-Sod ha-Yaḥid veha-Yaḥad*, 312–13.
32. Biography on Hayyim Soloveitchik: Ben Zion Eisenstadt, *Zaddik li-Verakhah* (1919); S. J. Zevin, *'Ishim ve-Shitot* (Jerusalem: Bet Hillel; 1979), 43–85, esp. 43–44; Kaplan, *Halakhic Man*, 24, 35, 36, 52, 73–75, 90–91; Karlinsky, *Rishon le-Shoshelet Brisk*, index.
33. Kaplan, *Halakhic Man*, 63, 24, 94.
34. See note 17.
35. "The Lonely Man of Faith," 6.
36. Ibid., 52 in note, quoting Maimonides, *Guide of the Perplexed* III:51.
37. See above, note 16, for full citations of "U-Vikashtem mi-Sham." Its dating is provided by Rabbi Soloveitchik's son-in-law, Aharon Lichtenstein, cited in Aviezer Ravitsky, "Kinyan ha-Da'at be-Haguto: Bein ha-Rambam le-Neyokantiyanim" [The Acquisition of Knowledge in the Thought of Rabbi Joseph B. Soloveitchik: Between Maimonides and Neo-Kantianism], *Jubilee Volume in Honor of Rabbi Soloveitchik*, vol. 1, p. 129, note 17. For statements on unification in "U-Vikashtem mi-Sham," see, in particular, 193, 198, 202, 204, 233–35 (rpt., *Galuei ve-Nistar*). For Soloveitchik's remembrance, see 230–32; "loneliness" quotation, 230; denouement, 232.
38. Peli, *On Repentance*.
39. *Halakhic Mind*, "Author's Note," vii.
40. Ibid., 56.
41. Ibid., 40.
42. Ibid., 44.
43. Ibid., 40–41.
44. Ibid., 73–74; cf. 127–28 (note 82).
45. Ibid., 78–80.
46. Ibid., 86–99; quotation, 96.
47. Ibid., 49.
48. Ibid., 89.
49. David Vital, *The Origins of Zionism* (Oxford: Oxford University Press, 1975).
50. David Vital, *Zionism: The Formative Years* (Oxford: Oxford University Press, 1982).
51. Letter to Rabbi Jacob Moses Karpas, August 25, 1899, Central Zionist

Archives (Jerusalem), A 9/154/13; cited in Vital, ibid., 212–13; Soloveitchik, *Five Addresses*, 34, 36.

52. Israel Kalusner, *Toledot ha-ʾAgudah Nes Ziona be-Volozhin* [History of the Nes Ziona Group in Volozhin] (Jerusalem: Mosad Harav Kuk, 1954). For a historical summary of early religious Zionism, see Vital, *Zionism: The Formative Years*, 213–29.

53. Biography on Meir Bar Ilan: Meir Bar Ilan, *Mi-Volozhin ʿad Yerushalayim* [From Volozhin to Jerusalem], 2 vols. (Tel Aviv, 1940). Karlinsky, *Rishon le-Shoshelet Brisk*, index.

54. Rabbi Isaac Zev Soloveitchik (1888-1960), Rabbi Hayyim Soloveitchik's eldest son, intellectual heir, and successor as rabbi of Brisk, was staunchly anti-Zionist. This ideology did not preclude his own emigration to Palestine during the Holocaust, nor did it preclude a family tradition initiated by him and adopted by his children and grandchildren never to leave Palestine for America. See Pinchas Biberfeld, "Yitzhak Ze'ev Soloveitchik," Leo Jung, ed., *Men of the Spirit*. On the continuing anti-Zionist tradition of Rabbi Joseph B. Soloveitchik's cousins, the children and grandchildren of Rabbi Isaac Zev Soloveitchik, see Meir Soloveitchik, Untitled Discourse (Jerusalem: xeroxed, 1985). This is a scathing attack on Karlinsky's claim in *Rishon le-Shoshelet Brisk* that Joseph B. Soloveitchik (1820–1897) supported the proto-Zionist Ḥibbat Zion, and an affirmation of the anti-Zionism that they (Rabbi Isaac Zev Soloveitchik's descendants) attribute to the nineteenth-century Joseph B. Soloveitchik.

55. Tension between father and son receded also in light of Moses Soloveitchik's retrospective appreciation of the advantages of his son's secular education. In a recommendation to the Tel Aviv rabbinate electoral commission in 1935, Moses Soloveitchik wrote: "A city such as Tel Aviv, in which different parties abound, requires a leader who can be a rabbi of all the people . . . a guide to all of the different parties. . . . [My son] is the one who can be a common denominator, from one end of the populace to the other—a gathering point for all camps. . . . Some will seek instruction from him in Torah, others in secular knowledge. . . ." " ʾAv Meʿid ʿal Beno," *Jubilee Volume in Honor of Rabbi Soloveitchik*.

Rabbi Soloveitchik's talmudic lectures on the anniversary of his father's death are dedicated to his memory and contain personal remarks of great reverence. *Shiʿurim le-Zekher Abba Mari Z'l* [Lectures in Memory of My Father and Master]; "Sacred and Profane," 23, 29.

56. Moses Soloveitchik, "ʾAv Meʿid ʿal Beno"; Zvi Kaplan, "ʾIyyunim be-ʾIshiyyuto uve-Yetzirutav" [Reflections on Rabbi Soloveitchik's Personality and Works], *Jubilee Volume in Honor of Rabbi Soloveitchik*, 3.

57. Joseph B. Soloveitchik, "Kol Dodi Dofek" [The Voice of My Beloved Knocks], Peli, *Be-Sod ha-Yaḥid veha-Yaḥad*, esp. 347–67, 390–400; idem, *Five Addresses*, 36, 116–17, 137–38, 150, 152, 170; cf. Soloveitchik's eulogy for Zev Wolf Gold (1889–1956), organizer of Mizrachi in America and, after emigration to Palestine, representative of Mizrachi on the executive of the Jewish Agency, "Be-Seter uve-Galui," 316–28. The praise of Zionism is never absolute. The State

of Israel is seen as a positive halakhic reality, but also as led by secularists who fail to recognize this. Their intentions must be carefully scrutinized and, when necessary, criticized. See *Five Addresses*, 35, 36, 79–81, 113–14, 117–23, 138.

58. Rabbi Soloveitchik's sympathetic and forceful defense of the ironclad opposition of his uncle, Rabbi Isaac Zev (note 54), to the institution of the chief rabbinate bespeaks typical contradiction. Rabbi Joseph B. Soloveitchik, Orthodox Jewry's most respected intellectual defender of religious Zionism and its movement, Mizrachi, sides with Rabbi Isaac Zev Soloveitchik, one of the most respected intellectual opponents of religious Zionism and of that institution most directly responsible for Judaism in the State of Israel, the chief rabbinate. Rabbi Joseph B. Soloveitchik, the conservative, wishes to retain the charismatic authority of the rabbinate of the Diaspora, and simultaneously to alter radically the political authority of the Jewish people by institutionalizing it in the State of Israel. See Joseph B. Soloveitchik, "Mah Dodekh mi-Dod," 246–50.

59. Symptomatic of the split is the table of contents of *Jubilee Volume* in Rabbi Soloveitchik's honor. The articles are divided into four sections, two in halakhic discourse and two in Jewish thought. Of the eighty-one contributors, only one contributed to both a section in Halakhah and a section in Jewish thought.

60. Moses Maimonides, *Mishneh Torah* [Code of Maimonides], Hilkhot Tefillah 1:1; Moses Nahmanides, commentary to Maimonides' *Sefer ha-Mitzvot* [Books of the Commandments], Mitzvah 5.

61. Ibid.

62. Besdin, *Reflections of the Rav*, 80–81.

63. Ibid., 81–82.

64. Ibid., 82.

65. The distinction between Maimonides and Nahmanides has been informatively summarized by Bernard Septimus, " 'Open Rebuke and Concealed Love': Nahmanides and the Andalusian Tradition," in Isadore Twersky, ed., *Rabbi Moses Nahmanides (Ramban): Explorations in His Religious and Literary Virtuosity* (Cambridge, Massachusetts, and London: Harvard University Press, 1983), 11:

> For a very long time there has been an almost irresistible urge to juxtapose Nahmanides to Maimonides. They were the two most influential teachers of the Hispano-Jewish tradition, differed on many crucial issues and represented rival spiritual tendencies. Sometimes one also suspects the old rhetorical pull of *paranomasia contrarium:* look how that little shift from *mem* to *nun* moves us from Rambam to his antithetical counterpart Ramban! In any case, rather than repeat such stale Rambam-Rambam oppositions as reason and faith, thought and feeling, philosophy and mysticism, I prefer to succumb to the traditional temptation with a contextual contrast: Maimonides was the last great figure formed by the "golden age" of Andalusia. Nahmanides was the first great Spanish figure belonging totally to the cultural environment of Christian Europe.

66. The impact of the death of his wife was deepened by the loss of his mother

and his brother, all three within a few months of each other. His move to openness progressed further in about 1975, when he mellowed. As one observer put it, "he graduated from fatherhood to grandfatherhood." He began to invite his Talmud students at Yeshiva University to visit his apartment there. It should be noted that the shift from closedness to confession, which came to punctuate his public lectures, was, however, already developing before the death of his wife. See "The Lonely Man of Faith" (1965), 5–10.

67. Fragility:
> In its very broad outlines, [Rabbi Soloveitchik's] philosophy or way of life finds great resonance among the modern Orthodox, who see in it a vindication of their own involvement in the secular world. But when Rabbi Soloveitchik attempts to apply this philosophy of life to reality, his position is often indecisive, vacillating, and quite contrary to expectations. It is the Orthodox who made of Rabbi Soloveitchik a charismatic leader; he disdains this role for himself.

Charles Liebman, "The Training of American Rabbis," 69. See note 29.

Enigma:
> Even though the Rov ['the Rabbi,' that is, Rabbi Soloveitchik] has stamped his seal individually and uniquely on generations of rabbis, yeshiva deans, educators, thinkers, and researchers, he has remained as God himself—cryptic and concealed (nish'ar be-geder tamir ve-ne'elam). It appears to me that autobiographical echoes permeate the Rov's comments in his use of the biblical Joseph the Righeous as an archetype to characterize one of the great leaders of the previous generation [Zev Wolf Gold; note 57]. As is well known, even the brothers of Joseph the Righteous did not fathom the secret buried within his multifaceted personality. "And they saw him from the distance" as possessed of a "coat of many stripes" since they were unable to penetrate to the essence of his closed, introversive personality. With respect to the Rov, we encounter the identical paradox: His coat of many stripes—his wondrous achievements in halakhah, aggadah, and philosophy—have acquired for him fame throughout the world; he is crowned with the crown of Torah, together with the crown of a good name, in splendrous and exemplary fashion; masses of admirers converge to hear his teaching. And yet, the famous halakhic man remains "the lonely man of faith."

Walter Wurzburger, "Ha-Metah ha-Dialekti bein 'Ish ha-Halakhah' u-ven 'Ish ha-'Emunah ha-Boded' " [The Dialectical Tension between 'Halakhic Man' and 'The Lonely Man of Faith' "], *Jubilee Volume in Honor of Rabbi Soloveitchik*, 56.

Liebman, defending Rabbi Soloveitchik, and Wurzburger, praising him, nonetheless felicitously express his fragility and enigma.

68. Kaplan, *Halakhic Man*, 74.

69. Dov Katz, *Tenu'at ha-Musar* [The Musar Movement], vol. 3 (Tel Aviv: Abraham Zioni, rev. ed., 1967), 21, 26–56.

70. Kaplan, *Halakhic Man*, 74.

71. This animating assumption in the writings of Rabbi Israel and his disciples

rises to explicit expression in a number of texts and terms, the most important of the latter being ʾ*adam ha-shalam,* "the harmonious man." It appears in Israel Salanter, *Tevunah* [Understanding] (Memel: August Stobbe, 1861–1862), 32 col. 2, 88 col. 2, 103. The term's place in Rabbi Israel's thought is elaborated in Hillel Goldberg, *Israel Salanter: Text, Structure, Idea—the Ethics and Theology of an Early Psychologist of the Unconscious* (New York: Ktav Publishing House, 1982), 116–17, 135, 137, 144–46, 150, 196.

72. Goldberg, ibid., Part Two, II:2; Part Four, IV.
73. Kaplan, *Halakhic Man,* 65.
74. Ibid., 74.
75. Ibid.
76. On Rabbi Blazer's spiritual tendencies, see his Introduction and "Shaʿarei ʾOr" [Gates of Light] in Isaac Blazer, ed., ʾ*Or Yisrael* (Vilna, 1900), esp. 4, 33, and 37. On these three pages Rabbi Blazer lists techniques of Musar study, cited in the name of his mentor Rabbi Israel. As Rabbi Benjamin J. Zilber has pointed out to me, Rabbi Blazer's listing does not fully tally with Rabbi Israel's (cf., for example, Rabbi Israel's second letter, ʾ*Or Yisrael,* 43 paragraph 2; and his postscript to letter 65 in Shraga Wilman, ʾ*Iggerot u-Mikhtavim* [Brooklyn, 1970], 73). To Rabbi Israel's techniques of learning Musar books "with a proper heart, with lips aflame, with impassioning of the soul" (ʾ*Or Yisrael,* 4), Rabbi Blazer adds a phrase nowhere found in Rabbi Israel's writings, "with a voice arousing sorrow and melancholy" *(tugah va-ʿetzev).* Whether this tonality represents Rabbi Blazer's own departure or an oral instruction from Rabbi Israel, it is clear that Rabbi Blazer dwelled on sin, on its debilitating effect on spiritual life, and on its transcendent consequence—Divine punishment. None of this and its variations prevented him or others—Eliezer Gordon, yeshiva dean in Telshe, to name but one—from making their mark as preeminent halakhic scholars. On Gordon's allegiance to Musar, even in the face of progressively violent student rebellion, see Jeruham Warhaftig, Introduction, *Shalmei Yeruham* (Jerusalem, 1941), and esp. Samuel Kol, ʾ*Eḥad be-Doro: Korot Ḥayyav, Maʾavako, u-Faʿalo shel Rabbi Yosef Shelomo Kahaneman ha-Gaon mi-Ponivech* [Unique in His Generation: The Life, Struggle, and Work of Joseph Solomon Cahaneman, Gaon from Ponevitch], vol. 1, no. 1 (Tel Aviv: Orot, 1970), 54–72. Blazer's halakhic work is *Peri Yitzhak,* 2 vols. in one (Kfar Hasidim, Israel: Yeshivat Knesset Hizkiyyahu, 2nd rev. ed., 1975); Gordon's, *Teshuvot R. Eliezer* (Pietrekow, 1923).

According to Isadore Twersky, Harry Austryn Wolfson used to overflow with remembrance of things past, such as Rabbi Blazer's last Musar talk in Slobodka (which was in 1903, not, as Twersky writes, prior to Blazer's assumption of the rabbinate in St. Petersburg, which was in 1862). Twersky, "Harry Austryn Wolfson, in Appreciation," Leo W. Schwarz, *Wolfson of Harvard: Portrait of a Scholar* (Philadelphia: Jewish Publication Society of America, 1978), xix–xx.

77. Katz, *Tenuʿat ha-Musar,* vols. 2–5.
78. Hillel Goldberg, "Early Modern Musar," *Immanuel,* no. 17 (Winter, 1983/84), 112–13.

79. Rabbi Israel's twentieth letter (Wilman, *Iggerot u-Mikhtavim*, 40) dates his presence in Berlin to 1864.
80. Wilman, ibid., letter 39 (Memel, 1876), 55; Emil Benjamin, *Jsrael Lipkin Salant* (Berlin, 1899), i; cf. Wilman, letter 33 (Memel, 1874), 47–48, on Rabbi Israel's knowledge of German, and analysis in Goldberg, *Israel Salanter*, Part Five, note 73, pp. 297–98.

6. Professor Abraham Joshua Heschel

1. Fritz A. Rothschild, "Abraham Joshua Heschel (1907–1972): Theologian and Scholar" [necrology], *American Jewish Yearbook*, vol. 74 (New York: American Jewish Committee, and Philadelphia: Jewish Publication Society of America, 1973), 533. On Heschel's mother's name, see dedicatory page, Abraham Joshua Heschel, *Torah min ha-Shamayim be-'Aspaklaryah shel ha-Dorot* [Theology of Ancient Judaism], vol. 1 (London and New York: Soncino Press, 1962).
2. Samuel H. Dresner, Introduction to Abraham Joshua Heschel, *I Asked for Wonder: A Spiritual Anthology*, ed. Samuel H. Dresner (New York: Crossroad, 1983), x.
3. Interview with Samuel H. Dresner, student of Heschel, March, 1985 (Jerusalem). See also Samuel H. Dresner, Introduction to Abraham Joshua Heschel, *The Circle of the Baal Shem Tov: Studies in Hasidism*, ed. Samuel H. Dresner (Chicago and London: University of Chicago Press, 1985), xxviii–xix.
4. Abraham Joshua Heschel, *A Passion for Truth* (New York: Farrar, Straus and Giroux, 1973), xiii–xv; *Kotsk: In Gerangl far Emesdikeit* [Kotsk: The Struggle for Integrity] (Tel Aviv: Hamenorah Publishing House, 1973), vol. 1, pp. 7, 10. For Heschel's ancestry, see Dresner, Introduction, *The Circle of the Baal Shem Tov*, xxviii note 35, xxix.
5. Interview with Wolfe Kelman, associate of Heschel, May, 1985 (Jerusalem). According to Dresner (*The Circle of the Baal Shem Tov*, xxvii–xxviii), Heschel's mother once entered Heschel's room after noticing that she no longer heard him chanting Talmud, and found him learning Polish. Apparently he then adopted his method of chanting declensions to talmudic singsong as a way of precluding maternal and larger familial distress.
6. *A Passion for Truth*, xv.
7. In *The Circle of the Baal Shem Tov*, xxviii, Dresner recounts a meeting between the Novominsker Rebbe and Heschel, prior to Heschel's leaving Warsaw. The Rebbe had tried to dissuade Heschel, unsuccessfully. He then told his nephew, "You can go, but *only* you." The faith in Heschel's capacity not to become polluted by secular society could only have heightened the perplexity at Heschel's decision to leave. For if secular society would not pollute him, then there was no reason for it to have tempted him. Such would run the logic of someone for whom hasidic society and teaching were self-validating and all absorbing.
8. See Heschel's tributes to Hebrew poet and translator, "Hillel Bavli: In

Memoriam," *Conservative Judaism*, vol. XVII, nos. 1–2 (Fall, 1962–Winter, 1963), and to Hebrew translator and scholar, "Zevi Diesendruck," *American Jewish Yearbook*, vol. 43 (Philadelphia: Jewish Publication Society of America, 1941), esp. 394–96. Heschel wrote his major study of Jewish theology in Hebrew; see below.

9. See Heschel's eulogy-tribute to the Polish-Jewish artist, "Ilya Schor z'l," *Conservative Judaism*, vol. XVI, no. 1 (Fall, 1961); and Yudel Mark, "Heschl un Yiddish" [Heschel and Yiddish], *Conservative Judaism*, vol. XXVIII, no. 1 (Fall, 1973). Heschel wrote his major study of Hasidism in Yiddish; see below.

10. Heschel was ordained in 1934 from the Hochschule, the Reform rabbinical seminary in Berlin, and was a teacher from 1940 to 1945 at the American Reform rabbinical seminary in Cincinnati. He resigned in 1945 because "I do not feel that my own interpretation of Judaism is in full accord with the teachings of the College," but at the end of his life he told the president of Hebrew Union College that "he was pleased with the developments within the School as of late and, indeed, if he were to have been a Professor at the College today, he would have seen no need to leave." Alfred Gottschalk, "Abraham Joshua Heschel: A Man of Dialogues," *Conservative Judaism*, vol. XXVIII, no. 1 (Fall, 1973), 24–25.

11. Heschel was chosen by the highest plurality of students at Conservative Judaism's Jewish Theological Seminary of America as "the rabbi who best reflects their own religious-philosophical-theological position." Charles Liebman, "The Training of American Rabbis," *American Jewish Yearbook*, vol. 69 (New York: American Jewish Committee, and Philadelphia: Jewish Publication Society of America, 1968), 84–85.

12. Heschel's views on the divine revelation of Torah and the indispensability of Halakhah, or Jewish law, which are scattered throughout his writings, were received as Orthodox, or close to it, by many Orthodox thinkers. In Heschel's writings, see, in particular, "Toward an Understanding of Halakha," *Yearbook, The Central Conference of American Rabbis*, vol. 63 (1953); *God in Search of Man: A Philosophy of Judaism* (New York: Farrar, Straus, and Cudahy, 1955; rpt., Foreward, Susannah Heschel, Northval and London: Aronson, 1987), chapters 17, 27, 33; and *Torah min ha-Shamayim*, 2 vols. (1962, 1965). For Orthodox response, see Marvin Fox, "Heschel, Intuition, and the Halakhah," *Tradition*, vol. 3, no. 1 (Fall, 1960); Zalman M. Schachter, "Two Facets of Judaism," *Tradition*, vol. 3, no. 2, esp. 210; Eliezer Berkovits, "Dr. A. J. Heschel's Theology of Pathos," *Tradition*, vol. 6, no. 2 (Spring–Summer, 1964), rpt. in idem, *Major Themes in Modern Philosophies of Judaism* (New York: Ktav Publishing House, 1974); Marvin Fox, "Heschel's Theology of Man," *Tradition*, vol. 8, no. 3 (Fall, 1966); Norman Lamm, "Abraham Joshua Heschel, Teacher," *Sh'ma*, vol. 3, no. 46 (January 19, 1973).

13. Abraham Joshua Heschel, "The Individual Jew and His Obligations" [paper presented in Hebrew to the Jerusalem Ideological Conference, The Hebrew University, 1957], "Israel and the Diaspora" [paper presented to the 58th convention of the Rabbinical Assembly of America, 1958], in *The Insecurity of Free-*

dom: Essays on Human Existence (New York: Schocken Books, 1975); "A Time for Renewal [address delivered to 28th World Zionist Congress, Jerusalem, 1972], *Midstream*, vol. XVIII, no. 5 (May, 1972).

14. Heschel's writings closest in form to *Wissenschaft des Judentums* are his early papers in medieval Jewish philosophy and his studies of four hasidic masters in the circle of the founder of Hasidism, the Baal Shem Tov. See "Der Begriff des Seins in der Philosophie Gabirols," in *Festschrift Jakob Friemann zum 70. Geburtstag* (Berlin, 1937), trans. and abridged, David Wolf Silverman, "The Concept of 'Beings' in the Philosophy of ibn Gabirol," *Conservative Judaism*, vol. XXVIII, no. 1 (Fall, 1973); "Der Begriff der Einheit in der Philosophie Gabirols," in *Monatsschrift fuer die Geschichte und Wissenschaft des Judentums*, vol. 82 (1938); "Das Wessen der Dinge nach der Lehre Gabirols," *Hebrew Union College Annual*, vol. 14 (1939); *A Concise Dictionary of Hebrew Philosophical Terms* (Cincinnati: Hebrew Union College, 1941) [mimeographed]; Dresner, ed., *The Circle of the Baal Shem Tov: Studies in Hasidism*.

15. Rothschild, "Abraham Joshua Heschel," 534. For a brief memoir of Heschel in this period, see Shlomo Beillis, "The Beginnings of Young Vilna," quoted in Dresner, *The Circle of the Baal Shem Tov*, xxx.

16. "Ich un Du; Beyn Hashmoshes; Vandlungen; Noyt; Oreman; Got Geyt Mir nokh Umetum," in *Berliner Bleter far Dikhtung un Kunst*, vol. 1, no. 1 (Berlin, November, 1931). The talmudic novellae appeared in *Sha'arei Torah: Kovetz Rabbani Hodshi* (Warsaw), vol. 13, no. 1 (Tishrei–Kislev, 5683 [1922]), vol. 13, no. 2 (Tevet–Adar, 5683 [1923]), vol. 13, no. 3 (Nisan–Iyar, 5683 [1923]).

17. *Der Sheym Hamfoyrosh: Mentsh* (Warsaw: Farlag Indsl, 1933); seven poems trans. Zalman M. Schachter, *Sh'ma*, vol. 3, no. 46 (January 19, 1973).

18. Rothschild, "Abraham Joshua Heschel," 534.

19. Louis Finkelstein, "Three Meetings with Abraham Joshua Heschel," *Conservative Judaism*, vol. XXVIII, no. 1 (Fall, 1973), 19.

20. "Toward an Understanding of Halakha," 386–87.

21. Ibid., 387–92. The critical analysis of Kant in this article is omitted in its republication in Abraham Joshua Heschel, *Man's Quest for God: Studies in Prayer and Symbolism* (New York: Charles Scribner's Sons, 1954; rpt. New York: Crossroad, 1982), 93–114.

22. "Toward an Understanding of Halakha," 387.

23. Ibid., 388.

24. Abraham Joshua Heschel, *Who is Man?* [The Raymond Fred West Memorial Lectures on Immortality, Human Conduct, and Human Destiny] (Stanford: Stanford University Press, 1965), 111.

25. Jacob Neusner, "Faith in the Crucible of the Mind," *America*, vol. 128, no. 9 (March 10, 1973), 209. I am indebted to this article for its analysis of Heschel's objections to Kant as ontological rather than epistemological. Somewhat revised, the article appears as "An American Jewish Life: Abraham Joshua Heschel as a Religious Thinker" in Jacob Neusner, *Israel in America: A Too-Comfortable Exile?* (Boston: Beacon Press, 1985).

26. Heschel, *God in Search of Man*, 31.
27. Ibid., 33–34.
28. Ibid., 38.
29. Ibid., 46.
30. Abraham Joshua Heschel, *Man is Not Alone: A Philosophy of Religion* (New York: Farrar, Straus, and Giroux, 1951; rpt. New York: Harper Torchbooks, 1966), 20.
32. Ibid.
32. Ibid., 8.
33. *God in Search of Man*, 74.
34. Neusner, "Faith in the Crucible of the Mind," 209.
35. Abraham Joshua Heschel, *Die Prophetie* [German] (Cracow: The Polish Academy of Sciences, 1936), esp. Part Three, 127–65.
36. Sylvia Heschel, Foreword to Abraham Joshua Heschel, *Maimonides: A Biography* (originally published as *Maimonides, Eine Biographie* [Berlin: Erich Reiss Verlag, 1935]), trans. Joachim Neugroschel (New York: Farrar, Straus, and Giroux, 1982), ix.
37. "My entire world outlook was crystalized in the atmosphere of Rambam [Maimonides' Code] and Rabad, of legal conceptualization." Joseph B. Soloveitchik, "And Joseph Dreamt a Dream," *Five Addresses* (Jerusalem: Tal Orot Institute, 1983), trans. (from Yiddish? Hebrew?) by S. M. Lehrman, 34.
38. Reuven Kimelman, "Abraham Joshua Heschel (1907–1972) zts'l," *Response* (Winter, 1972–1973), 20.
39. *Maimonides*, 34. The first quotation, cited by Heschel, is the words of Maimonides himself in Introduction, *Commentary on the Mishnah* (rpt. in Babylonian Talmud, standard editions).
40. *Maimonides*, 34.
41. "The wisdom of philosophers is not a commodity that can be produced on demand. Their books are not responsa. We should not regard them as mirrors, reflecting other people's problems, but rather as windows, allowing us to view the author's soul. Philosophers do not expend their power and passion unless they themselves are affected, originally or vicariously. The soul only communes with itself when the heart is stirred." Abraham Joshua Heschel, *The Quest for Certainty in Saadia's Philosophy* (New York: Feldheim, 1944), 1. See also *Maimonides*, 29, 131, 137, 161, for application of the approach that wisdom in books reflects stirrings in their authors.
42. *Maimonides*, 34.
43. Ibid., 76.
44. Ibid., 87, quoting Maimonides, in A. Lichtenberg, ed., *Kovetz Teshuvot ha-Rambam ve-ʾIggerotav* [Compendium of Maimonides' Responsa and Letters] (Leipzig, 1859), vol. 1, 25c ff.
45. Ibid.
46. *Maimonides*, 93.
47. Ibid., 91.

48. Ibid., 92.
49. Ibid., 242–43.
50. Ibid., 127, quoting Maimonides, in Lichtenberg, ed., *Kovetz*, vol. 2, 37d.
51. *Maimonides*, 137.
52. Ibid., 135.
53. He was publishing still earlier. His poem, "In Tog fun Has," was written on April 1, 1933, on the occasion of the book-burning by the Nazis in the Berlin Opernplatz, according to Heschel's bibliographer, Fritz Rothschild, in Abraham Joshua Heschel, *Between God and Man: An Interpretation of Judaism*, ed. Fritz Rothschild (New York: The Free Press, rev. ed., 1975), 278. The poem appeared under the pseudonym, "Itzig," in *Haynt* (Warsaw, May 10, 1933). Heschel's response to the Holocaust, with which we deal below, originated in an address in March, 1938, delivered at a conference of Quaker leaders in Frankfurt am Main (Rothschild, ed., *Between God and Man*, 262).

In 1937, Heschel had an eerie foreboding. The spiritual foundation of the passivity of most of the six million—that it was theirs to be killed rather than to kill—marked the conclusion of Heschel's study of Abravanel, the medieval Spanish scholar and diplomat whose high connections and strenuous efforts could not stave off the expulsion of Spanish Jewry. Dedicated to Abravanel's life and work, Heschel's short book ends abruptly, unexpectedly, with ironic hindsight both historical and theological:

> The Jews, who . . . had held imposing positions, left their Spanish homeland. The conquest of the New World was accomplished without their collaboration. Had they remained on the Iberian peninsula, they most probably would have taken part in the enterprises of the conquistadores. When the latter arrived on Haiti, they found over one million inhabitants. Twenty years later one thousand remained. The desperate Jews of 1492 could not know what a favor had been done for them.

Abraham Joshua Heschel, *Don Jizchak Abravanel* (Berlin: Erich Reiss Verlag, 1937), trans., abridged, William Wolf, "Witness to Sefardic Jewry's Descent to Agony," *Intermountain Jewish News Literary Supplement*, vol. 4, no. 2 (December 19, 1986).

54. *Yivo Annual of Jewish Social Science*, vol. 1 (New York: Yiddish Scientific Institute–Yivo, 1946), originally delivered at the annual conference of the Yiddish Scientific Institute, January, 1945 (see unnumbered end page in source cited in next note).
55. New York: Henry Schuman, 1950; rpt. New York: Harper Torchbooks, 1966.
56. Both Rothschild, ed., *Between God and Man*, 262, and Heschel, *Man's Quest for God*, x, list this article as having appeared in "a 1943 issue of *The Hebrew Union College Bulletin*." I have not located this. The article does appear in *Liberal Judaism*, vol. 11, no. 10 (February, 1944). It originated as an address delivered in 1938 (see above, note 53). In its republication in *Man's Quest for God*, all contemporaneous references to Jews in ghettoes and death camps, which

give the article its visceral power, are omitted.
57. "The Meaning of This War," 18.
58. Ibid.
59. Ibid., 19. My italics.
60. Ibid., 20.
61. Ibid.
62. Ibid., 21.
63. Ibid.
64. Ibid.
65. Heschel's later account of how agitated he was during World War II was not reflected in anything he wrote during that period, except for the few searing sentences, referring to the Holocaust, in "The Meaning of This War"—sentences now omitted in the postwar publication of that article. Clearly, Heschel was agitated; just as clearly he labored to transfigure agitation—which he was unable to put to any practical use—into a theological-political program for the future. Excerpts from an interview with Heschel by Gershon Jacobson, *Day-Morning Journal* (June 13, 1963), cited, trans. Dresner, ed., *The Circle of the Baal Shem Tov*, xxv, note 30:

"I was an immigrant, a refugee. No one listened to me. Let me mention three examples: In 1941 I met with a prominent Jewish communal leader, a devoted Zionist. I told him that the Jews of the Warsaw ghetto endure in the belief that American Jewry is working ceaselessly on their behalf. Were they to know of our indifference, the Jews in Warsaw would perish from shock. My words fell on deaf ears. In 1942 or 1941, I was at a convention of Reform rabbis. A representative of the Quakers appeared, demanding that the rabbis adopt a resolution to have food parcels sent to the Jews in the ghettoes and concentration camps. The appeal was turned down. The rabbis explained that they could not do it officially, because it might aid the Germans by sending food into their territory. In 1943 I attended the "American Jewish Conference" of all Jewish organizations, to appeal that they act to extinguish the flames which had engulfed Eastern European Jewry. The "Conference" had a long agenda—Eretz-Yisrael, fascism, finances, etc.—the last item of which was Jews under the Germans. By the time they reached this issue, almost all the representatives had left. I went away brokenhearted."

What then, in fact, did you do?

"I went to Rabbi Eliezer Silver's synagogue in Cincinnati [where Heschel resided], recited Psalms, fasted, and cried myself out. I was a stranger in this country. My word had no power. When I did speak, they shouted me down. They called me a mystic, unrealistic. I had no influence on leaders of American Jewry."

Heschel's efforts would have to be turned inward, in laying the theological ground for future influence.

66. Abraham Joshua Heschel, "The Inner World of the Polish Jew," in Roman

Vishniac, *Polish Jews: A Pictorial Record* (New York: Schocken Books, 1947; rpt. 1965), 17; rpt. of "The Eastern European Era in Jewish History," *Yivo Annual* (1946).

67. Dresner, ed., *The Circle of the Baal Shem Tov*. See Steven T. Katz, "Abraham Joshua Heschel and Hasidism," *Journal of Jewish Studies*, vol. 31, no. 1 (Spring, 1980), and the response of Zanvel E. Klein, "Heschel as a Hasidic Scholar," *Journal of Jewish Studies*, vol. 32, no. 2 (Autumn, 1981).

68. *Man* (New York: Farrar, Straus, and Young, and Philadelphia: The Jewish Publication Society of America, 1951); *God* (New York: Farrar, Straus, and Cudahy, 1955; rpt. with Foreword by Susannah Heschel, Northval and London: Aronson, 1987).

69. Cracow: The Polish Academy of Sciences [German].

70. New York: Harper and Row, and Philadelphia: The Jewish Publication Society of America, 1962.

71. "May I make a personal statement here? I've written a book on the prophets, a rather large book. I spent many years. And, really, this book changed my life. Because early in my life, my great love was for learning, studying. And the place where I preferred to live was my study and books and writing and thinking. I've learned from the prophets that I have to be involved in the affairs of man, in the affairs of suffering man." "A Conversation with Abraham Joshua Heschel" (New York: National Broadcasting Co., 1973), 6.

72. Rothschild, "Abraham Joshua Heschel," 534; Finkelstein, "Three Meetings," 19. Heschel's foremost student from the Hebrew Union College period is Samuel H. Dresner. For brief memoirs of Heschel at HUC, see Richard Rubenstein, *Power Struggle* (New York: Charles Scribner's Sons, 1974), and Lou H. Silberman, "Rebbe for Our Day," *Jewish Heritage*, vol. 13, no. 3 (Fall, 1971).

73. *The Earth is the Lord's*, 1950, *Man is Not Alone*, 1951, *The Sabbath: Its Meaning for Modern Man* (New York: Farrar, Straus, and Young, 1951; rpt. New York: Harper Torchbooks, 1966); *Man's Quest for God*, 1954, *God in Search of Man*, 1955.

74. Theodore H. White, *In Search of History: A Personal Adventure* (New York: Warner Books, 1978), 373.

75. Morris Dickstein, *Gates of Eden: American Culture in the Sixties* (New York: Basic Books, 1977), 51, citing D. H. Lawrence.

76. See Dickstein, ibid., ix.

77. See Harold Weisberg, "Ideologies of American Jews," in Oscar I. Janowsky, ed., *The American Jew: A Reappraisal* (Philadelphia: Jewish Publication Society of America, 1964); Norman Podhoretz, *Making It* (New York: Bantam Books, 1969), chapter four, esp. 90–92.

78. On the roots of Heschel's resonance in America, see Hillel Goldberg, "Abraham Joshua Heschel and His Times," *Midstream*, vol. XXVIII, no. 4 (April, 1982), and unpublished footnotes; S. Daniel Breslauer, *The Impact of Abraham Joshua Heschel as Jewish Leader in the American Jewish Community from the 1960s to His Death: A Social, Psychological, and Intellectual Study* (Ph.D. dis-

sertation: Brandeis University, 1974), 1, 134, 138; Jacob Neusner, "Faith in the Crucible of the Mind." Neusner argues that Heschel's writings generated his prominence; Breslauer argues that Heschel's charisma generated his prominence. For Neusner, Heschel was a leader with an intellectual constituency; for Breslauer, a leader without a constituency. I differentiated between an intellectual impact in the 1950s, and a skillful intervweaving in the 1960s of universalistic and particularistic ideology, and of ideology and charisma (depending on the constituency), which generated Heschel's prominence among several constituencies otherwise at odds with each other.

79. Heschel, *The Prophets*, 3, 5, 6, 11, 17.

80. Rothschild, "Abraham Joshua Heschel," 535–36; Finkelstein, "Three Meetings," 20–22; Naomi W. Cohen, *Not Free to Desist: The American Jewish Committee, 1906–1966* (Philadelphia: Jewish Publication Society of America, 1972), chapter 17, esp. 467, 469, 473. On Heschel's relations with Protestants, including his antimissionary efforts, see J. A. Sanders, "An Apostle to the Gentiles," *Conservative Judaism*, vol. XXVIII, no. 1 (Fall, 1973), and John C. Bennet, "Agent of God's Compassion," *America*, vol. 128, no. 9 (March 10, 1973). Heschel's appreciation of Reinhold Niebuhr is "Confusion of Good and Evil," *The Insecurity of Freedom* (rpt. of "A Hebrew Evaluation of Reinhold Niebuhr," in Charles W. Kegley and Robert Bretall, eds., *Reinhold Niebuhr: His Religious, Social and Political Thought* [New York: The Macmillan Co., 1956]), and "Reinhold Niebuhr: A Last Farewell," *Conservative Judaism*, vol. XXV, no. 4 (Summer, 1971). See also Abraham Joshua Heschel, "Protestant Renewal: A Jewish View," *The Insecurity of Freedom* (rpt. from *The Christian Century*, vol. 80, no. 49 [Dec. 4, 1963]); "The Ecumenical Movement" [address at dinner for Augustin Cardinal Bea, New York, N.Y., April 1, 1963], *The Insecurity of Freedom* (rpt. from *Catholic News*, vol. 78, no. 14 [New York, April 4, 1963]); "No Religion is an Island," *Union Seminary Quarterly Review*, vol. 21, no. 2, part 1 (January, 1966), rpt. Frank E. Talmage, ed., *Disputation and Dialogue: Readings in the Jewish-Christian Encounter* (New York: Ktav Publishing House and Anti-Defamation League, 1975), 249–50); [Discussion on Second Vatican Council and the Jews], John H. Miller, ed., *Vatican II: An Interfaith Appraisal* (Notre Dame and London: Notre Dame University Press, 1966), 373–74.

81. "Jews in the Soviet Union" [paper presented to the Conference on the Moral Implications of the Rabbinate, Jewish Theological Seminary of America, Sept. 4, 1963], *The Insecurity of Freedom* (rpt. from *The Day–Jewish Journal*, September 12–13, October 12, 1963). See also "A Declaration of Conscience" [paper read to New York Conference on Soviet Jewry, Hunter College, October 28, 1964], *The Insecurity of Freedom;* and Foreward, Ronald I. Rubin, ed., *The Unredeemed: Antisemitism in the Soviet Union* (Chicago: Quadrangle Books, 1968).

82. "The White Man on Trial" [paper read to Metropolitan Conference on Religion and Race, February 25, 1964], *The Insecurity of Freedom*, 106; rpt. from *Proceedings* of the conference. See also "Religion and Race" [opening address at

National Conference on Religion and Race, Chicago, January 14, 1963], *The Insecurity of Freedom* (rpt. from Mathew Ahmann, ed., *Race: Challenge to Religion* [Chicago: Henry Regnery Co., 1963]); and comments of Martin Luther King, Jr., with whom Heschel marched in Selma, Alabama, March, 1965, in "Conversation with Martin Luther King" [King's answers to questions, prefaced by remarks by King and Heschel, at 68th annual convention of Rabbinical Assembly, March 25, 1968], *Conservative Judaism*, vol. XXII, no. 3 (Spring, 1968).

83. Abraham Joshua Heschel, "The Moral Outrage in Vietnam," in Robert McAfee Brown, A. J. Heschel, and Michael Novak, *Vietnam: Crisis of Conscience* (New York: Association Press, Behrman House, Herder & Herder, 1967); [Address given at Riverside Church, New York City, April 4, 1967], *Dr. Martin Luther King, Jr., Dr. John Bennett, Dr. Henry Steele Commager, Rabbi Abraham Heschel Speak on the War in Vietnam* [pamphlet] (New York: Clergy and Laymen Concerned about Vietnam, 1967); John C. Bennet, "Agent of God's Compassion"; Dresner, Introduction, *I Asked for Wonder*, ix.

84. Jacob Neusner, correspondence, *Judaism*, vol. 15, no. 2 (Spring, 1966), 223–24, and vol. 16, no. 3 (Summer, 1967), 363; Emil Fackenheim, "Jewish Faith and the Holocaust: A Fragment," *Commentary*, vol. 46, no. 2 (August, 1968); Frank E. Talmage, "Christianity and the Jewish People," in Talmage, ed., *Disputation and Dialogue*.

85. New York: Farrar, Straus, and Giroux, 1969.

86. The period of gestation of the pertinent books, speeches, and activities of Heschel anteceded the emergence of the causes to which he became committed. It was not until the massive march on Washington in August, 1963, that most of the United States united behind the legislative goals of the civil rights movement. But Heschel's active involvement began much earlier in 1963 (see above, note 82), and his expanded English version of *Die Prophetie* was issued in 1962. It was not until 1968 that American involvement in Vietnam became an issue on most college campuses (see Riesman, below, note 96). But Heschel's anti–Vietnam War activities began in 1966 (see above, note 83). It was not until 1964 that the Student Struggle for Soviet Jewry was founded, not until 1966 that Elie Wiesel's influential *The Jews of Silence* was published, and not until the early 1970s that American Jewish leaders responded to student and scattered communal efforts on behalf of Soviet Jewry. But Heschel's advocacy of public activity on behalf of Soviet Jewry began in 1963 (see above, note 81). Heschel's ecumenical impulse stretched back to the early 1950s, in his relationship with Reinhold Niebuhr, and in his early involvement in negotiations with the Vatican (see above, note 80).

87. New York: Farrar, Straus, and Young, 1951; rpt. New York: Harper Torchbooks, 1966.

88. *Israel: An Echo of Eternity*, 218.

89. Charles Liebman, "The Training of American Rabbis," 84: ". . . students are usually not exposed a great deal to his thinking, for he plays only a small institutional role and does not expound his . . . theology in courses most students attend." For years Heschel was allowed to teach only 45 minutes weekly.

90. Heschel, "The Individual Jew and His Obligations" (1957), 187–90.

91. *Torah min ha-Shamayim be-ʾAspaklaryah shel ha-Dorot* [Theology of Ancient Judaism] (London and New York: Soncino Press, vol. 1, 1962; vol. 2, 1965).

92. Heschel, *Maimonides*, 58.

93. Emil Fackenheim, review of *God in Search of Man*, in *Conservative Judaism*, vol. XV, no. 1 (Fall, 1960), 50. Fackenheim's earlier review of Heschel is less sympathetic; see *Judaism*, vol. 1, no. 1 (January, 1952), 85–89.

The leading Israeli scholar of the thought of the talmudic sages does not even discuss Heschel's two-volume work, dismissing it in a footnote as a work of personal theology and deficient in all scholarly technique. See Ephraim Urbach, *Ḥazal* (Jerusalem: The Magnes Press, 1969), trans. Israel Abrahams, *The Sages: Their Concepts and Beliefs* (Jerusalem: The Magnes Press, 1975), vol. 1, p. 17, vol. 2 [notes], 695.

94. *Kotsk: In Gerangl far Emesdikeit* (Tel Aviv: Hamenorah Publishing House, 1973).

95. Ibid., Introduction, 7–10; mostly translated by Dresner, Introduction, *The Circle of the Baal Shem Tov*, xxii–xxiii.

96. ". . . whites disappeared from front ranks, and white paternalism in any department became anathema"; C. Van Woodward, *The Strange Career of Jim Crow* (New York: Oxford University Press, 3rd rev. ed., 1974), 194. Quotation in text is from David Riesman, "Ten Years On: The Higher Learning in America since the Events of 1968," *The New Republic*, vol. 179, no. 1 (July, 1978), 14.

97. Bertrand Russell, *A History of Western Philosophy* (New York: Simon and Schuster, 10th pb. ed., 1964), 516.

98. *A Passion for Truth*.

99. Ibid., 11.

100. Ibid., 87.

101. *Maimonides*, 126–31; 63.

102. Ibid., 115.

103. Ibid., 214. In this context Heschel equates Aristotle's statement with Maimonides' strictures against speaking about sexual intercourse. Since touch is disgraceful, even talking about sexual touch is disgraceful. In fact, Maimonides' attitude toward sexual matters was more complex. See Fred Rosner, *Sex Ethics in the Writings of Maimonides* (New York: Bloch, 1974), and *Medicine in the Mishneh Torah of Maimonides* (New York: Ktav Publishing House, 1984), 182–88.

104. *The Sabbath*, 18, 19, 48, 53–55, 61.

105. See Babylonian Talmud, *Ketubot* 62b. Cf. Maimonides, *Mishneh Torah, hilkhot ʾishut* 14:1, and Joseph Karo, *Shulḥan ʾArukh, ʾEven ha-ʿEzer* 76:2. Stating a truth, which is half the truth, Heschel disembodies: "The Jewish contribution to the idea of love is the conception of love of the Sabbath, the love of a day, of a spirit in the form of time" (*The Sabbath*, 16). In *Theology of Ancient Judaism* [Hebrew], vol. 1, p. 124, note 2, Heschel cites an opinion rejected by Saadia Gaon that one must separate from one's wife on Sabbath—rejected only because the method of exegesis is incorrect, not because of teachings about the joining of husband and wife on Sabbath.

In the free association and integrative manner of talmudic discourse, the attitude toward relations on the Sabbath imbeds itself in unexpected contexts. For example, in the laws of mourning a number of activities are forbidden during the week of mourning, among them sexual relations. But on the eve of the Sabbath in that week a number of these forbidden activities, such as wearing shoes, must be resumed in order that the Sabbath be publicly honored. The Talmud raises the question: must relations also be resumed, without which Sabbath honor is deficient? The answer is negative, but only because all private activities of mourning are not superseded by the honor of the Sabbath. In other words, marital relations honor a normal Sabbath. See Babylonian Talmud, *Mo)ed Katan* 24a, and cf. *Ketubot* 4a, Tosafot, s.v. *)aval devarim shel tzin (a noheg*.

106. *Torah min ha-Shamayim*, 2 vols., *God in Search of Man: A Philosophy of Judaism*.

107. Heschel, *Who is Man?*

108. "Depth Theology," 125; rpt. from *Cross Currents* (Fall, 1960).

109. Compare the relative elaboration on the laxity regarding fasts and time-bound prayer (414–15, 418), and the phrase on *shiv(a nekiyyim* (the mandatory seven days, free of menstrual blood, prior to immersion in a *mikveh*, or ritualarium, and resumption of sexual relations); *Kotsk*, vol. 2.

110. Ibid., vol. 1, 241–43. The corresponding treatment in *A Passion for Truth*, the *Kotsk* English adaptation, dwells at length on Kierkegaard's negative attitude to marriage and sexual relations altogether, in comparison to which the Kotsker's ascetic penchant within marriage seems quite positive. Marriage per se was positive, but "the libido was to be transferred to the realm of religious passion" (*A Passion for Truth*, 221).

111. Jewish law explicitly prohibits celibacy, even for Talmud scholars. See Babylonian Talmud, *Ketubot* 61–62; Maimonides, *Mishneh Torah, hilkhot)ishut*, 14; and Joseph Karo, *Shulhan (Arukh,)Even ha-(Ezer*, 76.

112. Vol. 2, 124–26. Heschel treats also *Song of Songs* theologically, probing for meaning in a metaphor of love between God and the Jewish people (vol. 1, 160–62). Similarly, in Heschel's final serious reference to sexuality, Heschel treats *Hosea* metaphorically. Harlotry is "political promiscuity," for example; more generally, marriage and sexual imagery are symbols for the relationshiop of love and rejection between God and the Jewish people ("*In the domain of the imagination* [my italics] the most powerful reality is love between man and woman"). Heschel does regard the unfaithfulness, departure, and return of Hosea's wife as actual events, not visions or parables, but here too the ultimate point has nothing to do with sex, marriage, human relationship.

> As time went by, Hosea became aware of the fact that his personal fate was a mirror of the divine pathos, that his sorrow echoed the sorrow of God. In this fellow suffering as an act of sympathy with the divine pathos the prophet probably saw the meaning of the marriage which he had contracted at the divine behest. . . . [The] meaning [of the marriage of Hosea] was not objective, inherent in the marriage, but subjective, evocative. Only by living through in his own life what the divine Consort of Israel experienced,

was the prophet able to attain sympathy for the divine situation. The marriage was a lesson, an illustration. . . . Its purpose was to educate Hosea himself in the understanding of divine sensibility.
The Prophets, vol. 1, 39–60; quotations, 41, 50, 56.

113. Vol. 1, 130.

114. *Maimonides*, 25–32; Abraham Joshua Heschel, "Ha-He'emin ha-Rambam she-Zakhah li-Nevu'ah?" [Did Maimonides Believe That He Attained Prophecy?], in *Louis Ginzberg Jubilee Volume*, Hebrew section (New York: The American Academy for Jewish Research, 1945).

115. In "The Problem of Polarity," chapter 33 in *God in Search of Man*, Heschel delineates a number of what he takes to be essential polarities in Judaism, which only "abstractly" are "mutually exclusive." "In actual living," however, tension is not inevitable, still less is it rooted in being, as it is for Rabbi Soloveitchik. The polarities involve each other and harmony is possible. Moreover, the harmony requires no transmutation of either self or the polarities, but, simply, "equilibrium," which is maintained if pairs of polarities "are of equal force." Quotations, 341.

7. Rabbi Joseph Zev Lipovitz

1. For documentation on Joseph Zev Lipovitz, the reader is referred to the sources listed in Bibliography II (Primary Sources) and in Bibliography I (Interviews). There are no footnotes for Lipovitz since the documentation on him, unlike the other figures in this book, is virtually nonexistent. The single article on Lipovitz, by Dov Katz, opens only a slight wedge into Lipovitz's chronology and personality and omits critical information, such as Lipovitz's studies in Berlin. Accordingly, I have relied heavily on interviews with his friends and disciples, as well as on Katz's article and on Lipovitz's works, all of which, as indicated, are listed in Bibliography I and II.

Katz's article is " 'Al ha-Rav ha-Meḥabber Zts'l" [On Rabbi Lipovitz, Author of *Nahalat Yosef*], in Joseph Z. Lipovitz, *Naḥalat Yosef* [The Heritage of Joseph], vol. 1 (Tel Aviv, 1966).

8. Conclusion

1. Kent Emery, Jr., "Mysticism and the Coincidence of Opposites in Sixteenth- and Seventeenth-Century France," *Journal of the History of Ideas*, vol. XLV, no. 1 (January–March, 1984), 22–23.

2. Samuel H. Dresner, Introduction to Abraham Joshua Heschel, *I Asked for Wonder: A Spiritual Anthology*, ed. Samuel H. Dresner (New York: Crossroad, 1983), xiv.

Bibliography

Prefatory Note

By its nature, the study of transition figures from Eastern Europe reaches into several disciplines. Modern Jewish law and theology, modern Zionism, the history of psychology, and the intellectual history of Lithuanian and American Jewry are but a few of the relevant areas. I have tried to include a wide sampling of the thousands of pertinent books and articles on the variety of arenas touched by the six figures selected for analysis in this book. These works, plus secondary literature on these transition figures and to a lesser extent on other ones, constitute the third part of the bibliography, "Part III: Secondary Sources."

"Part II: Primary Sources" lists only those writings of the six transition figures that are actually cited in the book. By three of these figures there are other writings that I have relied on even though they are not cited. The interested reader is referred to excellent bibliographies on Harry Austryn Wolfson (appendix to Leo W. Schwarz's *Wolfson of Harvard: Portrait of a Scholar*), Abraham Joshua Heschel (appendix to Fritz Rothschild, ed., *Between Man and God*), and Joseph Baer Soloveitchik, whose bibliography has been compiled and privately circulated by Zanvel E. Klein, a psychologist in the Department of Psychiatry at the University of Chicago. Klein, whose work is exhaustive and meticulous, has been especially considerate in responding to numerous queries. In the first four sections of the bibliography to my *Israel Salanter: Text, Structure, Idea* are extensive primary and secondary literature on Israel Salanter, as well the Musar works of his disciples.

"Part I: Interviews" lists those people who offered invaluable oral history: disciples of, or others who had contact with, the six transition figures treated in this book; and a number of people who helped to illuminate the thought and history of various schools in the Musar movement.

I. Interviews

Ben Artzi, Samuel. On Novorodock Musar. September, 1975. Jerusalem.
Borodianski, Ephraim. On Joseph Z. Lipovitz. June, 1982. Jerusalem.
Carmy, Shalom. On Joseph B. Soloveitchik. July, 1987. Denver–New York.
Dresner, Samuel H. On Abraham J. Heschel. March, 1985. Jerusalem.
Elazari, Hayyim. On the Elder of Slobodka. October, 1981. Petach Tikva, Israel.
Faskowitz, H.B. On Novorodock Musar. June, 1973. Jerusalem.
Feuerstein, Mordechai. On Joseph B. Soloveitchik and Alexander Altmann. March, 1982. Jerusalem.
Green, Arthur. On Abraham J. Heschel. June, 1985. Jerusalem.
Gurman, Abraham. On Joseph Z. Lipovitz. June, 1982. Tel Aviv.
Kaminecki, Jacob. On the Elder of Slobodka and Joseph Z. Lipovitz. March, 1984. Monsey, New York.
Katz, Dov. On Israel Salanter and the Elder of Slobodka. November, 1976. Jerusalem.
Kelman, Wolfe. On Abraham J. Heschel. May, 1985. Jerusalem.
Kimelman, Reuven. On Abraham J. Heschel. January, 1981. Jerusalem.
Kuk, Zvi Judah. On Abraham I. Kuk's relationship with Isaac Blazer and Naphtali Amsterdam. July, 1977. Jerusalem.
Lichtenstein, Aharon. On Joseph B. Soloveitchik and Isaac Hutner. January, 1982. Jerusalem.
Lipkin, Hayyim Isaac (Israel Salanter's great-grandson). On Israel Salanter. December, 1976, and October, 1977.
Peli, Penina. On Abraham J. Heschel. August, 1981. Jerusalem.
Schick, Marvin. On Isaac Hutner and Joseph B. Soloveitchik. October, 1987. Denver–New York.
Ullman, Moses. On Joseph Z. Lipovitz. June, 1982. Tel Aviv.
Waldshun, Raphael. On Novorodock Musar. July, 1973. Jerusalem.
Wolfson, Harry Austryn. August, 1972. Boston.
Yeshurun, Abraham. On Joseph Z. Lipovitz. June, 1982. Tel Aviv.
Twelve individuals who requested anonymity. On Isaac Hutner. Jerusalem, Denver, New York City, and Monsey, New York. 1982–1987.

NUMEROUS INTERVIEWS:
Bruk, Eliezer Ben Zion. On Novorodock Musar. Jerusalem.
Bulman, Nathan. On several figures. New York and Jerusalem.
Orlansky, Isaac. On the Elder of Novorodock. New York and Jerusalem.

Zaritsky, David. *On Novorodock Musar*. Jerusalem.
Zilber, Benjamin J. *On Israel Salanter and Novorodock Musar*. Jerusalem and Benei Berak, Israel.

II. PRIMARY SOURCES

ISRAEL SALANTER

Five letters (Hebrew). Kovno, 1849. Seventeen undated letters (Hebrew). In Isaac Blazer, ed. *ʾOr Yisrael*. Vilna, 1900.
ʾIggeret ha-Musar [The Musar Letter]. Appended to Moses Cordovero. *Tomer Devorah*. Koenigsberg, 1858. Rpt., slightly emended in Isaac Blazer, ed. *ʾOr Yisrael*. Vilna, 1900.
Introduction and two untitled articles (Hebrew). In Israel Salanter, ed. *Tevunah*. Memel: August Stobbe, 1861. Rpt. in *Sheloshah Sefarim*. Grossman's Publishing House, 1965.
"Maʾamar be-ʿInyan Ḥizzuk Lomedei Torateinu ha-Kedoshah" [Statement on Encouraging Students of Our Holy Torah]. In ʿ*Etz Peri*. Ed. anonymous [Nathan Zvi Finkel]. Vilna, 1881.
Eight untitled homilies. In Shneur Zalman Hirshowitz, ed. *ʾEven Yisrael*. Warsaw, 1883.
Wilman, Shraga, ed. *ʾIggerot u-Mikhtavim* [Letters and Epistles]. Brooklyn, 1970.

HARRY AUSTRYN WOLFSON

BOOKS:
Crescas' Critique of Aristotle: Problems of Aristotle's Physics in Jewish and Arabic Philosophy. Cambridge: Harvard University Press, 1929. Rpt. 1971.
The Philosophy of Spinoza: Unfolding the Latent Processes of His Reasoning. 2 vols. Cambridge: Harvard University Press, 1934. Rpt. 2 vols. in one, n.d.
Philo: Foundations of Religious Philosophy in Judaism, Christianity and Islam. 2 vols. Cambridge: Harvard University Press, 1947. 4th rev. ed., 1968.
The Philosophy of the Church Fathers: Faith, Trinity, Incarnation. Cambridge, Massachusetts, and London: Harvard University Press. 3rd rev. ed., 1970.

Religious Philosophy: A Group of Essays. Cambridge: Harvard University Press, 1961.
The Philosophy of the Kalam. Cambridge, Massachusetts, and London: Harvard University Press, 1976.
Studies in the History of Philosophy and Religion. Isadore Twersky, George H. Williams, eds. Cambridge, Massachusetts, and London: Harvard University Press. Vol. 1, 1973. Vol. 2, 1977.
Repercussions of the Kalam in Jewish Philosophy. Cambridge, Massachusetts, and London: Harvard University Press, 1979.

ARTICLES:
"The Tear" (Hebrew poem). *Ha-Le'om*. September 4, 1908.
"The American Trend in Hebrew Literature" (Hebrew). *Ha-Yom*. Av 22, 5669 [August, 1909].
"Hebrew Studies at Harvard" (Hebrew). *Ha-Yom*. Elul 4, 5669 [September, 1909].
"The Menorah Society at Harvard" (Hebrew). *Ha-Yom*. Elul 24, 5669 [September, 1909].
Review of *Encyclopaedia Britannica* (Hebrew). *Ha-Deror*. Vol. 1, no. 2. September 8, 1911.
"Before the Tent of Temurah" (Hebrew). *Ha-Deror.* Vol. 1, no. 6. October 6, 1911.
Bluebooks. Written for George Santayana, 1911. Houghton Library Archives. Harvard University.
"Maimonides and Halevi: A Study in Typical Jewish Attitudes towards Greek Philosophy in the Middle Ages." *Jewish Quarterly Review*, n.s. Vol. 2, no. 3. 1912. Rpt. Wolfson, *Studies*. Vol. 2.
"Jewish Students in European Universities." *Menorah Journal*. Part I, vol. 1, no. 1. January, 1915. Part II, vol. 1, no. 2. April, 1915.
"The Arch of Titus" (Hebrew poem). Trans. Horace M. Kallen. *Menorah Journal*. Vol. 1, no. 4. October, 1915.
"The Spirit of Hebraism" (Hebrew poem). Trans. H. B. Ehrmann. In Joseph Friedlander, George A. Kohut, eds. *The Standard Book of Jewish Verse*. New York: Dodd, Mead and Co., 1917.
"Pomegranates." *Menorah Journal*. Part I, vol. 4, no. 1. February, 1918. Part II, vol. 4, no. 3. June, 1918.
"Escaping Judaism." *Menorah Journal*. Part I, vol. 7, no. 2. June, 1921. Part II, vol. 7, no. 3. August, 1921.
Review of James Moffat, *The Old Testament: A New Translation*. *Boston Sunday Post*. December 14, 1924.

"How the Jews Will Reclaim Jesus." Introductory Essay in Joseph Jacobs, ed. *Jesus as Others Saw Him*. New York: Bernard G. Richards, 1925.

Letter to Isadore Singer. 1929. In Leo W. Schwarz. *Wolfson of Harvard: Portrait of a Scholar*. Philadelphia: Jewish Publication Society of America, 1978. P. 84.

"Spinoza's Mechanism, Attributes, and Panpsychism." In Wolfson, *Studies*. Vol. 2.

"Some Guiding Principles in Determining Spinoza's Medieval Sources." In Wolfson, *Studies*. Vol. 2.

—— and F.T. Lewis. "The Kosher Code." *Science*. August 23, 1940.

'Our Survival in the Modern World." *The Hebrew Union College Monthly*. Vol. 34. Chanuko [sic], 1946.

'Causality and Freedom in Descartes, Leibniz, and Hume." In Wolfson. *Religious Philosophy*.

'Extradeical and Intradeical Interpretations of Platonic Ideas." In Wolfson. *Religious Philosophy*.

'Immortality and Resurrection in the Philosophy of the Church Fathers." In Wolfson. *Religious Philosophy*.

'The Philonic God of Revelation and His Later-Day Deniers." In Wolfson. *Religious Philosophy*.

'Sermonette: The Professed Atheist and the Verbal Theist." In Wolfson. *Religious Philosophy*.

'Spinoza and the Religion of the Past." In Wolfson. *Religious Philosophy*.

"Philo Judaeus." In Wolfson, *Studies*. Vol. 1.

'Greek Philosophy in Philo and the Church Fathers." In Wolfson, *Studies*. Vol. 1.

Isaac Hutner

Letters. In "Zikhronot"; in Joseph Buxbaum, ed. *Sefer ha-Zikkaron le-Maran Ba'al ha-Paḥad Yitzhak Ztz'l*. Jerusalem: Machon Yerushalayim, and Brooklyn: Gur Aryeh Institute for Advanced Jewish Scholarship, 1984.

"Mi-Ma'amakim" [From the Depths]. In Isaac Hutner, ed.? *Sefer Zikkaron li-Kedoshei Yeshivat Ḥevron "Kneset Yisrael."* Jerusalem 1930. In *Paḥad Yitzhak: Letters and Writings*. #166.

Torat ha-Nazir [Law of the Nazirite]. Kovno, 1932.

Kuntres 'Osef ha-Halakhot ha-Meḥudashot ha-Nimtza'ot be-Sifra' 'Asher Lo' Ba' Zikhran be-Talmud Bavli [Monograph Collection of the Derived Laws Found in Sifra, Unmentioned in the Babylonian Talmud].

1938. Rpt. Appendix in Shachne Koleditsky, ed. *Sifra> de-Vei Rav, Torat Kohanim*. Vol. 2, Jerusalem, 1961.

Paḥad Yitzhak (Hebrew). 8 vols. Brooklyn: Gur Aryeh Institute for Advanced Jewish Scholarship. *Passover*, 1984. *Pentecost*, 1983. *New Year*, 1974. *Day of Atonement*, 1978. *Chanukah*, 1964. *Purim*, 1966. *Sabbath and Tabernacles*. 1982. *Letters and Writings*, 1981.

Commentary on Hillel of Verona's Commentary on Sifra> (Hebrew). Appendix in Schachne Koleditsky, ed. *Sifra> de-Vei Rav, Torat Kohanim*. Vol. 2. Jerusalem, 1961.

"Holocaust." Rendered into English, Chaim Feuerman, Yaakov Feitman. *Jewish Observer*. Vol. XXI, no. 8. October, 1977.

JOSEPH BAER SOLOVEITCHIK

(Solowiejczyk, Josef). *Das reine Denken und die Seinskonstituierung bei Hermann Cohen*. Berlin: Reuther & Reichard, 1932.

" >Ish ha-Halakhah." *Talpiot*. Vol. 1, nos. 3–4. 1944. Trans. Lawrence Kaplan. *Halakhic Man*. Philadelphia: Jewish Publication Society of America, 1983. Hebrew rpt. in Pinchas Peli, ed. *Be-Sod ha-Yaḥid veha-Yaḥad*. Jerusalem: Orot, 1976; and in Joseph B. Soloveitchik. *>Ish ha-Halakhah—Galui ve-Nistar*. Jerusalem: World Zionist Organization, 1979.

Five Addresses. Delivered to Conventions of the Mizrachi Religious Zionist Movement, 1962–1967. Trans. S.M. Lehrman, A.H. Rabinowitz (from Yiddish? Hebrew?). Jerusalem: Tal Orot Institute, 1983.

"Confrontation." *Tradition*. Vol. 6, no. 2. Spring–Summer, 1964.

"The Lonely Man of Faith." *Tradition*. Vol. 7, no. 2. Summer, 1965.

"Sacred and Profane: *Kodesh* and *Chol* in World Perspectives." *Gesher*. Vol. 3, no. 1. New York: Student Organization of Yeshiva University, 1966.

"A Eulogy for the Talner Rebbe." *Boston Advocate*. June 22, 29, 1972. Rpt. with corrections, elaborations in Joseph Epstein, ed. *Shi^curei Harav: A Conspectus of the Public Lectures of Rabbi Joseph B. Soloveitchik*. New York: Hamevaser, Student Publication of Jewish Studies Divisions of Yeshiva University, 1974.

Epstein, Joseph, ed. *Shi^curei Harav: A Conspectus of the Public Lectures of Rabbi Joseph B. Soloveitchik*. New York: Hamevaser, Student Publication of Jewish Studies Divisions of Yeshiva University, 1974.

Peli, Pinchas, ed. *^cAl ha-Teshuvah*. Jerusalem: World Zionist Organization, 1975. Trans. *On Repentance*. Jerusalem: Orot, 1980.

Peli, Pinchas, ed. *Be-Sod ha-Yaḥid veha-Yaḥad* [In Aloneness, In Togetherness]. Jerusalem: Orot, 1976.
"Be-Seter uve-Galui" [Concealed and Revealed]. In Peli, ed. *Be-Sod ha-Yaḥid veha-Yaḥad*.
"Kol Dodi Dofek" [The Voice of My Beloved Knocks]. In Peli, ed. *Be-Sod ha-Yaḥid veha-Yaḥad*.
"Mah Dodekh mi-Dod" [What is Your Beloved-Uncle More Than Another Beloved-Uncle]. In Peli, ed. *Be-Sod ha-Yaḥid veha-Yaḥad*.
"Peleitat Sofreihem" [Remnant of the Scribes]. In Peli, ed. *Be-Sod ha-Yaḥid veha-Yaḥad*. Trans., abridged. Shalom Carmy. "A Eulogy for R. Hayyim Heller." In Epstein, ed. *Shi'ruei Harav*.
"U-Vikashtem mi-Sham" [And from There You Shall Seek]. *Hadorom*. Vol. 47. 1978. Rpt. Joseph B. Soloveitchik. *'Ish ha-Halakhah—Galui ve-Nistar*. Jerusalem: World Zionist Organization, 1979.
Besdin, Abraham R., ed. *Reflections of the Rav: Lessons in Jewish Thought Adapted from Lectures of Rabbi Joseph B. Soloveitchik*. Jerusalem: World Zionist Organization, 1979.
Kovetz Ḥiddushei Torah [Anthology of Talmudic Investigations]. Jerusalem: Machon Yerushalayim, 1983.
Shi'urim le-Zekher Abba Mari Z'l [Talmudic Lectures in Memory of My Father and Master]. Jerusalem: Machon Yerushalyim, 1983.
Kuntres be-'Inyan Yom ha-Kippurim [Talmudic Monograph on Yom Kippur]. Jerusalem, 1986.
The Halakhic Mind: An Essay on Jewish Tradition and Modern Thought. New York: The Free Press, 1986.

Abraham Joshua Heschel

BOOKS:

Der Sheym Hamfoyrosh: Mentsh [God's Ineffable Name: Man]. Warsaw: Farlag Indsl, 1933. Seven poems trans. Zalman M. Schachter. *Sh'ma*. Vol. 3, no. 46. January 19, 1973.
Maimonides, Eine Biographie. Berlin: Erich Reiss Verlag, 1935. Trans. Joachim Neugroschel. *Maimonides: A Biography*. New York: Farrar, Straus, and Giroux, 1982.
Die Prophetie. Cracow: The Polish Academy of Sciences, 1936.
Don Jizchak Abravanel. Berlin: Erich Reiss Verlag, 1937. Trans., abridged. William Wolf. "Witness to Sefardic Jewry's Descent to Agony." *Intermountain Jewish News Literary Supplement*. Vol. 4, no. 2. December 19, 1986.

The Quest for Certainty in Saadia's Philosophy. New York: Feldheim, 1944.
The Earth is the Lord's: The Inner World of the Jew in East Europe. Henry Schuman, 1950. Rpt. New York: Harper Torchbooks, 1966.
Man is Not Alone: A Philosophy of Religion. New York: Farrar, Straus, and Giroux, 1951. Rpt. New York: Harper Torchbooks. 1966.
The Sabbath: Its Meaning for Modern Man. New York: Farrar, Straus, and Young, 1951. Rpt. New York: Harper Torchbooks, 1966.
Man's Quest for God: Studies in Prayer and Symbolism. New York: Charles Scribner's Sons, 1954. Rpt. New York: Crossroad, 1982.
God in Search of Man: A Philosophy of Judaism. New York: Farrar, Straus, and Cudahy, 1955. Rpt. Foreward. Susannah Heschel. Northval and London: Aronson, 1987.
Rothschild, Fritz, ed. *Between God and Man: An Interpretation of Judaism*. New York: The Free Press, 1959. Rev. ed., 1975.
The Prophets. New York: Harper and Row, and Philadelphia: The Jewish Publication Society of America, 1962.
Torah min ha-Shamayim be-ʾAspaklaryah shel ha-Dorot [Theology of Ancient Judaism]. London and New York: Soncino Press. Vol. 1, 1962. Vol. 2, 1965.
The Insecurity of Freedom: Essays on Human Existence. New York: Schocken Books, 1965.
Who is Man? The Raymond Fred West Memorial Lectures on Immortality, Human Conduct, and Human Destiny. Stanford: Stanford University Press, 1965.
Kotsk: In Gerangl far Emesdikeit [Kotsk: The Struggle for Integrity]. Tel Aviv: Hamenorah Publishing House, 1973.
A Passion for Truth. New York: Farrar, Straus, and Giroux, 1973.
Dresner, Samuel H., ed. *I Asked for Wonder: A Spiritual Anthology*. New York: Crossroad, 1983.
Dresner, Samuel H., ed. *The Circle of the Baal Shem Tov: Studies in Hasidism*. Chicago and London: University of Chicago Press, 1985.

ARTICLES:

Talmudic Novellae. *Shaʿarei Torah: Kovetz Rabbani Ḥodshi*. Warsaw. Vol. 13, no. 1. Tishrei–Kislev, 5683 [1922]. Vol. 13, no. 2. Tevet–Adar, 5683 [1923]. Vol. 13, no. 3. Nisan–Iyar, 5683 [1923].
"Ich und Du" [I and You]. "Beyn Hashmoshes" [Twilight]. "Wandlungen" [Changes]. "Noyt" [Need]. "Oreman" [A Poor Man]. "Got Geyt Mir Nokh Umetum" [God Follows Me Everywhere]. (Poems). *Berlinger*

Bleter far Dikhtung un Kunst. Vol. 1, no. 1. Berlin, Nov., 1931.
Itzig (pseudonym). "In Tog fun Has" [In the Day of Hatred]. *Haynt.* Warsaw. May 10, 1933.
"Der Begriff des Seins in der Philosophie Gabirols." In *Festschrift Jakob Friemann zum 70. Beburtstag.* Berlin, 1937. Trans., abridged. David Wolf Silverman. "The Concept of 'Beings' in the Philosophy of ibn Gabirol." *Conservative Judaism.* Vol. XXVIII, no. 1. Fall, 1973.
"Der Begriff Der Einheit in der Philosophie Gabirols." *Monatsschrift fuer die Geschichte und Wissenschaft des Judentums.* Vol. 82. 1938.
"Das Wessen der Dinge nach der Lehre Gabirols." *Hebrew Union College Annual.* Vol. 14. 1939.
"A Concise Dictionary of Hebrew Philosophical Terms." Mimeographed. Cincinnati: Hebrew Union College, 1941.
"Zevi Diesendruck." *American Jewish Yearbook.* Vol. 43. Philadelphia: Jewish Publication Society of America, 1941.
"The Meaning of This War." *Liberal Judaism.* Vol. 11, no. 10. February, 1944. Rpt., abridged, "The Meaning of This Hour." In Heschel. *Man's Quest for God.*
"Ha-He'emin ha-Rambam she-Zakhah li-Nevu'ah?" [Did Maimonides Believe that He Attained Prophecy?]. In *Louis Ginzberg Jubilee Volume,* Hebrew section. New York: The American Academy for Jewish Research, 1945.
"The Eastern European Era in Jewish History." *Yivo Annual of Jewish Social Science.* Vol. 1. 1946. Rpt. "The Inner World of the Polish Jew." In Roman Vishniac. *Polish Jews: A Pictorial Record.* New York: Schocken Books, 1947. Rpt. 1965.
"Toward an Understanding of Halakha." *Yearbook, The Central Conference of American Rabbis.* Vol. 63. 1953.
"The Individual Jew and His Obligations." Paper presented in Hebrew to the Jerusalem Ideological Conference. The Hebrew University, 1957. In A. J. Heschel, *The Insecurity of Freedom.*
"Israel and the Diaspora." Paper presented to the 58th convention of the Rabbinical Assembly of America, 1958. In Heschel. *The Insecurity of Freedom.*
"Ilya Schor z'l." *Conservative Judaism.* Vol. XVI, no. 1. Fall, 1961.
"Hillel Bavli: In Memoriam." *Conservative Judaism.* Vol. XVII, nos. 1–2. Fall, 1962–Winter, 1963.
"The Ecumenical Movement." Address at dinner for Augustin Cardinal Bea. New York City, April 1, 1963. In Heschel. *The Insecurity of Freedom.*

"Jews in the Soviet Union." Paper presented to the Conference on the Moral Implications of the Rabbinate. Jewish Theological Seminary of America, September 4, 1963. In Heschel. *The Insecurity of Freedom*.

"A Declaration of Conscience." Paper presented to New York Conference on Soviet Jewry. Hunter College, October 28, 1964. In Heschel. *The Insecurity of Freedom*.

"The White Man on Trial." Paper presented to Metropolitan Conference on Religion and Race. February 25, 1964. In Heschel. *The Insecurity of Freedom*.

"Religion and Race." Opening address at National Conference on Religion and Race. Chicago, January 14, 1963. In Heschel. *The Insecurity of Freedom*.

"Depth Theology." In *The Insecurity of Freedom*.

"A Hebrew Evaluation of Reinhold Neibuhr." Rpt. "Confusion of Good and Evil." In Heschel. *The Insecurity of Freedom*.

"Protestant Renewal: A Jewish View." In Heschel. *The Insecurity of Freedom*.

"No Religion is an Island." *Union Seminary Quarterly Review*. Vol. 21, no. 2, part 1. January, 1966. Rpt. Frank E. Talmage, ed. *Disputation and Dialogue: Readings in the Jewish-Christian Encounter*. New York: Ktav Publishing House and Anti-Defamation League, 1975.

Discussion on Second Vatican Council and the Jews. John H. Miller, ed. *Vatican II: An Interfaith Appraisal*. Notre Dame and London: Notre Dame University Press, 1966.

"The Moral Outrage of Vietnam." In Robert McAfee Brown, A.J. Heschel, and Michael Novak. *Vietnam: Crisis of Conscience*. New York: Association Press, Behrman House, Herder & Herder, 1967.

Address at Riverside Church, New York City, April 4, 1967. In *Dr. Martin Luther King, Jr., Dr. John Bennett, Dr. Henry Steele Commager, Rabbi Abraham Heschel Speak on the War in Vietnam*. Pamphlet. New York: Clergy and Laymen Concerned about Vietnam, 1967.

Foreward. Ronald I. Rubin, ed. *The Unredeemed: Antisemitism in the Soviet Union*. Chicago: Quadrangle Books, 1968.

"Reinhold Niebuhr: A Last Farewell." *Conservative Judaism*. Vol. XXV, no. 4. Summer, 1971.

"A Time for Renewal." Address delivered to 28th World Zionist Congress. Jerusalem, 1972. *Midstream*. Vol. XVII, no. 5. May, 1972.

"A Conversation with Abraham Joshua Heschel." New York: National Broadcasting Co., 1973.

Joseph Zev Lipovitz

Megillat Rut ʾim Perush Naḥalat Yosef [The Scroll of Ruth and Commentary, "The Heritage of Joseph"]. Tel Aviv: Abraham Zioni, 1977.
Naḥalat Yosef. (Commentaries on the Pentateuch.) 2 vols. Tel Aviv: Committee for Publication of the Works of Joseph Zev Lipovitz, 1966, 1972.
Naḥalat Yosef. (Philosophical, Historiographical, and Homiletical Writings.) Tel Aviv: Committee for Publication of the Works of Joseph Zev Lipovitz, 1969.
Naḥalat Yosef. (Talmudic Investigations.) Tel Aviv: Committee for Publication of the Works of Joseph Zev Lipovitz, 1966.

III. Secondary Sources

Abramowitz, Molly. *Elie Wiesel: A Bibliography*. Metuchen, New Jersey: Scarecrow Press, 1974.
Adelson, Saul. "From Volozhin to Jerusalem: An Appreciation of Rabbi Meir Bar Ilan (Berlin)." *Jewish Life*. June, 1949.
Adler, Cyrus. *I Have Considered the Days*. Philadelphia: The Jewish Publication Society of America, 1941.
Agnon, S.Y. *Kol Sippurav shel Shemuel Yosef Agnon* [The Complete Works]. 8 vols. Tel Aviv: Schocken, 1966.
Agus, Jacob. *Banner of Jerusalem*. New York: Bloch Publishing Co., 1946.
Ahren, Yitzhak. "Rabbi Israel Salander und das Unbewusste." *Udim*. 1975/76.
Albert, Phillis Cohen. *The Modernization of French Jewry: Consistory and Community in the Nineteenth Century*. Hanover: Brandeis University Press, 1977.
Albo, Joseph. *Sefer ha-ʿIkkarim* [Book of Roots]. Philadelphia: Jewish Publication Society of America, 1930.
Alexander, Sidney. *Marc Chagall: A Biography*. New York: G.P. Putnam's Sons, 1978.
Allon, Yigal. *My Father's House*. Trans. Reuven Ben-Yosef. New York: W. W. Norton, 1976.
Alter, A.M., and Yitzhak M. Alter. *Bet Gur* [House of Ger].
Alter, Israel [Gerer Rebbe]. *Bet Yisrael* [House of Israel]. 5 vols. Jerusalem, 1978.
Altmann, Alexander. *Moses Mendelsohn: A Biographical Study*. Univer-

sity, Alabama: University of Alabama Press, 1973. Rpt. Philadelphia: Jewish Publication Society of America, 1973.

———. *Essays in Jewish Intellectual History*. Hanover: University Press of New England, 1981.

———. "Commentary" to Moses Mendelssohn. *Jerusalem*. Hanover: University Press of New England, 1983.

Amsterdam, Naphtali. Letter (Hebrew). In Isaac Blazer. "Netivot ʾOr," in Isaac Blazer, ed. ʾ*Or Yisrael*. Vilna, 1900.

———. "Yesod ha-Teshuvah" [Foundation of Repentence]. In ʾ*Or ha-Musar*. Vol. 1. Poland: Central Student Organization of Yeshivot Novorodock, n.d. Rpt. Benei Berak: Ḥokhmah u-Musar, 1966.

———. "Zavaʾah" [Last Will and Testament]. In ʾ*Or ha-Musar*. Vol. 2. Poland: Central Student Organization of Yeshivot Novorodock, n.d. Rpt. Benei Berak: Ḥokhmah u-Musar, 1966.

———. "Ha Sekhel veha-Ḥush" [The Intellect and the Senses]. Vol. 1. *Ḥayyei ha-Musar*. Ostrov: Student Organization of Yeshivat Bet Yosef, n.d. Rpt. Benei Berak: Ḥokhmah u-Musar, 1966.

———. "Ḥeshbon ha-Nefesh" [Accounting of the Soul]. Vol. 2. *Ḥayyei ha-Musar*. Ostrov: Student Organization of Yeshivat Bet Yosef, n.d. Rpt. Benei Berak: Ḥokhmah u-Musar, 1966.

———. Letters (Hebrew). In Isaac Blazer. *Kokhvei ʾOr*. Jerusalem, 1974.

Arama, Isaac. ʿ*Akedat Yitzhak* [The Binding of Isaac]. Salonica, 1552. Rpt. Pressberg, 1849. New York, 1960.

Arendt, Hannah. "Rahel Varnhagen. Zum 100. Todestag." *Kölnische Zeitung*, no. 131, March 7, 1933. Rpt. *Judische Rundschau*, no. 28/29, April 7, 1933.

———. *Eichmann in Jerusalem: A Report on the Banality of Evil*. New York: Viking, 1963. Rev. and enlarged, 1965.

———. "Eichmann in Jerusalem." *Encounter*. January, 1964. (An Exchange of letters between Arendt and Gershom Scholem).

———. *The Jew as Pariah: Jewish Identity and Politics in the Modern Age*. Ed., intro. Ron H. Feldman. New York: Grove Press, 1978.

Asher b. Yehiel (Rosh). *Halakhot* (talmudic commentary). Standard editions of the Talmud.

Ashkenazi, Léon. "Un Enseignement sur le 'Chabatt.' " *Tenth Anniversary Souvenir Journal*. Gur Aryeh Institute. Brooklyn, 1966.

Atlas, Samuel. "Ha-Gaon Rabbi Yehiel Yaakov Veinberg Ztz'l: Kavvim li-Demuto" [The Gaon Rabbi Jehiel J. Weinberg: Elements of a Portrait]. *Sinai*. Vol. 58, nos. 4–6. 1966.

Aviad, Janet O'Dea. *Return to Judaism: Religious Renewal in Israel*.

Chicago and London: The University of Chicago Press, 1983.
Avineri, Shlomo. "Marx and Jewish Emancipation." *Journal of the History of Ideas*. Vol. XXV, no. 3. July–Sept, 1964.
———. *The Making of Modern Zionism: The Intellectual Origins of the Jewish State*. New York: Basic Books, 1981.
———. *Moses Hess: Prophet of Communism and Zionism*. New York and London: New York University Press, 1985.
'*Avot de-Rabbi Natan*. Solomon Schechter, ed. Vienna, 1877. Corrected ed., New York, 1967. Trans. Judah Goldin. *The Fathers according to Rabbi Nathan*. New Haven: Yale University Press, 1955.
Avraham b. David (Rabad). *Hassagot on Mishneh Torah*. Standard editions of *Mishneh Torah*.
Babylonian Talmud, standard editions. Trans. Isadore Epstein, general ed. *The Babylonian Talmud*. 35 vols. London: Soncino, 1935–1952.
Baer, Fritz. *A History of the Jews of Christian Spain*. 2 vols. Philadelphia: Jewish Publication Society, 1961–1966.
Bahya Ibn Pakuda. *Ḥovot ha-Levavot*. Trans. into Hebrew. Yehudah ibn Tibbon; A. Zifroni, ed. Jerusalem, 1928. Trans. into English. M. Hyamson. New York, 1925. Menahem Mansoor. London, 1973.
Bakan, David. *Sigmund Freud and the Jewish Mystical Tradition*. Boston: Beacon Press, 1975.
Bar Ilan, Meir. *Mi-Volozhin 'ad Yerushalayim* [From Volozhin to Jerusalem]. 2 vols. Tel Aviv, 1940.
———. *Rabban shel Yisrael* [Rabbi of Israel; Naphtali Zvi Judah Berlin]. New York, 1943.
Barnard, Harry. *The Forging of an American Jew: The Life of Judge Julian Mack*. New York: Herzl Press, 1974.
Barrett, William. *Irrational Man: A Study in Existential Philosophy*. Garden City, New York: Doubleday, Anchor Books, 1962.
———. *The Truants: Adventures Among the Intellectuals*. Garden City, New York: Doubleday, Anchor Books, 1982.
Baruch, Bernard M. *Bernard M. Baruch: My Own Story*. New York: H. Holt, 1957.
———. *Bernard M. Baruch: The Public Years*. New York: Holt, Rinehart and Winston, 1960.
Barzilay, I. "The Treatment of the Jewish Religion in the Literature of the Berlin Haskalah." *Proceedings of the American Academy of Jewish Research*. Vol. XXIV. 1955.
———. "The Ideology of the Berlin Haskalah." *Proceedings of the American Academy of Jewish Research*. Vol. XXV, 1956.

Baylin, Bernard, and Donald Fleming. *The Intellectual Migration: Europe and America, 1930–1960*. Cambridge: Harvard University Press, 1969.

Bayme, Steven. *Jewish Leadership and Anti-Semitism in Britain, 1898–1918*. Ph.D. dissertation. Columbia University, 1977.

Beck, Mordechai. *Learning to Learn: A Guide to the New Yeshivot in Israel*. Second ed. Jerusalem: Israel Economist and World Union of Jewish Students, 1977.

Becker, Carl L. *The Heavenly City of the Eighteenth-Century Philosophers*. New Haven and London: Yale University Press, 1965.

Bein, Alex. *Theodor Herzl: A Biography*. Trans. Maurice Samuel. Philadelphia: Jewish Publication Society of America, 1943. Rpt. Cleveland: World Publishing Co., 1962.

———. "The Origin of the Term and Concept 'Zionism.'" *Herzl Yearbook: Essays in Zionist History*. Vol. 2. 1959.

Belkin, Samuel, *Philo and the Oral Law*. Cambridge, Massachusetts: Harvard University, 1940.

Ben-Amos, Dan, and Jerome R. Mintz, eds. *In Praise of the Baal Shem Tov [Shivḥei ha-Besht]*. Bloomington: Indiana University Press, 1970.

Ben Artzi, Samuel. *Shivti* [I Sit Eternally in the Study of Torah]. Jerusalem: Kiryat Sepher, 1967.

Ben Chaim, Binyomin (pseudonym). "The Sefer Torah of the Azoroh: Rav Yitzhak Hutner Zts'l." *Jewish Women's Outlook*. January–February, 1981.

Benjamin, Emil. *R. Jsrael Lipkin Salant: Sein Leben und Werken*. Berlin, 1899.

Bennet, John C. "Agent of God's Compassion." *America*. Vol. 128, no. 9. March 10, 1973.

Bentwich, Norman. *Solomon Schechter: A Biography*. Philadelphia: Jewish Publication Society, 1948.

———. *My First Seventy Years: An Account of My Life and Times, 1883–1960*. London, 1962.

———. *Claude Montefiore and His Tutor in Rabbinics*. London, 1966.

Berenbaum, Michael. *The Vision of the Void: Theological Reflections on the Works of Elie Wiesel*. Middletown: Wesleyan University Press, 1979.

Bergman, Samuel Hugo. *Faith and Reason: An Introduction to Modern Jewish Thought*. Trans., ed. Alfred Jospe. New York: Schocken Books, 1963.

Berkovits, Eliezer. "Dr. A. J. Heschel's Theology of Pathos." *Tradition*. Vol. 6, no. 2. Spring–Summer, 1964. Rpt. idem. *Major Themes in Modern Philosophies of Judaism*. New York: Ktav Publishing House, 1974.

———. "Rabbi Yechiel Yakov Weinberg Zts'l: My Teacher and Master." *Tradition*. Vol. 8, no. 2. Summer, 1966.

———. "A Contemporary Rabbinical School for Orthodox Jewry." *Tradition*. Vol. 13, no. 1. Fall, 1971.

Berlin, Isaiah. *Russian Thinkers*. London: Hogarth Press, 1978.

———. "Benjamin Disraeli, Karl Marx and the Search for Identity." *Against the Current: Essays in the History of Ideas*. New York: Viking Press, 1979.

———. "The Life and Opinions of Moses Hess." *Against the Current: Essays in the History of Ideas*. New York: Viking Press, 1979.

———. *Personal Impressions*. London: Hogarth Press, 1980.

Berlin, Naphtali Zvi Judah. *He'amek Davar*. [Commentary on *She'iltot*]. 3 vols. Jerusalem, 1948–1953.

———. *He'amek Davar*. 5 vols. Jerusalem, 1975.

Bernstein, Eliezer Zalman. "Ha-Rav ve-Histadrut ha-Rabbanim" [Rabbi Soloveitchik and the Rabbinical Council of America]. In Saul Yisraeli, Norman Lamm, Yitzhak Rafael, eds. *Sefer ha-Yovel li-Khvod Morenu ha-Gaon Rabbi Yosef Dov ha-Levi Soloveitchik*. Jerusalem: Mosad Harav Kuk, and New York: Yeshiva University, 1984.

Biale, David. *Gershom Scholem: Kabbalah and Counter-History*. Cambridge, Massachusetts, and London: Harvard University Press, 1979. Abridged paperback, Harvard University Press, 1982.

———. *Power and Powerlessness in Jewish History*. New York: Schocken Books, 1986.

Bialik, Chaim Nachman. *Selected Poems of Hayyim Nahman Bialik*. Israel Efros, ed. Rev. ed. New York: Bloch Publishing Co., 1965.

———. *Shirim* [The Collected Poems]. Tel Aviv: Dvir, 1966.

Biberfeld, Pinchas. "Yitzhak Ze'ev Soloveitchik." In Leo Jung, ed. *Men of The Spirit*. New York: Kymson Publishing Co., 1964.

Bieber, Hugo, and Moses Hadas, eds. *Heinrich Heine: A Biographical Anthology*. Philadelphia: Jewish Publication Society of America, 1956.

Billington, James Hadley. *Fire in the Minds of Men: Origins of the Revolutionary Faith*. New York: Basic Books, 1980.

Birnbaum, Ruth. "The Man of Dialogue and the Man of Halakhah" [on Joseph B. Soloveitchik]. *Judaism*. Vol. 26, no. 1. Winter, 1977.

Birnbaum, Solomon. "Nathan Birnbaum." In Leo Jung, ed. *Men of the Spirit*. New York: Kymson Publishing Co., 1964.
Blake, Robert. *Disraeli's Grand Tour: Benjamin Disraeli and the Holy Land, 1830–31*. London: Weidenfield and Nicolson, 1982.
Blazer (Peterburger), Isaac, ed. *Peri Yitzhak* [The Halakhic Fruit of Isaac]. 2 vols. in one. Kfar Hasidim, Israel: Yeshivat Knesset Hizkiyyahu, 2nd rev. ed., 1975.
——. *)Or Yisrael* [Light of Israel]. Vilna, 1900.
——. Introduction, "Sha(arei)Or" [Gates of Light], "Netivot)Or" [Paths of Light], "Kokhvei)Or" [Stars of Light]. In Isaac Blazer, ed. *)Or Yisrael*. Vilna, 1900.
——. *Kokhvei)Or* [Stars of Light]. Jerusalem, 1974.
Blumel, André. *Léon Blum: Juif et Sioniste*. Paris, 1951.
Bokser, Ben Zion. *From the World of the Cabbalah: The Philosophy of Rabbi Judah Loew of Prague*. New York: Philosophical Library, 1954.
Borowitz, Eugene. "The Typological Theology of Rabbi Joseph B. Soloveitchik." *Judaism*. Vol. 15, no. 2. Spring, 1966. Rpt. Idem. *A New Jewish Theology in the Making*. Philadelphia: The Westminster Press, 1968.
Bradford, Sarah. *Disraeli*. London: Weidenfield and Nicolson, 1982.
Brandeis, Frederika. *Reminiscences of Frederika Dembitz Brandeis*. Prepared at the Request of Her Son, Louis, During the Years Dec. 12, 1880–Dec. 27, 1886. Trans. Alice Goldmark Brandeis, for her grandchildren, 1943. Privately printed, 1944. Copies in Yale University Library. Radcliffe College (Schlesinger Library). Brandeis University (Goldfarb Library).
Braude, William G. "Harry Wolfson as Mentor." *Rhode Island Jewish Historical Notes*. Vol. 7, no. 1. November, 1975.
Breslauer, Daniel. *The Impact of Abraham Joshua Heschel as Jewish Leader in the American Jewish Community from the 1960s to His Death: A Social, Psychological, and Intellectual Study*. Ph.D. dissertation. Brandeis University, 1974.
Brodetsky, Selig. *Memoirs: From Ghetto to Israel*. London, 1960.
Brown, Robert McAfee. *Elie Wiesel: Messenger to All Humanity*. Notre Dame: Notre Dame University Press, 1973.
Buber, Martin. "Kafka and Judaism." Ronald Douglas Gray, ed. *Kafka: A Collection of Critical Essays*. Englewood Cliffs, New Jersey: Prentice-Hall, 1962.
Bulman, Nachman. "Reason, Emotion and Habit in the Training of a Torah Personality." Joseph Kaminetsky and Murray I. Friedman,

eds. *Building Jewish Ethical Character*. New York, 1975.
Butler, Eliza Marian. *Henrich Heine: A Biography*. London: Hogarth Press, 1956.
Carlebach, Alexander. *Adass Yeshurun of Cologne*. Belfast, 1964.
Carlebach, Ezriel. "Musar. Notizen zur Geschichte einer Bewegung." *Jarbuch der Jüdisch-Literarischen Gesellschaft*. Frankfurt a.M., 1931–32.
———. "R. Yisrael mi-Salant" [Rabbi Israel of Salant]. *Sefer ha-Demuyyot*. Tel Aviv, 1959.
Caro, Robert A. *The Years of Lyndon Johnson: The Path to Power*. New York: Vintage Books, 1983.
Carson, Clayborne. *In Struggle: SNCC and the Black Awakening of the 1960's*. Harvard University Press. Cambridge, Massachusetts and London, 1981.
Cayton, Mary Kupiec. "The Making of an American Prophet: Emerson, His Audiences, and the Rise of the Culture Industry in Nineteenth-Century America." *The American Historical Review*. Vol. 92, no. 3. June, 1987.
Chagall, Bella. *Burning Lights*. New York: Schocken Books, 1946.
Chagall, Marc. *Ma Vie*. Paris: Stock, 1931.
Clark, Ronald W. *Freud: The Man and the Cause*. New York: Random House, 1980.
Cody, John. *After Great Pain: The Inner Life of Emily Dickinson*. Cambridge: Harvard University Press, 1971.
Cohen, Arthur A. "The Rhetoric of Faith: Abraham Joshua Heschel." *The Natural and the Supernatural Jew: An Historical and Theological Introduction*. New York: Random House, 1962. 3rd rev. ed. New York: Behrman House, 1979.
———. Ed. *The Jew: Essays from Martin Buber's Journal "Der Jude," 1916–1928*. University: University of Alabama Press, 1980.
Cohen, Gavirel Hayyim. "Devarim le-Zikhro shel Harahag Dr. Yehiel Yaakov Veinberg Zts'l" [Words in Memory of the Gaon, Rabbi Dr. Jehiel J. Weinberg]. *De'ot*. No. 31. Winter–Spring, 1966.
Cohen, Henry J. "Theodor Herzl's Conversion to Zionism." *Jewish Social Studies*. Vol. 32, no. 1. January, 1970.
Cohen, Hermann. *Jüdische Schriften*. 3 vols. Berlin, 1924.
———. *Religion of Reason out of the Sources of Judaism*. Trans. Simon Kaplan. New York: Frederick Ungar, 1972.
Cohen, Morris Raphael. *A Dreamer's Journey*. Boston: Beacon Press, 1949.
Cohen, Naomi W. *Not Free to Desist: The American Jewish Committee,*

1906–1966. Philadelphia: Jewish Publication Society of America, 1972.

Cohen, Stuart A. *English Zionists and British Jews: The Communal Politics of Anglo-Jewry, 1895–1920*. Princeton: Princeton University Press, 1982.

Cohen-Yashar, Johanan. *Bibliografyah Shimmushit shel Kitvei ha-Maharal mi-Prag* [Select Bibliography of the Writings of the Maharal of Prague]. Jerusalem, 1967.

Colton, Joel. *Léon Blum: Humanist in Politics*. New York: Random House, 1966.

Conkin, Paul Keith, and John Higham, eds. *New Directions in American Intellectual History*. Baltimore: Johns Hopkins University Press, 1979.

Coser, Lewis A. *Refugee Scholars in America: Their Impact and Their Experiences*. New Haven and London: Yale University Press, 1984.

Cowan, Paul. *An Orphan in History: Retrieving a Jewish Legacy*. New York: Bantam, 1983.

Crescas, Hasdai. *ʾOr ʾAdonai*. Vienna, 1860.

Cuddihy, John Murray. *The Ordeal of Civility: Freud, Marx, Levi-Strauss, and the Jewish Struggle with Modernity*. New York: Basic Books, 1974. Rpt. Boston: Beacon Press, 1987.

Daiches, David. "My Father and His Father." *Commentary*. Vol. 20, no. 6. December, 1955.

———. *Two Worlds*. New York, 1956.

Dalby, Louise. *Léon Blum: Evolution of a Socialist*. New York: Thomas Yoseloff, 1963.

Dan, Joseph. "Ethical Literature." *Encyclopedia Judaica*. Vol. 3. Jerusalem: Keter, 1971.

Dash, Joan. *Summoned to Jerusalem: The Life of Henrietta Szold*. New York, Hagerstown, San Francisco, London: Harper & Row, 1979.

Davis, Moshe. *The Emergence of Conservative Judaism: The Historical School in 19th Century America*. Philadelphia: Jewish Publication Society of America, 1965.

Dawidowicz, Lucy. *The Golden Tradition: Jewish Life and Thought in Eastern Europe*. New York: Holt, Rinehart and Winston, 1967.

———. *The War Against the Jews, 1933–1945*. New York: Holt, Rinehart and Winston, 1975.

Debré, Moses. *The Image of the Jew in French Literature 1800–1908*. New York: Ktav Publishing House, 1970.

Dembitz, Lewis N. "The Free Coinage Problem." *Present Problems*. Vol.

1, no. 1. August 1, 1896.

———. "Results of Bad Teaching." *Nation*. Vol. 43, no. 4. October 14, 1886.

Dessler, Eliyahu E. *Strive for Truth!* [Michtav Me-Eliyyahu rendered into English]. Ed., trans., annot. Aryeh Carmell. Jerusalem, New York: Feldheim Publishers. Part One, 1978. Part Two, 1985.

Deutsch, Akiva W. "The Development of Social Work as a Profession in the Jewish Community in Eretz Israel." Ph.D. dissertation. Jerusalem: The Hebrew University, 1970.

Deutscher, Isaac. *The Non-Jewish Jew and Other Essays*. Ed., intro. Tamara Deutscher. New York: Hill and Wang, 1967.

Diamond, Sigmund. "Sigmund Freud, His Jewishness, and Scientific Method: The Seen and the Unseen as Evidence." *Journal of the History of Ideas*. Vol. XLIII, no. 4. October–December, 1982.

Dickstein, Morris. *Gates of Eden: American Culture in the Sixties*. New York: Basic Books, 1977.

Dienstag, Jacob I. "Ha-ʾIm Hitnagged ha-Gra le-Mishnato ha-Philosofit shel ha-Rambam" [Did the Vilna Gaon Oppose the Philosophic Teaching of Maimonides?] *Talpiot*. Vol. 4, nos. 1–2. 1949.

Domb, Cyril, ed. *Memories of Kopul Rosen*. London, 1970.

Drachman, Bernard. *The Unfailing Light: Memoirs of an American Rabbi*. New York: Rabbinical Council of America, 1948.

Dresner, Samuel H. "Is Bashevis Singer a Jewish Writer?" *Midstream*. Vol. XXVII, no. 3. March, 1980.

Dreyfus, Theodor. *Dieu parle aux hommes: la révélation selon le Maharal de Prague*. Paris: C. Klincksieck, 1969.

Drury, Betty, and Stephen Duggan. *The Rescue of Science and Learning: The Story of the Emergency Committee in Aid of Displaced Foreign Scholars*. New York: Macmillan, 1948.

Dubnow, Simon. *Nationalism and History: Essays on Old and New Judaism*. Koppel S. Pinson, ed. Philadelphia: Jewish Publication Society, 1958.

Dukas, Helen, and Banesh Hoffman. *Albert Einstein: Creator and Rebel*. London: Mac Gibbon, 1972. Rpt. New York: Hart-Davis, 1973.

———. *Albert Einstein: The Human Side*. Princeton: Princeton University Press, 1979.

Dushkin, Alexander M. *Living Bridges: Memoirs of an Educator*. Jerusalem: Keter, 1975.

Ebner, Eliezer. "Simhah Zissel Broida (Ziff)." In Leo Jung, ed. *Guardians of Our Heritage*. New York: Bloch Publishing Co., 1958.

Edel, Leon. "The Biographer and Psychoanalysis." *International Journal of Psycho-Analysis*. Vol. 42, pts. 4–5 (1961).
Edels, Samuel Eliezar (Maharsha). *Ḥiddushei Halakhot ve-ʾAggadot*. Standard editions of the Talmud.
Editors. *Commentary* Magazine. *The Condition of Jewish Belief*. New York: The Macmillan Co., 1966.
Ehrmann, Herbert B. "Felix." In Wallace Mendelson, ed. *Felix Frankfurter: A Tribute*. New York: Reynal, 1964.
Einstein, Albert. *About Zionism: Speeches and Letters*. Trans., ed., intro. Leon Simon. London: Soncino Press, 1930.
Eisen, Arnold. *Galut: Modern Jewish Reflections on Homelessness and Homecoming*. Bloomington and Indianapolis: Indiana University Press, 1986.
Eisenstadt, Ben Zion. *Zaddik li-Verakhah* (on Hayyim Soloveitchik). 1919.
Eisner, Isi Jacob. "Reminiscences of the Berlin Rabbinical Seminary." *Leo Baeck Institute Yearbook*. 1967.
Elbaum, J. "Rabbi Judah Loew of Prague and His Attitude to the Aggadah." *Scripta Hierosolymitana*. Vol. XXII. 1971.
Elijah, Gaon of Vilna. *Beʾur ha-Gra*. Standard editions of *Shulḥan ʿArukh*.
———. *Haggahot ha-Gra*. Standard editions of the Talmud.
Elkana, Yehuda, and Gerald Holton, eds. *Albert Einstein: Historical and Cultural Perspectives*. Princeton: Princeton University Press, 1982.
Ellenberger, Henri. *The Discovery of the Unconscious: The History and Evolution of Dynamic Psychiatry*. New York: Basic Books, 1970.
Elon, Amos. *Herzl*. New York: Holt, Rinehart and Winston, 1975.
Epstein, Baruch. *Mekor Barukh* [Baruch's Sources]. 4 vols. New York, 1954.
Epstein, Joseph. *Masters: Portraits of Great Teachers*. New York: Basic Books, 1981.
Epstein, Moses Mordechai. *Levush Mordekhai* [Mordechai's Talmudic Garment]. On *Bava Kamma*. Warsaw, 1901. Rpt. Jerusalem: Yeshivat Ḥevron, 1957. On *Bava Metziʿa*. Jerusalem, 1929. On *Zevaḥim, Menaḥot*. Jerusalem, 1937. On *Yevamot, Gittin*. Jerusalem, 1948. On *Ketubot, Shabbat*. Jerusalem, 1969. *Responsa*. Jerusalem, 1946.
Erikson, E.H. *Young Man Luther: A Study in Psychoanalysis and History*. New York: W.W. Norton, 1962.
Etkes, Immanuel. *R. Yisrael Salanter ve-Reshitah shel Tenuʿat ha-Musar* [Rabbi Israel Salanter and the Beginning of the Musar Movement]. Jerusalem: The Magnes Press, 1982.

———. "Ha-Gra veha-Haskalah—Tadmit u-Metzi'ut" [The Vilna Gaon and Enlightenment—Image and Reality]. In Etkes and Y. Salmon, eds. *Studies in the History of Jewish Society in the Middle Ages and in the Modern Period*. Jerusalem: The Magnes Press, 1980.

Fackenheim, Emil. Review of A. J. Heschel, *Man is Not Alone: A Philosophy of Religion*. *Judaism*. Vol. 1, no. 1. January, 1952.

———. Review of A. J. Heschel, *God in Search of Man: A Philosophy of Judaism*. *Conservative Judaism*. Vol. XV, no. 1. Fall, 1960.

———. "Jewish Faith and the Holocaust: A Fragment. *Commentary*. Vol. 46, no. 2.

Feingold, Henry L. " 'Courage First and Intelligence Second': The American Jewish Secular Elite, Roosevelt and the Failure to Rescue." *American Jewish History*. Vol. 72, no. 4. June, 1983.

Feldberg, Yosef. *Kedosh Yisrael* [Holiness of Israel (Salanter)]. Vilna, 1884.

Feldman, Emanuel. "Reflections of the Rav: Lessons in Jewish Thought." *Tradition*. Vol. 19, no. 1. Spring, 1981. Rpt. idem. *The Biblical Echo: Reflections on Bible, Jews, and Judaism*. Hoboken: Ktav Publishing House, 1986.

Fermi, Laura. *Illustrious Immigrants: The Intellectual Migration from Europe. 1930–1941*. Chicago: University of Chicago Press, 1968.

Feuer, Lewis S. "Recollections of Harry Austryn Wolfson." *American Jewish Archives*. Vol. XXVIII, no. 1. April, 1976.

———. "The Professionalization of Philosophy." Review of Bruce Kuklick, *The Rise of American Philosophy: Cambridge, Massachusetts, (1860–1930)*. In *The Chronicle of Higher Education*. Vol. XVI, no. 2. March, 1978.

———. "The Stages in the Social History of Jewish Professors in American Colleges and Universities." *American Jewish History*. Vol. 71, no. 4. June, 1982.

Fine, Ellen S. *Legacy of Night: The Literary Universe of Elie Wiesel*. Albany: State University of New York Press, 1982.

Finkel, Nathan Zvi (The Elder of Slobodka). *Siḥot ha-Sava mi-Slobodka* [Intimate Addresses of the Elder of Slobodka]. Zvi Kaplan, ed. Tel Aviv: Abraham Zioni, 1955.

———. "Naḥpesah Derakheinu" [Let Us Search Our Ways]. Joseph Zev Lipovitz, ed. In Lipovitz, *Nahalat Yosef*. Vol. 2. Tel Aviv, 1972. Aviv, 1972.

———. *'Or ha-Zafun* [The Hidden Light]. Dov Katz, ed. Vol. 1. Jerusalem, 1958. Rpt. E. Hoffman and Z. Weinrib, 1978. Vol. 2. Jeru-

salem: Committee for Publication of the Addresses of the Elder of Slobodka, 1968. Vol. 3. Jerusalem. E. Hoffman and Z. Weinreib, 1978.
Finkelstein, Louis. "Three Meetings with Abraham Joshua Heschel." *Conservative Judaism*. Vol. XXVIII, no. 1. Fall, 1973.
Fiske, Edward B. "Rabbi's Rabbi Keeps the Law up to Date" (on Joseph B. Soloveitchik). *New York Times*. June 23, 1972.
Flexner, Bernard. *Mr. Justice Brandeis and the University of Louisville*. Louisville: University of Louisville, 1938.
———. "Brandeis and the Palestine Economic Corporation." *The New Palestine*. Vol. 32. November 14, 1941.
Fox, Everett. "The Bible Needs to be Read Aloud." *Response*. Vol. XI, no. 1. Spring, 1977.
Fox, Marvin. "Heschel, Instution, and the Halakha." *Tradition*. Vol. 3, no. 1. Fall, 1960.
———. "Heschel's Theology of Man." *Tradition*. Vol. 8, no. 3. Fall, 1966.
Fraenkel, Josef, ed. *The Jews of Austria: Essays on their Life, History, and Destruction*. London: Vallentine, Mitchell, 1967. Rpt. 1970.
Frank, Phillip. *Einstein: His Life and Times*. Trans. George Rosen. New York: Knopf, 1947.
Freier, Recha. *Let the Children Come: The Early History of Youth Aliyah*. London: Weidenfeld & Nicholson, 1961.
Freud, Sigmund. *The Standard Edition of the Complete Psychological Works of Freud*. New York, 1973.
Freund, Paul. "Mr. Justice Brandeis." *Harvard Law Review*. Vol. 55. 1941.
———. "Mr. Justice Brandeis: A Centennial Memoir." *Harvard Law Review*. Vol. 70. 1957.
Freundlich, Charles H. *Peretz Smolenskin, His Life and Thought: A Study of the Renascense of Jewish Nationalism*. New York: Bloch Publishing Co., 1965.
Friedenwald, Harry. *Jewish Luminaries in Medical History, and Catalogue of Works Bearing of the Subject of Jews and Medicine from the Private Library of Henry Friedenwald*. Baltimore, 1946. Rpt. New York: Ktav Publishing House, 1967.
Friedman, Isaiah. "Dissensions over Jewish Identity in West European Jewry." In Jacob Katz, ed. *The Role of Religion in Modern Jewish History*. Cambridge: Harvard University Press, 1975.
Friedman, Maurice. *Martin Buber's Life and Work*. Vol. 1. *The Early*

Years, 1878–1923. Vol. 2. *The Middle Years, 1923–1945*. Vol. 3. *The Later Years, 1945–1965*. New York: E.P. Dutton, 1981, 1982, 1983.

Friesel, Evyatar. "Ha-Ma'avak ben Brandeis u-Veizman" [The Brandeis-Weizmann Struggle]. Beersheba: Ben Gurion University of the Negev, n.d.

Frischman, David. "Sheloshah she-'akhlu" [Three Who Ate]. *Kol Kitvei David Frischman*. Vol. 1. Warsaw and New York, 1929.

Gabirol, Solomon ibn. *Goren Nakhon (Tikkun Middot ha-Nefesh)* [Repair of Qualities of the Soul]. Vilna, 1844.

Gartner, Lloyd P. *The Jewish Immigrant in England, 1870–1914*. New York: Columbia University Press, 1957. Rpt. London: Simon Publications, 1973.

Gay, Peter. *Weimar Culture: The Outsider as Insider*. New York: Oxford University Press, 1974.

———. *Freud, Jews and Other Germans: Masters and Victims in Modernist Culture*. New York: Oxford University Press, 1978.

———. *Freud for Historians*. New York: Oxford University Press, 1985.

Gelis, Yaakov. *Shiv'im Shanah bi-Yerushalayim* [Seventy Years in Jerusalem]. Jerusalem, 1967.

Gershuni, Ben Zion. *Bi-Metzudah ha-Perusah* [In the Citadel of a Slice of Bread]. Jerusalem: Mosad Harav Kuk, n.d.

Gerz, M. (Gershon Movshovich). *Musarnikes: Tipn un Geshtaltn* [Musarniks: Types and Images]. Riga, 1936. Partially trans. Lucy Dawidowicz. "The Old Man of Slobodka." *The Golden Tradition: Jewish Life and Thought in Eastern Europe*. New York, Chicago, San Francisco: Holt, Rinehart and Winston, 1967.

Gilbert, Martin. *Auschwitz and the Allies*. New York: Holt, Rinehart and Winston, 1981.

Gilman, Sender L. "Karl Marx and the Secret Language of Jews." *Modern Judaism*. Vol. 4, no. 3. October, 1984.

Ginzberg, Eli. *Keeper of the Law: Louis Ginzberg*. Philadelphia: Jewish Publication Society of America, 1966.

Ginzberg, Louis. *Students, Scholars, and Saints*. Philadelphia: Jewish Publication Society, 1928. Rpt. several editions.

———. *A Commentary on the Palestinian Talmud* (Hebrew). 4 vols. New York, 1941–1961.

Glaser, Edward. "Invitation to Intolerance: A Study of the Portuguese Sermons Preached at Autos-Da-Fé." *Hebrew Union College Annual*. Vol. 27. 1956.

Glatzer, Nahum N. *Franz Rosenzweig: His Life and Thought*. New York:

Schocken Books, 1961. Rpt. several editions.

———. "The Beginnings of Modern Jewish Studies." In Alexander Altmann, ed. *Studies in Nineteenth-Century Jewish Intellectual History*. Cambridge: Harvard University Press, 1964.

———. *Hillel the Elder: The Emergence of Classical Judaism*. New York: Schocken Books, 1966.

Glenn, Menahem G. *Israel Salanter: Religious-Ethical Thinker*. New York: Bloch Publishing Co., 1953.

Glick, Leonard B. "Types Distinct from our Own: Franz Boas on Jewish Identity and Assimilation." *American Anthroplogist*. Vol. 84, no. 3. September, 1982.

Goldberg, Hillel. "Toward an Understanding of Rabbi Israel Salanter." *Tradition*. Vol. 16, no. 1. Summer, 1976.

———. "Joseph Yozel Hurvitz." *Encyclopedia Judaica Year Book*, 1977/78.

———. Review. Leo W. Schwartz. *Wolfson of Harvard: Portrait of a Scholar*. In *Association for Jewish Studies Newsletter*. No. 24. March, 1979.

———. Review. Alexander Altmann. *Essays in Jewish Intellectual History*. In *The Jerusalem Post Magazine*. August 21, 1981.

———. *Israel Salanter: Text, Structure, Idea—The Ethics and Theology of an Early Psychologist of the Unconscious*. New York: Ktav Publishing House, 1982.

———. "Abraham Joshua Heschel and His Times." *Midstream*. Vol. XXVIII, no. 4. April, 1982.

———. "An Early Psychologist of the Unconscious." *Journal of the History of Ideas*. Vol. XLII, no. 2. April-June, 1982.

———. "From Berkeley to Jerusalem." *Midstream*. Vol. XXVIII, no. 6. June-July, 1982. Rpt. *Jewish Action*. Vol. 46, no. 2. Spring, 1986.

———. "The Early Buber and Jewish Law." *Tradition*. Vol. 21, no. 1. Spring, 1983.

———. "The Mute Radiance of Eliyahu Sobel." *Intermountain Jewish News*. Vol. 70, no. 25. June 24, 1983. Rpt. *Jewish Tradition*. Vol. 32, no. 4. April, 1987.

———. "Early Modern Musar: Its Coherence and Relevance." *Immanuel*. No. 17. Winter, 1983/84.

———. Review. Dennis B. Klein. *Jewish Origins of the Psychoanalytic Movement*. In *The American Historical Review*. Vol. 89, no. 2. April, 1984.

———. "Musar's Twin Gestures." *Midstream*. Vol. XXX, no. 10. December, 1984.

―――. Review. Abraham Joshua Heschel. *The Circle of the Baal Shem Tov: Studies in Hasidism*. Samuel H. Dresner, ed. In *Midstream*, Vol. XXXII, no. 1. January, 1986.

―――. "Israel Salanter's Suspended Conversation." *Tradition*. Vol. 22, no. 3. Fall, 1986.

―――. *The Fire Within: The Living Heritage of the Musar Movement*. New York: Mesorah Publications, 1987.

―――. Contribution. Symposium on Musar. *Jewish Action*. Vol. 47, no. 3. Rosh Hashanah, 1987.

―――. "Israel Salanter and ʾOrḥot Zaddikim: Restructuring Musar Literature." *Tradition* vol. 23, no. 4, Summer, 1988.

Goldin, Judah. "On the Sleuth of Slobodka and the Cortez of Kabbalah." *American Scholar*. Summer, 1980.

Goldmark, Josephine. *Pilgrims of '48: One Man's Part in the Austrian Revolution of 1848 and a Family Migration to America*. New Haven: Yale University Press, 1930. Rpt. New York: Arno Press, 1975.

Goldstein, Herbert S., ed. *Forty Years of Struggle for a Principle: The Biography of Harry Fischel*. New York: Bloch Publishing Co., 1928.

Golomb, Abraham A. "Jewish Self-Hatred." *Yivo Annual of Jewish Social Science*. Vol. 1. 1946.

Gordon, Eliezer. *Teshuvot R. Eliezer* [Responsa of Rabbi Eliezer]. Pietrekow, 1923.

Gottschalk, Alfred. "Abraham Joshua Heschel: A Man of Dialogues." *Conservative Judaism*. Vol. XXVIII, no. 1. Fall, 1973.

Grade, Chaim. Musernikes [Musarniks] (poems). Vilna, 1939. Rpt. idem. *Dorot*. New York, 1945.

―――. "Mein Krig mit Hersh Rasseyner." *Yiddisher Kemfer*. Vol. 32, no. 923. Erev Rosh Hashanah, 5712 [1951]. Trans., abridged. "My Quarrel with Hersh Rasseyner." In Irving Howe, Eliezer Greenberg, eds. *A Treasury of Yiddish Stories*. New York: Fawcett, 1968.

―――. *Tsemakh Atlas*. 2 vols. New York, 1967. Trans. Curt Leviant. *The Yeshiva*. Vol. 1, 1976. Vol. 2, 1977. Indianapolis and New York: The Bobbs-Merrill Co.

Green, Arthur. *Tormented Master: A Life of Rabbi Nahman of Bratzlav*. New York: Schocken Books, 1981.

Grieder, Jerome B. *Intellectuals and the State in Modern China: A Narrative History*. New York: Free Press, 1981.

Grodzinski, Abraham. *Torat Avraham* [The Teachings of Abraham]. Benei Berak: Kolel Torat Avraham, 1978.

Grodzinski, Hayyim Ozer. *Haskamah* [Letter of Approbation]. For Isaac Hutner. *Torat ha-Nazir*. Kovno, 1932.

Grunfeld, Frederic. *Prophets Without Honor: A Background to Freud, Kafka, Einstein and Their World*. New York: Holt, Rinehart, and Winston, 1979.

Ha-Kohen, Shabbetai. *Siftei Kohen* (Commentary on Joseph Karo's Shulḥan ʿArukh). Standard editions of *Shulḥan ʿArukh*.

Hadda, Janet. "The Double Life of Isaac Bashevis Singer." *Prooftexts*. Vol. 5, no. 2. May, 1985.

Halevi, Judah. *The Kuzari*. Trans. into Hebrew. Yehudah ibn Tibbon; A. Zifroni, ed. Tel Aviv, 1948. Trans. into English. H. Hirschfeld. New York, 1968.

Halkin, Hillel. *Letters to an American Jewish Friend*. Philadelphia: Jewish Publication Society, 1977.

Hall, A. Rupert. *Philosophers at War: The Quarrel Between Newton and Leibniz*. New York: Cambridge University Press, 1980.

Halpern, Ben. *The American Jew: A Zionist Analysis*. New York: Theodor Herzl Foundation, 1956.

———. *The Idea of the Jewish State*. Cambridge: Harvard University Press, 1961.

———. "Brandeis's Way to Zionism." *Midstream*. Vol. XVII, no. 8. October, 1971.

———. *A Clash of Heroes: Brandeis, Weizmann, and American Zionism*. New York: Oxford University Press, 1987.

Handler, Andrew. *Dori: The Life and Times of Theodor Herzl in Budapest, 1860–1878*. University, Alabama: University of Alabama Press, 1983.

Hapgood, Hutchins. *The Spirit of the Ghetto: Studies of the Jewish Quarter of New York*. With drawings from life by Jacob Epstein. New York: Funk and Wagnalls, 1902. Rpt. Moses Rischin, ed. Cambridge: Harvard University Press, 1967.

Hapgood, Norman. *The Changing Years: Reminiscences of Norman Hapgood*. New York: Farrar & Rinehart, 1930.

Harlan, Louis R. *Booker T. Washington: The Making of a Black Leader 1856–1901*. New York: Oxford University Press, 1972.

———. *Booker T. Washington: The Wizard of Tuskegee, 1910–1915*. New York: Oxford University Press, 1983.

Harvey, Warren Zev. "The Return of Maimonideanism." *Jewish Social Studies*. Vol. 42, nos. 3–4. Summer–Fall, 1980.

———. "Hebraism and Western Philosophy in H.A. Wolfson's Theory of History." *Immanuel*. No. 14. Fall, 1982.

Hayyim of Volozhin. *Nefesh ha-Ḥayyim* [The Soul of Life]. Vilna, 1824,

1937. Jerusalem, 1973.
Heer, Friedrich. "Freud, the Viennese Jew." In Jonathan Wolfe Miller, ed. *Freud: The Man, His World, His Influence*. Boston, Toronto: Little, Brown and Co., 1972.
Heilbut, Anthony. *Exiled in Paradise: German Refugee Artists and Intellectuals in America, From the 1930s to the Present*. New York: Viking Press, 1983.
Heinemann, Isaac. *Philon's griechische und jüdische Bildung*. Breslaw, 1929–1932.
Heller, Celia S. *On the Edge of Destruction: Jews of Poland Between the Two World Wars*. New York: Columbia University Press, 1977.
Heller, Hayyim. "Al ha-Targum ha-Yerushalmi la-Torah" [On the Jerusalem Translation of the Torah]. 1911.
———. *Untersuchungen ueber die Peshitta*. 1911.
———. Critical edition of Maimonides' *Sefer ha-Mitzvot*. 1914. 1946.
———. *Le-Ḥikrei Halkhot* [Talmudic novellae]. 1924–32.
———. Annotated *Peshitta* of Genesis, Exodus. 1927–29.
———. *Untersuchungen zur Septuaginta*. 1932.
———. *Kuntres be-Hilkhot Loveh u-Malveh* [Novellae on Maimonides' Code]. 1946.
———. *Peri Ḥayyim* [The Halakhic Fruit of Hayyim]. In Maimonides' Code. New York: Schulsinger, 1946.
Heller-Wilensky, Sara. *R. Yitzhak Arama u-Mishnato* [Rabbi Isaac Arama and His Thought]. Jerusalem: Mosad Bialik, 1956.
Helmreich, William B. *The World of the Yeshiva: An Intimate Portrait of Orthodox Jewry*. New York: The Free Press, 1982.
Hensel, S. *Die Familie Mendelssohn, 1729–1847*. Berlin: B. Behr, 1896–1898. Rpt. Leipzig: Hesse, 1929.
Hertzberg, Arthur. *The French Enlightenment and the Jews*. New York: Columbia University Press, 1968.
Herzl, Theodor. *The Complete Diaries of Theodor Herzl*. Raphael Patai, ed. Trans. Harry Zohn. 5 vols. New York: Herzl Press, 1960.
———. *The Jewish State*. Trans. Harry Zohn. New York: Herzl Press, 1970.
———. *Zionist Writings*. Trans. Harry Zohn. 2 vols. New York: Herzl Press, 1973.
Herzog, Chaim. *The Arab-Israeli Wars: War and Peace in the Middle East*. Random House. New York, 1982.
Heschel, Sylvia. Foreward. A. J. Heschel, *Maimonides: A Biography*. New York: Farrar, Straus and Giroux, 1982.

Hess, Moses. *The Sacred History of Mankind by a Young Disciple of Spinoza*. 1837.

———. *The European Triarchy*. 1841.

———. *Rome and Jerusalem*. 1862. Trans. Meyer Waxman. New York: Bloch, 1943.

Hillquit, Morris. *Loose Leaves from a Busy Life*. New York: The Macmillan Co., 1934.

Hirsch, H.N. *The Engima of Felix Frankfurther*. New York: Basic Books, 1981.

Hirsch, Samson Raphael. *The Nineteen Letters on Judaism*. Trans. Bernard Drachman. New York: Feldheim, 1969.

Hirschler, Eric E., ed. *Jews from Germany in the United States*. Intro. Max Gruenwald. New York: Farrar, Straus and Cudahy, 1955.

Hollander, Paul. *Political Pilgrims: Travels of Western Intellectuals to the Soviet Union, China and Cuba, 1928–1978*. New York: Oxford University Press, 1981.

Horowitz, Aryeh Leib. *Ḥayyei Aryeh* [The Life of Aryeh, Israel Salanter's son]. Vilna, 1907.

Howe, Irving. *World of our Fathers*. New York: Harcourt, Brace, Jovanovich, 1976.

———. *A Margin of Hope: An Intellectual Autobiography*. New York: Harcourt, Brace, Jovanovich, 1982.

Howe, Irving, and Eliezer Greenberg, eds. *A Treasury of Yiddish Poetry*. New York: Holt, Rinehart, and Winston, 1969.

———. *A Treasury of Yiddish Stories*. New York: Viking, 1954.

Hurvitz, Joseph Jozel. *Madregat ha-ʾAdam* [The Stature of Man]. New York: The Foundation for the Advancement of Torah and Ethics of the Central Yeshiva "Beth Joseph," 1947. Rpt., emended Moshe Yemini. Jerusalem, 1970. 12th chapter trans. Shraga Silverstein. *To Turn the Many to Righteousness*. Jerusalem and New York: Feldheim Publishers, 1970, 1987.

Hyman, Arthur. "Harry Austryn Wolfson: 1887–1974." *Jewish Book Annual*. Vol. 33. 1975–1976.

Hyman, Paula. "Joseph Salvador: Proto-Zionist or Apologist for Assimiliation." *Jewish Social Studies*. Vol. 34, no. 1. January, 1972.

———. *From Dreyfus to Vichy: The Remaking of French Jewry, 1906–1939*. New York: Columbia University Press, 1979.

Israeli, Shaul, Norman Lamm, and Yitzhak Raphael, eds. *Jubilee Volume in Honor of Moreinu Hagaon Rabbi Joseph B. Soloveitchik Shelita*. 2 vols. Jerusalem: Mosad Harav Kuk, and New York: Yeshiva University, 1984.

Isser, Natalie, and Lita Linzer Schwartz. "Minority Self-Hatred: A Psychohistorical Study." *Journal of Psychology and Judaism*. Vol. 7, no. 2. Spring/Summer, 1983.
Jackman, Jarrell C., and Carla M. Borden. *The Muses Flee Hitler: Cultural Transfer and Adaptation, 1930–1945*. Washington, D.C.: Smithsonian Institution Press, 1983.
Jacob b. Asher. *Turim*. Standard editions.
Jacobs, Rose G. "Justice Brandeis and Hadassah." The *New Progressive*. Vol. 32. November 14, 1941.
Jacobson, Gershon. Interview with A. J. Heschel (Yiddish). *Day-Morning Journal*. June 13, 1963. Trans., abridged, Samuel H. Dresner, ed. A. J. Heschel. *The Circle of the Ba'al Shem Tov*.
"Joseph Baer Soloveitchik." *Encyclopedia Judaica*. Vol. 15. Jerusalem: Keter Publishing House, 1971.
Jung, Leo, ed. *Men of the Spirit*. New York: Kymson Publishing Co., 1964.
Kafka, Franz. *Complete Stories*. Nahum Glatzer, ed. New York: Schocken, 1983.
Kagan, Israel Meir ha-Kohen (Hofetz Hayyim). *Mishnah Berurah* (Commentary on Joseph Karo's *Shulḥan ʿArukh, ʾOraḥ Ḥayyim*). Standard editions.
Kallen, Horace M. *Zionism and World Politics: A Study in History and Social Psychology*. Garden City and Toronto: Doubleday, Page and Co., 1921.
———. *The Faith of Louis D. Brandeis, Zionist*. New York: Hadassah, n.d.
———. *Culture and Democracy in the United States: Studies in the Group Psychology of the American Peoples*. New York: Boni and Liveright, 1924. Rpt. New York: Arno Press, 1970.
———. *Judaism at Bay: Essays toward the Adjustment of Judaism to Modernity*. New York: Bloch Publishing Co., 1932. Rpt. New York: Arno Press, 1972.
———. *Cultural Pluralism and the American Idea: An Essay in Social Philosophy* (with comments by eight scholars). Philadelphia: University of Pennsylvania Press, 1956.
Kaplan, Avraham Eliyahu. "Shetei Derakhim" [Two Paths]. *Be-ʿIkvot ha-Yirʾah*. Jersualem, 1960.
Kaplan, Edward K. "Language and Reality in Abraham J. Heschel's Philosophy of Religion." *Journal of the American Academy of Religion*. Vol. XLI, no. 1. March, 1973.

Kaplan, Lawrence. "Rabbi Isaac Hutner's 'Daat Torah Perspective' on the Holocaust: A Critical Analysis." *Tradition*. Vol. 18, no. 3. Fall, 1980.

Kaplan, Zvi. "'Iyyunim be-'Ishiyyuto uve-Yetsirutav" [Reflections on Joseph B. Soloveitchik's Personality and Works]. In Shaul Israeli, et al., eds. *Jubilee Volume in Honor of Rabbi Soloveitchik*. Vol. 1.

Karlinsky, Chaim. *Ha-Rishon le-Shoshelet Brisk: Toldot Hayyav u-Fa'alav shel ha-Gaon Rabbi Yosef Dovber ha-Levi Soloveitchik Ztz'l* [First in the Geneological Chain of Brisk: The Gaon Rabbi Yoseph Ber Soloveitchik, His Life, Times, and Activities]. Jerusalem: Machon Yerushalayim, 1984.

Karo, Joseph. *Bet Yosef* (Commentary on Jacob B. Asher's *Turim*). Standard editions of *Turim*.

―――. *Kesef Mishneh* (Commentary on Maimonides' Code). Standard editions of *Mishneh Torah*.

―――. *Shulḥan 'Arukh*. Standard editions.

Katz, Dov. *Tenu'at ha-Musar: Toldotehah, 'Ishehah, ve-Shitotehah*. Vol. 1. Jerusalem: Abraham Zioni, 5th rev. ed., 1969. Trans. in 2 vols. Leonard Oschry. *The Musar Movement: Its History, Leading Personalities and Doctrines*. Vol. 1. Tel Aviv: Orly, 1975. Vol. 2. Tel Aviv: Orly, 1977.

―――. *Tenu'at ha-Musar*. Vols. 2–5. Tel Aviv: Abraham Zioni, 1954, 1967 (rev. ed.), 1963, 1963.

―――. "'Al ha-Rav ha-Meḥabber Ztz'l" [On Rabbi Joseph Zev Lipovitz, Author of *Naḥalat Yosef*]. Vol. 1. Tel Aviv, 1966.

―――. *Pulmus ha-Musar* (Polemics over the Musar Movement). Jerusalem: Abraham Zioni, 1972.

Katz, Jacob. *Tradition and Crisis: Jewish Society at the End of the Middle Ages*. New York: Free Press of Glencoe, 1961.

―――. *Exclusiveness and Tolerance*. New York: Schocken Books, 1962.

―――. *Out of the Ghetto: The Social Background of Jewish Emancipation, 1770–1870*. Cambridge: Harvard University Press, 1973.

―――. *From Prejudice to Destruction: Antisemitism, 1700–1933*. Cambridge: Harvard University Press, 1980.

Katz, Steven T. "Abraham Joshua Heschel and Hasidism." *Journal of Jewish Studies*. Vol. 31, no. 1. Spring, 1980.

Kaufmann, Yehezkel. *Golah Ve-Nekhar* [Exile and Alienation]. 2 vols. Tel Aviv: Dvir, 1962.

Kellner, Leon. "Herzl and Zangwill in Vienna: A Contrast in Personalities and Types." In *Theodor Herzl: A Memorial*. 1929.

Kellner, Menahem. "Dogmas in Medieval Jewish Thought: A Bibliographical Survey." *Studies in Bibliography and Booklore*. 1984.

———. *Dogma in Medieval Jewish Thought: From Maimonides to Abravanel*. New York: Oxford University Press, 1986.

Kimelman, Reuven. "Abraham Joshua Heschel (1907-1972) zts'l." *Response*. Winter, 1972–1973.

Kimmel, M. "The History of Yeshivat Rabbi Hayyim Berlin" [Hebrew]. *Shevilei ha-Hinukh*. Fall, 1948.

King, Martin Luther Jr. "Conversation with Martin Luther King." King's answers to questions, prefaced by remarks by King and A. J. Heschel, at 68th annual convention of Rabbinical Assembly. March 25, 1968. *Conservative Judaism*. Vol. XXII, no. 3. Spring, 1968.

Kirzner, Yisroel Mayer. "By the Writing Desk of the Master: Reflections on Pachad Yitzhok: Igaros Ukesavim." *Jewish Observer*. Vol. XV, no. 10. December, 1981.

Kisch, F.H. *Palestine Diary*. London: Victor Gollancz, 1938.

Klapperman, Gilbert. *The Story of Yeshiva University*. New York: Macmillan, 1969.

Klausner, Israel. *Toledot ha-)Agudah Nes Ziona be-Volozhin* [History of the Nes Ziona Group in Volozhin]. Jerusalem: Mosard Harav Kuk, 1954.

Klein, Dennis B. *Jewish Origins of the Psychoanalytic Movement*. New York: Praeger, 1981.

Klein, Zanvel E. "Heschel as a Hasidic Scholar." *Journal of Jewish Studies*. Vol. 32, no. 2. Autumn, 1981.

Kleinberger, Aaron F. *Ha-Mahashavah ha-Pedagogit shel ha-Maharal mi-Prag* [The Educational Thought of the Maharal of Prague]. Jerusalem: The Magnes Press, 1962.

Kohler, Kaufmann. *Jewish Theology: Systematically and Historically Considered*. New York: Macmillan, 1928.

Kol, Samuel. *)Ehad be-Doro: Korot Hayyav, Ma'avako, u-Fa'alo shel Rabbi Yosef Shelomo Kahaneman ha-Ga'on mi-Ponivech* [Unique in His Generation: The Life, Struggle and Work of Joseph Solomon Cahaneman, Gaon from Ponevitch]. Vol. 1, no. 1. Tel Aviv: Orot, 1970.

Kook [Kuk], Abraham Isaac. *The Lights of Penitence, the Moral Principles, Lights of Holiness, Essays, Letters, and Poems*. Trans., ed., intro. Ben Zion Bokser. New York, Ramsey, Toronto: Paulist Press, 1978.

———. *Haskamah* [Letter of Approbation]. For Isaac Hutner. *Torat ha-Nazir*. Kovno, 1932.

———. "Kedosh Yisrael" [Israel (Salanter) the Holy.] *Sha'arei Zion*. Vol. 13, nos. 3–5. 1933.
Korzec, Pawel. "Antisemitism in Poland as an Intellectual, Social, and Political Movement." In Shikl Fishman, ed. *Shtudies vegn Yidn in Polyn. 1919–1939*. New York, 1974.
Kotler, Aaron. *Mishnat Rabbi Aharon*. [Teachings of Rabbi Aaron Kotler]. Jerusalem: Machon Yerushalayim, 1982.
Kranzler, George. *Williamsburg: A Jewish Community in Transition*. New York: Philipp Feldheim, 1961.
Kraut, Benny. *From Reform Judaism to Ethical Culture: The Religious Evolution of Felix Alder*. Cincinnati: Hebrew Union College Press, 1979.
———. "Living in Two Civilizations: Hope and Confrontation: A Review Essay." *Modern Judaism*. Vol. 4, no. 3. October, 1984.
Kuklick, Bruce. *The Rise of American Philosophy: Cambridge, Massachusetts, 1860–1930*. New Haven: Yale University Press, 1977.
Kunzli, A. *Karl Marx, Psychographie*. Vienna, Frankfurt, Zurich, 1966.
Lamm, Norman, *Faith and Doubt*. New York, 1971. Hebrew. *Torah Lishmah*. Jerusalem, 1972.
———. "Abraham Joshua Heschel, Teacher." *Sh'ma*. Vol. 3, no. 46. January 19, 1973.
Lash, Joseph P., ed. *From the Diaries of Felix Frankfurter*. New York: W. W. Norton, 1975.
Laub, Morris. "Tuesday Evenings with the Rav [Rabbi Joseph B. Soloveitchik]." *Congress Bi-Weekly*. Vol. 38, no. 11. November 12, 1971.
Lefin, Menahem Mendel. *Ḥeshbon ha-Nefesh* [Inspection of the Soul]. Vilna, 1844.
Lesin, Jacob Moses. *Derekh Hayyim*. New York, 1947.
———. *'Orah la-Ḥayyim*. New York, 1952.
———. *Ha-Ma'or sheba-Torah*. Vol. 1. 1956. Vols. 2–5, Jerusalem, 1960, 1962, 1966, 1970.
Levin, Alexandra Lee. *The Szolds of Lombard Street: A Baltimore Family, 1859–1909*. Philadelphia: Jewish Publication Society of America, 1960.
———. "Henrietta Szold and the Jewish Publication Society." Paper delivered at the 73rd annual meeting of JPS. *JPS Bookmark*. June, 1961.
———. "Henrietta Szold and the Russian Immigrant School." *Maryland Historical Magazine*. March, 1962.
———. *Vision: A Biography of Harry Friedenwald*. Philadelphia: Jewish

Publication Society of America, 1964.

Levinas, Emmanuel. "Franz Rosenzweig." *Midstream.* Vol. XXIX, no. 9. November, 1983.

Levinger, Elma Ehrlich. *Fighting Angel: The Story of Henrietta Szold.* New York: Behrman House, 1946.

Lewin, Abraham. *Kantonistn* [Cantonists; On the Drafting of Jews in Russia in the Times of Tsar Nicholas I, 1827–1856]. Warsaw, 1934.

Liberles, Robert. *Religious Conflict in Social Context: The Resurgence of Orthodox Judaism in Frankfurt am Main, 1838–1877.* Westport and London: Greenwood Press, 1985.

Lichtenstein, Aharon. *Henry More: The Rational Theology of a Cambridge Platonist.* Cambridge: Harvard University Press, 1962.

———. "Joseph Soloveitchik." In Simon Noveck, ed. *Great Jewish Thinkers of the Twentieth Century.* Vol. 3. Washington, D.C.: B'nai B'rith Department of Adult Education, 1963.

Lieberman, Saul. *Greek in Jewish Palestine: Studies in the Life and Manners of Jewish Palestine in the II–IV Centuries C.E.* New York: The Jewish Theological Seminary of America, 1942.

Liebman, Charles. "Orthodoxy in American Jewish Life." *American Jewish Yearbook.* Vol. 66. New York: American Jewish Committee, and Philadelphia: Jewish Publication Society of America, 1965.

———. "The Training of American Rabbis." *American Jewish Yearbook.* Vol. 69. New York: American Jewish Committee, and Philadelphia: Jewish Publication Society of America, 1968.

Lief, Alfred. *Brandeis: The Personal History of an American Ideal.* New York and Harrisburg: Stackpole Sons, 1936.

Lindheim, Irma. *Parallel Quest.* New York: Thomas Yoseloff, 1962.

Lipkin, Aryeh Leib. [Commentary to] *Ḥiddushei ʾAggadot Maharal.* Jerusalem, 1906.

Lipkin, Isaac. (Israel Salanter's son.) "Mi-Derakhav u-Feʿulotav shel Maran ʾOr Yisrael mi-Salant Ztz'l" [On the Demeanor and Deeds of Our Master, the Light of Israel from Salant]. *Tevunah.* No. 7. Nisan, 1941.

Lipkin, Zev Wolf. *Hagahot ben Aryeh* [Aryeh's Son's Glosses]. Standard editions of Babylonian Talmud and Maimonides' Codex.

———. Commentary on *Ha-ʿIttur* and Responsa of Alfasi (Hebrew). Unpublished.

Lippmann, Walter. *The Stakes of Diplomacy.* New York: Holt, 1915. Rpt. "Patriotism in the Rough." *The New Republic.* Oct. 16, 1915.

———. "Public Opinion and the America Jew." *American Hebrew.* April

14, 1922.
Lipschitz, Jacob. *Zikhron Yaakov* [Jacob's Memoirs]. Vol. 3. Kovno, 1930.
Lipsett, Seymour M., and Everett C. Ladd, Jr. "Jewish Academics in the United States: Their Achievement, Culture and Politics." *American Jewish Yearbook*. Vol. 72. New York: American Jewish Committee, and Philadelphia: Jewish Publication Society of America, 1971.
Litvin, Joseph. "Naphtali Tzevi Berlin (The Netziv)." In Leo Jung, ed. *Men of the Spirit*. New York: Kymson Publishing Co., 1964.
Litvinoff, Barnet. *Weizmann: Last of the Patriarchs*. New York, 1972.
Loew, Judah (Maharal). *The Book of Divine Power, Introductions: On the Diverse Aspects and Levels of Reality*. Trans., annotated, illustrated Shlomo Mallin, in collaboration with Aryeh Carmell. Jerusalem and New York: Feldheim, 1975.
Loewenberg, Peter. "A Hidden Zionist Theme in Freud's 'My Son, the Myops. . . .' Dream." *Journal of the History of Ideas*. Vol. XXXI, no. 1. January–March, 1970.
———. "Theodor Herzl: A Psychoanalytic Study in Charismatic Political Leadership." In Benjamin B. Wollman, ed. *The Psychoanalytic Interpretation of History*. New York: Harper Torchbooks, 1973.
———. "Walter Rathenau and Henry Kissinger: The Jew as a Modern Statesman in Two Political Cultures." *The Leo Baeck Memorial Lecture #24*. New York: Leo Baeck Institute, 1980.
———. *Decoding the Past: The Psychohistorical Approach*. New York: Alfred A. Knopf, 1983.
Low, Alfred David. *Jews in the Eyes of the Germans: From Enlightenment to Imperial Germany*. Philadelphia: Institute for the Study of Human Issues, 1979.
Lowenthal, Marvin. *Henrietta Szold, Life and Letters*. New York: Viking Press, 1942.
Luzzato, Moshe Hayyim. *Mesillat Yesharim*. Trans. Shraga Silverstein. *Path of the Just*. New York: Feldheim, 1965.
Macht, D. "Moses Maimonides, Physician and Scientist." In M. Soltes, ed. *Jewish Academy of Arts and Sciences Jubilee Volume*. New York, 1954.
Mahler, Raphael. *Yehudei Polin ben Shetei Milḥamot 'Olam* [The Jews of Poland between the Two World Wars]. Tel Aviv, 1968.
Mahrer, Grete. "Herzl's Return to Judaism." *Herzl Yearbook*. Vol. 2. 1959.
Maimonides, Moses B. Maimon (Rambam). Commentary on the Mishnah (Hebrew). In *Babylonian Talmud*. Standard editions.

———. *Guide of the Perplexed.* Trans. S. Pines. Chicago: University of Chicago Press, 1963.

———. *Mishneh Torah* [The Code of Maimonides]. 14 vols. Standard editions.

———. *Sefer ha-Mitzvot* [Book of the Commandments]. Standard editions.

———. A Lichtenberg, ed. *Kovetz Teshuvot ha-Rambam ve-)Iggerotav* [Compendium of Maimonides' Responsa and Letters]. Leipzig, 1859.

Malter, Rudolf. "*Critique of Pure Reason:* German Interpreters." *Journal of the History of Ideas.* Vol. XLII, no. 3. July–September, 1981.

Mark, Jacob. *Gedoylim fun Unzere Tseyt* [Our Generation's Greats]. Trans. to Hebrew. Samuel Haggai. *Bi-Meḥitzatam shel Gedolei ha-Dor* [In the Sanctum of the Generation's Greats]. Jerusalem: Gevil, 1958.

Mark, Yudel. "Heschl un Yiddish" [Heschel and Yiddish]. *Conservative Judaism.* Vol. XXVIII, no. 1. Fall, 1973.

Mauskopf, Aaron. *Religious Philosophy of the Maharal of Prague.* Brooklyn: Hammer Publishing Co., 1949.

May, Henry Farnham. *The End of American Innocence: A Study of the First Years of our own Time, 1912–1917.* New York, 1959. Rpt. New York: Oxford University Press, 1979.

———. *Coming to Terms: A Study in Memory and History.* Berkeley, Los Angeles and London: University of California Press, 1987.

Mazlish, Bruce. *The Revolutionary Ascetic: Evolution of a Political Type.* New York: McGraw-Hill, 1977.

McCormick, John. *George Santayana: A Biography.* New York: Knopf, 1987.

Meinertzhagen, Richard. *Middle East Diary.* London: Cresset Press, 1959.

Meir Simhah of Dvinsk. *)Or Sameaḥ* (Commentary on Maimonides' Code). New York, 1963.

Melamed, Samuel M. "L. D. Brandeis and Chaim Weizmann." *The Reflex.* Vol. 2. May, 1928.

Mellow, James Robert. *Charmed Circle: Gertrude Stein and Company.* London: Phaidon Press, 1974.

———. *Nathaniel Hawthorne in his Times.* Boston: Houghton Mifflin Co., 1980.

Mendelsohn, Ezra. "Jewish Assimilation in Lvov—The Case of Wilhelm Feldman." *Slavic Review.* Vol. 28, no. 4. 1969.

———. "The Politics of Agudas Yisroel in Inter-War Poland." *Soviet*

Jewish Affairs. Vol. 2, no. 2. 1972.

———. *Zionism in Poland: The Formative Years, 1915–1926*. New Haven and London: Yale University Press, 1981.

Mendelssohn, Moses. *Jerusalem*. Trans. A. Jospe. New York: Schocken, 1969.

Mersky, Roy. *Louis Dembitz Brandeis, 1856-1941: A Bibliography.* New Haven: Yale Law School, 1958.

Merton, Robert K. "Resistance to the Systematic Study of Multiple Discoveries in Science." *European Journal of Sociology*. Vol. 4, no. 4. 1963.

Meyer, Franz. *Marc Chagall: Life and Work*. Trans. Robert Allen. New York: Harry Adams, n.d.

Meyer, Isidore S., ed. *Early History of Zionism in America*. New York: American Jewish Historical Society and Theodor Herzl Foundation, 1958.

Meyer, Michael A. *The Origins of the Modern Jew: Jewish Identity and European Culture in Germany, 1759–1824*. Detroit: Wayne State University Press, 1967. Rpt. 1975.

———. "Alienated Intellectuals in the Camp of Religious Reform: The Frankfurt Reformfreunde, 1842–1845." *AJS* [Association for Jewish Studies] *Review*. Vol. 6. 1981.

Midrash Rabbah. 2 vols. Vilna, 1878.

Midrash Tanḥuma. Constantinople, 1520–22. Facsimile, Jerusalem, 1972. Solomon Buber, ed. Vilna, 1885. Rpt. New York, 1946.

Miller, Jonathan Wolfe, ed. *Freud: The Man, His World, His Influence*. Boston and Toronto: Little, Brown and Co., 1972.

Mintz, Alan. "Mordecai Zev Feierberg and the Reveries of Redemption." *Association for Jewish Studies Review*. Vol. 2. 1977.

Mirsky, Mark Jay. *My Search for the Messiah: Studies and Wanderings in Israel and America*. New York: Macmillan, 1977.

Momigliano, Arnoldo. *Jacob Bernays*. Amsterdam and London: North-Holland Publishing Company, 1969.

Moore, Deborah Dash. *At Home in America: Second Generation New York Jews*. New York: Columbia University Press, 1981.

Muhlstein, Anka. *Baron James: The Rise of the French Rothschilds*. New York: Vendome Press, 1982.

Murphy, Bruce Allen. *The Brandeis/Frankfurter Connection: The Secret Political Activities of Two Supreme Court Justices*. New York: Oxford University Press, 1982.

Nahmanides, Moses B. Nahman (Ramban). Commentary to Maimonides'

Sefer ha-Mitzvot (Hebrew). *Sefer ha-Mitzvot*. Standard editions.
———. *Commentary on Pentateuch* (Hebrew). C.B. Chavel, ed. 2 vols. Jerusalem: Mosad Harav Kook, 1954–1959.
———. *Milḥamot ha-Shem*. Standard editions of the Rif.
———. *Torat ha-ʾAdam*. C.B. Chavel, ed. Jerusalem, 1963.
Nardi, Noach. *Zionism and Education in Palestine*. New York: Teachers' College, Columbia University, 1934.
Navon, Yitzhak. "On Einstein and the Presidency of Israel." In Yehuda Elkana, Gerald Holton, eds. *Albert Einstein: Historical and Cultural Perspectives*.
Neher, Andre. *Le Puits de l'Exil; la théologie dialectique du Maharal de Prague*. Paris: A. Michel, 1966.
Neriyah, Moses Zvi, ed. *Moʿadei ha-Reʾiyah: Ḥaggim u-Zemanim be-Haguto uve-ʾOraḥ Ḥayyav* [Jewish Holy Days according to Rabbi Abraham Isaac ha-Kohen Kuk: Holidays and Special Times in His Thought and Life]. Jerusalem: Moriah, 1982.
———. *Ḥayyei ha-Reʾiyah: ʾOrḥotav ve-Haguto* [The Life of Rabbi Abraham Isaac ha-Kohen (Kuk): His Ways and His Thought]. Tel Aviv: Moriah, 1983.
———. *Bi-Sedeh ha-Reʾiyah: ʿAl Demuto ve-Darko ve-ʿAl Neʾemanei Ruḥo shel Mara de-ʾArʿaʾ de-Yisraʾel* [In the Field of Rabbi Abraham Isaac ha-Kohen Kuk: Portrait, Path, and Those Faithful to the Spritit of the Master of the Land of Israel]. Kfar Haroeh, 1987.
Netanyahu, Ben Zion. *Don Isaac Abarbanel: Statesman and Philosopher*. Philadelphia: Jewish Publication Society of America, 1953. Rpt. 1972.
Neusner, Jacob. Correspondence. *Judaism*. Vol. 15, no. 2. Spring, 1966. Vol. 16, no. 3. Summer, 1967.
———. "Faith in the Crucible of the Mind." *America*. Vol. 128, no. 9. March 10, 1973. Rev. "An American Jewish Life: Abraham Joshua Heschel as a Religious Thinker." In Jacob Neusner. *Israel in America: A Too-Comfortable Exile?* Boston: Beacon Press, 1985.
———. *Ancient Israel after Catastrophe: The Religious World View of the Mishnah*. Charlottesville: University Press of Virginia, 1983.
Nietzsche, Friedrich. *Basic Writings of Nietzsche*. Trans. Walter Kaufman. New York, 1968.
Niewyk, Donald L. *The Jews in Weimar Germany*. Baton Rouge: Louisiana State University Press, 1980.
Obchinski, Levi. *Toledot ha-Yehudim be-Kurland* [History of the Jews in Courland]. Vilna, 1912.

Omer-Man, Jonathan. "The Great Transition." *Parabola*. Vol. 5, no. 3. Summer, 1980. Rpt. *Response*. Vol. XIII, nos. 1–2. Fall–Winter, 1982.
Oren, Dan A. *Joining the Club: A History of Jews and Yale*. New Haven and London: Yale University Press, 1985.
Pachter, Mordechai. Introduction, ed. *Kitvei R. Yirael Salanter* [Writings of Rabbi Israel Salanter]. Jerusalem, 1972.
Palestinian Talmud. Standard editions.
Parrish, Michael Emerson. *Felix Frankfurter and His Times: The Reform Years*. New York: Free Press, 1982.
Parzen, Herbert. *Architects of Conservative Judaism*. New York: Jonathan David, 1964.
Patai, József. "Herzl's School Years." *Herzl Year Book*. Vol. 3. New York: Herzl Press, 1960.
Pelcovits, N.A. "What about Jewish Anti-Semitism? A Prescription to Cure Self-Hatred." *Commentary*. Vol. 3 no. 2. February, 1947.
Peli, Pinchas. ")Aḥarit Davar" [Epilogue]. In Joseph B. Soloveitchik. ʿAl ha-Teshuvah. Jerusalem: World Zionist Organization, 1975. Trans. "Repentant Man—A High Level in Rabbi Soloveitchik's Typology of Man." *Tradition*. Vol. 18, no. 2. Summer, 1980.
Penkower, Monty Noam. *The Jews Were Expendable: Free World Diplomacy and the Holocaust*. Urbana and Chicago: University of Illinois Press, 1983.
Peretz, I.L. *Ale Verk fun Y.L. Peretz*. S. Niger, ed. 11 vols. New York: CYCO, 1947–1948.
Philipson, David. *The Reform Movement in Judaism*. New York, 1907.
Phillips, Harlan Buddington, ed. *Felix Frankfurter Reminisces*. New York: Reynal, 1960.
Philo. *Works*. 10 vols. London: Loeb Classical Library, 1929–1962.
Podhoretz, Norman. *Making It*. New York: Random House, 1967.
Poppel, Stephen M. *Zionism in Germany, 1897–1933: The Shaping of a Jewish Identity*. Philadelphia: The Jewish Publication Society of America, 1977.
Preschel, Tuvia. "Rabbi Yisrael Salanter ve-Tirgum ha-Shas le-Sefat)Ever" [Rabbi Israel Salanter and the Translation of the Talmud to Hebrew]. *Ha-Do)ar*. No. 53. 1974.

Rabad (Abraham b. David). *Glosses on Maimonides' Code* (Hebrew). Standard editions of *Mishneh Torah*.
Raisin, Jacob. *The Haskalah Movement in Russia*. Philadelphia, 1913.

Rakefet-Rothkoff, Aaron. *Bernard Revel: Builder of American Jewish Orthodoxy*. Philadelphia: The Jewish Publication Society of America, 1972.

Rather, L.J. *The Dream of Self-Destruction: Wagner's Ring and the Modern World*. Baton Rouge: Louisiana State University Press, 1979.

"A Reexamination of a Classic Work in American Jewish History: Marshall Sklare's *Conservative Judaism*, Thirty Years Later." Six-article symposium. *American Jewish History*. Vol. LXXIV, no. 2. December, 1984.

Reinharz, Jehuda. *Fatherland or Promised Land: The Dilemma of the German Jew, 1893–1914*. Ann Arbor: University of Michigan Press, 1975.

Reissner, Hanns. "Rebellious Dilemma: The Case Histories of Edward Gans and Some of His Partisans." *Leo Baeck Institute Yearbook*. Vol. 2. London: East and West Library, 1957.

Rieff, Philip. *Freud: The Mind of the Moralist*. New York: Viking Press, 1959.

Riesman, David. "Ten Years On: The Higher Learning in America since the Events of 1968." *The New Republic*. Vol. 179, no. 1. July, 1978.

Rischin, Moses. *The Promised City: New York's Jews, 1870–1914*. Cambridge, Massachusetts: Harvard University Press, 1962.

Rivlin, Eliezer. *Ha-Zaddik R. Yosef Zundel mi-Salant ve-Rabbotav* [The Righteous Rabbi Joseph Zundel of Salant, and His Teachers]. Jerusalem: Gross Bros., 1926.

Robert, Marthe. *From Oedipus to Moses: Freud's Jewish Identity*. Trans. Ralph Manheim. Garden City: Anchor Books, 1976.

Ronnen, Meir. "Schatz' Bezalel." *The Jerusalem Post Magazine*. Vol. L, no. 15705. December 10, 1982.

Rosen, Kopul. *Rabbi Israel Salanter and the Musar Movement*. London, 1945.

Rosenblatt, Bernard A. *Two Generations of Zionism: Historical Recollections of an American Zionist*. Intro., amplified background (in italicized insertions). Gedalyahu Cornfeld. New York: Shengold Publishers, 1967.

Rosenfeld, Samuel. *R. Yisrael Salanter* [Rabbi Israel Salanter]. Warsaw, 1911.

Rosenzweig, Franz. *Judaism despite Christianity: The "Letters on Christianity and Judaism" between Eugen Rosenstock-Huessy and Franz Rosenzweig*. Eugen Rosenstock-Huessy, ed. New York: Schocken Books, 1971.

―――. *The Star of Redemption*. Trans. William W. Halo. Boston: Beacon Press, 1972.
Roskies, David. *Against the Apocalypse: Responses to Catastrophe in Modern Jewish Culture*. Cambridge, Massachusetts, and London: Harvard University Press, 1984.
Rosner, Fred. *Sex Ethics in the Writings of Maimonides*. New York: Bloch Publishing Co., 1974.
―――. *Medicine in the Mishneh Torah of Maimonides*. New York: Ktav Publishing House, 1984.
Rosovsky, Nitza. Contrib. Pearl K. Bell, Ronald Steel. *The Jewish Experience at Harvard: Introduction to Exhibition, Harvard Semitic Museum*. Cambridge: Harvard University Press, 1986.
Rotenstreich, Nathan. *Tradition and Reality: The Impact of History on Modern Jewish Thought*. New York: Random House, 1972.
Roth, Cecil. *A History of the Marranos*. Philadelphia: Jewish Publication Society of America, 1947.
Rothschild, Fritz A. "Abraham Joshua Heschel (1907–1972): Theologian and Scholar." *American Jewish Yearbook*. Vol. 74. New York: American Jewish Committee, and Philadelphia: Jewish Publication Society of America, 1973.
Rubenstein, Richard. *Power Struggle*. New York: Charles Scribner's Sons, 1974.
Ruppin, Arthur. *Memoirs, Diaries, Letters*. London: Weidenfeld & Nicolson, 1971.
Russell, Bertrand. *A History of Western Philosophy*. New York: Simon and Schuster, 1964.
Saadia Gaon. *)Emunot ve-De(ot*. Yosefov, 1885. Trans. Samuel Rosenblatt, *The Book of Beliefs and Opinions*. New Haven, 1948.
Sacher, Howard M. *The Emergence of the Middle East, 1914–1924*. New York: Alfred A. Knopf, 1969.
―――. *Europe Leaves the Middle East, 1936–1954*. New York: Alfred A. Knopf, 1972.
Salmon, Joseph. *Yaḥas ha-Ḥaredim la-Tenu(ah ha-Zionit be-Reshitah: Rusya-Polin 1882–1900* [The Attitude of the Orthodox to the Early Zionist Movement: Russia-Poland, 1882–1900]. Ph.D. dissertation. The Hebrew University of Jerusalem, 1974.
Samuel, Maurice. *The Worlds of Maurice Samuel: Selected Writings*. Ed., intro. Milton Hindus. Foreword Cynthia Ozick. Philadelphia: Jewish Publication Society of America, 1977.
Sanders, J.A. "An Apostle to the Gentiles." *Conservative Judaism*. Vol.

XXVIII, no. 1. Fall, 1973.
Sarachek, Joseph. *Don Isaac Abravanel*. New York: Bloch Publishing Co., 1938.
Sarna, Jonathan. *Jacksonian Jew: The Two Worlds of Mordechai Noah*. New York: Holmes and Meier, 1981.
Schachter, Zalman M. "Two Facets of Judaism." *Tradition*. Vol. 3, no. 2. Spring, 1961.
Schapiro, Meyer. "Chagall's Vision of the Old Testament." *Harper's Bazaar*. November, 1956.
Schechter, Solomon. *Seminary Address and Other Papers*. New York: Burning Bush Press, 1959.
Schisha, A. "Hermann Adler, Yeshiva Bahur, Prague, 1860–1862." In John M. Shaftesley, ed. *Remember the Days: Essays in Honor of Cecil Roth*. London: 1966.
Schlipp, Paul Arthur. *Albert Einstein: Philosopher-Scientist*. La Salle, Illinois: Open Court, 1969–1970.
Schmidt, Sarah L. *Horace M. Kallen and the Americanization of Zionism*. Ph.D. dissertation. University of Maryland, 1973.
Scholem, Gershom. "Mitzvah ha-Ba)ah be-(Averah" [A Commandment Fulfilled through Its Violation]. *Knesset*. Vol. 2. 1938. Rpt. idem. *Studies and Texts Concerning the History of Sabbetianism and its Metamorphoses* (Hebrew). Jerusalem: Mosad Bialik, 1974. Trans. Michael A. Meyer. "The Holiness of Sin." *Commentary*. Vol. 51, no. 1. January, 1971.
———. *Major Trends in Jewish Mysticism*. New York: Schocken Books, third rev. ed., 1961.
———. *The Messianic Idea in Judaism and Other Essays on Jewish Spirituality*. New York: Schocken Books, 1972.
———. *Sabbatai Sevi: The Mystical Messiah, 1626–1676*. Princeton: Princeton University Press, 1973.
———. *Kabbalah*. Jerusalem 1974.
———. "Against the Myth of the German-Jewish Dialogue." In *On Jews and Judaism in Crisis: Selected Essays*. New York: Schocken Books, 1976.
———. *On Jews and Judaism in Crisis: Selected Essays*. Werner J. Dannhauser, ed. New York: Schocken Books, 1976.
———. "Once More: The German-Jewish Dialogue." In *On Jews and Judaism in Crisis: Selected Essays*. New York: Schocken Books, 1976.
———. *Zur Kabbala und ihrer Symbolik*. Frankfurt am Main: Suhrkamp, 1977.

———. *From Berlin to Jerusalem: Memories of My Youth*. New York: Schocken Books, 1980.

Schorske, Carl E. *Fin-de-Siècle Vienna: Politics and Culture*. New York: Vintage Books, 1981.

Schorsch, Ismar. *Jewish Reactions to German Anti-Semitism, 1870–1914*. New York and London: Columbia University Press; Philadelphia: Jewish Publication Society of America, 1972.

Schopenhauer, Arthur. *Complete Essays of Schopenhauer*. Trans. T. Bailey Saunders. New York, 1942.

———. *The World as Will and Idea*. Trans. R. B. Haldane and J. Kemp. London, n.d.

Schwarz, Jordan A. *The Speculator: Bernard M. Baruch in Washington, 1917–1965*. Chapel Hill: University of North Carolina Press, 1981.

Schwarz, Leo. W. "Harry A. Wolfson, Master of Prose." *Jewish Book Annual*. Vol. 20. 1962–63.

———. *Wolfson of Harvard: Portrait of a Scholar*. Philadelphia: Jewish Publication Society of America, 1978.

Schwarzchild, Steven S. "An Introduction to the Thought of R. Isaac Hutner." *Modern Judaism*. Vol. 5, no. 3. October, 1985.

Schwob, Rene. *Chagall et l'ame juive*. Paris: R. A. Correa, 1931.

Seder Eliyyahu Rabba—Seder Eliyyahu Zuta (Tanna de-Vei Eliyyahu). M. Friedman, ed. Vienna, 1902. Rpt. Jerusalem, 1960.

Seidman, Hillel. "Rabbi Hayyim Heller, 1878–1960" (Hebrew). In S. Federbush, ed. *Ḥokhmat Yisrael be-Ma'arav 'Eropah*. Vol. 2. Jerusalem and Tel Aviv: Ogen, 1963.

Seigel, Jerrold E. *Marx's Fate: The Shape of a Life*. Princeton, New Jersey: Princeton University Press, 1978.

Seltzer, Robert. *Jewish People, Jewish Thought: The Jewish Experience in History*. New York: Macmillan Publishing Co., 1980.

Septimus, Bernard. *Hispano-Jewish Culture in Transition: The Career and Controversies of Ramah*. Cambridge, Massachusetts, and London: Harvard University Press, 1982.

———. " 'Open Rebuke and Concealed Love': Nahmanides and the Andalusian Tradition." In Isadore Twersky, ed. *Rabbi Moses Nahmanides (Rambam): Explorations in His Religious and Literary Virtuosity*. Cambridge, Massachusetts, and London: Harvard University Press, 1983.

Shapira, Abraham Dovber Kahane. *Haskamah* [Letter of Approbation]. For Isaac Hutner. *Torat ha-Nazir*. Kovno, 1932.

———. Ordination Diploma of Joseph B. Soloveitchik. Abridged in Moses

Soloveitchik. " ʾAv Meʿid ʿal Beno." In Shaul Israeli, et al., eds. *Jubilee Volume in Honor of Rabbi Soloveitchik*. Vol. 1.

Shapiro. Chaim. "Torah Pioneers." *Jewish Observer*. Vol. X, no. 2. June, 1974.

———. "Rabbi Yerucham Levovitz." *Jewish Observer*. Vol. XIII, no. 2. June 1977.

Shapiro, David S. "Secular Studies and Judaism." *Tradition*. Vol. 16, no. 1. Summer, 1966.

Shapiro, Yonathan. *Leadership of the American Zionist Organization 1897–1930*. Urbana, Chicago, London: University of Illinois Press, 1971.

Sharot, Stephen. "Religious Change in Native Orthodoxy in London, 1870–1914." *Jewish Journal of Sociology*. Vol. 15. December, 1973.

Sherwin, Byron L. *Mystical Theology and Social Dissent: The Life and Works of Judah Loew of Prague*. Rutherford, N.J.: Farleigh Dickenson University Press and Associated University Presses, 1982.

Shlomo b. Yitzhak (Rashi). *Perush*. Standard editions of Hebrew Bible.

Shneiderman, S.L. "The Crucifixion Theme in the Works of Marc Chagall." *Midstream*. Vol. XXIII, no. 6. June–July, 1977.

Sifraʿ (Torat Kohanim). I.H. Weiss, ed. New York, 1947. Photostat of Vienna, 1862 edition.

Silberman, Lou H. "Rebbe for Our Day." *Jewish Heritage*. Vol. 13, no. 3. Fall, 1971.

Silberner, Edmund. "Was Marx an Anti-Semite?" *Historia Judaica*. Vol. XI, no. 1. April, 1949.

———. *Moses Hess: Geschichte Seines Lebens*. Leiden: E. J. Brill, 1966.

Silvera, Alain. *Daniel Halévy and His Times*. Ithaca: Cornell University Press, 1966.

Simon, Ernest. "Sigmund Freud, the Jew." *Leo Baeck Institute Yearbook*. Vol. 2. London: East and West Library, 1957.

Simpson, Eileen. *Poets in their Youth: A Memoir*. New York: Vintage Books, 1983.

Singer, Isaac Bashevis. *In My Father's Court*. New York: Farrar, Straus and Giroux, 1966.

Sklare, Marshall. *Conservative Judaism: An American Religious Movement*. Glencoe: The Free Press, 1955. Rev. ed. New York: Schocken Books, 1972.

Slutsky, Y. "Bet ha-Midrash le-Rabbanim be-Vilna" [The Rabbinical Seminary in Vilna]. *He-ʾAvar*. Vol. 7. 1960.

Smith, Morton. *Presentation to Harry Austryn Wolfson*. New York, 1962.

In Leo W. Schwartz, *Wolfson of Harvard: Portrait of a Scholar*. Philadelphia: Jewish Publications Society of America, 1978.

Soloveitchik, Hayyim. Letter to Jacob Moses Karpas. August 25, 1899. Central Zionist Archives, Jerusalem. A 9/54/3.

———. *Ḥiddushei Rabbenu Ḥayyim ha-Levi: Ḥiddushim u-Vi)urim (al ha-Rambam* [The Talmudic Investigations of Our Master Rabbi Hayyim ha-Levi: Interpretations and Clarifications of Maimonides' Code]. Brisk, 1936.

Soloveitchik, Meir. Untitled Discourse (polemic against Chaim Karlinsky. *Rishom le-Shoshelet Brisk*). Jerusalem, 1985 (xerox).

Soloveitchik, Moses. ")Av Me(id (al Beno" [A Father Testifies about His Son]. In Shaul Israeli, et al., eds. *Jubilee Volume in Honor of Rabbi Soloveitchik*. Vol. 1.

Stampfer, Shaul. *Shalosh Yeshivot Lita)iot be-Me)ah ha-19* [Three Lithuanian Yeshivas in the Nineteenth Century]. The Hebrew University of Jerusalem. Ph.D. dissertation, 1981.

Stanislawski, Michael. *Tsar Nicholas I and the Jews: The Transformation of Jewish Society in Russia 1825–1855*. Philadelphia: Jewish Publication Society of America, 1983.

Stannard, David E. *Shrinking History: On Freud and the Failure of Psychohistory*. New York: Oxford University Press, 1980.

Stearns, Harold E. *The Street I Know*. New York: Lee Furman, 1935.

Steel, Ronald. *Walter Lippmann and the American Century*. Boston: Little, Brown, 1980.

Steiner, George. *In Bluebeard's Castle: Some Notes Towards the Redefinition of Culture*. New Haven: Yale University Press, 1971.

Steinschneider, Hillel Noah Maggid. *(Ir Vilna* [The City of Vilna]. Vilna, 1900.

Stern, Fritz Richard. *Gold and Iron: Bismarck, Bleichröder and the Building of the German Empire*. New York: Alfred A. Knopf, 1977.

———. "Einstein's Germany." In Yehuda Elkana and Gerald Holton, eds. *Albert Einstein: Historical and Cultural Perspectives*. Princeton: Princeton University Press, 1982.

Stern, Moses. ")Ish)Eshkolot" [Multifaceted Personality, Jehiel J. Weinberg]. *De'ot*. No. 31. Winter–Spring, 1966.

Stern-Taübler, Selma. "The Jew in Transition from Ghetto to Emancipation." *Historia Judaica*. Vol. 2, no. 2. October, 1940.

Sternbuch, Moses. *Mo(adim u-Zemanim ha-Shalem* [Jewish Holidays and Special Times: The Complete Works]. 9 vols. Benei Berak: rev. ed., Netivot ha-Torah veha-Ḥesed, 1981.

Storrs, Ronald. *The Memoirs of Sir Ronald Storrs*. New York: G.P. Putnam's Sons, 1937.
Strum, Philippa. *Louis D. Brandeis: Justice for the People*. Cambridge, Massachusetts, and London: Harvard University Press, 1984.
Sulloway, Frank J. *Freud, Biologist of the Mind: Beyond the Psychoanalytic Legend*. New York: Basic Books, 1979.
Swetschinski, Daniel M. "The Portuguese Jews of Seventeenth-Century Amsterdam: Cultural Continuity and Adaptation." In Frances Malino, Phyllis Cohen Albert, eds. *Essays in Modern Jewish History: A Tribute to Ben Halpern*. New York: Herzl Press, and London and Toronto: Associated University Presses, 1982.
Sykes, Christopher. *Crossroads to Israel*. London: Collins, 1965.
Synnott, Marcia Graham. *The Half–Opened Door: Discrimination and Admissions at Harvard, Yale, and Princeton, 1900–1970*. Westport and London: Greenwood Press, 1979.
Szajkowski, Zosa. "Quarrels between the Orthodox and the Reform in France" (Hebrew). *Horeb*. Vols. XIV–XV. 1960.
———. *An Illustrated Sourcebook of Russian Anti-Semitism, 1881–1978*. 2 vols. New York: Ktav Publishing House, 1980.
Szold, Henrietta. *Recent Jewish Progress in Palestine*. Philadelphia: Jewish Publication Society of America, 1915.
Tal, Uriel. *Christians and Jews in Germany*. Trans. Noah Jonathan Jacobs. Ithaca: Cornell University Press, 1975.
———. "Jewish and Universal Social Ethics in the Life and Thought of Albert Einstein." In Elkana, Holton, eds. *Albert Einstein: Historical and Cultural Perspectives*.
Talmage, Frank E. "Christianity and the Jewish People." In idem, ed. *Disputation and Dialogue: Readings in the Jewish-Christian Encounter*. New York: Ktav Publishing House and Anti-Defamation League, 1975.
———. *David Kimhi: The Man and the Commentaries*. Cambridge, Massachusetts, and London: Harvard University Press, 1975.
Taylor, John Russell. *Strangers in Paradise: The Hollywood Emigrés. 1933–1950*. New York: Holt, Rinehart, and Winston, 1983.
Teller, Judd. "America's Two Zionist Traditions." *Commentary*. Vol. 20, no. 4. October, 1955.
Tishbi, Yeshayahu (with Yosef Dan). *Mivḥar Sifrut ha-Musar* [Anthology of Musar Literature]. Jerusalem, 1970.
Todd, A.L. *Justice on Trial: The Case of Louis D. Brandeis*. New York, Toronto, London: McGraw-Hill, 1964.

Tramer, Hans. "Prague—City of Three Peoples." *Leo Baeck Institute Yearbook*. Vol. 9. London: East and West Library, 1964.
Twersky, Isadore. "Harry Austryn Wolfson, in Appreciation." In Leo W. Schwarz. *Wolfson of Harvard*.
———. *Rabad of Posquières: A Twelfth-Century Talmudist*. Cambridge: Harvard University Press, 1962. Rpt. Philadelphia: Jewish Publication Society of America, 1980.
———. "Necrology: Harry Austryn Wolfson (1887–1974)." *Proceedings of the American Academy for Jewish Research*. Vols. XLI–XLII. 1975.
———. *Introduction to the Code of Maimonides*. New Haven: Yale University Press, 1980.
———. *Studies in Jewish Law and Philosophy*. New York: Ktav Publishing House, 1982.
Underhill, Evelyn. *Mysticism*. New York, 1961.
Urbach, Ephraim. *Ḥazal*. Jerusalem: The Magnes Press, 1969. Trans. Israel Abrahams. *The Sages: Their Concepts and Beliefs*. 2 vols. Jerusalem: The Magnes Press, 1975.
Urofsky, Melvin I. *A Mind of One Piece: Brandeis and American Reform*. New York: Charles Scribner's Sons, 1971.
———. *American Zionism from Herzl to the Holocaust*. Garden City, New York: Anchor Press, 1975.
———. *A Voice that Spoke for Justice: The Life and Times of Stephen S. Wise*. Albany: State University of New York Press, 1982.
Ury, Zalman F. *The Musar Movement*. New York, 1970. Rpt. "Salanter: The Musar Movement." Leon D. Stitskin, ed. *Studies in Judaica in Honor of Dr. Samuel Belkin as Scholar and Educator*. New York, 1974.
Vital, David. *The Origins of Zionism*. Oxford: Oxford University Press, 1975.
———. *Zionism: The Formative Years*. Oxford: Oxford University Press, 1982.
Vital, Hayyim. *ʿEtz Ḥayyim* [Tree of Life]. Warsaw, 1890.
Walsh, W.H. "*Critique of Pure Reason:* English Interpreters." *Journal of the History of Ideas*. Vol. XLII, no. 4. October–December, 1981.
Weinberg, Jehiel J. *Seridei ʾEsh* [Remnants of a Conflagration]. 4 vols. Jerusalem: Mosad Harav Kook, 1961–1966. Rpt. in 2 vols., 1977.
———. "Tenuʿat ha-Musar" [The Musar Movement]. "Baʿalei ha-Musar" [Musar Personalities]. *Seridei ʾEsh*. Vol. 4. Jerusalem: Mosad Harav Kook, 1969. Trans., slightly abridged. Leo Jung, Howard Levine. "The 'Mussar' Movement and Lithuanian Jewry." In Leo Jung, ed.

Men of the Spirit. New York: Kymson Publishing Co., 1964.

———. *'Et 'Aḥai 'Anokhi Mevakkesh: Rashei Perakkim le-Hidabberut ben Palgei Yahadut* [I am My Brothers's Keeper: Outlines toward a Dialogue between the Factions of Judaism]. Benei Berak: Netzaḥ, 1966.

Weinraub, Bernard. "The Artistry of Ruth Prawer Jhabvala." *The New York Times Magazine*. September 11, 1983.

Weinstein, Lewis H. "Epilogue." In Schwarz. *Wolfson of Harvard: Portrait of a Scholar*.

Weisberg, Harold. "Ideologies of American Jews." In Oscar I. Janowsky, ed. *The American Jew: A Reappraisal*. Philadelphia: Jewish Publication Society of America, 1964.

Weiss, Gershon. "A European Mashgiach in an American Yeshiva." *Jewish Observer*. Vol. 10, no. 8. March, 1975.

Weizmann, Chaim. *Trial and Error: The Autobiography of Chaim Weizmann*. New York: Schocken Books, 1966.

Weltsch, Felix. "The Rise and Fall of the Jewish-German Symbiosis: The Case of Franz Kafka." *Leo Baeck Institute Yearbook*. Vol. 1. London: East and West Library, 1956.

Werblowsky, R. J. Zwi. *Joseph Karo: Lawyer and Mystic*. The Jewish Publication Society of America. Philadelphia, 1977.

Werner, Eric. "New Light on the Family of Felix Mendelssohn." *Hebrew Union College Annual*. Vol. 26. Cincinnati, 1955.

White, Theodore. *In Search of History: A Personal Adventure*. New York: Harper and Row, 1978.

Whitehead, Alfred North. *Science and the Modern World*. New York, 1967.

Whittaker, Cynthia H. *The Origins of Modern Russian Education: An Intellectual Biography of Count Sergei Uvarov*. DeKalb: Northern Illinois University Press, 1984.

Whyte, Lancelot L. *The Unconscious before Freud*. London, 1972.

Wiesel, Elie. *Un Di Velt Hot Geshvign* [And the World Was Silent]. Buenos Aires: Tzentral-Farband fun Poylishe Yidn in Argentine, 1956.

———. *Night*. Trans, Stella Rodway. Foreword, François Maurice. New York: Hill and Wang, 1960.

———. *Souls on Fire: Portraits and Legends of Hasidic Masters*. Trans. Marion Wiesel. New York: Random House, Vintage Books, 1973.

———. *Somewhere a Master: Further Hasidic Portraits and Legends*. Trans. Marion Wiesel. New York: Summit Books, 1982.

Wiernik, Peter. "Musarnikes." *The Jewish Encyclopedia*. New York and London, 1907.

Wieseltier, Leon. "Philosophy, Religion, and Harry Wolfson." *Commentary*. Vol. 61, no. 4. April, 1976.
Wilman, Shraga. *)Iggerot u-Mikhtavim* [Letters and Epistles of Israel Salanter]. Brooklyn, 1970.
Winston, David. Introduction. In David Winston, John Dillon, eds. *Philo of Alexandria: The Contemplative Life, The Giants and Selections*. New York, Ramsey, Toronto: Paulist Press, 1981.
Wise, Stephen S. *Challenging Years: The Autobiography of Stephen Wise*. New York: G.P. Putnam's Sons, 1949.
Wohl, Robert. *The Generation of 1914*. Cambridge: Harvard University Press, 1979.
Wohlgelernter, Maurice. *Israel Zangwill: A Study*. New York, 1964.
Wolbe, Solomon. *Ha-)Adam bi-Kar: Kavvin le-Toledot Ḥayyav)Admor)Or ʿOlam Maran R. Yeruham ha-Levi Levovitz mi-Mir* [Precious Man: Toward the History of the Life and Thought of Our Teacher Rabbi Yeruham ha-Levi Levovitz of Mir]. Jerusalem: Bet ha-Musar, 1982.
Woodward, C. Vann. *The Strange Career of Jim Crow*. New York: Oxford University Press, 3rd rev. ed., 1974.
Wurzburger, Walter. "The Maimonidean Matrix of Rabbi Joseph B. Soloveitchik's Two-Tiered Ethics." In Jonathan V. Plaut, ed. *Through the Sound of Many Voices*. Toronto: Lester and Orpen Dennys, 1982.
———. "Ha-Metaḥ ha-Dialekti ben ')Ish ha-Halakhah' u-ven ')Ish ha-)Emunah ha-Boded' " [The Dialectical Tension between 'Halakhic Man' and 'The Lonely Man of Faith']. In Shaul Israeli, et al., eds. *Jubilee Volume in Honor of Rabbi Soloveitchik*. Vol. 1.
Wyman, David S. *The Abandonment of the Jews: America and the Holocaust, 1941–1945*. New York: Pantheon Books, 1984.
Yahrblum, Moshe. *Peretz Smolenskin: The Impact of Peretz Smolenskin's Writings on Hebrew Literature and Jewish Nationalism*. Ph.D. dissertation. New York University, 1970.
Yalkut Shimoni. 1527. Facsimile, Jerusalem, 1973. Standard edition, Jerusalem, 1952.
Yaron, Zvi. "Introduction: Toward a Biography of Rabbi [Abraham Isaac] Kuk" (Hebrew). *Mishnato shel ha-Rav Kuk*. Jerusalem: World Zionist Organization, 1974.
Yerushalmi, Yosef Hayim. *From Spanish Court to Italian Ghetto: Isaac Cardoso, A Study in Seventeenth-Century Marranism and Jewish Apologetics*. New York: Columbia University Press, 1971. Rpt. Seattle and London: University of Washington Press, 1981.

———. *Zakhor: Jewish History and Jewish Memory*. Seattle: University of Washington Press, 1982.
Yona b. Avraham Gerondi. *Shaʿarei Teshuvah*. Trans. Shraga Silverstein. *Gates of Repentance*. New York: Feldheim, 1967.
Young-Bruehl, Elisabeth. *Hannah Arendt: For Love of the World*. New Haven: Yale University Press, 1982.
Zaitchik, Hayyim Ephraim. *Ha-Meʾorot ha-Gedolim* [The Great Luminaries]. Jerusalem: 4th rev. ed., 1969. Retold Ester van Handel. *Sparks of Musar*. Jerusalem: Feldheim Publishers, 1985.
Zaritsky, David. *Gersher Zar* [Narrow Bridge]. 2 vols. Benei Break: Netzaḥ, 1968.
Zeitlin, Hillel. *ʿAl Gevul Shenei ʿOlamot* [On the Boundary of Two Worlds]. Tel Aviv: Yavneh, 1965.
Zeitlin, Rose. *Henrietta Szold: Record of a Life*. New York: Dial Press, 1952.
Zevin, S.J. *Ha-Moʿadim be-Halakhah* [The Jewish Holidays in Jewish Law]. Jerusalem: Mosad Harav Kuk, 1954.
———. *ʾIshim ve-Shitot* [Modern Talmudic Personalities and Methods]. Jerusalem: Bet Hillel, 1979.
"Zikhronot" [Memories of Isaac Hutner]. In Joseph Buxbaum, ed. *Sefer ha-Zikkaron le-Maran Baʿal ha-Paḥad Yitzhak Ztz'l*. Jerusalem: Machon Yerushalayim, and Brooklyn: Gur Aryeh Institute for Advanced Jewish Scholarship, 1984.
Zimmern, Alfred. *The Greek Commonwealth*. Oxford: Clarendon Press, 1912, 1931.
Zinsser, William, ed. *Extraordinary Lives. The Art and Craft of American Biography*. New York: American Heritage, 1986.
Ziv (Broida) Simhah Zisl. *Ḥokhmah u-Musar* [Wisdom and Musar]. 2 vols. New York, 1957, 1964.
———. *ʾOr Rashaz* [The Light of Rabbi Simhah Zisl]. 5 vols. Jerusalem: 1960–1965.
———. *Kitvei ha-Sava mi-Kelem: Pinkas ha-Kabbalot* [Writings of the Elder of Kelm: Diary of Resolutions]. Benei Berak: Sifsei Chachamin, 1984.
Zohn, Harry. "The Jewishness of Franz Kafka." *Jewish Heritage*. Vol. 7, no. 1. Summer, 1964.
Zolti, Bezalel. *Rabbi Shemuel Salant Ztz'l*. Jerusalem, 1962.

INDEX

Abu Bekr ibn Turfail, 55
Abulfaraj, 55
Adad al-Din al-Iji, 55
Aggadah, approach of Isaac Hutner, Israel Salanter, and J.B. Soloveitchik to, 81-82
Agudath Israel, 32
Alfandari, Solomon Eliezer (1826-1930), 86
Alfarabi, 55
Alfasi, code of, and commentary of Z.W. Lipkin on, 17
Algazali, 55
Alkalai, Judah (1798-1878), 106
Altabrizi, 55
"The American Trend in Hebrew Literature," 41
Amiel, Moses Avigdor (1883-1946), 107
Amsterdam, Naphtali (1823-1916): disciple of Israel Salanter, 25-26; Musar teachings of, 35; and J.Z. Salanter, 26
Anti-Semitism, at Harvard University, 47
Apostasy, alternative to transition, 12
Arama, Isaac, 84
Aramaic-Hebrew dictionary, other projects, proposed by Israel Salanter, 30
Asher, code of, and commentary by Z.W. Lipkin on, 17
Ashkenazi Jewry, 2, 12
Assimilation: alternative to transition, 12; and immigrants, 4
Averroes, 55
Avicenna, 55

Baal Shem Tov (Israel ben Eliezer; 1700-1760), 17, 95, 118
Bar Ilan (Berlin), Meir (1880-1949), 107
Ben Gurion, David (1886-1973), 138-39
Berlin: Hayyim Heller's advanced talmudic institute Beth Midrash Elyon in, 93; as concept, 92-93; *see also* University of Berlin
— and A.J. Heschel, 6, 92-93, 120
— and Isaac Hutner, 69-71, 92
— and J.Z. Lipovitz, 10, 92, 144

— and Lubavitcher Rebbe (M.M. Schneerson), 92
— and Israel Salanter, 112
— and J.B. Soloveitchik, 8, 9, 92-94, 106
— and J.J. Weinberg, 69-70, 92, 141
Berlin, Naphtali Zvi Judah ("Netziv"; 1817-1893), 91-94, 106
Bialystock, Poland, J.Z. Lipovitz in, 6
Biblical and talmudic sources: Deuteronomy 4:29, 102; Genesis 2:18, 62; 12:1, 11; Babylonian Talmud, *Nedarim* 20b, 135; *ʾAvot de-Rabbi Natan*, chapter 31, 82
Birnbaum, Nathan (1864-1937), 70
Blau, Amram, 80
Blazer, Isaac (1838-1906), 112; disciple of Israel Salanter, 25-27; and Musar movement, 26-27; Musar teachings of, 35; in St. Petersburg, 26
Book of the Commandments, 93
Boston: J.B. Soloveitchik in, xii, 6, 38, 89, 106, 108; Maimonides school of, xii, 108; H.A. Wolfson, 38
Brandeis, Louis D. (1856-1941), role of H.A. Wolfson in embrace of Zionism by, 43, 45
Brisk (Brest Litovsk), Lithuania, 52, 99, 106, 108
Brisker method, *see* Talmud
Broide, Zvi Hirsh (teacher of Israel Salanter), 17
Buber, Martin (1878-1965), xv, 92

Cambridge, Mass., H.A. Wolfson in, 5, 59
Chicago, 93
Cholera epidemic, and Israel Salanter's approach to, 23-25
Christianity, 149; conversion to, as non-transition experience, 3; unable to live with contradictions, 150-51
Cincinnati, A.J. Heschel in, 6, 119-20, 129
Code of Joseph Karo (*Shulḥan ʿArukh*), 94
Code of Maimonides (*Mishneh Torah*), 94; as springboard to Brisker method of talmudic analysis, 52; as J.B. Soloveitchik's

INDEX

"friend" and focus, 103, 123; commentary of Z.W. Lipkin on, 17; *see also:* Maimonides
Cohen, Hermann (1842-1918), xv, 106; neo-Kantian epistemology of, as metaphor for Hayyim and J.B. Soloveitchik's Brisker method of talmudic analysis, 57, 99-100; epistemology of, as subject of J.B. Soloveitchik's doctoral dissertation, 95
Commentary on the Mishnah, 82-83, 123-24
Conservative Judaism: A.J. Heschel, 79, 84, 129, 132, 135; Isaac Hutner, 78-80
Crescas, 44
Crescas' Critique of Aristotle, 49, 55, 59, 70
Cultural pluralism, Horace Kallen and H.A. Wolfson, 45

Da(at Torah, 32
David al-Mukammis, 55
Dresner, Samuel, quoted on A.J. Heschel, 152

The Earth is the Lord's: The Inner World of the Jew in East Europe, 126, 129, 149
"The Eastern European Era in Jewish History," 126, 129
Einstein, Albert, 3, 75, 92
Elder of Slobodka, *see* Slobodka
Eliezer b. Hyrcanus, 145
Elijah of Vilna, *see* Vilna Gaon
Emery, Kent Jr., quoted on Christianity, 150
Enlightenment, and natural law, 83; *see also* Haskalah
Epstein, Moses Mordechai (1866-1933), dean of Slobodka yeshiva: contrasted to Hayyim Heller, 93; intellectual backbone of Slobodka, xv, 27, 65; *Levush Mordekhai*, 50-51; and J.Z. Lipovitz, 140; quoted, 58; H.A. Wolfson's scholarly method patterned after that of, 50-59, 99; H.A. Wolfson sees as kindred intellectual spirit, 26, 40-41
"Escaping Judaism," 42, 45, 47-48
)*Eretz Yisra)el*, and Isaac Hutner, 65, 85-87; *see also* Palestine
Eternal People, 70

Fear of Heaven, *see* Pietism
Feuer, Lewis, 47; quoted, 44
Finkel, Hayyim Zev (grandson of Elder of Slobodka), 142
Finkel, Nathan Zvi, *see* Slobodka, Elder of
France, Israel Salanter in, 5, 29

Frank, Golda, 27
Frank, Shraga, 27
Freud, Sigmund (1856-1939), 3

Germany: and Haskalah, 29; Israel Salanter in, 5, 29, 31
Ginsberg, Allen (born 1926), 130
Goldin, Judah, quoted on H.A. Wolfson, 41-42, 61
God in Search of Man: A Philosophy of Judaism, 129-30
God's Ineffable Name: Man, 120
Goodman, Paul, 130
Grodzinski, Hayyim Ozer (1863-1940), 107

Halakhah, and Aggadah, 81-82
"Halakhic Man," 94-105, 111-12
The Halakhic Mind: An Essay in Jewish Tradition and Modern Thought, 104-106
Halivni, David Weiss, 77
Halusk, Russia, 6
Harvard University, and H.A. Wolfson, 5, 8, 10, 38-39, 43, 47-49, 51, 60, 147-48
Hasidism, 17, 31; and A.J. Heschel, 6, 9, 12, 115, 117-19, 128, 132; and Isaac Hutner, 64, 69, 72, 76, 80; and J.Z. Lipovitz, 140; Lubavitcher Hasidism and Lubavitcher Rebbe, 17, 78-79, 92; and Israel Salanter, 17; Stoliner Hasidism, 17
Haskalah ("Enlightenment"): in Germany, 29; in Kovno and Vilna, 27-28; and Musar movement, 27-28; emphasis on secular studies of Lithuanian, 27-28; and Israel Salanter, 16, 24, 27-29; *see also* Enlightenment
Haslovitz, Lithuania, 92
Hayyim of Volozhin (1749-1821), student of Vilna Gaon, teacher of J.Z. Salanter, 17, 96
Hebrew Union College, A.J. Heschel teaching at, 129, 131
Heichal Rabbenu Hayyim Ha-Levi, talmudic institute, 108
Heller, Hayyim (1878-1960), xv; biography, 93
— and A.J. Heschel, 120
— and J.Z. Lipovitz, 138, 140, 144
— and J.B. Soloveitchik, 93
Herzl, Theodor (1860-1904), 106
Heschel, Abraham Joshua (1907-1972): activism, civil rights movement, 6, 12, 120, 126, 130-33, 135; association with secular poets, 6, 9; birth, 6; and Christianity, 151; in Cincinnati, 6, 119-20, 129; and Cohenian idealism, 121; and Conservative Judaism,

INDEX

79, 84, 129, 132, 135; childhood, 7, 9; complexity of, 115-16; development of, precipitated by travel, 6; displaced influence of, 6; and ecumenicism, 129-31, 151; exaggerated estimation of, by disciples, 11; and Hasidism, xiii, 6, 9, 12, 115, 117-19, 128, 132; Hebrew Union College, teaching at, 129, 131; Holocaust, response to, 120, 122, 126-30. 133, 135; impact of Maimonides on, 123-26, 128, 132-35; inappropriateness of personal titles for, 79; Jewish Theological Seminary of America, teaching at, 79, 129, 132, 135; Kantianism, 121-22; languages, 7, 9, 118, 120; literary style, 7, 115-16, 139, 143, 152-53; in New York City, 6; philosophic study, 120; quoted 115, 118, 120-22, 124-28, 130-31, 134; and Reform Judaism, 120, 132; representative of Ashkenazi Jewry in transition, 2; silence about teenage years, 9-10; in the specter of failure, 12; study as youth, 117-18; twofold legacy, as activist and hasid, 12; at University of Berlin, 92-93, 120; views on being, reality, 121-23, 128; in Vilna, 118; in Warsaw, 6, 79; "Young Vilna," 120, 135; Zionism, 130-31

— works of, xv; *The Earth is the Lord's: The Inner World of the Jew in East Europe*, 126, 129, 149; "The Eastern European Era in Jewish History," 126, 129; *God in Search of Man: A Philosophy of Judaism*, 129-30; *God's Ineffable Name: Man*, 120; *The Insecurity of Freedom: Essays on Human Existence*, 134; *Israel: An Echo of Eternity*, 131; *Kotsk: The Struggle for Integrity*, 132, 134; *Maimonides: A Biography*, 123-25; *Man is Not Alone: A Philosophy of Religion*, 129; "The Meaning of This War," 127; *The Prophets*, 129, 132; *Die Prophetie*, 122, 129; *The Sabbath: Its Meaning for Modern Man*, 131; *Theology of Ancient Judaism*, 134; *Who is Man?* 134, 136

— and Hayyim Heller, 120
— and Isaac Hutner, 79, 84, 115-16, 119, 135, 148, 152-53
— and J.Z. Lipovitz, 115, 139, 143, 148, 152
— and Israel Salanter, 115, 135, 148, 152-53
— and J.B. Soloveitchik, 115-16, 119-21, 135, 148, 151-53
— and H.A. Wolfson, 115-16; 135-36, 152-53

Heschel, Moses Mordechai, *see* Peltzovizner Rebbe

Heschel, Rebeccah Reisel (A.J. Heschel's mother), 117

Heschel, Sylvia (A.J. Heschel's wife), quoted on A.J. Heschel, 123

Hess, Moses (1812-1875), 106

Ḥibbat Zion, 106-107

Hillel of Verona, 70, 73

Hitler, Adolph, 92

Holocaust, 6, 7; A.J. Heschel's response to, 120, 122, 126-30, 133, 135; "The Meaning of This War," 127

Horney, Karen, quoted, 23

Hugenberg, Alfred, 92

Hurvitz, Joseph Jozel (Elder of Novorodock; c. 1850-1919), 27

Hutner, Isaac (1906-1980): approach to Aggadah, 81-82; in Berlin 69-71, 92; biography, 5, 8-11, 63-65; childhood, 7-8; and Conservative Judaism, 78-80; and definition of modern Orthodox Judaism, 79; development of, precipitated by travel, 6; and discipleship, 74; displaced influence of, 6; and ecumenicism, 151; and ʾ*Eretz Yisra*ʾ*el*, 65, 85-87; exaggerated estimation of, by disciples, 11; at Gerer *shtibl*, Warsaw, 72; and Hasidism, 64, 69, 72, 76, 80; in Israel, 6, 65, 85-87; in Kovno, 65; languages, 7; literary style, 63-64, 67, 116, 139, 143, 153; in Lomza yeshiva, Poland, 65; marriage, 71; Mesivta Rabbi Chaim Berlin, 75-77, 80; and Maharal, 75-76, 82; and Musar, xiii, 5-6, 65, 67-68, 72-73, 78; in New York City, 65; and piety, 8, 64-68, 72-73, 78-79; pre-Holocaust influence of, 6-7; principal, Yeshiva Rabbi Jacob Joseph High School, 75; quoted, 64, 67, 69, 71-73, 75, 79, 82-83, 85-86; and Reform Judaism, 78; representative of Ashkenazi Jewry in transition, 2; scholarly interests, 70-71, 73; and secular study, 6, 78-80; and Slobodka, 5, 26, 65-69, 71-73, 79, 119; silence about teenage years, 9-10; thought of, 80-85; twofold legacy, as dialectician and sermonizer, 12; in Warsaw, 6, 65, 69, 71-72; as yeshiva dean, Rosh Yeshiva, 5, 74, 76; and Zionism, 5-6, 64, 107-108

— works of; xv; letters and diary notations, 63-64, 67, 69, 71-73, 75, 85-86; notebooks of, 83; *Paḥad Yitzḥak*, 81, 85, 143; *Torat ha-Nazir (Law of the Nazirite)*, 71
— and S.E. Alfandari, 86
— and Amram Blau, 80
— and A.J. Heschel, 79, 84, 115-16, 119,

135, 148, 152
— and Jacob Kaminecki, 66, 86
— and Aaron Kotler, 66, 76, 80, 86
— and A.I. Kuk, 67-69, 76, 80, 86, 144
— and J.Z. Kuk, 80
— and Saul Lieberman, 79-80
— and J.Z. Lipovitz, 139, 141, 143-44, 148-49, 151-52
— and Lubavitcher Rebbe, 78-79
— and I.Z. Meltzer, 86
— and I.J. Ruderman, 66
— and Israel Salanter, 18, 81, 83, 110, 148-49, 152
— and Satmarer Rebbe, 80
— and A.D.K. Shapiro, 86
— and J.B Soloveitchik, 78-79, 81, 90, 107-108, 110, 148-49, 151-52
— and J.H. Sonnenfeld, 86
— and H.A. Wolfson, 61-62, 148, 152-53
— and Menahem Ziemba, 86
Hypothetico-deductive method, *see* Talmud

Ibn, Daud, Abraham, 55
The Insecurity of Freedom: Essays on Human Existence, 134
Intercollegiate Menorah Association, 43
Isaac Abravanel, 55
)Ish ha-Halakhah, see "Halakhic Man"
Israel: An Echo of Eternity, 131
Israel: cultural transition in, 137; J.Z. Lipovitz and, 142; see also *)Eretz Yisra)el*; Palestine
Israel ben Eliezer, *see* Baal Shem Tov

"Jewish Students in European Universities," 44
Jewish Theological Seminary of America, A.J. Heschel teaching at, 79, 129, 132, 135
Joseph ibn Aknin, 55
Joseph al-Basir, 55
Joseph ibn Zaddik, 55
Judah Abravanel, 55
Judah ha-Levi, 92, 95
Judah ha-Nasi, 123-25

Kallen, Horace, cultural pluralism and H.A. Wolfson, 45
Kaminecki, Jacob (1892-1986), colleague of Isaac Hutner, 66, 87
Kant, Immanuel (1724-1804), 57, 151
Kantianism: and M.M. Epstein, 57; and A.J. Heschel, 121-22; and J.B. Soloveitchik, 99-101, 113; and H.A. Wolfson, 57; *see also* neo-Kantianism

Kaplan, Abraham Elijah, 92, 141
Kariv, Abraham, 142
Karo, Joseph (1488-1575), Code of Rabbi Joseph Karo *(Shulḥan (Arukh)*, 94
Kelm, Musar academy or yeshiva of, 26-27
Kirzner, Yisrael Mayer, quoted on Isaac Hutner, 76-77
Knesset Bet Yitzhak, in Kovno, 40
Kotler, Aaron (1892-1962), and Isaac Hutner, 66, 76, 80
Kotsk: The Struggle for Integrity, 132, 134
Kotsker Rebbe (Menahem Mendel Morgenstern; 1787-1859), 118, 132; *see also* Rebbes
Kovno, Lithuania: Israel Salanter in, 5, 24-25, 27; and Haskalah, 27-28; Knesset Bet Yitzhak, 40; Musar academy, yeshiva of, 24, 27; Israel Salanter in, 5, 16, 25-27, 39; H.A. Wolfson in, 5
Kuk, Abraham Isaac (1865-1935), and Isaac Hutner, 67-69, 76, 80, 86, 144; and J.Z. Lipovitz, 144
Kuk, Zvi Judah, 80

Lasker-Schueler, Else, 92
Law of the Nazirite (Torat ha-Nazir), 71
League of Nations Mandate (for Palestine), 137
Lebowitz, Baruch Ber, 58
Lesin, J.M., xiii
Levush Mordekhai, 50-51
Lichtenstein, Aaron, 77
Lieberman, Saul, 70, 79-80
Lipkin, Israel, *see* Israel Salanter
Lipkin, Lippman (Israel Salanter's son), *Lippman parallelogram*, 31
Lipkin, Zev Wolf (father of Israel Salanter; died 1858), commentaries of, 17
Lipovitz, Baylah, 140; quoted, 142
Lipovitz, Joseph Zev (1889-1962): in Berlin, 10, 92, 144; in Bialystock, Poland, 6; and cultural transition in Palestine, 137-40, 145; development of, precipitated by travel, 6; disciple of Elder of Slobodka, 138-40, 142, 150; exaggerated estimation of, by disciples, 11; and Hasidism, 140; literary style, 7, 143-44, 154; and Musar, xiii, 6, 138, 141, 145; and piety, 141-44; and Ponavitch yeshiva, 142; quoted, 137; representative of Ashkenazi Jewry in transition, 2; in Rituva, Lithuania, 6, 140; silence about teenage years, 9-10; and Slobodka, 6, 26, 138-39, 140-42; in Tel Aviv, 141-44; teacher, 142; twofold legacy, as self-con-

scious commentator and unself-conscious believer, 12; at University of Berlin, 141, 144; and Zionism, 6, 141-42
— works of, xiii, xv; *Naḥalat Yosef (The Heritage of Joseph)*, 140, 143; *Scroll of Ruth*, 7, 140, 142-43
— and Hayyim Heller, 138, 140, 144
— and A.J. Heschel, 115, 139, 148, 152, 154
— and Isaac Hutner, 139, 141, 143-44, 148-49, 151-52
— and Israel Salanter, 18, 139, 141, 144, 148-49, 151-52
— and J.B. Soloveitchik, 139, 143-44, 148-49, 151-52, 154
— and H.A. Wolfson, 139, 148, 152
Loew, Judah (Maharal; c. 1526-1609), model for Isaac Hutner, 75-76, 82; quoted, 75
Lomza, Poland, 65, 93
"The Lonely Man of Faith," 101-103
Lubavitcher Rebbe (Menahem Mendel Schneerson; born 1902): and Isaac Hutner, 78-79; in Berlin, 92; and definition of modern Orthodox Judaism, 79; *see also* Rebbes
Lurianic mystical tradition, 17
Lyon, David Gordon, 44

McCarthy, Joseph R., 129
Maimonides, Moses ben Maimon (1135-1204), 55, 59, 92; *Book of the Commandments*, 93; *Commentary on the Mishnah*, 82-83, 123-24; *Guide of the Perplexed*, 123; impact on A.J. Heschel, 123-26, 128, 132-35; quoted, 87; views on prayer analyzed by J.B. Soloveitchik, 109-110
— Code of Maimonides (*Mishneh Torah*), 94; springboard to Brisker method of talmudic analysis, 52; J.B. Soloveitchik's "friend" and focus, 103, 123; commentary of Z.W. Lipkin on, 17
Maimonides: A Biography, 123-25; quoted, 123
Maimonides School, Boston, xii, 108
Man is Not Alone: A Philosophy of Religion, 129
Marcuse, Herbert, 130
"The Meaning of This War," 127
Meltzer, Isser Zalman (1870-1954), 86
Menahem Mendel of Kotsk, *see* Kotsker Rebbe
Mendelssohn, Moses (1729-1786), xv, 2
Menorah dinner, 43
Menorah Journal, 48

Mesivta Rabbi Chaim Berlin, Isaac Hutner at, 75-77, 80
Mizrachi-Hapoel Mizrachi World Organization, 107
Moore, George Foote, 48
Morgenstern, Julian, 129
Muehsam, Erich, 92
Muhlhausen, Yom Tov Lippman, 84
Musar: contrasted to Hasidism, 72; dispute over, 40; and ego, 64, 72-73; given to excessive self-criticism, 31; as halakhic norm, 31; and Haskalah, 27-28; Kelm academy, yeshiva of, 26-27; *kolel* of, 26; Kovno academy of, 24, 27; introspection and occupational hazard thereof, 22, 40; personality of, 34-35; Slobodka yeshiva of, 26-27; H.A. Wolfson's hypothetico-deductive method of text interpretation originating in third-generation school of, 38; and Zionism, 141; *see also* Piety and pietists
— and Isaac Blazer, 26-27
— and Isaac Hutner, xiii, 5, 65, 67-68, 72-73, 78
— and J.Z. Lipovitz, 6, 138, 141, 145
— and Israel Salanter, xiii, 5, 8, 16, 18-20, 22-25, 28-30, 40
— and Hayyim Soloveitchik, 26
— and J.B. Soloveitchik, xiii, 26, 111-12
— and H.A. Wolfson, xiii, 40-42, 50-51

Naḥalat Yosef (The Heritage of Joseph), 140, 143
Nahmanides (1194-1270), views on prayer analyzed by J.B. Soloveitchik, 109-110
"The Needs of Jewish Scholarship in America," 45-46
Neo-Kantianism, 57, 78, 99-101, 113, 151-52; *see also* Kantianism
Neusner, Jacob, quoted on A.J. Heschel, 121
New York City: A.J. Heschel in, 6; H.A. Wolfson in, 5, 8; Hayyim Heller in, 93; J.B. Soloveitchik in, 89, 93, 108
Nicholas I, Tsar (1796-1855), offering seminary post to Israel Salanter, 24

Ortega y Gasset, Jose, 1-2; quoted, 1
Orthodox Judaism: Agudath Israel, political movement of, 32; and Amram Blau, 80; East European, in transition, 92-93; elusive definition of, 79; and Haskalah, 28-29; and Isaac Hutner, 78-80; and J.Z. Kuk, 80; Lithuanian, 20, 29; and nonconformity, 149; Israel Salanter's image as iconoclastic

representative of, 24, 30; and J.B. Soloveitchik, 6, 78-79; and Synagogue Council of America, 78; unalloyed, alternative to transition, 12; H.A. Wolfson and, 10, 38

Paḥad Yitzhak, 81, 85, 143
Palestine, xiii, 8, 65-67, 72, 93, 115, 132; cultural transition in, 137-40, 145; League of Nations Mandate for, 137; and J.Z. Lipovitz, 138-40, 145; see also ʾEretz Yisraʾel; Israel
Paris, Israel Salanter in, 29, 31
Peltzovizner Rebbe (Moses Mordechai Heschel, A.J. Heschel's father), 117; see also Rebbes
Peri Yitzhak, 112
Perlow, Alter Israel Simon, 117
Philo, 49
Philo of Alexandria, xiv, 92
Philosophy: and Cambridge Platonists, in Israel Salanter, 22; and Halakhah and Aggadah, in Isaac Hutner, 8, 81-84; and history of, in H.A. Wolfson, 7, 37-38, 44, 46-51, 55-56; and Kantianism, in A.J. Heschel, 120-22; and neo-Kantianism, in J.B. Soloveitchik, 94-101, 104, 113; and piety, in J.Z. Lipovitz, 6, 143
The Philosophy of the Church Fathers: Faith, Trinity, Incarnation, 46, 49
The Philosophy of the Kalam, 49, 55
The Philosophy of Spinoza: Unfolding the Latent Processes of His Reasoning, 48-50, 57
Piety and pietists, 3; and Isaac Hutner, 8, 64-68, 72-73, 78-79; and J.Z. Lipovitz, 6-7, 10, 141-44; and Israel Salanter, 5, 7-8, 15-16, 18, 22, 24-25, 33, 40; and J.Z. Salanter, 10, 18; and H.A. Wolfson, 40; see also Musar
Planck, Max, 92
Plotinus, 55
Plutarch, 55
Poetry, H.A. Wolfson and Hebrew poetry, 38, 41
"Pomegranates," 44-45
Die Prophetie, 122, 129
The Prophets, 129, 132
Psychologist of the unconscious, Israel Salanter, 12, 15-16, 21-23, 25, 28, 33

Rabad of Posquieres, 52-53
Rabbi Isaac Elchanan yeshiva, 41; see also Yeshiva University
Rabbinical Seminary for Orthodox Judaism, 69

Rameiles Yeshiva, Vilna, 20
Rebbes: Kotsker, 118, 132; Lubavitcher, 78-79, 92; Peltzovizner, 117; Satmarer, 80
Reform Judaism: A.J. Heschel, 120, 132; Isaac Hutner, 78
Reisman, David, quoted, 132-33
Reiss, Erich, 123
Religious Zionists of America, 107
Ritual slaughter, 31
Rituva, Lithuania, 6, 140
Rosenzweig, Franz (1886-1929), xv
Rubenstein, Richard, 77
Ruderman, Isaac Jacob (1901-1987), colleague of Isaac Hutner, 66
Russel, Bertrand, quoted, 133
Russian Orthodox Church, 24

Saadia, 55
The Sabbath: Its Meaning for Modern Man, 131
Sabbath law, and Israel Salanter, 23-25
St. Petersburg, 26
Salant, Lithuania, Israel Salanter in, 8, 17, 20
Salanter, Israel (1810-1883): in Berlin, 112; biography, 17-21; childhood, 7-8; and cholera epidemic in Vilna, 23-25; death of, 16, 35; and daʿat Torah, 32; development of, precipitated by travel, 6; displaced influence of, 6; exaggerated estimation of, by disciples, 11; exaggerated estimation of failure of, by Israel Salanter himself, 11; his father, as his first Talmud teacher, 17; in Germany, 15, 29, 31; and Hasidism, 17; and Haskalah, 16, 24, 27-29; hypothetico-deductive Talmudic method originating in his third-generation Musar school, 38; instinct and intellect, 21-24; introspection, and hazards thereof, 40; in Kovno, 5, 16, 25-27, 39; languages, 7; literary style, 15-16, 21-22, 139, 152-53; in Lithuania, 6, 15, 19-20, 39; and Musar, xiii, 5, 8, 16, 18-20, 22-25, 28-30, 40; Tsar Nicholas I offering seminary post to, 24; Orthodox iconoclast, 24, 30; in Paris, 29, 31; philosophy and Cambridge Platonists, 22; piety, pietism, 5, 7-8, 15-16, 18, 22, 24-25, 33, 40; polarity and dialectics, 16, 21-24; proposes Aramaic-Hebrew dictionary, other projects, 30; psychologist of the unconscious, 12, 15-16, 21-23, 25, 28, 33; quoted, 15, 22-23, 25, 29, 34-35; at Rameiles Yeshiva, Vilna, 20; representative of Ashkenazi Jewry in transition, 2; rhetoric, 21-22; Sabbath law and confrontation with authorities, 23-25; in Salant, 8, 17, 20; self-

revelation, self-concealment, 20, 29-30, 72; silence about teenage years, 10; study with talmudic scholars, 5, 16-17; teaching laymen, 20, 27; and *Tevunah*, 30; twofold legacy, as psychologist and talmudist, 12; in Vilna, 5, 16, 20-21, 23-24, 39; West European travel, 29-31; and women, 8, 16, 20
— works of, xv-xvi; articles of 1861-62, 5; essay of 1881, 5; homilies of 1845-1846, 21; letters of 1849, 5, 21
— and Naphtali Amsterdam, 25-26
— and Isaac Blazer, 25-27
— and Elder of Slobodka, 18, 149-50
— and A.J. Heschel, 115-16, 135, 148, 152-53
— and Isaac Hutner, 18, 81, 83, 110, 148-49, 152
— and J.Z. Lipovitz, 18, 139, 141, 144, 148-49, 151-52
— and J.Z. Salanter, 17-21
— and J.B. Soloveitchik, 18, 89, 110, 112, 148-49, 151-52
— and H.A. Wolfson, 18, 39-40, 148, 152-53
— and S.Z. Ziv, 25-26
Salanter, Joseph Zundel (1786-1866), 91; and Naphtali Amsterdam, 26; influence on Israel Salanter, 17-21
Santayana, George (1863-1952), teaching H.A. Wolfson, 43; quoted, 43
Satmarer Rebbe (Joel Teitelbaum; 1888-1980), 80; *see also* Rebbes
Saul ha-Kohen Ashkenazi, 55
Savitz, Harry Austryn, 62
Schneerson, Menahem Mendel, *see* Lubavitcher Rebbe
Scholem, Gershom, 61, 69
Scranton, Penn., H.A. Wolfson in, 5, 8, 38, 41, 59
Scroll of Ruth, 7, 140, 142-43
Secular studies: and Haskalah, 27-28; A.J. Heschel, 6, 9-10; Isaac Hutner, 6, 78-80; at Kelm Academy, 26; J.B. Soloveitchik, 78, 90, 92; H.A. Wolfson, 5
Self-effacement, Musar goal, 40
Self-sacrifice, Musar goal, 72
Self-scrutiny, and Musar, 22-23, 72
Self-transcendence, and J.J. Hurvitz, 27
Septimus, Bernard, quoted, 1
Shapiro, Abraham Dov Ber Kahane, 86
Sharastani, 55
Shulevitz, Eliezer, 34
Simhah, Meir, 140
Simplicius, 55

Slobodka, 65; as concept, xv, 92-93; *gadlut ha-ʾadam*, 73; Musar piety of, 40, 65, 141; talmudic methodology of dean of yeshiva of, 50-59, 99; yeshiva of, splits in two, 40; and Zionism, 141
— Elder of Slobodka (Nathan Zvi Finkel; 1849-1927), xv, 86, 93; affects Kelm academy, 26; charismatic leader, 119; Hayyim Zev Finkel, grandson of, 142; independent, 27, 65; penchant for secrecy, 66, 87; and Israel Salanter, 18, 149-150; taught by S.Z. Ziv, 66; teachings of, 72-73, 111, 149-50
— Isaac Hutner, affected by Elder of, 26, 66-68, 119; teachings of, 72-73, 79; in yeshiva of, 5, 65-66, 69, 71
— A.E. Kaplan, teaching talmudic methodology of, 141
— J.Z. Lipovitz, affected by Elder of, 26, 138-39; in yeshiva of, 6, 140; teaching talmudic methodology of, in Hebrew, 141-42
— J.Z. Salanter, ultimate progenitor of, 18
— J.B. Soloveitchik, and teachings of, 111
— J.J. Weinberg, student in, 69, 92; teaching talmudic methodology of, 141
— H.A. Wolfson, affected by piety of, 40-41; affected by talmudic dean of, 26, 50-59, 65; surreptitiously studied in yeshiva of, 40-41, 50
Social activism, and A.J. Heschel, 12, 120
Soloveitchik, Hayyim (J.B. Soloveitchik's grandfather; 1853-1918), 91, 100, 106-107; attitude to Musar, 26; originator of "Brisker," critico-conceptual method of talmudic analysis, 52-54, 58, 92
Soloveitchik, Isaac (J.B. Soloveitchik's uncle; 1886-1960), 91
Soloveitchik, Joseph Baer (J.B. Soloveitchik's great-grandfather; 1820-1897), 91
Soloveitchik, Joseph Baer (born 1903), 52; attitude to Musar, xiii, 26, 111-12; in Berlin, 8-9, 92-94, 106; in Boston, xii, 6, 38, 89, 106, 108; childhood, 7-9; creation and dual Adam, 101-102; and definition of modern Orthodox Judaism, 79; development of, precipitated by travel, 5; displaced influence of, 6; and ecumenicism, 151; exaggerated estimation of, by disciples, 11; in Halusk, Russia, 6; languages, 7; literary style, 90, 116, 139, 153-54; and neo-Kantianism, 78, 99-101, 113, 151-52; in New York City, 89, 93, 108; personal reminiscence of, xi-xiii; philosophy as epistemology of Halakhah, 94-101; pre-

Holocaust influence of, 6-7; on prayer, 109-110; quoted, 38, 89, 96-105, 109-113; representative of Ashkenazi Jewry in transition, 2; and secular studies, 78, 90, 92; silence about teenage years, 9-10; in specter of failure, 11-12; spiritual disharmony, 102-103; talmudic study, 6-7, 90, 92-94, 108; teaching at Heichal-Rabbenu Hayyim Ha-Levi, talmudic institute, 108; teenage education, 92; and *Tradition*, 95; twofold legacy, as existentialist and talmudist, 12; unification of opposites, 102-103, 106; at University of Berlin, 8, 9, 92; at Yeshiva University, xi-xiii, 108, 113; and Zionism, 91, 106-108
— works of, xv; "Halakhic Man," 95-105, 111-12; *The Halakhic Mind: An Essay in Jewish Tradition and Modern Thought*, 104-106; "The Lonely Man of Faith," 101-103; "U-Vikashtem mi-Sham," 102-103, 106
— and Hayyim Heller, 93
— and A.J. Heschel, 115-16, 118, 120-21, 135, 148-49, 151-52
— and Isaac Hutner, 78-79, 81, 90, 107-108, 110, 148, 151-52
— and J.Z. Lipovitz, 139, 143-44, 148, 151-52, 154
— and Israel Salanter, 18, 89, 110, 112, 148, 149, 151-52
— and H.A. Wolfson, 89-90, 98-99, 148, 151
Soloveitchik, Joseph Ha-Levi (first of Soloveitchik family; eighteenth century), 90-91
Soloveitchik, Joseph Ha-Levi (2), 91
Soloveitchik, Moses (J.B. Soloveitchik's father; 1876-1941); 91, 99, 107, 119
Sonnenfeld, Joseph Hayyim (1849-1932), 86
State of Israel, *see* Israel
Stearns, Harold E., quoted on H.A. Wolfson, 43
"Structure and Growth of Philosophic Systems from Plata to Spinoza," 56, 61
Synagogue Council of America, 78-79
Szold, Henrietta, 138-39

Talmud: and *da'at Torah*, 32; Brisker method of study of, 52-54, 56-58; hypothetico-deductive method of study of, 38, 50-54, 56-59; commentary of Z.W. Lipkin on, 17; Israel Salanter's innovative suggestions regarding study of, 30, 32
Talmudic sources, *see* Biblical and Talmudic sources

Teitelbaum, Joel, *see* Satmarer Rebbe
Tel Aviv, J.Z. Lipovitz in, 6, 141-44
Tevunah, 30
Theology of Ancient Judaism, 134
Torat ha-Nazir (Law of the Nazirite), 71
Tradition, 95
Transition: distinguished from prototypical medieval and modern Jewish experiences, 2-3; double cultural inclusion, 3-4; excludes J.J. Hurvitz, 27; excludes apostasy and assimilation, 12: in Palestine, 137-40, 145; and Orthodox Judaism, 92-93; requires broad-based and inductive research, xiii-xiv, 4; simultaneous persistence of the culturally old and new, 1-2; thesis about, xiv-xv; *see also* Transition figures; A.J. Heschel; Isaac Hutner; J.Z. Lipovitz; Israel Salanter; J.B. Soloveitchik; H.A. Wolfson
Transition figures:
— development of, precipitated by travel, 5-6
— displacement of influence, 6-7
— disciplined and disrupted childhoods, 7-9
— erudition, 149
— exaggerated estimation of, by disciples, 11-12
— geographical dislocation of, 5-6
— link between style and personality, work and writer, 152-54
— nonconformity, 147-49
— in the specter of failure, 11-12
— talent at languages, 7
— twofold legacy of, 12-13
— silence about teenage years, 9-10; *see also* Transition; A.J. Heschel; Isaac Hutner; J.Z. Lipovitz; Israel Salanter; J.B. Soloveitchik; H.A. Wolfson
Tsar Nicholas I, *see* Nicholas I
Twersky, Isadore, quoted, 53

Ukraine, and Hasidism, 17
University of Berlin: J.Z. Lipovitz at, 144; J.B. Soloveitchik at, 8-9, 92; Heschel at, 92-93, 120; *see also* Berlin
University of California, Berkeley, x
University of Giessen, J.J. Weinberg at, 69
Uvarov, Sergei, 24
"U-Vikashtem mi-Sham," 102-103, 106

Vilna, Lithuania: Israel Salanter in, 5, 16, 20-21, 23-24, 39; A.J. Heschel in, 6, 118; H.A. Wolfson in, 5, 8; and Haskalah, 27-28; Rameiles Yeshiva, 20

Vilna Gaon, Elijah of Vilna (1720-1797), 17, 76, 91, 94
Vilna Gymnasium, 118
Volhynia, White Russia, and Hasidism, 17
Volozhin Yeshiva, 107

Warsaw: Isaac Hutner in, 5, 65, 69, 71-72, 79; A.J. Heschel in, 6, 79
Weinberg, Jehiel Jacob (1885-1966), 69-70, 92, 141
White, Theodore, quoted, 129
Who is Man? 134, 136
Wohl, Robert, 1
Wolfson, Harry Austryn (1887-1974): birth, 39; in Boston, 38; childhood, 8; cultural pluralism and Horace Kallen, 45; development of, precipitated by travel, 5; displaced influence of, 6; essay writing, 38, 42, 44; exaggerated estimation of, by disciples, 11; and Harvard, 5, 8, 10, 38-39, 43, 47-49, 51, 60, 147-48; Hebrew poetry, 38, 41-43; hypothetico-deductive method of text interpretation, 38, 51-60; and Intercollegiate Menorah Association, 43; in Kovno, 5, 40; languages, 7, 38, 41-42, 60; literary style, 41-42, 55, 116, 139, 153; in Lithuania, 8, 39; and Musar, xiii, 40-42; in New York City, 5, 8; and Orthodoxy, 10, 38, 44-45, 142; and history of philosophic texts, 7, 37-38, 44, 46-51, 55-56, 60, 70; pre-Holocaust influence of, 6-7; quoted, 21, 32, 37-38, 42-52, 54, 56-57, 59-60, 62; in Rabbi Isaac Elchanan yeshiva, 41; on religious reform, 36; renunciation of halakhic observance, 10, 38, 42; representative of Ashkenazi Jewry in transition, 2; George Santayana teaching, 43; in Scranton, Penn., 5, 8, 38, 41, 59; self-hatred, 44; Sheldon Travel Fellowship, 44; short-story writing, 41; silence about teenage years, 9-10; in Slobodka yeshiva, 26, 40-41, 50-51, 65; in specter of failure, 11; "Structure and Growth of Philosophic Systems from Plato to Spinoza," 56, 61; twofold legacy, as objective scholar and Jewish partisan, 12, 60-61; in Vilna, 5, 8; wit of, 60-61; and Yiddish, 45, 48, 147; and Zionism, 38, 42-45; "Zvi Hirsh" Wolfson, 49-51
— works of, xv; "The American Trend in Hebrew Literature," 41; *Crescas' Critique of Aristotle*, 49, 55, 59, 70; "Escaping Judaism," 42, 45, 47-48; "Jewish Students in European Universities," 44; "The Needs of Jewish Scholarship in America," 45-46; *Philo*, 49; *The Philosophy of the Church Fathers: Faith, Trinity, Incarnation*, 46, 49; *The Philosophy of the Kalam*, 49, 55; *The Philosophy of Spinoza: Unfolding the Latent Processes of His Reasoning*, 48-50, 57; "Pomegranates," 44-45; untitled undergraduate essay on philosophy of art, 41
— and A.J. Heschel, 115-16, 135-36, 152-53
— and Isaac Hutner, 61-62, 148, 153
— and J.Z. Lipovitz, 139, 148, 152
— and Israel Salanter, 18, 39-40, 148, 152-53
— and J.B. Soloveitchik, 89-90, 98-99, 148, 151
Wolfson of Harvard, 49; quoted, 41, 56
Women, and Musar study, 8, 16, 20
World Zionist Organization, 107

Yeshiva College, Yeshiva University (New York City), J.B. Soloveitchik at, xi-xiii; 108, 113
Yeshiva Knesset Israel, *see* Slobodka
Yeshiva Rabbi Jacob Joseph High School, Isaac Hutner principal of, 75
Yom Kippur, Israel Salanter confronting authorities on, 23-25
"Young Vilna," and A.J. Heschel, 120, 135

Ziemba, Menahem, 86
Zionism, 80; and A.J. Heschel, 130-31; First Zionist Congress, 106; Ḥibbat Zion, 106-107; Religious Zionists of America, 107; role of H.A. Wolfson in Louis D. Brandeis' embrace of, 43, 45
— Isaac Hutner's attitude to, 5-6, 64, 107-108
— J.B. Soloveitchik's attitude to, 91, 106-108
— H.A. Wolfson's attitude to, 38, 42-45
— J.Z. Lipovitz's attitude to, 6, 141-42
Ziv, Simhah Zisl (1824-1898), disciple of Israel Salanter, 25-26; at Kelm academy, 26-27; Musar teachings of, 34; teaching Elder of Slobodka, 66